The Evolution of
Educational Thought

Emile Durkheim

The Evolution of Educational Thought

Lectures on the formation and
development of secondary education
in France

Translated by

Peter Collins

Department of Philosophy
University of Cape Town

Routledge & Kegan Paul
London, Henley and Boston

First published as L'Evolution pédagogique en France
in 1938 by Presses Universitaires de France
Second French edition 1969.

This English translation
first published in 1977
by Routledge & Kegan Paul Ltd
39 Store Street,
London WC1E 7DD,
Broadway House,
Newtown Road,
Henley-on-Thames,
Oxon RG9 1EN and
9 Park Street,
Boston, Mass. 02108, USA
Set in Baskerville
by Computacomp (UK) Ltd,
Fort William
and printed in Great Britain by
Lowe & Brydone Ltd
French edition © Presses Universitaires de France 1938
This translation © Routledge & Kegan Paul 1977
No part of this book may be reproduced in
any form without permission from the
publisher, except for the quotation of brief
passages in criticism

British Library Cataloguing in Publication Data

Durkeim, Emile

The evolution of educational thought.

1. Education, Secondary — France — History
I. Title   II. Collins, Peter
373.44   LA695

ISBN 0-7100-8446-3

For Don Crompton, who for three years at Westminster College, Oxford, taught me at least 'that we must fashion rationalists, that is to say men who are concerned with clarity of thought; but they must be rationalists of a new kind who know that things, whether human or physical, are irreducibly complex and who are yet able to look unfalteringly into the face of this complexity' (p.348).

Contents

part two

Acknowledgments

There are so many people to whom I am grateful for help in the production of this book that I can only mention those to whom I am most outstandingly indebted: to Prof. Basil Bernstein for initiating and encouraging me to undertake the project, as well as for innumerable conversations to which I owe whatever little understanding of sociology I may possess; to Peter Hopkins and Carol Gardiner of Routledge, the former for patience and sympathy, the latter for some invaluable corrections; to Dr Steven Lukes for criticism, encouragement, advice and generosity in allowing me to learn from his own translations; and finally in chronological order to Mrs Winifred Newnham, Miss Brenda Farmer, Mrs Toni Tattersall, Mrs Dot Howard and Miss Mary Pritt, all of whom uncomplainingly contributed to the laborious business of transcription of tape and manuscript.

Peter Collins

Introduction by Maurice Halbwachs to the French edition of 1938

The work here offered to our readers is the text of a course on the *History of Education in France* which was first given by Durkheim in 1904-5 and which he repeated in subsequent years until the war. It had been decided, at the time of the 1902 reform, to organise a professional course in educational theory for all *'agrégation'* candidates. The University of Paris had entrusted the running of this course to Durkheim.

It is a fact which needs to be remembered without being exaggerated that sociology was not admitted wholesale to the Sorbonne but rather insinuated itself through the narrow gate of educational theory. In 1902 Durkheim was appointed as the deputy of Ferdinand Buisson, whom he succeeded in 1906, and given responsibility for teaching the science of education. Moreover, his teaching at Bordeaux had prepared him for this since a large part of it had always been devoted to this discipline. It will be seen that this course only partially comprised new work. It came after long years in the course of which he did not cease to be concerned with the problems of education and teaching. Moral education, child psychology, the history of educational doctrines: Durkheim had successfully adopted these three perspectives which constitute classical educational theory. There is scarcely a province in this area which he did not explore. And not only in order to carry out a task which was required of him. It was a part, and also one of the essential practical applications, of the science of man which he believed fully deserved the effort he devoted to it.

The 'course of education in France' had absorbed and was imbued by all this. But we have here something else besides. Durkheim has furnished us with a model example of what can be made of a study of educational institutions carried out within an historical framework by a great sociologist. Just as there is a sociology of religion, a sociology of politics, etc., there is in fact a sociology of education which is by no means the least important. For education is the most powerful instrument a society possesses for fashioning its members in its own image. Certainly, the family takes the child in its entirety first of all, envelops him wholly and forms him in its own way. But if we think of the revolutions which take place in him when he goes to school for the first time, we realise that his way of being and even almost his very nature change. From this moment onwards he contains within himself a veritable duality. When he goes home, his parents feel that he belongs less and less to them. Fathers and children: the generation gap is established at this point. Subject to the regimen of the school environment, the child, the young man progressively discovers a whole social world which is exterior to his family and in which he can only take a place if he adapts to it and incorporates it. The family itself is gradually modified by this.

Like all major functions of society, education has its own spirit which is expressed in programmes of study, of subjects taught, teaching methods and a physical body, a material structure which partially expresses this spirit but which also influences it, sometimes leaves its imprint upon it and temporarily serves to confine it. From the Cathedral schools to the mediaeval universities, from these latter to the Jesuit colleges, and then from there to our own *lycées* there have certainly been many transformations. This is because the organs of education are in every age closely related to the other institutions of the body social, to customs and beliefs, to the major intellectual movements.

But they also have a life of their own, an evolution which is relatively autonomous in the course of which they conserve many of the features of their former structure. Sometimes they defend themselves against influences acting upon them from the outside by relying on their past. For example it would be impossible to understand the division of universities into faculties, the systems of examinations and degrees, the boarding system, the use of sanctions in the academic world, unless we go right back to the time when the institution was being constructed whose outward forms, once they have come into being, tend to endure through time whether by some kind of force of inertia or because they successfully adapt to new circumstances. Seen from this point of view the organisation of education appears to be more hostile to change, more conservative and traditional even perhaps than the Church itself because its function is to transmit to the new generation a culture whose roots reach back into the distant past. But as against this the organisation of education has always been subject at certain periods to more radical changes brought about by genuine revolutions which have sometimes proved excessive. As

Durkheim noticed the men of the Renaissance in their hostility towards scholasticism failed to preserve that aspect of mediaeval education which deserved to be retained, namely its concern for a vigorous training in logic, and thus they paved the way for a purely literary, Greco-Latin curriculum designed primarily to fashion sophisticated writers, masters of eloquence, and accomplished conversationalists.

It is a complex and eventful story which is also vast in its scale since it embraces the whole period stretching from the Carolingian era to the end of the nineteenth century. Of course Durkheim was not an historian by profession. But he was thoroughly familiar with modern historical methods, having been a pupil, and a highly valued pupil, of Fustel de Coulanges at the Ecole Normale. He studied primary scources; for example, he read Alcuin in the original. No less eminent a historian than Christian Pfister, who was familiar with the two lectures on the Carolingian renaissance, found them unexceptionable. His documentation was as substantial as possible: the majority of his lectures included bibliographies which bore witness to massive reading and which we have not reproduced here because of course they are now out of date.

However it is of crucial importance to understand what Durkheim intended. When he had agreed to run this course he had clearly specified that he would not treat educational problems in doctrinal fashion as a psychologist or a moralist. He would demonstrate rather how they arose in the course of events under the pressure of circumstances and the social environment, what solutions triumphed, what their consequences were and what we should learn from them. He sought in the past the lessons from which the present was to take advantage. This way history for him furnished the subject-matter for reflection on a certain number of great educational experiments whose structure and outline it presents. He needed to evoke them, to imagine them, to relive them in thought and, above all, to understand them and to interpret them in their relationships and their development. As Auguste Comte said of positivism, sociology could do ample justice to the views which have preceded it and which it believes itself destined to replace. Durkheim recognised the gaps, the excesses, the congenital vices of the earlier systems of educational thought. But he was also sensitive to an understanding of those qualities in them which were novel and fruitful and which had constituted the legitimate reasons for their more or less sustained success.

All this can be found in the large bold fresco which covers ten centuries of history, in this kind of sustained discourse on the progress of the human mind in France which only Durkheim was capable of constructing.

It is our belief that by making known this aspect of his thought, of his intellectual activity, we are rendering good service to his memory. His opponents have sometimes represented him as having a scholastic mind, narrow, nourished by abstractions, incapable of insight into anything beyond the confines of his own system. It has also been urged against him by people who have concentrated on one part of his work despite the extensiveness and diversity of the whole that he attended too exclusively to savage and archaic societies. To those who read this book, he will appear as he really was, that is as a mind free from all preconceived ideas, subject first and foremost to the authority of facts and moreover quite at ease working on a large canvas. It will also be seen how for him the history of education in France is constantly illuminated by the history of French and European thought over more than ten centuries. Could anything be more concrete and more relevant, closer to our own contemporary concerns?

Besides there is an additional factor apart from the above mentioned which has decided us at this particular time not to let the work slumber and disappear into obsolescence as is the fate of so many forgotten manuscripts. This is the fact that the book provides direct answers to questions which we ourselves pose today with greater urgency than ever so that it is only fitting to reintroduce it into the main stream of contemporary life, into the world of argument and debate which is its only habitat.

This course was undertaken immediately after the great parliamentary enquiry into education where qualified representatives from all parts of society, from all walks of life, from all political parties and from every kind of school, came to give evidence which culminated in the 1902 reform. It took place at a time when another reform of secondary education or, as we say now, of the 'secondary level', was being prepared. Durkheim described in one of his final lectures the variations in the curricula of the nineteenth century. He would not have been surprised that in the first third of the twentieth century, these endless toings and froings, despite being somewhat chaotic and contradictory, between one system and another, one conception and another, one extreme and another, have continued. But on the other hand he thought that this simply constituted a state of uncertainty which could not last indefinitely, that a state of crisis would soon be reached and that instead of timorous and partial reforms which failed to penetrate to the heart of things, it would be necessary to undertake a total reorganisation of our educational system. At that moment, it would be necessary to review the problem of educational thought in its entirety and it was precisely to the task of specifying fully the terms of the problem and to indicate the ways in which solutions were to be sought that Durkheim wished to contribute when at the conclusion of this long historical study he wrote two long prescriptive chapters. In them he distinguished the two great objects of education, namely persons and things, and examined successfully what benefit should be derived in this respect from the study of the sciences, of history and of languages. These pages contain a comprehensive educational theory which is simultaneously positive and systematic and well fitted to the needs of the moment. We present it with complete confidence to those responsible for the structural reforms which the ancient edifice of our school and university system requires as well as to academics and teachers at all levels. These latter in particular will be all the better able to contribute to making these reforms a reality, if they have a clearer conception of that portion of the evolutionary curve which has been hitherto traversed. In this way they will at least know how the academic organism of which they are a part has been gradually constituted, where it comes from, even if not where it is going and what principles emerge from a well-conducted examination of an already long period in the history of educational thought in France.

Translator's introduction

Preamble

I shall make no attempt, in introducing the present text to the English-speaking reader, either to set these lectures within the context of Durkheim's achievement as a whole or to provide a synoptic guide to their principal places of interest. I am not sufficient of a Durkheim scholar, a sociologist or an historian to attempt the former and there is a more urgent prefatory task than the latter which needs to be undertaken.[1] For this book consists of a series of twenty-seven lectures originally delivered in 1904 as part of the compulsory curriculum for that élite cadre of French graduates destined to compete in the *agrégation* where success would lead, in the majority of cases, to academic careers to be begun by filling the year's vacant positions in the *lycées*. *Prima facie*, therefore, there would seem to be good grounds for doubting whether the book can be of much interest to present-day, English-speaking students of education. It may, indeed, be that such doubts on the part of publishers and even students of Durkheim have brought about the situation which Steven Lukes characterises by saying: 'It [the book] has been almost completely ignored by writers on Durkheim and on the history and sociology of education, though it is unquestionably a major work that deserves to be translated.'[2] Nevertheless, I wish to claim not only that Lukes's evaluation is more than amply justified — the book will show that — but also and more surprisingly that Durkheim's treatment of large-scale but always concrete educational issues has as much to teach us about the problems which confront us today as almost anything we are likely to encounter in the writings of modern educational theorists. Far from being irrelevant, parochial, out-of-date, narrowly historical and only of interest to Durkheim scholars, this book is imbued with that insight and wisdom which transcend spatio-temporal limitations and which are characteristic of the genuine classic.

In his opening lecture Durkheim speaks of 'meeting an urgent contemporary need' by carrying out the investigation he is about to embark on. I shall argue that the turbulent state of educational theory and practice in the Western World in the last quarter of the twentieth century generates a need no less urgent than that to which Durkheim felt himself to be responding. Moreover, I shall claim that that response in the very earliest years of the century still goes a very long way towards meeting the same need. In particular, I shall try to show how much we have to learn from Durkheim with respect to four major areas of current educational controversy: the preparation of teachers and the content of the curriculum, then, though more briefly, styles of discipline and the distribution of education.

The preparation of teachers

The very existence of a compulsory course in educational theory for aspirant teachers continues to generate controversy in all quarters. Conservatives are suspicious lest it provide an opportunity for educational ideologues to indoctrinate the future teachers of their children with dangerously 'progressive' views. Radicals see it as yet another device whereby the priestly guild of teachers seek to enhance their monopoly power and prestige by insisting upon yet another vacuously mysterious initiation rite. And ordinary practitioners and interested spectators of the everyday business of educating the young enquire irritably or wistfully how long, O Lord, how long before some real expert will appear and actually and accurately tell us how to deal with discipline problems, how to ensure that our charges grow up to be moral and well-adjusted citizens, what to teach to whom — when, how and why. It is possible that sensitivity to all these issues accounted for Durkheim's reported reluctance to take responsibility for the course in the first place. Nevertheless, once having accepted it, he made no attempt to evade the issues.

In trying to elucidate what Durkheim thought the justification of educational theory to be, it is necessary to begin by saying something about what he took the nature of that activity to consist in. The French word which I have usually translated by the phrase 'educational theory' is 'pédagogie'. In one important respect, the translation is seriously defective in that Durkheim himself, as Lukes points out, proposed a threefold distinction between '(1) the scientific study of education; (2) the art of education, consisting of "ways of acting, practices, systematized skill" — the "savoir-faire of the educator, the practical skill of the teacher"; and (3) pedagogy, seeking to "combine, as conscientiously as possible all the data science puts at its disposal, at a given time, as a guide to action". Pedagogy is thus a "practical theory" — "an intermediary between art and science"' (Lukes, op. cit., p.111n). I have, however, avoided the word 'pedagogy' on the grounds that its colloquial use in English is extremely vague and certainly the cognate 'pedagogue' would be quite wrong, whereas its current technical use in the sociology of education gives it a sense more akin to 'educational ideology'. Moreover, I am far from certain that I can share Lukes's enthusiasm for the usefulness of this tripartite distinction and I am certain that the commonly-made distinction between that part of education courses for teachers which is 'academic' and that which is 'professional' is disastrously superficial. In fact, for better or worse, 'educational theory' is the name given to the kind of practically-orientated course, which Durkheim designated 'pédagogie' and which is found in most institutions in the English-speaking world concerned with the preparation of teachers, and for that reason I have chosen to use it.

What then is this educational theory which Durkheim regards as an essential part of the modern student teacher's preparation? It is perhaps easiest to begin trying to answer this question by looking to the results Durkheim hoped to achieve. Durkheim's absolutely fundamental premise is that an educational system is only as good as the teachers who operate it. It is crucial, therefore, that in the course of his preparation the teacher acquire a critical self-consciousness of the activity he is engaged in and of the framework within which he is functioning. Otherwise he is doomed to a mindless and mechanical repetition of the principles and procedures which governed his own education, and education itself is condemned to a stifling and degenerate conservatism. The teacher, then, must be prepared both to see how and why the present system came to be what it is and also to challenge it in the light of contemporary social need. But though he will not be this kind of servile conservative he will be no naive radical either believing that the present system can be scrapped completely and that we can start afresh from first principles. Durkheim saw too clearly the complexity of social reality and also knew full well that revolution typically destroys as much of what is good as it does of what is bad, as was so notably the case when the men of the Renaissance rejected the mediaeval system in its entirety. The successfully prepared teacher, then, would be progressive, but (to adapt a phrase of Burke's) he would attend to the ills of the body educational as to the wounds of a beloved father; moreover he would have a powerful insight into the social distortions which had produced those ills in the first place.

An important point related to this, and indeed it is the point which explains the need for caution in setting about the task of educational reform, is that the teacher both as an individual and a species is essentially an adaptive animal. If he were not, like other biological and social creatures, subject to the law of evolution, then in principle it might be that the preparation of teachers should consist in the transmission of eternal pedagogical verities. Indeed some such verities may indeed be timeless, such as the ab-solutely indispensable role of dialectic in the transmission and in-deed the creation of knowledge. But, in general, educational ideals and consequently the appropriate means of attaining them will change as social conditions and hence societies' values change. The good teacher consequently will be aware of the legitimate needs of his own society and to gain this awareness he will need to study how these needs have evolved in the history of that society. This is the sense in which it is correct to describe Durkheim as an 'ethical conventionalist'. He is not arguing just that social forces do in fact determine ethical ideals, still less for the extreme ethical relativism which ultimately says 'Anything goes'. But he does believe, in an important sense, that when in Rome not only does one do as the Romans do but actually that this is what one *should* do. This position is to be distinguished again from that of the Social Darwinists which ultimately makes it analytically true that what is to be socially valued are those values which in fact survive. Rather Durkheim regards man as an essentially social creature, such that what counts as the good for the individual is determined by the norms of his society. This is why Durkheim talks so fre-quently about 'responding' or 'meeting' new needs created by changing social circumstances. In particular, contemporary society, he believes, celebrates the cult of the individual and, though it is not clear what the precise educational consequences of this are, it is clear that Durkheim regarded it as vital that teachers become aware, primarily by studying educational systems responding to different needs, of the popular moral demands that the educational system of their own society was required to meet, in virtue of the popular legitimate needs of that society itself.

This profoundly moral emphasis, which is characteristic of Durkheim's whole approach to social science, leads to the final point that needs to be made concerning Durkheim's conception of the aim of educational theory. For ultimately Durkheim hoped that these lectures would result not merely in the acquisition of knowledge by future teachers but in the generation of a new educational faith — a secular faith, certainly, but nevertheless one which would issue in passionate commitment to the vocation of teaching and would engage and sustain the individual teacher at the deepest level of his heart and mind. It was the kind of faith which Durkheim, the teacher, himself possessed in such abundance and adhered to with such rigorous devotion. It is significant in this connection to note, though Durkheim does not himself make the point explicitly, that the educational systems whose effectiveness Durkheim is most impressed by are, he thinks, ultimately to be explained as the product of profound systems of religious belief. This is true not only of mediaeval education and classical education as developed by the Jesuits but also of the regrettably short-lived 'Realist' system whose theoretical progenitors were most notably Comenius and, to some extent, Rousseau, and which had rediscovered the insight of Greek religious thought which celebrates as sacred the particulars of concrete, physical nature as opposed to the Christian emphasis on general truths about human nature.

What, however, is to be the subject-matter which the future teacher must study in order that these aims may be achieved? The now so familiar distinctions between history, psychology, sociology and philosophy of education — the four horses of the apocalypse of educational theory — Durkheim was, mercifully, spared. It was not that such distinctions were foreign to him: on the contrary he is quite emphatic that the present can only be studied in historical perspective, that though the social sciences are too 'young' to provide precise educational analysis, educational systems are nevertheless to be understood in their social context, and it is to be expected that, for example, Freud's discovery of the unconscious will have important educational implications. Moreover and more importantly, not only is Durkheim's knowledge of philosophy clearly extensive but he characteristically concludes his historical analyses with the kind of evaluative statement which we might typically regard as philosophical and indeed the book as a whole culminates in two superb chapters of educational prescription.

The fact of the matter is that intellectual life in Durkheim's France was much less troubled by border disputes concerning what theoretical territory rightly belonged to whom. Polymathy was thought to be both possible and desirable and, purely as an example of the deployment of polymathic power, this book constitutes an outstanding achievement. Thus, although Durkheim himself places the emphasis on history, it is history so interpreted and so treated that it embraces and is suffused with the perspectives of the social sciences and of philosophy. There are in the end no distinct disciplines of educational theory for the future teacher to study: there is only the investigation of how education has been in the past, why it is as it is in the present and what it could and should become in the future. The important thing is that the future teacher's theoretical training should equip him to analyse his particular educational situation critically, knowledgeably and in depth, and to plan and prescribe with wisdom and insight.

There is a final point to be made concerning Durkheim's views on the preparation of teachers which is in some ways the most important of all. For the work is like an 'Ars Poetica' which itself exemplifies the doctrines it is proclaiming. Nowhere else that I am aware, do we get so clear an impression of what it must have been like actually to be taught by Durkheim. Thus, if the study of education is supposed to be comprehensive and embrace several intellectual perspectives, then Durkheim's own treatment of education is comprehensive and multi-faceted. If teaching, to be effective, must strike at the heart of the pupil's being, then Durkheim exerts all the resources of a rich and subtle prose style to strike up the appropriate chords and resources in the minds of his audience. Above all, if education is a process of striving to sensitise the young imagination so that it can grasp new modes of conceiving the world then this imaginative sensitising Durkheim engages in, with respect to education itself.

The content of the curriculum

Since Durkheim's concept of education is often thought to be élitist, which proposition I shall examine below, it is perhaps well to begin a consideration of his prescription regarding the content of the curriculum, by stressing that Durkheim regarded it as a healthy evolutionary phenomenon that secondary education by developing out of the original Arts faculty of the university should have required and retained an essentially general and non-vocational character. Of course, education must have as its overall aim the socialising of individuals into the role in society which they are destined to fill, and this includes preparing those individuals to play a particular part in the division of labour. But this in no wise implies that Durkheim thought education, and especially secondary education, should be narrowly vocational. However, that Durkheim should be thought to hold crudely utilitarian views on the reform of the curriculum is attributable to his sustained hostility to the hegemony of the 'classical' education; and it is worth examining his position in this respect more closely.

Durkheim made a characteristically radical distinction between studying the form of reality and the study of reality itself. The former in one guise or another had dominated the secondary school curriculum since its inception. Thus the trivium of the early mediaeval period had been seriously flawed by its exclusive concentration on grammar. This was in fact at yet a farther remove from the study of reality than the study of its form, for to study grammar is to study the language in which the form of reality finds expression. To that extent Durkheim regarded it as extremely arid and certainly quite unsuited to the general education by means of which the student was to prepare himself for the more practically orientated studies of the quadrivium. It was only redeemed by the fact that close attention to grammatical form issued inevitably in insight into, and appreciation of logical form. Thus the study of grammar paved the way for the next and, in Durkheim's view, great period of the Middle Ages when the curriculum came to be dominated by dialectical logic. Then, in a highly original and persuasive historical analysis of the Renaissance, Durkheim argues that revolt against the excesses of an education based almost entirely on dialectic resulted in over-reaction and excessive destruction. Everything about the mediaeval curriculum was rejected and this included the good as well as the bad. In its place there appeared, exemplified in the work of Rabelais, what might be called 'the cult of useless information'. It is true that this constituted an improvement in that reality could, as it were, peep through the study of what the authors of antiquity had said about the world of nature but it was still far removed from Durkheim's own ideal because of its indiscriminateness and because in the end, it allowed a study of reality only indirectly through the medium of what classical authors had said about it. Worse still was the other major strand in Renaissance educational thought whose most important exponent Durkheim identified as Erasmus and which might be termed 'the cult of the emptily elegant'. Here all the emphasis was on developing the arts of self-expression so that one might become well thought of in polite society. Both strands, however, were equally guilty in the banishment of dialectical debate from the curriculum. This, Durkheim felt, was the right and necessary method for generating and assaying opinions which did not fall within the province of scientific knowledge. As such, it would always need to be studied, though, of course, not in its exclusive and excessive mediaeval form.

In the emergence of classical education, largely under the influence of the Jesuits, French education congealed into a new formalism from which it continued to suffer in Durkheim's own day. This formalism might be described as 'the cult of human generality'. It was distinguished by its concern to convey, through a study of classical history and literature, especially the Roman, an understanding of the eternally enduring features of human nature. Now, the hegemony of such a curriculum Durkheim deplored on at least two crucial grounds. First, it excluded study of the world of nature through the natural sciences — and Durkheim points to the truly staggering fact that it took some two and a half centuries before the vast and revolutionary advances in natural science of the Renaissance gained even a foothold in the school curriculum. Second, it rested on a radically misguided notion of how it is appropriate to study the world of persons, for in its artificial emphasis on what is the same, it ignored the crucial fact about human nature, namely the almost limitless diversity of its manifestation. To gloss over the differences between the ancient Roman and the modern Frenchman was not only to mislead the pupil about human nature as it was exemplified in Roman culture, it also prevented him from understanding human nature in the peculiar particularity of his own situation. Moreover, there was the further corollary that other, allegedly more 'primitive' ancient cultures could safely be ignored since they would only be of interest, in as far as they exemplified in embryonic form that human nature which found fully-fledged expression only with the Greeks and the Romans.

Now, it was by exposing these two radical flaws in classical education — the exclusion of natural science and the serious misconception of human nature — that Durkheim hoped to show the traditional arts-science dichotomy to be a false one, with the consequence that competition between them for scarce curricular resources could be eliminated.

The reconciliation of conflict between the arts and the sciences can be brought about if we see that the pedagogical justification for neither of them is what it is too often taken to be and for both of them it is the same. The essential function of education is to develop neither aesthetic nor utilitarian skills, its goal rather must be the essentially moral one of cultivating the seeds of humanity which repose within each of us. Now, to achieve this not only must the world of persons be studied through a historical perspective on the extant literature of other cultures and other ages, but the world of nature will also form an essential object of study if our goal is an understanding of human consciousness. This for at least four reasons. First, activity occurs and the conceptions we have concerning the world about us affect the whole basis upon which we govern our lives. Second, it is in the world of nature that we have our origins and our roots and consequently to attempt to study man apart from the immense universe which surrounds him is to commit the anthropocentric fallacy. Third, the works of scientists no less than that of artists constitute human achievements and to that extent need to be understood if humanity itself is to be understood. Finally, the natural sciences have developed a logic of their own in the course of their development and the pupil can only acquire the art of inductive reasoning by direct experience through reliving for himself that course of development. With the emergence of the social sciences this logic will be indispensable for the study and understanding of man himself.

In this way, therefore, Durkheim proposes a curriculum which retains the phenomena of human consciousness as the central object of study, while reinterpreting and reassessing the role of the humanities within it and complementing that role with a fresh conception of the role of the natural sciences.

To the study of man in his variety and science in its humanity Durkheim only adds the study of forms of human thought through the medium of their modes of linguistic expression. In proposing such a curriculum Durkheim was fully aware that he was conforming with one of the traits which had dominated French educational thought throughout its development, namely the striving after encyclopaedic comprehensiveness. It is no doubt also true that in proposing such a radical reform of the curriculum he found it politic not to be dismissive of the great traditional bastions of education, classical studies and languages. Nevertheless, Durkheim was clearly sincere in his conviction that a comprehensive, indeed a complete intellectual diet was not only desirable for the health of education but also both possible and necessary. I am not aware of any persuasive argument or evidence to suggest that Durkheim was wrong about this: perhaps the only thing wrong with educational encyclopaedicism is that, like Christianity, it has never been tried.

Discipline

Durkheim's most important and detailed work on discipline in the context of the school is to be found elsewhere, particularly in the work on the application of the science of morality to the teaching situation. There are nevertheless a number of important clues to Durkheim's views on discipline to be discovered in the present work and together they are sufficient to reveal both the subtlety and the essential humanity of Durkheim's educational thought. First of all, Durkheim held that what, in the widest sense, he meant by 'discipline' constituted half of what needed to be studied with respect to any educational system. Roughly speaking, his division was between intellectual education and moral education. He emphasises that one of the earliest, most enduring and most fundamental features of education as it developed out of the Christian tradition was the concern of the teacher to influence children at the deepest level of their being, and this concern remains a legitimate one. The teacher, like a secular priest, is responsible for the moral welfare of his charges, no matter what his particular academic specialism, and it is part of his duty to get the child to understand that true freedom consists in the self-mastery that enables a man to do his duty. This sounds somewhat austere and there is no doubt that Durkheim would have regarded as suicidally anarchic the more extreme prescriptions of modern permissivists. What the discipline of a school and an individual teacher must seek to do is to facilitate the child's emergence from the private world of the family into the public world of organised society. This, as was evidenced by the staggering success of Jesuit education, required intensive control over the whole domain of the child's conduct, although no less important, in Durkheim's view, was the complementary feature of education, almost wholly neglected in the classical system, namely the extensive exploration of experience.

However, to characterise Durkheim as harshly authoritarian with respect to discipline would be a serious mistake. This can be seen by looking to relevant aspects of the educational systems he admires. Thus the total surveillance exercised by the Jesuits enables the teaching to be tailored to the needs and nature of the individual; in as far as this system was essentially personal and frequently led to sincere and enduring friendships between teachers and taught. Durkheim considered it more humane and more effective than the almost wholly impersonal system which had prevailed during the mediaeval period. It was rather the fanaticism which bred both curricular vacuity and the ruthless exploitation of children's egoistic propensities that Durkheim deplored. By contrast, he writes with evident sympathy of many features of mediaeval education which would today be regarded as distinctly 'progressive' in relation to discipline. In particular he appears to have approved of treating adolescent students substantially as adults from the age of about fourteen onwards, with college principals being elected democratically, with little or no corporal punishment after the primary level and, most striking of all, the complete absence of any pedagogical exploitation of the competitive spirit. The rationale underlying all this is not hard to find for Durkheim thought that the essential function of school discipline was to express, convey and reinforce the moral values of society and indeed awareness of the ultimate value of social life itself. Fear and egoism had neither of them any contribution to make in this direction; and moreover, to the standard objection that permissive discipline is unrealistic about human nature Durkheim would have replied both that the claim is historically falsified and that, in any case, the supposition that there is any single immutable phenomenon called 'human nature' is disastrously mistaken. As in other areas, Durkheim's attitude to discipline is characteristically complex, profound, rationally and vigorously argued and a reflection of his own brand of passionately and nobly held humanistic morality.

Access to education

We need finally to consider briefly what light the present work has to shed on the problem of access to education or what is more commonly called the problem of educational opportunity. We need to do this because it is too easily thought that Durkheim was élitist in his educational prescriptions and that therefore his analysis can be of little value in a society which has recognised the critical link between educational opportunity and life-chances. Now it is perfectly true that Durkheim envisaged that his audience would eventually be concerned with the education of those destined for middle-class jobs. It is also true that he does not seem at any point to have questioned whether secondary education as a selection mechanism, which determines first access to itself and thence to the life-styles which go with fulfilling different functions in the division of labour, may in fact serve to reinforce the very inequality to whose elimination it is supposed to contribute. Now, there are four points I want to make on Durkheim's behalf in mitigation of this charge. First, Durkheim is writing in a society where access to material goods was in the first place substantially less determined by the nature of the person's work than it is today and, moreover, access to different kinds of work was substantially less dependent upon access to education. In such a society (the France of both Zola and Proust) it is surely fair to claim that at least a start should, in the interests of justice and social solidarity, be made in the direction of meritocracy, so that trained ability rather than influence or privilege will determine the individual's role in the division of labour. To deny this is to commit the perfectionist fallacy: because it is logically or practically impossible to implement the meritocratic principle in its entirety, it doesn't follow that it is undesirable to try to implement as far as possible. Second, Durkheim's élitism, if such it is, is of a purely intellectual kind: he sees universities as places which generate a concentration of the best researchers and teachers the culture has produced, but there is no suggestion that because of this they should enjoy any special status other than that conferred upon them by their role as transmitters and creators of a society's knowledge. This is made clear by Durkheim's contemptuous account of the Erasmian strand in Renaissance education where the life of the mind is prostituted and valued only as an adornment for the participant in polite society. Less vigorously the Rabelaisian system is also radically flawed by being based ultimately upon a vainglorious concern for what other people think of one. Third, we should again note Durkheim's approbation of the mediaeval university, not the least impressive feature of which was precisely its cosmopolitanism and its classlessness.

Fourth and perhaps most important of all, there is a general point to be made about egalitarianism and élitism in education, a point which picks out a mistake which is actually avoided by Durkheim, as it is by Plato, even though both have frequently been castigated by egalitarians for making it. Indeed, it constitutes the Gordian knot of the excellence-equality debate. For, of course, no one concerned with social reality will want to deny that equality of educational attainment is either possible in practice or even desirable in principle, since presumably the most ardent egalitarian will not deny that people will in fact differ in their preferences even if he denies that there are any ineradicable reasons why they should differ in their prowess (implausible hypothesis though that is). But it in no wise follows from that that educational attainment should in any way be correlated, with social privilege whether this be measured in terms of material rewards, prestige or political power. In fact, Plato did notoriously want to make maximal educational attainment the sole prerequisite for the exercise of political power but, of course, for Plato the exercise of political power was anything but a privilege because not only incompatible even with relative economic superiority but also a painful distraction from the life of contemplation. Durkheim, arguably with a firmer grasp of, and concern with the art of the immediately possible, also nowhere wants to correlate educational attainment with social privilege, in the sense required by his egalitarian critics. What he rather wants to do, as is evident from the extreme sensitivity of his historical analyses of succeeding epochs, is to see social policy as the negotiation of constantly evolving aspirations and expectations. The just society is one where rewards are distributed in accordance with consensual agreement about the value of different kinds of labour, the secure society is one where there is maximal realisation of expectation. Presumably, therefore, it is part of the function of the educator, with his calling to a new secular faith, to generate rationalism rather than rationalisation in this area too.

Notes

1 However, a model introductory chapter which meets both these needs is to be found as Chapter 19 of Steven Lukes's major and, for the foreseeable future, authoritative study. *Emile Durkheim: His Life and Work*, Allen Lane The Penguin Press, London, 1973.
2 Loc. cit., p.357.

Translator's apologia

All translations are more or less bad translations; for the ideal translation is one in which the symbols of the translation-language exactly reproduce for the translation-audience all and only those responses which the original symbols would elicit from the original intended audience, and this ideal is an impossible one outside the realm of formal languages. The translator in fact must walk a tight-rope between the fluent and the accurate, the elegant and the literal, the readable and the written; and this is a tight-rope from which he must inevitably fall periodically into the saving net of compromise. All he can do in mitigation is to explain the principles he has striven to follow in seeking to meet the ultimately irreconcilable demands of fidelity to his author and concern for his public. Thus the endeavours of the humble translator, no less than those of the exalted poet, are never completed, only abandoned.

In translating the present work, I have been acutely conscious of handling material that was written to be spoken, and spoken in a teaching situation at that. This accounts for one detail of Durkheim's style that I have sought to reproduce, namely his constant exploitation of synonymy: he will typically make a point by offering three synonymous (or nearly so) words or expressions for the key concept, as if he is deliberately allowing time for the point to be absorbed while at the same time offering the student different linguistic modes of access to the ideas he is seeking to convey. More generally, my awareness that I am dealing with the lecture-form, has led me on the whole and where irresoluble conflict occurs to opt for readability rather than strict technical but clumsy correctness. To render the lucid obscurely or the elegant ponderously is no less to do violence to an original than to distort matters of more obvious substance.

I have also made the general — and surely uncontroversial —

assumption that there is little point in producing a translation for those who are in a position to criticise the translation rather than for those who are not so placed because they do not have the language of the original. This has involved me in a certain amount of vulgarisation, but then vulgarisation in the etymological sense is precisely what gives translation its point. More specifically, I have usually sought contemporarily intelligible equivalents for, for example, mediaeval Latin academic terms, and I have also translated words in foreign languages other than French.

Finally I have tried to produce a translation which can be read with profit and pleasure by people who have in common with Durkheim's original audiences that they are young and that they are destined to become teachers and for whom, therefore, inspiration is no less important than information.

part one

chapter 1

The history of secondary education in France

This year we are going to study a subject which has long intrigued me. Even at a time when I was not as I am today, exclusively concerned with teaching educational theory, I was already attracted by the idea of researching into how our secondary school education emerged and developed, because this study seemed to me to be one of very great general interest. And if this project was never realised it was both because I was deflected by other concerns and because I was aware of the great difficulties of the subject. If today I have decided to embark upon this venture it is not only because I now feel better prepared for it, but also, and more importantly, because circumstances seem to demand it of me since it meets, I believe, an urgent contemporary need.

It has been announced that a great reform of secondary education is at hand. After having spent the last twenty-odd years moulding and remoulding, in every possible direction, our secondary school curricula, it has finally been realised that, however valuable and interesting the innovations which have been successively introduced might be from other points of view, there is one consideration which is far more important than all the others and which ought by rights to have preceded them, for it constitutes the condition on which alone the others can succeed. It has been realised that if it is necessary to show discrimination in prescribing the different subjects to be taught, to transmit them in prudent dosages and to apportion them with care, it is even more essential to communicate to the teachers, who will be called upon to carry out this teaching, the spirit which is supposed to animate them in their task. It has been realised that the value of a programme is wholly dependent on the way in which it is carried out; for if it is carried out with reluctance or a passive resignation either it will defeat its object or it will remain a dead letter. It is essential that the teachers entrusted with the task of transforming the programme into a reality approve of it and take an interest in it. Only if they themselves live it, will they be able to bring it to life. Thus it is not enough to prescribe to them in precise detail what they will have to do; they must be in a position to assess and appreciate these prescriptions, to see the point of them and the needs which they meet. In brief, they must be familiar with the problems for which these prescriptions provide provisional solutions. This means that it is essential to initiate them into the great problems involved in the education for which they will be responsible, no less than into the methods whereby it is proposed to solve them, so that they may be able to make up their own minds with a knowledge of the issues involved. Such an initiation can only come from a study of educational theory which, if it is to be of value, must be given at the appropriate time: namely, when the intending teacher is still a university student. This is how the idea emerged that we need to organise through our various faculties the study of education, by means of which the future secondary school teacher can prepare for his functions.

A simple enough idea, I admit, indeed one which is to all appearances a mere truism; but nevertheless one which is still going to meet with a great deal of resistance from a variety of quarters. First of all, there is an old French prejudice which looks with a kind of contempt on the whole business of educational theory. It seems to be a very inferior form of study. By some strange illogical process, whereas political systems interest us and we argue passionately about them, educational systems inspire indifference in us, or even a kind of instinctive aversion. This is a quirk in our national temperament, which I shall not take it upon myself to explain. I am content simply to note it; I shall not waste more time showing the extent to which this kind of indifference and contempt is unjustified. There are some truths which one cannot go on harping back to indefinitely. Educational theory is nothing more than reflection applied as methodically as possible to educaional matters. How then can there be any form of human activity which can do without reflection? There is today no field of action in which science, theory, that is to say reflection, does not increasingly explore and illuminate practice. Why should the activity of education be an exception? No doubt one can attack the scandalous use to which more than one educational theorist has put his reasoning powers; one may think that the systems are often very abstract, making little contact with the world of reality; one can say that, given the present state of the human sciences, speculations about education cannot proceed too cautiously. But simply from the fact that it has been distorted by the way in which it has been understood, it does not follow that the activity is impossible; from the fact that it has been deliberately modest and circumspect one cannot conclude that it is pointless. What, after all, is more futile than telling men that they should lead their **lives** as if they weren't endowed with reason and reflection? **Reflection** has been stimulated; it cannot help but apply itself to those educational problems which have arisen in its path. The question is not whether it is to be used, but whether it is to be used haphazardly or methodically. Now, to use reflection methodically is to do educational theory.

But there are some who, while willing to admit that educational theory has some sort of general use, deny that it can be of any use as far as secondary education is concerned. It is currently said that a theoretical preparation is necessary for the primary school teacher but that, thanks to some special providence, the secondary school teacher has no need of it. On the one hand he has seen, in the example of his teachers, how one teaches and, on the other, the wide cultural grounding which he gets at university enables him intelligently to exercise this technique which he has observed in operation throughout his school days, so that he needs no further initiation. One may well ask, however, how it is that simply because the young student can explicate ancient texts, understand the subtleties of languages whether living or dead, is an erudite historian — how, in consequence of this alone, he should know what procedures are necessary in order to transmit to children the education which he himself has received. We have here two quite different types of activity which cannot be learned by the same processes. Acquiring knowledge does not entail acquiring the art of communicating it to others. It does not even entail acquiring the fundamental principles on which this art is grounded. But surely, it is said, the young teacher will organise his teaching on the basis of what he remembers of his school and student days. But is it not clear that this is to decree the eternal perpetuation of existing practices, for it follows that tomorrow's teacher can do nothing but repeat the practices of his own teacher of yesterday, just as he too was merely imitating his own teacher; and it is consequently impossible to see how, in this endless series of self-reproducing models, there can be any innovation at all. The scourge and enemy of routine is reflection. This alone can prevent habits from becoming immutable, rigid and sacrosanct. This alone can keep them vital and sustain them in such a condition of flexibility and malleability that they will be able to change, evolve and adapt themselves to variations in circumstance and situation. In as far as one restricts the role of reflection in education, one condemns it to stagnation; and perhaps here is to be found at least a partial explanation of the surprising fact, which we shall have cause to notice later; namely, the strange neophobia which has characterised our secondary education for centuries. We shall see in fact how in France, whereas everything has changed, whereas the political, economic and ethical system has been revolutionised, there has nevertheless been something which has remained palpably immutable until quite recent times: this is the educational presuppositions and procedures of what has come to be called a classical education.

But there is more. Not only is there no reason why secondary education should enjoy the sort of privilege which allows it to do without any knowledge of educational theory, but in my view there is nowhere where it is more essential. It is precisely in those school situations where it is most lacking, that there is the greatest need of it.

In the first place, secondary education is a more complex organism than primary education. Now, the more complex an organism is, the more it needs reflection in order to adapt itself to its environment. In the elementary school, at least in theory, every class is in the hands of one and only one teacher; consequently his teaching tends to have a quite natural unity which is very straightforward and therefore does not need to be intellectually planned: it is indeed the unity of the person teaching. The same is not true of secondary schools, where the same pupil is generally taught by a variety of teachers. Here there is a genuine division of pedagogic labour. There is one teacher for literature, another for languages, another for history, another for mathematics and so on. How, short of a miracle, can unity emerge from this diversity, unless it is contrived? How can all these different teachers adapt to one another and complement each other so that they create a unified whole, if the teachers themselves have no notion of what the whole is? It is not a question, especially in secondary schools, of producing mathematicians and men of letters, physicists and naturalists, but of developing the mind through the medium of literature, history, mathematics and the natural sciences. But how can each teacher fulfil his function, as regards his own specialised part in the total enterprise, if he does not know what this enterprise is and how his various colleagues are supposed to collaborate with him in it, in such a way that all his teaching is related to it? People often argue as if all this went without saying, as if everybody knew instinctively what is involved in developing a mind.

But there is no problem more complicated. It is not enough to be a literary sophisticate, a good historian or an ingenious mathematician in order to understand the diverse elements out of which an intelligence is formed, the basic conceptions which constitute it and how they can be called forth in the various educational disciplines. Add to this the fact that the word 'education' changes its meaning depending whether the child we are talking about is of one age rather than another, is at primary or secondary school, is destined for one sort of activity in life as opposed to another. Now, if it is important to explain the goals which all education should serve and the routes by which the goals can be reached, then we need the study of educational theory; and it is for lack of this that so many teachers in our secondary schools are working in a situation where their efforts are dissipated, and they find themselves paralysed by their isolation from one another. They shut themselves up in their specialism and expound the subject of their choice as if it existed alone, as if it was an end in itself, when it is really only a means to an end which it should constantly have in view and to which it should always be subordinated. Indeed, how should it be otherwise as long as, while they are at university, each group of students are taught their chosen subject separately from the rest and there is nothing to encourage these colleagues of tomorrow to meet and to reflect together on the common task which awaits them.

But that is not all. Secondary education has for more than half a century been undergoing a serious crisis which has by no means reached its conclusion. Everybody feels that it cannot remain as it is, without having any clear idea about what it needs to become. Hence all these reforms which follow one another with almost cyclical regularity, which are carried out and revised and sometimes even contradict one another. They bear witness both to the difficulty and to the urgency of the problem. Moreover the question is not peculiar to France; there is no major European state in which it has not arisen in almost identical terms. Everywhere educationalists and statesmen are aware that the changes which have occurred in the structure of contemporary societies, in their domestic economies as in their foreign affairs, require parallel transformations, no less profound, in the special area of the school system. Why is it that the crisis is most acute in the case of secondary education? This is a fact that for the moment I am content to note without trying to explain. We shall understand it better in what follows. Whatever it may be, in order to emerge from this period of turmoil and uncertainty, we cannot rely on the sole effectiveness of decrees and regulations. As I argued at the beginning, decrees and regulations can only connect with reality if they are supported by conviction. I would go further and claim that they cannot have any real authority unless they have been proposed, planned, publicised and in some way pleaded for by informed opinion, unless they express it in a thoughtful, clear and co-ordinated way, instead of trying to create and control it through the medium of officialdom. For as long as the spirit of doubt reigns in the minds of men, there is no mere administrative decision, however wise, which can cure it. It is essential that this great task of reconstruction and reorganisation be the work of the same body of people as that which is being called upon to be the subject of the reorganisation and reconstruction. Ideals cannot be legislated into existence; they must be understood, loved and striven for by those whose duty it is to realise them. Thus there is no task more urgent than that of helping future secondary school teachers to reach a consensus as to what is to become of the education for which they will be responsible, what goals it might pursue, what method it should use. Now, there is no way of achieving this other than by confronting future teachers with the questions which arise and with the reasons why they arise, by equipping them with all the pieces of factual knowledge which might help them in reaching solutions to the problems, and by guiding their reflections with liberal teaching methods. Moreover, this constitutes a necessary condition for revitalising, without any kind of artificiality, the somewhat ailing condition of our secondary education. For it is no use trying to conceal the fact that secondary education finds itself intellectually disorientated between a past which is dying and a future which is still undecided, and as a consequence lacks the vigour and vitality which it once possessed. To say this is not to imply that anyone is to blame but rather to take note of something which is a product of the nature of things. The old faith in the perennial virtue of the classics has been definitively shaken. Even those who by inclination look most naturally towards the past have a strong sense that something has changed, that needs have arisen which will have to be satisfied. As against this, however, no new faith has yet appeared to replace the one which is disappearing. The task of educational theory is precisely to help in the development of this new faith and, consequently, of a new life. For an educational faith is the very soul which animates a teaching body.

Thus the necessity for study of educational theory turns out to be far more pressing in the case of the secondary school teacher than in that of the primary. It's not a question of simply instructing our future teachers in how to apply a number of sound recipes. They must be confronted with the problems of secondary school culture in its entirety. This is precisely what the course of study we are going to begin this year seeks to achieve.

I know that both those who over-generalise and those who are meticulously scholarly (for in this instance diametrically opposed types of mind find themselves in agreement) will claim that nothing of practical utility can be learned from history. What on earth, they ask, can the colleges of the Middle Ages tell us about secondary schools today? In what way can the scholasticism of the trivium and the quadrivium help us to discover what, here and now, we ought to be teaching to our children and how we ought to be teaching it? It is sometimes even additionally suggested that these retrospective studies can only have disadvantageous consequences; since it is the future for which we have to prepare, it is the future to which we should be looking and on which we should be concentrating our attention; excessive contemplation of the past can only hold us back. I believe, by contrast, that it is only by carefully studying the past that we can come to anticipate the future and to understand the present; consequently a history of education provides the soundest basis for the study of educational theory.

Indeed is it not already highly instructive to survey the various sorts of education which have followed one another in the course of our history. Of course — as is too often the case — the successive variations are attributed to the feebleness of the human intellect which has failed to grasp the one-and-for-all-time ideal system, if they are regarded simply as a series of mistakes painfully and imperfectly correcting themselves one after the other, then this whole history can only be of marginal interest. At most it could put us on our guard against repeating old mistakes; but then again, since the realm of errors knows no bounds, error itself can appear in an infinite variety of forms; a knowledge of the mistakes made in the past will enable us neither to foresee nor to avert those which may be made in the future. We shall see, however, that there was nothing arbitrary about any of these theories and these systems, which have undergone the test of experience and been incarnated in reality. If one of them has not survived, this was not because it was merely the product of human aberration but rather that it was the result of specific and mutually interacting social forces. If it has changed, this is because society itself has changed. Thus one comes to realise on the basis of first-hand experience that there is no immutable form of education, that yesterday's cannot be that of tomorrow, that while on the one hand, the systems are in a state of perpetual flux, these continual changes (at least when they are normal) connect at any given moment in time with a single fixed and determining reference-point: namely, the condition of society at the relevant moment. In this way we can get away from the prejudices, both of neophobia and of neophilia: and this is the beginning of wisdom. For while, on the one hand, one acquires immunity from that superstitious respect which traditional educational practices so easily inspire, one comes to feel at the same time that the necessary innovations cannot be worked out *a priori* simply by our imagination which longs for things to get better, but rather that they must be, at every stage of development, rigorously related to a totality of conditions which can be objectively specified.

The history of education, however, does not consist merely in a kind of introduction to educational theory, excellent in itself but of only very general relevance. We can and should expect it to furnish us with certain essential requirements which nothing else can provide.

In the first place, isn't it obvious that in order to play his part in that organism which is the school, the teacher needs to know what the organism is, what are the component parts out of which it is constituted and how they are interrelated so as to form a unity? Since this is the environment in which he will have to live it is critically important that he be familiar with it; but now the question arises, how are we to set about giving him this familiarity? Are we to restrict ourselves to explaining to him the legal rules and regulations which determine both the material and moral aspects of the way our academic institutions are organised, by pointing out to him the various cog-wheels and showing how they interlock? Certainly a course of this sort wouldn't be a waste of time; indeed it might justly be thought surprising that we allow our young teachers to enter the academic world without any knowledge of the laws which govern it. But this sort of knowledge would not really be knowledge, for these teaching institutions did not come into existence on the same day that the legislation defining them was drafted. They have a past which is the soil which nourished them and gave them their present meaning, and apart from which they cannot be examined without a great deal of impoverishment and distortion. If we are to know what they are really like and how consequently we shall behave towards them, it is not enough to be apprised of the letter of the laws which stipulate the relevant form they are to take and lay down (in theory) how they are to be organised. What we need to know is, as it were, the inner life of the institutions, how they are motivated and what goals they seek to achieve. For they have acquired a momentum of their own, which drives them in some particular direction and it is this which we need to know about more than anything else. Now just as we need more than one point in order to specify any particular line (especially a relatively tortuous one), so the geometrical point which is constituted by the present moment is by itself quite useless if what we wish to do is to plot the trajectory of a particular institution. What tends to make it move in one direction rather than another are forces which are internal to it, which give it life, but which do not reveal themselves clearly on the surface. In order to understand them we need to see them at work in the course of history, for only in history do they manifest themselves through the accumulation of their effects. This is why no educational subject can be truly understood except by placing it in the context of the institutional development, the evolutionary process of which it forms a part but of which it is only the contemporary and provisional culmination.

But it is not only the organisation of education which history helps us to understand; it also illuminates the educational ideals which this organisation was designed to achieve, the aims which determine and justify its existence.

Here again, it looks on the surface as if so much historical investigation was really unnecessary for solving the problem. Isn't the object of education to turn our pupils into men of their times, and in order to know what we need to produce a man of his own times is it really necessary to investigate the past? The model of man which today's education must seek to construct was not fashioned in the Renaissance, the seventeenth or eighteenth centuries. So it is modern man that we should be studying. It is ourselves that we should be scrutinising and our contemporaries that we need to investigate, and it is the conception of man that we form after this kind of study of ourselves and our neighbours which we ought to use in determining the aim of education. But although this method is often advocated by the intelligentsia as being the only one which will enable us to prepare for the future, I believe that on the contrary it is virtually certain to lead to a multitude of dangerous errors. Indeed what do we even mean when we talk about contemporary man, the man of our times? It is simply the agglomeration of those characteristic traits whereby today's Frenchman can be identified and distinguished from the Frenchman of former times. But this cannot really give us a picture of the whole modern man; for in each one of us, in differing degrees, is contained the person we were yesterday, and indeed in the nature of things it is even true that our past *personae* predominate, since the present is necessarily insignificant when compared with the long period of the past because of which we have emerged in the form we have today. It is just that we don't directly feel the influence of these past selves precisely because they are so deeply rooted within us. They constitute the unconscious part of ourselves. Consequently we have a strong tendency not to recognise their existence and to ignore their legitimate demands. By contrast, with the most recent acquisitions of civilisation we are vividly aware of them just because they are recent and consequently have not had time to be assimilated into our collective unconscious. This is particularly true of those which are in the process of developing, those of which we are not yet fully in possession, which still partially elude us, for these, more than any others, make overwhelming demands on the totality of our intellectual energies. Precisely because we don't fully grasp them we train our conscious mind actively upon them, thus spotlighting them so that we form a mental image of them as constituting the most essential feature of reality, that which is of greatest price and value and consequently most worthy of research. All other things are relegated to the shadows, despite the fact that they are, none of them, any less real or important. Science is the great novelty of our century, and for all those who experience it as such, scientific culture seems to form the basis of all culture whatsoever. Should we notice that we are short of practical people with technical skills, then we shall conclude that the aim of education is to develop practical capabilities. It is this sort of situation which gives rise to educational theories which are exaggerated, one-sided and incomplete, expressing only temporary needs and transitory aspirations, theories which in any case cannot long endure, for they soon generate others to correct, complete and modify them. The man of his times is a man who is dominated by the needs and inclinations of the moment, and these are always one-sided and tomorrow will be replaced by others. The result is all sorts of clashes and revolutions which can do nothing but harm to the steady process of evolution. What we need to understand is not the man of the moment, man as we experience him at a particular point in time, influenced as we are by momentary needs and passions, but rather man in his totality throughout time.

To do this we need to cease studying man at a particular moment and instead try to consider him against the background of the whole process of his development. Instead of confining ourselves to our own particular age, we must on the contrary escape from it in order to escape from ourselves, from our narrow-minded points of view, which are both partial and partisan. And that is precisely why a study of the history of education is so important and worthwhile. Instead of starting out by what the contemporary ideal ought to be we must transport ourselves to the other end of the historical time-scale; we must strive to understand the educational ideology most remote in time from our own, the one which was the first to be elaborated in European culture. We will study it, describe it and, as far as we are able, explain it. Then, step by step, we will follow the series of changes which it has undergone, parallel to changes in society itself, until finally we arrive at the contemporary situation. That is where we must end, not where we must begin; and when, by travelling along this road, we arrive at the present-day situation it will appear in a light quite different from that in which we would have seen it, had we abandoned ourselves at once and unreservedly to our contemporary passions and prejudices. In this way we shall avoid the risk of succumbing to the prestigious influence exercised by transitory passions and predilections, because these will be counter-balanced by the newly acquired sensitivity to differences in needs and necessities — all equally legitimate — with which the study of history will have furnished us. Thus the problem, instead of being arbitrarily over-simplified, will become susceptible of a dispassionate examination, in all its complexity and in a form which is no less relevant for the student of the social ethos of our own age than it is for the historian.

This kind of historical enquiry will even on occasions enable us to revise our ideas about history itself. For the development of educational theory, like all human development, has been far from following a steady, regular course. In the course of the struggles and conflicts which have arisen between opposing sets of ideas, it has often happened that basically sound ideas have floundered, whereas, judged from the point of view of their intrinsic worth, they ought to have survived. Here as elsewhere the struggle for survival has led to results which are only crude and approximate. In general it is the best adapted and the most gifted which survive, but as against that, this whole history is littered with a multitude of lamentable and unjustified triumphs, deaths and defeats. How many healthy ideas which ought to have survived to maturity have been cut down in their prime! New educational theories — no less than moral or political ones — are so full of the fire and energy of youth that they adopt a stance of violent aggressiveness towards those which they seek to replace. They regard them as implacable enemies, so conscious are they of the burning hostility which divides them, and they strive to the limits of their capacity to subdue and, as far as possible, exterminate them. The champions of new ideas will willingly believe that there is nothing worth preserving in the older ideas which are really their progenitors and allies, since it is from them that they descend. The present does battle with the past, despite the fact that it derives from it and constitutes its continuation. Thus it is that aspects of the past disappear which could have and should have become standard features of the present and the future. The men of the Renaissance were convinced that Scholasticism should be totally eliminated, and indeed as a consequence of their violent campaign very little does in fact remain. We shall have later to consider whether this revolutionary attitude did not lead to a very serious deficiency in the set of educational ideals which the men of the Renaissance handed down to us. Thus the study of history will enable us not only to communicate our own principles but also, from time to time, discover those amongst our predecessors that it is crucial for us to take into account since they are our forebears and we are their heirs.

These then are the lines along which we shall pursue our enquiry. It will be evident that we are not concerned with a scholarly investigation into the archaeology of educational theory: if we depart from the present our final aim is to return; if we flee from it, we do so in order to see it better and to understand it better. But in fact we shall never lose sight of it. It will be the goal towards which we are constantly tending, and it will emerge gradually in the course of our advance. After all, what is history if it is not an analysis of the present, since the constituent components of the present are only to be found in the past? And that is why I believe that the ensuing historical enquiry can be of immense value to the student of education.

chapter 2

The early Church and education (I)

It is widely believed that anyone who concerns himself with practical matters should cease to contemplate the past in order to concentrate his entire attention upon the present. Since the past no longer exists and there is nothing we can do about it, it seems that it can be of interest to us only as a curiosity. It belongs, people think, to the realm of scholarship. What we need to know about is not what was once the case but what is now the case, and — better still — what is likely to become the case: this latter is what we must strive to foresee in order to be able to satisfy the demands which our present circumstances make on us. In the last lecture I concentrated on trying to show the extent to which this method is unfruitful. For the truth is that the present, to which we are invited to restrict our attention, is by itself nothing: it is no more than an extrapolation of the past, from which it cannot be severed without losing the greater part of its significance. The present is composed of an infinite number of elements which are so closely intertwined that it is difficult for us to see clearly where one begins and another ends, what each of the elements is by itself and what are the relationships which hold between them. By direct scrutiny we can only arrive at a very crude and confused conception. The only way in which we can distinguish and analyse these elements, and consequently succeed in shedding some light on all this confusion, is by carrying out historical research into the manner whereby they have progressively come to cluster together, to combine and to form organic relationships. Just as we instinctively regard matter as homogeneously extended until scientific analysis has disclosed to us the principle of intellectual categorisation whereby we order our perceptions, so our immediate awareness of the present inhibits us from realising its complexity until this has been revealed to us by historical analysis. But what is perhaps more dangerous still is the exaggerated importance which such an attitude inclines us to attribute to the aspirations of the present moment when these have ceased to be subject to any critical checking procedures. For it is precisely by their topicality that they hypnotise us, absorb us, and cripple our ability to be aware of anything other than they themselves. Our awareness of what we lack is always very intense; consequently it tends to occupy an exaggerated position in our consciousness by refusing to take cognisance of everything else, which it casts into the shadows. As the exclusive object of our desires it appears to us to be the sole supreme value, the ideal to which everything else in existence ought to be subordinated. However, the truth is that what we lack according to this criterion is either no more essential or is even less essential than what we already have; and so it is that, in the interests of our transient and relatively unimportant needs, we are tempted to sacrifice genuinely essential and vital necessities. Rousseau was aware that in his time education left too little room for the spontaneity of the child; he therefore makes a systematically negative methodology the one essential feature of any sound educational theory. Solely on the basis of the fact that children are not sufficiently involved with natural phenomena, he virtually makes education through contact with natural phenomena the exclusive basis of any education whatsoever. If we are to resist the prestigious influence of our present preoccupations (both inevitable and one-sided, as they are) we must let them be counterbalanced by a knowledge of all those other human needs to which we must be no less alive; and this knowledge can only be acquired by a study of history; for this shows us how to complete our understanding of the present by linking it to the past whose continuation it is.

The arguments I have advanced to show that a historical study of education is of practical value are, however, not the only ones. Not only does this method enable us to guard against possible future mistakes, but also we may anticipate that it will furnish us with the means of correcting certain mistakes which have been committed in the past and from whose consequences we are still suffering. Indeed the development of educational theory, like all human development, has not always been regular. In the course of the struggles that have been waged between the different views which historically have succeeded one another, there are several sound ideas which have been killed off whereas, judged by the criterion of their intrinsic value, they ought to have survived. Here as elsewhere the struggle for survival yields only very crude results. As a general rule it is the fittest, the best endowed who survive; but as against that, how many unworthy successes have there been, how many lamentable deaths and defeats due to some accidental combination of circumstances. In the history of ideas, there is one cause which is more efficacious than all others in producing this effect. When new ideas come into being, whether they are educational, moral, religious, or political, they quite naturally possess the aggressive fire and vitality of contemporary youth in any culture: they come to display themselves as violently hostile to the older ideas which they seek to replace. They therefore reject them *in toto*. The champions of new ideas, carried away by the heat of battle, are only too ready to believe that there is nothing worth preserving in the older ideas against which they are fighting. They make war on them totally and mercilessly; and yet the truth is that here as elsewhere the present is the progeny of the past from which it derives and whose continuation it constitutes. Between any new historical situation and the one which preceded it there is no great gulf fixed but rather a close familiar relationship since, in a certain sense, the former is the offspring of the latter. But men do not realise the existence of this relationship: they feel only the antagonism which separates them from their predecessors, and they are blind to what they both have in common. They believe that there are no limits to the destruction which they are justified in wreaking upon a tradition to which they are opposed and which resists them. This has resulted in deplorable acts of destruction; features of the past disappear when they ought to have become features of the future. The Renaissance succeeds Scholasticism: the men of the Renaissance immediately took it as self-evident that there was nothing worth preserving in the system of the Scholastics. We shall have to ask whether this revolutionary approach did not produce certain gaps in our educational ideology which have been handed on down to our own times; thus by studying education historically we shall be enabled not only to understand the present better, but also we shall have the chance of revising the past itself and of bringing to light mistakes which it is important for us to recognise, since it is we who have inherited them.

However, in addition to its practical relevance, which I have been at pains to emphasise at the outset because it is most frequently misunderstood, the enquiry on which we are about to embark is also of considerable theoretical and scientific importance. At first glance, the history of secondary education in France might appear to be a highly specialised study of interest only to a narrow circle of school-teachers. However, as the result of something peculiar to France, it happens that throughout the major part of our history secondary education has provided the focus for the whole of our academic life. Higher education, after having given birth to secondary education, very soon became extinct and was only reborn in the aftermath of the 1870 war. Primary education appears only very late in our history and only really got off the ground after the Revolution. Thus, throughout a large period of our national existence the entire educational scene is dominated by secondary education. The consequence of this is, first, that we cannot write the history of secondary education without at the same time writing a general history of education and educational theory in France. What we are going to try and chart is the development of all the most essential features of the French educational ideal, by scrutinising the doctrines in which it has from time to time sought to articulate itself self-consciously as well as the academic institutions whose function it was to realise it. Moreover, since the most important intellectual forces of the nation were, from the fourteenth or fifteenth century onwards, formed in our secondary schools, we shall, as we progress, be driven to what almost amounts to writing a history of the French intellectual. It is additionally true that this disproportionate role played by secondary education in the totality of that social life which is peculiar to our nation and which is not to be found anywhere else to the same extent, will, as we can be sure in advance, derive from some personally distinctive characteristic, some idiosyncrasy in our national temperament which we shall come to uncover simply because we shall be seeking the causes of this peculiarity in the history of our educational thought. The history of educational thought and the study of social *mores* are indeed closely linked.

Having thus specified how we understand the subject-matter with which we shall be dealing and the manifold ways in which it is of interest, we now set about tackling it. But where to begin? At what moment of time should we begin this history of secondary education?

In order fully to understand the development of any living phenomenon, in order to explain the different forms which it assumes at successive moments in its history, we should need to begin by discovering the composition of the initial germ which stands at the origin of its entire evolution. Of course, nobody would any longer claim today that a living being exists in perfected embryonic form in the egg from which it issues. We know that the effect of the environment, of all manner of external circumstances, is indeed considerable. It is nevertheless still true that the egg exerts substantial influence over the whole of what it eventually becomes. The moment when the first living cell is constituted is a moment of unique and absolutely radical significance whose effect is felt throughout the whole of the rest of life. What is true of living beings is equally true of social institutions, whatever they may be. Their future, the direction in which they develop, their vigour at various stages in their subsequent existence, all these depend crucially upon the nature of the first germ from which they originate. Thus, in order to understand the way in which the educational system which we are to study has developed, in order to understand what it has become, we must not shrink from tracing it to its most remote origins. We must go back beyond the Renaissance and even beyond the time of the Scholastics. We must go on backwards until we have reached the first nucleus of educational ideas and the first embryo of an academic institution which are to be discovered in the history of modern societies. As soon as we have carried out this study we shall see clearly that retrospective research of this kind is by no means useless, and that certain essential peculiarities in our modern convictions still bear the stamp of these very remote influences.

But this nucleus, this original germinative cell, where is it to be found?

The entire substance of our early intellectual culture came to us from Rome. It is therefore reasonable to expect that our educational thought, the fundamental principles of our educational system, came to us from the same source, since education itself is only a digest of adult intellectual culture. But by what path and in what manner was this transmission effected? The Germanic peoples (i.e., the Franks) — if not all of them, at least those who gave their name to our country — were barbarians quite unable to appreciate any of the refinements of civilisation. They attached no value at all to literature, the arts or philosophy: we know that even the buildings and sculpture of the Romans inspired in them only hatred and contempt. There was thus a veritable moral gulf fixed between them and the Romans which, it appears, rendered impossible between these two peoples any kind of communication or mutual influence. Since these two civilisations were so intensely alien one to another they were apparently only able to reject one another. Fortunately, however, there appeared — not of course immediately but still very quickly — a flank on which these two societies, who were so antagonistic to one another on all other fronts and whose relations were those of mutual hostility and exclusion, were able to find something in common, which drew them closer to one another and enabled them to communicate with one another. At a very early period one of the most essential institutions of the Roman Empire took root in French society and expanded and developed there without, however, undergoing any change in its nature: this was the Church. And it was the Church which served as a mediator between heterogeneous peoples, it was the channel along which the intellectual life of Rome gradually flowed into the new societies which were in their formative stages. And it was precisely by means of education that this transfusion was effected.

At first sight, admittedly, it may seem surprising that the Church, without in any way losing its unique identity, was able to take root and flourish equally in such radically different social milieux. The most essential characteristic feature of the Church and of the morality which it introduced to the world was contempt for the joys of this world, for material and psychological luxury; it undertook to substitute for the joys of living the more astringent joys of renunciation. It was entirely natural that such a doctrine should suit the Roman Empire, weary as it was after long centuries of over-civilisation. All it did was to translate and consecrate the feeling of satiety and disgust which had for a long time gnawed at Roman society and to which both Epicureanism and Stoicism had, in their own ways, given expression. All the pleasure which can be extracted from the refinements of culture had been exhausted; people were thus quite ready to welcome as the means of salvation a religion which claimed to reveal to men a quite different source of felicity. But how could this religion, which had been born in the midst of an aging and decaying society, effect such easy acceptance in young nations, which, far from having over-indulged in the delights of this world, had not yet even tasted them and which, far from being weary of life, were only just embarking upon it?

How could such robust, vigorous societies, overflowing with vitality, subject themselves so spontaneously to a depressing rule of life which ordered them above all to practise continence, self-privation and renunciation? How could fiery appetites which bridled at all moderation and all restraint reconcile themselves to a doctrine which prescribed above all else moderation and self-restraint? The contract is so striking that Paulsen, in his *Geschichte des gelehrten Unterrichts*, goes so far as to claim that the whole civilisation of the Middle Ages contained, as a result, an internal contradiction in the principle of its development and constituted a living antinomy. According to him, the content and the container, the substance and the form of this civilisation, were mutually contradictory and incompatible. The content was the real life of the Germanic peoples with their violent untamed passions, their thirst for life and for pleasure, and the container was the Christian ethic with its notions of sacrifice and renunciation and its powerful inclination towards a life of restraint and discipline. However, if mediaeval civilisation had indeed nurtured in its bosom a contradiction so flagrant, an antinomy so irreconcilable, it would not have lasted. The substance would have shattered the form which was so ill-adapted to it; the content would have burst through the container; the needs felt by human beings would have rapidly overwhelmed the rigid ethic which sought to suppress them.

The fact is that there was one aspect of the Christian doctrine which harmonised perfectly with the aspirations and the state of mind of the Germanic societies. For Christianity was supremely the religion of those who were not great, of the humble, of the poor, the poor whose poverty was both material and cultural. It exalted the virtues of humility, of unpretentiousness in both material and intellectual matters. It extolled simple hearts and simple minds. Now the Germanic peoples, because they were still in their infancy, were themselves simple and humble. It would be a mistake to imagine that they led a life of passionate abandon. Rather was their existence made up of involuntary fasting, forced privations and heavy toil which was only interrupted when the opportunity arose by violent but spasmodic debauches. Peoples which had only recently been nomadic could not but live in conditions of harsh poverty with simple customs, so that they quite naturally welcomed with joy a doctrine which glorifies poverty and which extols a simple manner of life. This pagan civilisation which the Church was fighting was no less odious to the Germans themselves than it was to the Church, Christians and Germans alike shared a common enemy in the Romans, and this common feeling of antagonism and hatred created close bonds between them because they both found themselves confronted by the same enemy. Thus the Church in its infancy gladly placed the barbarians above the Gentiles and gave evidence of a genuine preference for the former: 'The barbarians,' says Salvien to the Romans, 'the barbarians are better than you.'

There was thus a powerful affinity and a secret sympathy between the Church and the barbarians; and it is this which explains how the Church was able to implant and establish itself so firmly amongst them. It was because it answered their needs and their aspirations; because it offered them a moral consolation which they could not find elsewhere. On the other hand, its origins were Greco-Latin and it could not but remain more or less faithful to its origins. It had acquired its form and organisation in the Roman world, the Latin language was its language, it was thoroughly impregnated with Roman civilisation. Consequently in implanting itself in barbarian environments it at the same time introduced the very civilisation of which it could not rid itself, whatever the circumstances, and thus became the natural tutor of the peoples which it converted. Of the new religion these peoples asked only a faith, a moral framework; but at the same time they found a culture which was the corollary of this faith. At all events,

if the Church really did play this role it was at the cost of a contradiction against which it has fought for centuries without ever
achieving a resolution. For the fact was that in the literary and artistic monuments of antiquity there lived and breathed the very
same pagan spirit which the Church had set itself the task of
destroying, to say nothing of the more general fact that art,
literature and science cannot but inspire profane ideas in the
minds of the faithful and distract them from the only thought to
which they should be giving their entire attention: the thought of
their salvation. The Church could not therefore provide a place
for the writings of the ancients without scruple and anxiety.
Hence the insistence of the early fathers on the dangers to which
the Christian is exposed when he gives himself immoderately over
to profane studies. They multiply their proscriptions in order to
reduce such studies to the minimum. On the other hand, they
could not do without them altogether. In spite of themselves they
were forced not to proscribe them, as is evidenced by the rule
enunciated by Minucius Felix: *Si quando cogimur litterarum secularium
recordari et aliquid ex his discere, non nostrae sit voluntatis sed, ut ita dicam,
gravissimae necessitatis* (If ever we are compelled to bring to mind
secular literature and to learn something from it, let it not be at
our desire, but, I would say, under the gravest necessity). First of
all, circumstances demanded that Latin be the language of the
Church, the sacred language in which the canons of the faith were
composed. Now where can Latin be learned unless in the monuments of Latin literature? These could indeed be chosen with discrimination and only a very small number permitted, but one way
or another it was necessary constantly to return to them. In addition to this, whereas paganism was above all a system of ritual
practices backed up no doubt with a mythology, but vague, incon-
sistent and without any expressly obligatory authority, Christianity by contrast was an idealistic religion, a system of ideas and
a body of doctrines. To be a Christian was not a matter of carrying
out certain material operations according to the traditional
prescriptions, it was rather a question of adhering to certain articles of faith, of sharing certain beliefs, of accepting certain ideas.

In order to inculcate a particular practice, a simple method of
training is an effective and perhaps even the only effective
method; but ideas and feelings cannot be communicated except
by means of education, whether this education is addressed to the
emotions or to the reason or to both at the same time. And this is
why from the moment of the foundation of Christianity, preaching (which was quite unknown in antiquity) immediately began to
play a crucially important part, for to preach is to teach. Now,
teaching presupposes a culture, and at that time there was no

culture other than pagan culture. It was therefore necessary for the Church to appropriate it. Teaching and preaching presuppose in him who is teaching or preaching certain linguistic skills, a certain capacity for dialectic, and a certain familiarity with man and with history. All this knowledge was only to be found in the works of the ancients. The single fact that Christian doctrine is complexly involved in books, that it expresses itself daily in prayers which are said by each of the faithful and which are required to be known not only in the letter but also in the spirit, rendered it necessary not only for the priest but also even for the layman to acquire a certain amount of culture. This is strikingly demonstrated by St Augustine in his *De doctrina Christiana*. He explains that, truly to understand Holy Scripture, one must have knowledge in depth of the language and of the things themselves which are expressed by the words. For how many are the symbols and the figures of speech which are unintelligible so long as we have no notion of the things which appear in these symbols or figures of speech? History is indispensable for chronological studies. Rhetoric itself is a weapon which the defender of the faith cannot afford to be without, for why should he remain feeble and unequipped when confronted by the error which it is his duty to combat?

Such then were the higher necessities which forced the Church to open schools and to create a place in these schools for pagan culture. The first schools of this type were those which opened in the environs of the cathedrals. The pupils, for the most part, were young people preparing for the priesthood, but simple laymen were also accepted who had not yet decided to embrace the sacred ministry. In them the pupils lived together in *convicts*, which were a very new and very special sort of scholastic establishment, the significance of which we shall have an opportunity of reverting to later. In particular we know that St Augustine founded at Hippo a *convict* of this type which, according to Possidius who wrote the saint's biography, produced ten bishops renowned for their learning and who in their turn founded in their own bishoprics similar establishments. Quite naturally, under the pressure of circumstances, the institution spread to the West; its fortunes we shall be describing later.

The secular clergy, however, was not alone in creating schools. As soon as the religious orders appeared, they played the same role; the educational influence of monasticism was no less great than that of the episcopacy.

We know well the way in which during the first centuries of Christianity the doctrine of renunciation gave birth to the monastic institution. Was not the best way of escaping from the corruption of the age to leave it altogether? Thus from the third and fourth centuries onwards we see communities of men and women multiplying everywhere from the East to as far as Gaul. The resulting invasions and upheavals of every kind accelerated the movement. It seemed as if the world was going to end: *orbis ruit*, the world is crumbling away in every quarter; and multitudes of people were taking refuge in deserted places. But Christian monasticism distinguished itself at the outset from, for example, Hindu monasticism, in that it was never purely contemplative. What the Christian is charged to watch over is not only his personal salvation but also the salvation of humanity. His role is to prepare for the reign of truth, the reign of Christ; not only in his own inner life but also in the world. The truth which he possesses is not to be piously or jealously guarded by himself alone for his own benefit, but rather actively propagated all around him. He must open blind eyes so that they see the light, he must carry the gospel to those who have misunderstood it or who have not heard it. He must recruit new soldiers for Christ. To achieve this it is essential that he does not shut himself up in egoistical isolation; he must, even while he shuns the world, retain a relationship with it.

The monk's life was consequently not one of simple solitary meditation but rather one which involved the active propagation of the faith: he was a preacher, a proselytiser, a missionary. This is also why alongside the majority of monasteries there arose schools to which not only candidates for the monastic life but also children from all sorts of different backgrounds and with all sorts of different vocations came, to receive an education which was at once religious and secular.

Cathedral schools and cloister schools, very humble and very modest as they were, were the kind from which our whole system of education emerged. Elementary schools, universities, colleges; all these derived from there; and that is why it is here that we have had to make our starting-point. Moreover because it was from this primitive cell that the whole of our academic organisation in all its complexity originated, this and this alone does and can explain certain essential features which our education has exhibited in the course of its history, or which it has retained right down to our own times.

In the first place, we can now see why education remained for so long in our society, and indeed in that of all the peoples of Europe, a Church affair and, as it were, an annex of religion; why, even after the time when teachers had ceased to be priests, they nevertheless retained for a very long time indeed something of the priestly physiognomy and even priestly duties (notably the duty to remain celibate). When we notice at a slightly later date the total absorption of education by the Church, we might be tempted to attribute it to political prudence. One might think that the Church seized the schools in order to be able to block any culture which tended by its nature to embarrass the faith. In truth, however, this relationship results quite simply from the fact that the schools began by being the work of the Church; it is the Church which called them into existence, with the result that they found themselves from the moment of their birth, one might even say from the moment of their conception, stamped with an ecclesiastical character which they subsequently had so much difficulty in erasing. And if the Church played this role, it is because the Church alone could perform it successfully. It alone could serve as the tutor of the barbarian peoples and initiate them into the only culture which then existed, namely classical culture. For since it was linked both with Roman society and with the Germanic societies; since, to some extent, it had two faces and two aspects; since, although it retained its links with the past, it was nevertheless orientated towards the future, it was able and it alone was able to serve as a bridge between these two such disparate worlds.

But at the same time we have seen that this embryo of education contained within itself a sort of contradiction. It was composed of two elements, which no doubt, in some sense, complememted and completed one another but which were at the same time mutually exclusive. There was on the one hand the religious element, the Christian doctrine; on the other, there was classical civilisation and all the borrowings which the Church was obliged to make from it, that is to say the profane element. In order to defend and propagate itself the Church, as we have seen, was forced to rely on a culture and this culture could not but be pagan since there wasn't any other. But the ideas which emerged from it patently conflicted with those which were at the basis of Christianity. Between the one and the other there stretched the whole of that abyss which separates the sacred from the profane, the secular from the religious. This enables us to explain a phenomenon which dominates the whole of our academic and educational development: this is that if schools began by being essentially religious, from another point of view as soon as they had been constituted they tended of their own accord to take on an increasingly secular character. This is because from the moment that they appeared in history they contained within themselves a principle of circularity. This principle was not something which they acquired (we know not how) from outside in the course of their evolution: it was innate in them. Feeble and rudimentary to begin with, it grew and developed; from being in the background it passed gradually into the foreground, but it existed from the very beginning. From their origins the schools carried within themselves the germ of that great struggle between the sacred and profane, the secular and the religious, whose history we shall have to retrace.

But the outward organisation of this nascent form of education already reveals an essential peculiarity which characterises the whole system which followed it.

In antiquity the pupil received instruction from different teachers who had no connection with one another. He went to a teacher of grammar or letters in order to learn grammar, to the teacher of either to learn music, to the rhetorician to learn rhetoric, and to the other teachers for other subjects. All these different forms of teaching met together inside him but outwardly they were isolated. It was a mosaic of different types of teaching, which were only formally connected. We saw that exactly the opposite is the case in the first Christian schools. All the teaching which took place in them was given in one and the same place and was consequently subjected to one and the same influence, tended in one and the same moral direction. This was that which emanated from Christian doctrine, that which shaped men's souls. Whereas formerly teaching had been dispersed, it now acquired a unity. The contact between the pupils and the teacher was continuous; it is indeed this permanence in the relationship which is characteristic of the *convict*, the earliest type of boarding school. Now, this concentration of teaching in one place constitutes an innovation of crucial importance and bears witness to a profound change which had come about in man's conception of the nature and role of intellectual culture.

chapter 3

The early Church and education (II)

Monastic schools up to the time of the Carolingian Renaissance

In our last lecture we saw what has been the seed of which our present-day system of education is but the flowering. It was in the closes of the cathedrals and the monasteries that those schools were opened which constituted the first embryo of our educational life. And, just as the seed already contains in itself in rudimentary form the characteristic properties of the living being which one day will emerge from it, so we have seen in this first seed of our educational system the origin of certain peculiarities which characterise its subsequent development. Indeed, since these schools were born in the Church, since they are the work of the Church, it is easy to see why they were originally essentially religious in their nature and imbued with the spirit of religion. But, as against this, because they already contain within themselves an element of the profane, specifically all those things which the Church borrowed from pagan civilisation, we can understand why, from the moment of their foundation, they were to some extent striving to rid themselves of their ecclesiastical character and to become more and more secular. The fact is that the principle of secularity which was contained within them from this moment tended to develop. This development is unintelligible as long as one fails to realise the need of the early Church to borrow the subject-matter of its educational system from paganism; that is, the Church's need to lay itself open to ideas and feelings which contradicted its own teaching.

Nor is this all; and an analysis of this early educational system will help us to understand one of the characteristics of our present organisation which we do not normally notice because we are so used to it, but which, nevertheless, is worth examining.

In antiquity, whether Greek or Latin, the pupil received his instruction from different masters who were in no way connected with one another. Each of his teachers taught in his own home and in his own way, and if the variety of things that the pupil learned in this way eventually coalesced in his head, they had been taught independently by teachers who took no account of each other's existence. There was no common motive or goal. Each teacher did his job on his own; one would teach reading, another the art of correct speaking, yet another would teach music, and another the art of speaking as a learned person. But each of these activities was pursued separately. This is in dramatic contrast to what happened as soon as the first Christian schools were founded. The Christian school, from the moment it first appears, claims to be able to give the child everything which it needs to know for its particular age. It takes over the child in his entirety. The child finds in the school everything which he needs. He is not even obliged to leave it in order to satisfy other material needs; he spends his whole life there; he eats and sleeps there and he applies himself there to his religious duties. This is, indeed, the distinguishing feature of the *convict*, the earliest type of boarding school. Thus the extreme diversification of earlier times is followed by an extreme concentration. And since this school is dominated by a single overwhelming influence, namely the ideals of the Christian faith, the child finds himself subject to this solitary influence at every moment of his life.

This innovation in the organisation of education itself derives from a novel conception of education and teaching.

In antiquity the education of the mind took as its aim the passing on to the child of a certain number of specific talents, whether these talents were thought of as a sort of adornment designed to heighten the aesthetic value of the individual or whether they were seen, as was the case in Rome, from a utilitarian point of view, as tools which people need in order to play their part in life. In both cases it was a question of inculcating in the pupil certain portions of knowledge and modes of behaviour.

These specific portions of knowledge and particular modes of behaviour could be acquired, without disadvantage, from quite separate teachers. It was not a question of making an impact on that part of the personality which gives it its fundamental unity but rather, as it were, of dressing it up in a kind of external suit of armour, different pieces of which could be forged quite independently, so much so that each workman could operate separately. Christianity, by contrast, very soon developed an awareness that underlying the particular condition of our intelligence and sensibility there is in each one of us a more profound condition which determines the others and gives them their unity; and it is this more profound condition which we must get at if we are truly to do our job as educators and have an effect which will be durable.

Christianity was aware that the forming of a man was not a question of decorating his mind with certain ideas, nor of getting him to contract certain specific habits; it is a question of creating within him a general disposition of the mind and the will which will make him see things in general in a particular light.

It is easy to understand how Christianity came to have this insight. It is because, as we have shown, in order to be a Christian it is not enough to have learned this or that, to be able to go through certain rites or utter certain formulae, to be familiar with certain traditional beliefs. Christianity consists essentially in a certain attitude of the soul, in a certain *habitus* of our moral being. To nurture this attitude in the child will thus henceforth be the essential aim of education. This is what explains the emergence of an idea which was totally unknown in the ancient world and which by contrast played a substantial role in Christianity: the idea of conversion. A conversion, as Christianity understands it, is not really a question of adhering to a particular set of beliefs and specific articles of faith. True conversion involves a profound movement as a result of which the soul in its entirety, by turning in a quite different direction, changes its position, its stance, and as a result modifies its whole outlook on the world. So little is it a matter of acquiring a certain number of true beliefs that this movement can be the work of a moment. It can happen that, shaken to its foundations by a sudden strong blow, the soul effects this movement of conversion, that is to say, changes its orientation suddenly and at a stroke. This is what happens when, to use theological terminology, it is suddenly touched by grace. Then, as the result of a kind of 'right-about-turn', it finds itself in the twinkling of an eye confronted with a wholly new outlook; unsuspected realities and unknown worlds are revealed before it; it sees, it knows things of which only a moment before it was wholly ignorant. But this same shift of perspective can come about slowly as a result of gradual and imperceptible pressure; this is what happens as a result of education. However, to be able to act thus powerfully on the deepest recesses of the soul it is patently essential that the different influences to which the child is subjected are not dispersed in different directions but are, rather, vigorously concentrated towards one and the same goal. This can be achieved only by making children live in one and the same moral environment, which is constantly present to them, which enshrouds them completely, and from whose influence they are unable, as it were, to escape. This explains the concentration of the whole of the child's education, indeed of his whole life, once Christianity had taken over the organisation of schooling.

Even today we have no other conception of education. For us

too, the principal aim is not to give the child a more or less large number of pieces of knowledge but to imbue in him some deep and internal state of mind, a kind of orientation of the soul which points it in a definite direction, not only during childhood but throughout life. Of course, we do not take the aim of education to be the production of Christians since we have abandoned confessional aims, but still we regard the aim of education as being the production of men. For just as to become a Christian it is necessary to acquire a Christian way of thinking and feeling, so too in order to become a man it is not enough to have a mind furnished with a certain number of ideas, but rather must one above all have acquired a truly human manner of feeling and thinking. Our conception of the aim has become secularised, consequently the means employed must also change; but the abstract outline of the educational process is not changed. It is still a question of getting down to these deep recesses in the soul about which antiquity knew nothing.

This also explains our present concept of the school. For we believe that school should not be the sort of hostel where different teachers, who are not known to one another, come to give a host of different types of instruction to pupils who meet only transiently and who have no links between them. We too believe that school, at every level, ought to provide a morally cohesive environment which closely envelops the child and which acts on his nature as a whole. We compare school to a social community, we speak of the social community of the school; and it is indeed a social group with a unity of its own, its own make-up, its own organisation, just like the society of adults. All of this clearly shows that it is not simply constituted as in ancient times by a collection of pupils who, in a more than physical sense, were gathered together in a single location. This conception of the school as an organised moral environment has become so familiar to us that we find it difficult to believe that it has not existed since the beginning of time. Yet, in fact, we have seen that it is a relatively late development, that it did not and could not appear until a particular moment in history, that it is bound up with a specific condition of civilisation, and we can now see what that condition is. School, as we know it, could only emerge with the emergence of peoples in whose view the essence of human culture consists not in the acquisition of certain specific abilities or habits of mind but rather in a general orientation of the mind and the will; in short, it is the moment when peoples have reached a sufficient degree of idealism. Henceforth, the goal of education was essentially to give to the child the necessary impetus so that he would travel in the right direction; and it consequently had to be organised in such a way as to be able to produce the profound and lasting effect which was demanded from it.

This observation has an important corollary. When we describe the Middle Ages as that historical period which elapsed between the fall of the Roman Empire and the Renaissance, we are clearly conceiving of it as a merely intermediate epoch, whose sole function was to serve as a hyphen between classical antiquity and modern times, between the moment when ancient civilisation burned itself out and the moment when it was reborn in order to embark again upon a new career. Apparently it had no other historical function than, as it were, that of holding the fort, of occupying the stage during a sort of interval. Nothing could be further from the truth than this view of the Middle Ages, and consequently nothing is more inappropriate than the name which we give to this epoch. Far from its being a mere period of transition without any originality of its own between civilisations which were brilliantly original, it is rather the period of gestation for the fertile seeds of an entirely new civilisation. And the most notable proof of this is to be found in this history of education and of educational theory. The school such as we find it at the beginning of the Middle Ages does indeed constitute a great and important innovation. It is distinguished by characteristics wholly alien to everything which the ancients called by the same name. Of course, as we have said, it borrowed from paganism the subject-matter of what was taught there; but this subject-matter was expounded in a brand new way and from this exposition something quite new resulted, as I have just shown. Moreover, it can be argued that it is only during this period that school, in the real sense of the term, emerged. For a school is not simply a place where a teacher teaches; it has a moral life of its own, a moral environment, saturated with certain beliefs and feelings, an environment which envelops the teacher no less than the pupils. Antiquity knew nothing like this. It had teachers, but it did not have genuine schools. The Middle Ages was thus a period of innovation in educational theory and practice. We shall be seeing later on the full significance of this remark.

Now that we have characterised the birth of the Christian school in a general way, we must now seek to trace its history in our own country.

Following the Roman occupation Gaul was exposed to Latin literature. Naturally this transformation did not come about all of a sudden on the day following the occupation. First of all Gaul learned from its conquerors how to transform its soil and the material aspect of its cities; it built, ploughed, grew rich. But in the fourth century it was ripe for acquiring an intellectual culture, and it did so. The municipalities attracted teachers, and schools were founded many of which showed outstanding brilliance: this was the case with the schools at Marseille, at Bordeaux, at d'Autun, at Trèves. Many of the Christian bishops of Gaul were nurtured in those schools and learned there to love classical literature, and consequently strove to reconcile the cult of literature with the demands of the new faith. This brilliance survived even the first invasions by the barbarians. Some of them, such as the Goths and the Burgundians, were already Christians anyway, and quickly came to envy the sophistication of Gallic manners and had themselves initiated into literature, science and the arts. One saw Theodoric at Toulouse, studying rhetoric and Roman law; Gondebaud, king of the Burgundians was learning Greek, and summoned to him Roman scholars to whom he entrusted the highest posts. No doubt there was at first a period of strife and disarray, but very soon we see the schools opening again and life returning to its normal course.

It was a quite different story when the Franks, in their turn, crossed the Rhine and spread through Gaul. They swarmed like a raging torrent all over the peoples who had successively established themselves in the country, Romans, Gauls, Goths and Burgundians, leaving nothing behind them but ruins. 'It would be difficult,' say the authors of *The Literary History of France*, 'to list in detail all the dire consequences which resulted from the fearsome temperament of these new inhabitants of Gaul.' If we are ignorant of the details of all these devastations it is because these dark times have no history: 'no-one wrote any more because no-one knew any more how to write'. '*Vae diebus nostris*,' exclaims Gregory of Tours, '*quia periit studium litterarum a nobis* (Woe unto us, for the taste of literature has disappeared from amongst us).' And indeed this same Gregory of Tours, who was nevertheless considered by his time as a man of learning and a great orator, admits himself that he has no knowledge of letters (*nullam litterarum scientiam*). He never learns either rhetoric or grammar (*Sum sine litteris rhetoricis et arte grammatica*). One cannot imagine the speed with which all this terrible destruction was carried out. Between Gregory of Tours and Sidonius Apollinaris (died in 489), there is a gap of fifty years only. If we compare what was produced in the period before and the period afterwards, they appear, as has been said, 'to belong to two different epochs'. At that moment if the Church had not existed human culture would have been done for, and one may well ask what would have happened to civilisation itself. However, the Frankish conquerors, as soon as they set foot in Gaul, were converted to the new faith; and the Church became a ruling power in the new state which was being formed. Consequently everything to which it gave shelter, all the vestiges of the past to which it was able to give sanctuary, shared in the protection which it enjoyed and benefited from the privileged situation which had been created for it.

As we have shown, the Church could not make do entirely without classical letters, even if it was only in order to be able to speak and understand the language which henceforth became the language of the cult. And so it happened that something of antiquity was saved by the Church. Of all the municipal schools which had rendered Gaul illustrious from the beginning of the fourth century, nothing remains. They were completely swept away by the torrent of the invasion; only the cathedral and monastic schools remained open. They were the sole organs of public education, the only places of refuge for intellectual activity; and it is thanks to them that there was not a complete halt, an irreparable break in the continuity of human progress.

We must not exaggerate the importance of the literary life which managed to survive. We have seen that if the Church was obliged to have recourse to classical antiquity this was despite itself: we have given the reasons which the Church had for viewing secular studies with suspicion. Moreover, the barbarians for their part felt no need of them. It is easy to imagine the fate of these studies in the midst of this double indifference, or rather in the midst of this double hostility. Revulsion which the Church felt instinctively for all this profane learning, reinforced by the equally strong revulsion which the barbarians experienced, no longer knew any bounds. The Church continued to teach a little Latin and a few essential items of knowledge, but taught as little as possible. Never, either before or since, have its attempts to cultivate the human mind been reduced to such a pathetic minimum. Everything which went beyond what was strictly necessary was severely prohibited, and even the study of grammar in some slight depth was regarded as a culpable luxury. One of the greatest minds of the seventh century, Pope Gregory the Great, having learned that Didier, Archbishop of Vienne, had in what had once been one of the most literate cities of Gaul undertaken to receive scholarly study by teaching grammar himself, wrote to him: 'My brother, I have been told, and I cannot repeat it without shame, that you have thought it your duty to teach grammar to certain people (*Sine verecundia memorare non possumas fraternitatem grammaticam quibusdam exponere*).'

However deep the darkness into which Gaul was plunged at that time, there are nevertheless certain points of light gathered here and there: they are these humble schools which survive in the cloisters and in the cathedrals. We shall now see how these feeble glimmers of light gradually came to revitalise themselves, to grow little by little in strength and brilliance; then, instead of remaining in isolation somewhere or other, coming closer together, amalgamating, mutually reinforcing one another as a result of this concentration until they became, as colleges and universities, powerful centres of brightness. We are accustomed to reserving the name 'Renaissance' for the great movement of intellectual and moral reconstruction which was effected in the sixteenth century. The truth is that the history of thought and the history of education has been nothing other than an uninterrupted series of renaissances; and we shall encounter one at the beginning of the present study.

Civilisation in Gaul had fallen so low that, abandoned to its own devices, it would probably have climbed out of the abyss only with the greatest of difficulty. It is from abroad that there came to us a part of those forces which revitalised our country. By a happy coincidence of circumstances, outside of Gaul all shrouded in darkness, two important cultural centres had established themselves and developed, one in the south of Italy, the other in the north of Ireland. It is the light which emanated from them into France which caused or which, at least, prepared the first renaissance, the first step forward along the path of our academic organisation.

In the nature of things, Latin civilisation was so deeply embedded in Italian soil that invaders always had much greater difficulty in uprooting it and, in as far as they did uproot it, always did so much less completely than in the other countries of Europe. Along with the material remains of antiquity something of its intellectual life survived to be handed down from one age to the next. There were memories which never completely disappeared, which were always ready to re-emerge. Thus the taste for literature was always much easier to revive there than in other parts. That is why it is often from Italy that the first impetus has come for more than one educational revolution; and it is for this reason significant that, from the sixth century onwards, an order established itself there which was to contribute more than any other to the revival of scholarship. This was the order of the Benedictines, whose founder was St Benedict.

It is not certain that St Benedict deliberately set out to defend the cause of literature and intellectual culture. As an orthodox Catholic he subordinated all profane interests, whatever they might be, to the interests of faith. But by the force of circumstances he came to give an important place in the monastic life to study. In order not to leave his monks idle he made them work hard at active material tasks but there are in the day times, which vary according to the seasons, when such work is impossible. These periods were to be spent reading. It is true that in theory the monk was not supposed to read anything other than holy books. *Certis temporibus occupari debent fratres in labore manuum, ceteris iterum horis in lectione divina.* (At certain times the brothers must be occupied in manual labour; at other hours again in divine reading.) But amongst holy books it was necessary to include, in addition to the Old and New Testaments, all the commentaries and all the expositions which had been made by the most reputed of the early fathers (*et expositiones earum quae a nominatissimis doctoribus orthodoxis et catholicis paribus factae sunt*). But this alone was enough to open the door to study and to reflection. For who can say where the list of early fathers who were the most orthodox and the most reputable begins? Then in order to understand their commentaries and their controversies it was necessary to know the theories which they were discussing and which they rejected. This is how profane literature inevitably found its way into the monasteries.

If the Benedictines had been abandoned to the spirit of their order, if they had developed only in conformity with their own earliest internal principles, it is probable that progress would have been extremely slow. But an external cause appeared to stimulate their literary and educational activity, and obliged them to renew themselves and to expose themselves to new ideas and interests. This was their meeting with the monks and the Church of Ireland. This constituted a cross-fertilisation of influences which played a role of considerable importance in the intellectual development of the Christian monks.

Christianity had been imported into Ireland at a relatively early date and, although we do not know exactly how, its origins were Eastern. For a long time the Irish Church remained on many points closer to the Eastern Church than to the Roman Church. The first Irish Christians thus brought with them elements of Greek culture of which the West was more or less wholly ignorant. On the other hand, the peace which the island had enjoyed at a time when the European continent was being ravished by invasions allowed these seeds of civilisation to develop. There quickly sprang up all over the country monasteries which, while still practising a strict asceticism, attached considerable importance to intellectual education. Astronomy, dialectic, versification, were all taught; Greek was studied in addition to Latin. Thus people came from all over to visit 'the island of saints and sages'.

However if the Irish Church had remained immured within the confines of the island, then, despite its growing reputation, it would probably never have exercised any great influence on the intellectual life of the Continent. But the mediaeval monk was essentially a traveller. Nor was this characteristic peculiar to him. We find the same temperament amongst the knights, amongst the teachers in the first universities. We have here a peculiarity in the mediaeval character which we will need later to explore. This explains how it was possible for the Irish monks to establish colonies even on the Continent. The Benedictines, motivated by the same tendency, sent their own missionaries into England; and there they found themselves in the presence of the Irish. The moving principles of these two monastic organisations were quite different. The order of St Benedict was entirely devoted to the cause of Papacy; the principle which it represented was that of the unity of the Catholic Church, the supremacy of the Holy See. The Irish, by contrast, had very pronounced individualistic tendencies; they had special rites; and an awareness of all that they had achieved on their own, of the substantial results which they had produced unaided, gave them a strong sense of their own autonomy. This resulted in a struggle which was not without violence. It was the order of St Benedict, more active and more strongly organised, which carried the day. But although it was the victor it allowed itself to be infiltrated by the spirit of the vanquished. Indeed, in order to win, it had to imitate its adversaries, to borrow from them their own weapons, and consequently to offer to the peoples they wished to conquer an education which was less meagre and paltry than that which was given on the Continent. This is how the Anglo-Saxon Church became established, which had and retained its own special character within the totality of the Catholic Church. Its distinguishing mark is its taste for things intellectual, which is found nowhere else to the same degree. In it and through it the level of academic studies was raised. And as it continued to send missionaries out into the rest of Europe they brought with them this new spirit. Thus Continental monasticism itself felt the need to pay more attention in its schools to secular studies.

Thus stimulated by the example of the Irish monks, the Benedictines prepared the way for the intellectual renewal of Europe. But they only prepared the way for it; they did not themselves bring it to pass. They helped a little in shaking people out of their intellectual torpor; thanks to their propaganda a little more teaching was more widely carried out. But they could not be the instruments of a truly profound transformation. First of all, education did not have for them any intrinsic value. It was little more than a weapon of war, a means of extending the circles of their influence and winning over people's intellect. Then again, all that they did and all that they could do was to propagate this teaching peripatetically, by a sort of silent dissemination and slow diffusion. Inexorably they extended the trenches leading to the pagan world, which they had dug; they added monastery to monastery, school to school; as a result these few bright points which flecked with light the darkness covering Gaul increased in number at the same time as they grew somewhat in their brilliance.

But this constant swarming across Europe could not lead to the formation of great teaching institutions. And it was institutions of this sort which were lacking. In order that they might come into existence it was necessary that all the intellectual forces in the country be brought together and concentrated in a small number of places in order that they could mutually reinforce one another. A cultural centre of any importance can only result from an energetic movement of concentration. Thus in order for an important step forward to be possible along the road of academic and educational progress it was essential that new social arrangements rendered instruction more necessary and made the need of it more keenly felt. Moreover, it was above all essential that a single strong hand should gather together, in one and the same cluster, the intellectual resources which were scattered all over the place. This was the educational achievement of Charlemagne. Without spending a long time over it, it is very necessary to understand Charlemagne's work, for it was the prelude to another concentration still more intense, from which there resulted somewhat later the university and the colleges; that is, higher education and secondary education with all the essential characteristics which they have retained until quite recent times. However far removed in time the Carolingian Renaissance may appear, it is nevertheless clear that by examining it we shall be in a better position to understand the process of evolution which has led to even our modern form of educational organisation.

chapter 4

The Carolingian Renaissance (I)

We saw in the last lecture how secular studies, which had so drastically declined by the end of the seventh century, began to take an upward turn thanks to the Benedictines, stimulated by the example and the competition of the Irish monks. But these early stages of educational advance, no matter how real they may have been, took place in a way which was, as it were, deaf and dumb because it was unconscious. It was like a slow invasion which stops nowhere but continues steadily at an even pace, and is extended ever further without its ever becoming clear from what precise point it originally emanated. The instruction, for all the rudimentariness which it still retained, which the monks brought with them came to cover ever increasingly extensive territories without either having or establishing any major centre from which it could derive nourishment. The intellectual powers at the disposal of the Order were scattered in every direction throughout Europe and never concentrated themselves in a single specific place or places where they would have been able mutually to reinforce each other as a result of being associated together. The first concentration of this type which we encounter in the history of education is that which we associate with the name of Charlemagne.

The Carolingian Empire has sometimes been presented as the personal achievement of a man of genius. Charles is somehow supposed to have created it out of nothing through sole power of his own will. But such an explanation, in my view, misses both its significance and its influence. It involves reducing an event which exercised so vast an influence on the whole of subsequent history to the fortuitous appearance of a single individual. Besides, to imagine the European state could emerge from nothing in this way, solely as a result of the appeal of an individual, entails the postulation of a miracle in an historical explanation. Such a gigantic society could never have been formed, and been formed in such a way as to last for a significant period of time, except in as far as it responded to certain sociological facts. And indeed it had its deepest roots in nothing other than the condition of Europe at that time and it was the consequence of this condition; this fact is of crucial importance if we are to understand what follows.

We do not need to judge what the various peoples of Europe were like according to the criteria of what they are like today; in other words, we must not see them as having collective characters powerfully constituted and sharply differentiated from one another, with a vivid awareness of their own existence, distinguishing themselves from, and even conflicting with one another in the same clear way which applies to individual persons. For several centuries Europe had been rather like a kaleidoscope ceaselessly in flux and appearing quite different from one period to another. The different peoples successively formed the greatest variety of combinations and, with the greatest ease, passed from the hands of one state into that of another, and from domination by one set of people to that of another. Under these conditions how could they be expected to retain a homogeneous character? In the shuffle which invariably followed the great swarm of invasions they inevitably lost a large part of their distinctive features in the ensuing clashes. The frontiers which separated them were more or less obliterated under the feet of conquerors. On the other hand, as Christianity developed all these groups, which on their own lacked stability and durability, became constituent elements of a much larger society which enveloped them all and which possessed or at least increasingly acquired this moral unity and this stability which they lacked; this society was the Church. Increasingly Christianity became the sole civilisation where all these societies which lacked any civilisation of their own came to communicate with one another. In one sense then, Europe was morally more unified than today since there was, so to speak, no national civilisation to be set over against that civilisation which was common to all the peoples of Europe. It is this which explains the remarkably substantial role played by monasticism in the moral and intellectual formation of Europe. The monk, in fact, belongs to no particular country and no particular society other than the great society of Christendom. This is what gave him his great mobility, travelling from one country to another, moving like a veritable nomad from one extremity of Europe to the other. Wherever he went he carried his own homeland within him. Thus he became the schoolmaster of Europe. Does this entail that there was a very substantial degree of European cosmopolitanism since education in Europe was international?

Here we need to make the reservation that European society

was still something latent, lacking in self-awareness because it lacked organisation. All the peoples of Christendom had a vague feeling of belonging to a single whole, without this feeling generating any specific institution to express it. Certainly there was the Papacy, but this lacked the material strength necessary for transforming a vast political agglomeration into a genuine political society. It was Charlemagne who, for a time, was to provide Christendom with this central institution which it lacked. In him and through him European Christendom became a state. This idea of the unity of Christendom, which had been slumbering in a state of semi-consciousness, was given substance by him and became a historical reality. That was his achievement. He did not create this unity out of nothing by some sort of magic artifice. Rather he expressed it and organised it; but this fact of organisation itself was a novelty which entailed others, particularly with regard to the intellectual life.

The fact is that living creatures increase in self-awareness the better organised they are. An animal which lacks a central nervous system is only aware in a confused kind of way of what is going on in the further reaches of his body. Human beings, by contrast, or the higher animals, thanks to their central nervous system, are at every instant alerted to any goings-on of importance taking place within them. So it is with societies. When a society has a central institution in which the whole of its life both internal and external culminates, then it knows itself better. It has a greater awareness of what it is experiencing, of what affects it, of the sufferings it endures and of their causes, of the needs under which it labours. We have seen that in the nature of things Christianity had need of education; that it could not do without it. The monks of St Benedict were trying to satisfy this obscure need with their teachings, however rudimentary these may have been. In the person of Charlemagne, representing Christendom, this need surfaced into full consciousness. Now it was no longer merely a vague feeling, but an idea which has been clearly apprehended. And at the same time it was intensified; for consciousness, while adding clarity to the tendencies which it illuminates, also strengthens them. Our desires are more vital and more vigorous when we clearly know what it is that we desire. Additionally, a large organised society has need of greater consciousness and more reflection, and consequently of more education and knowledge; for the mechanism which it constitutes, being more complex, cannot function purely automatically. For all these reasons the creation of the Carolingian Empire was inevitably to bring about important educational reforms.

As the product of a movement of concentration designed to

gather together in a single hand and beneath a single law the whole Christian world, the new state was naturally inclined to concentrate all the intellectual forces which it contained in such a way as to form a cultural and intellectual centre, capable of influencing the whole Empire. This centre was the Ecole du Palais. Much discussion has ranged round the question of whether the Ecole du Palais was founded by Charlemagne or whether it did not already exist before his accession. We shall not pause long to examine this purely academic controversy. It is infinitely probable that the Ecole du Palais was not born one fine day without anything having prepared for it. We know that the Merovingians summoned to their court the sons of their principal lords, and had them brought up there in such a way as to bind them to themselves with stronger ties, whilst at the same time guaranteeing them in return substantial advantages; this meant, in effect, that the most important positions in the state were reserved for them. This group of young people brought up communally already formed a kind of privileged school. In any case, under Pépin le Bref, it is fairly certain that an education was already being given at the court which, if we believe the biographer D'Adalard, a cousin of Charlemagne, drew on all fields of human knowledge (*omnis mundi prudentia*). But what is certain is that with Charlemagne the Ecole du Palais took on an importance which it had not had until then, and developed accordingly. Not, of course, that we should picture it as we would a modern school. Thus the question which has been raised about which part of the Empire it resided in is patently futile. It moved around with the court of which it formed an integral part, and consequently followed the emperor on all his frequent journeys. It was a nomadic school but it was no longer the preserve of the sons of noble lords; it was open to young clerics who were recruited from all ranks of society, as is proved by the famous incident reported by the monk from Saint-Gall. Moreover, it placed in charge of the education teachers chosen from amongst the most eminent scholars which Europe then possessed. Such were the grammarian Pierre de Pise, the Greek scholar Paul Warnefrid, or Paul Diacre, and Clement d'Irlande.

Amongst these teachers there was one who eclipsed them all by the importance of his role and by the influence which he exercised over Charles; this was Alcuin. Alcuin was precisely one of the faithful of that Anglo-Saxon Church of which we have already spoken, and which distinguished itself from the other Christian Churches by its pronounced and avaricious taste for matters intellectual. He had been brought up in the very famous school of York; he had there received an education palpably superior to that which was then being given in the schools on the Continent. The tastes and the knowledge which he had there acquired he brought to the Ecole du Palais, whose director he became in 782; and the outstandingly important role that he played in the entourage of Charlemagne allowed him to make his influence felt beyond the court and throughout the rest of the kingdom.

But Charles did not stop at the creation of this model school, this central institution; he prodded his bishops into multiplying within their dioceses institutions of the same type. Even before meeting Alcuin he was writing to Lull, archbishop of Mayence: 'You are working with God's help to win over souls and yet I cannot but be astounded that you are not the slightest bit bothered about teaching literature to your clergy. All around you you see those who have frequently plunged themselves into the darkness of ignorance; and at a time when you could enable them to share the light of your knowledge you leave them buried in the darkness of their blindness...So teach your sons the liberal arts in order to satisfy our wishes in a matter which concerns us most particularly.' But it is above all in a letter written in 787, addressed to Bangulfe, the Abbot of Fulva, that we find the best exposition of his plans together with the reasons which seem to him to justify them. 'We have adjudged it useful,' he writes, 'that in the bishoprics and the monasteries whose government Christ in his goodness has entrusted to us there should be, in addition to the observance of a regular life and the practices of holy religion, literary studies (*litterarum meditationes*); and that those who through a gift of God are able to teach should consecrate, each according to his ability, their mission to teaching.' These studies are necessary first of all in order to give 'regularity and beauty to the language'. Not that Charles was sensible of the aesthetic value of style; what concerned him was the influence of words on ideas, and the fact that one cannot think clearly and distinctly as long as one cannot express clearly and distinctly one's thoughts: 'The Soul understands that much better what it wants to do in proportion as the tongue is not glibly uttering falsehoods.' In the second place, it is necessary to be initiated into all the secrets of language in order to be able to understand the Holy Scriptures: 'We exhort you not only not to neglect the study of letters but also to apply yourselves zealously and with a perseverance which is full of humility and pleasing unto God, in order that you may be able to penetrate more easily and more accurately the mysteries of the Holy Scriptures. Since these contain images, tropes, and other similar figures, no one can doubt that the reader will not elevate himself all the more quickly to the spiritual meaning in proportion as he is steeped in a grammatical understanding of the text.' Here we have a mystical conception of the Bible, the Bible being treated as a cabbalistic book. According to Cassin this mystical meaning reveals itself only to the saint who has reached, through the practice of asceticism, to the highest degree of illumination. Alcuin and Charles had a more rationalistic conception of it. According to them, in order to understand these allegorical mysteries it was enough to have the mind sharpened and exercised by a scholarly training. But this training was indispensable. Moreover, these two reasons by which Charlemagne justifies his recommendations led to a third, which was more political in nature and which summarises and contains in itself the first two. It was essential above all that the clergy should have in the eyes of the people a prestige which would assure its authority. For this was the necessary condition for the maintenance of faith, and with it that of the unity of the Church and the Empire. Now, in order that the people believe in its priests it is not enough that the priests should entertain in the depth of their hearts interior sentiments of piety. They must be intellectually superior to their flock, and these latter must feel that authority. 'We wish that, as is fitting for soldiers of the Church, you be animated by an internal devoutness and that externally you appear scholarly...eloquent in your words, so that whoever for the love of God and in search of holy conversation, may desire to see you shall be edified by your appearance and instructed by your learning.'

In response to these appeals, repeated in successive capitularies, new schools were founded near the cathedrals, the abbeys and the monasteries, and distinguished teachers arrived from Italy and Ireland in order to provide in them a broader education than that which was customary. The bishops in their turn followed up the policy of the day and everywhere founded under the auspices of simple parish churches more modest schools where an elementary education could be received. We have a letter by Theodulse Bishop of Orleans, urging the priests of the boroughs and villages to give free instruction to the children of their parishioners. Thus there was established a whole scholastic hierarchy with three stages. At the bottom there was the parish school, where the most elementary matters were taught; above that there were the cathedral schools and those of the large monasteries; finally right at the top there was the model school reserved for the élite the Ecole du Palais. In his capacity as Director of this school Alcuin was like some sort of special minister, responsible to the administration for the oversight of this public education which was in its infancy and just beginning to find its feet.

This organisation was not only more complex and more learned than the one which had preceded it; it was also distinctive on account of the more marked element of secularity which it possessed. Of course, education remained in the hands of the priests; but it was a layman who provided its intellectual driving force. It was temporal power which had generated this educational renewal, and consequently the temporal preoccupations of education found a place which they had never hitherto had. It is quite true that for Charles the interests of faith and the interests of the state were intermingled. It remains nevertheless true that it was the interests of the state which became the goal to which everything else was to be subordinated. No longer did one teach only that which was indispensable for the practice of religion: one was chiefly concerned with that which could be of service to the Empire. This is why Charles had the idea of arranging for the teaching of Greek, solely in order to facilitate his relations with the East. Even the way in which the Ecole du Palais was made up was not without influence from this point of view; it included amongst its pupils not only young people but also adults; and amongst these adults there were not only clerics but also courtiers, men of the world who would not be satisfied with an education which was purely ecclesiastical. One fact shows beyond all doubt how far the nature of this environment influenced the education which was given within it. The time came when Alcuin left the court of Charlemagne and withdrew to the monastery at Tours. Immediately he became, as we would say today, a reactionary as far as education was concerned. His former liberalism vanished. The reading of pagan authors was almost entirely forbidden to his pupils. Finally there was another important change in that cathedral schools which, in the preceding period, had been overshadowed by the monastic schools now began from the time of Charlemagne to take precedence. The cathedrals and their clergy stood in a much closer relationship with the outside world than the monasteries and the abbeys; they were more exposed to secular interests, they had more contact with lay situations. We shall have occasion shortly to see this again, since it was from the cathedral schools that the universities emerged.

Having now examined what this new educational system consisted in and how it became established, let us now look at the content of the education which was given within it. From the container let us move on to the contents; from the organ to its function. We shall inevitably say nothing about the parochial school, about which in any case we know very little, in order to concentrate on the cathedral schools, in particular the Ecole du Palais which was their paradigm example; for only these schools are connected with the secondary education whose history we are seeking to trace. We know a great deal about the Ecole du Palais, for we still possess the works in which Alcuin summarised his educational theory (*Didascalica*, Reg., 191). And since the cathedral schools merely reproduced with variations of detail what was happening in the Palace school we shall be describing the entire educational system of the time.

The first characteristic feature of this education is that it was or strove to be encyclopaedic. Its goal was not to instruct the pupil in a certain number of branches of knowledge, but in the totality of human learning. As soon as the Church began to become established (that is, from the beginning of the sixth century), we see the appearance of writers all of whom set themselves the task of collecting together into a sort of synthesis, and of condensing into the smallest volume possible, all the results of ancient science. Already this had been tried by Boethius (died 525), but Boethius was first and foremost a dialectician, so he did not exert his full influence until the time when dialectic studies were fully in vogue, namely during the Scholastic period. Until that time Boethius was known mainly through the works of Cassiodorus (562), whose treatise *De septem artibus* embraces the whole of contemporary learning. But work which reveals more fully this encyclopaedic character is that of a seventh-century writer who died in 636, Isidore of Seville. His treatise *De originibus*, under the pretext of researching into the origins of words, is in fact a summary of all the knowledge which classical antiquity possessed. From words he moves on to things and thus surveys, on the pretext of doing etymology, all the branches of learning, all the human disciplines from the most humble onwards; from grammar to medicine, jurisprudence, natural history and theology. It is these works, particularly the last two, which were the classics of the whole mediaeval period. Education in the Middle Ages never ceased to make use of them, to comment upon them and to paraphrase them. Right up to the fifteenth century they had all sorts of imitators, but these did nothing other than reproduce the original models. The teacher confined himself to borrowing from one or another of these basic books certain ready-made expositions of a subject, without even altering the language. Monnier has compared whole passages from the didactic works of Alcuin with the corresponding part of the *De originibus*; they are often literally identical. They were so unfamiliar with the concept of originality that these plagiarists felt no scruples. They saw in these works, as it were, a fund of common wisdom like a collective treasure which was not the property of anyone in particular, and which everyone could freely make use of.

A no less general and persistent tendency must clearly be connected with something about the essential character of Christian thought. One might wonder, first of all, if it does not result from the vivid if by no means lucid attitude that Christianity instinctively adopted with respect to the unity of both science and the truth. For Christianity the truth is not an abstract name given to a plurality or a totality of particular truths. The truth is essentially a unity; for it is the word of God, and God is one. Just as moral truth is entirely contained in a single book, the Holy Scriptures, it must have appeared entirely natural to the Christian thinker that temporal truths, scientific truths, must also have the same unity and find their expression in a single book, in a breviary which would function in the domain of the profane as an equivalent to the Holy Scriptures in the domain of the sacred.

In addition to this awareness there is another cause which must have contributed significantly to the phenomenon which we are seeking to understand. We have seen that for Christianity education has as its object not the development of this or that particular skill but rather the shaping of the mind in its entirety. In exactly the same way science as a whole is needed in order to shape the mind as a whole. An education which is incomplete can only form an intellect which is incomplete, and cannot touch the fundamentals of human thought. Educative action can only really be effective on condition that it is not purely parochial, that it does not set its sights on certain particular points but rather envelops the intelligence in its entirety, without leaving out anything at all. In a word, teaching, according to Christianity, must be educative; and it cannot be educative unless it is encyclopaedic. This idea, which we come across in modern educational writers, was in reality present throughout the evolution of our educational ideas from their earliest origins. I am certainly not claiming that modern authors have done nothing other than to restore an age-old conception; far from it. If this idea has been present since that time it was then so in a very confused, very obscure, very unconscious form. We will have occasion to follow the way in which it has developed, been rendered specific and transformed; we shall also have to take note of the eclipses which it has undergone. But it is very important to establish that it was immanent in all the educational developments which were to succeed it. We shall see shortly how the universities gave it reality in a new form.

But this encyclopaedic education, what did it consist of? How was it organised?

The whole of human knowledge was divided into seven branches or seven fundamental disciplines; these are the *septem artes liberales*, which name was used as a title for the great works of Cassiodorus. This division into seven reaches back to the latter days of classical antiquity; we find it for the first time in Martianus

Capella, at the beginning of the sixth century. But in the Middle Ages it was no longer the transitory view of a single individual; it became a veritable institution. For centuries it was to remain as the basis of education. In this way it took on in the eyes of the people of the time a kind of mystical character. The seven arts were compared with the seven pillars of wisdom, with the seven planets, with the seven virtues. The number seven itself was deemed to have a mystical meaning.

The seven arts did not all enjoy equal status; they were divided into two groups whose educational significance was very different, and which the Middle Ages always distinguished from one another with the greatest care.

First of all there were three disciplines, grammar, rhetoric and dialectic, which formed what was called the 'trivium'. Here is the origin of the word which has had such a varied fate. In Rome they called *trivialis scientia* the elementary subject-matter which was taught by a teacher of letters. It was common knowledge, plebeian, such as would be available to the man in the street. Perhaps also it was an allusion to the fact that these primary schools usually were sited *in triviis*, at the crossroads. But when the word 'trivium' had entered common usage its origins were forgotten; it was thought that it referred exclusively to the tripartite division of primary education and simply meant an education which included three branches of learning, three paths. The result was that in order to designate the four arts which were not included in the trivium the expression 'quadrivium' was used. The quadrivium included geometry, arithmetic, astronomy and music.

These two cycles were not only distinguished by the number of disciplines which they included. There was also a profound difference in the nature of the disciplines which were taught within the two cycles. The trivium was intended to instruct the mind about the mind itself, that is to say the laws which it obeys when it thinks and when it expresses itself, and the rules which it ought to follow in order to think and express itself correctly. These are in effect the goals of grammar, of rhetoric and of dialectic. The triple curriculum is thus entirely formal. It deals exclusively with general forms of reasoning, with abstractions made from their application to things, or perhaps with what is even more formal than thought, namely language. Thus the arts of the trivium were called *artes sermonicinales* or *logica*. The quadrivium, by contrast, consisted of a set of branches of learning related to things. Its role was to generate understanding of external realities and the laws which govern them, the laws of number, the laws of space, the laws concerning the stars, and those which govern sounds. For this reason the arts which it included were called *artes reales* or *physica*. The trivium and the quadrivium were thus oriented in two quite different directions: the one towards the human mind, the other towards things in the real world. The function of the first was to shape the intelligence in a general way, to expose it in its normal state and stance; the goal of the second was to furnish it and to nourish it. It will be readily seen that we have already here that opposition between the two great branches of learning which we shall encounter again later fighting for pre-eminence; on the one hand we have the humanities which relate to truth about man; on the other hand we have the natural sciences. Here we have classical education and the education of the Realschulen, also called specialist education. Thus these words 'trivium' and 'quadrivium' which at first sight seem so archaic, so remote from ourselves, are found in fact to connote ideas which in a way are still with us today, questions which we still ask. How fascinating it is to find them in their ancient state! For as a result of this alone, we are less likely to attach undue prestige to the contingent and transitory guise in which we find them today, and which very often actually disguises from us the realities to which they give expression.

Now that we have characterised these two fundamental cycles, we need to ascertain the respective places which they were accorded in education.

Despite the fact that respect for religion was the object of the seven arts, despite the unity which they were felt to possess, it is far from true that the trivium and the quadrivium played roles of equal importance in academic life. The quadrivium was a kind of *de luxe*, supererogatory curriculum, reserved for a small élite of specialists and initiates. How this position came about is easily explained with reference to the way in which the four constituent disciplines were understood and practised. They were still conceived of in part as mystical arts analogous to those of the magician. For example, the goal of arithmetic was to discover the mystical properties of numbers. Thus we find that Alcuin, amongst others, following the example of Isidore of Seville, attached allegorical significance to them. Some were a portent of evil, others were good omens. The numbers three and six were the key to all the secrets of nature; they would yield perfect knowledge to anyone who could penetrate their occult significance. This science was the one which fascinated Alcuin the most: 'He only spoke of it in whispers; but he spoke of it all the time.' He had even taught something of it to King Charles, who was quite astounded by it. Exactly the same was true in the case of astrology, which Alcuin again defined as the study of the stars, of their nature, and of their power. Thus he still admitted that the stars have an influence on human events. Comets were thought of as bearded stars which proclaimed events of outstanding importance: new dynasties, plague, and so on. Finally, one of the reasons why the men of the Middle Ages were fascinated by the scientific study of music was that it opened up to their imaginations vast mystical horizons. The laws of harmony, they thought, must explain the harmony of the universe, of the seasons, of the different parts of the human soul, or that which results from its unity with the body. Such studies, surrounded as they were with so much mystery, were clearly not suitable for being brought out into the open in the schools; they could not form the subject-matter of a common curriculum, but could only be treated by a handful of initiates.

Thus it was the trivium (grammar, rhetoric and dialectic) which exclusively constituted what one might call the normal course of studies of the period, the substance of what was taught in the cathedral and abbey schools. Now, as we have seen, the sciences of the trivium were wholly formal in character; they looked exclusively towards man. From this it follows that if education had at that time a tendency to be encyclopaedic, its encyclopaedic nature turned out in reality to consist in a variety of systems of purely formal studies. It is not difficult to gain an insight into what it was that gave rise to this formalism. The object of education as it was henceforth understood was to train the mind in large generalities, about essential and fundamental principles, irrespective of the many and various ways in which these might be concretely applied. It seemed that the only way of achieving this goal was to get humanity to reflect upon its own nature, to understand itself and to be conscious of itself. It was not that the natural sciences could not have served this same goal. But, for reasons which we shall be investigating, it was only very slowly that people came to realise the services which the natural sciences could render in this connection. For centuries it seemed self-evident that only studies relating to human beings could really serve to shape human beings. Thus we reach the important conclusion that there was a logical necessity in the process which led to education's being at first wholly formal. One can readily imagine what difficulty it subsequently had in order to get rid of this congenital formalism. Indeed, we shall see it passing from one sort of formalism to another (for there are different sorts of formalism) without managing to escape from it, sometimes even exacerbating, under the pressure of circumstances, this initial tendency, so much so that the question still remains an open one today.

chapter 5

The Carolingian Renaissance (II)

The teaching of grammar

In the last chapter I began by characterising the first organised system of education to appear in the history of our country and indeed, more generally, in the history of European societies: I am referring to the one which began to emerge at the end of the eighth century, partially under the influence of Charlemagne. What is characteristic of this education is the fact that it sought to embrace the totality of human knowledge, that its aim was to be encyclopaedic. However, we also saw that the different disciplines of which it was composed did not play roles of equal importance in academic life. Those studies which dealt with man, with the human mind, with the mechanism of thought or even the mechanism through which thought is expressed — namely, grammar, rhetoric and dialectic — dominated the scene more or less completely; those whose subject-matter was things — arithmetic, geometry, mechanics, music, the external world — formed the substance of a kind of supplementary education reserved for a relatively small number of élites. The quadrivium was a kind of higher education, whereas the trivium corresponded more nearly to our own secondary education. From this it followed that in actual academic practice teaching was made up of a set of totally formal disciplines whose aim was to generate reflection on the most general forms of thought (logic), or through the still more external forms which ideas take when they are expressed (language).

It is not difficult to explain how such a system for all its incompleteness could have been taken for an encyclopaedic curriculum; this is because from one point of view it did play this role. It is indeed true that the world only exists for us in as far as it is represented or is capable of being represented to our minds; in as far as it cannot affect our intelligence it is as if it did not exist. In a sense, therefore, everything which is, is to be found in the most general forms, the most general framework of thought; all the things that exist in the universe are comprehensible within one or another of the major categories of the understanding, since these categories are only higher-order classes which include all things and outside of which there is nothing. Thus when we understand the nature of these categories or fundamental concepts, their relationships with one another, the ways in which they operate in reasoning and the making of judgments (for this was the object of the mental sciences), we come at the same time to understand reality as a whole and from a point of view of maximum generality. The mind, it has often been said, is a microcosm, a universe reduced to scale and portraying in miniature the greater one outside. Consequently to understand the mind is, from a certain point of view, to understand the world; and the sciences and disciplines whose subject-matter is the mind constitute a kind of abridged encyclopaedia.

However, this initial portrait of the education which was given in the cathedral and monastic schools during the eighth and ninth centuries is inadequate. For even in the succeeding centuries, when the university and the colleges had been founded, the trivium was to remain the essential part of the curriculum. And yet these two phases in our academic history are very different. The educational formalism of the eighth century is by no means the same as that of the twelfth. What is it then that is so peculiar about the former?

It is the fact that amongst the disciplines of the trivium itself there were some which were later to make great strides forward academically and to become the central part of the curriculum, but which at that time were accorded only minor importance. This is the case, first of all, with rhetoric. To demonstrate this we need only read Alcuin's treatise on the subject. It is a scanty, frigid and feeble reproduction of Cicero's *De Oratore*. It is clear that Alcuin is talking about this subject without any great interest. The picture of the ideal orator with which, one feels, Cicero's whole book is imbued and which gives it its life and its unity has vanished in Alcuin's version. All that remains is an arid enumeration of abstract definitions and lifeless formulae. The examples intended to illustrate these formulae are not borrowed from antiquity, whether Greek or Roman, which was so fertile in models of eloquence; they are dug out of the Scriptures. Thus the passage in Genesis where it said that God accepted the offerings of Abel and refused those of Cain is presented as an example of the assertoric mode; the conflicting pieces of advice given by Achitofel and Chusai to Absalom on the question of whether or not to betray David are offered as examples of the deliberative mode. The accusations of the Jews against Paul and his defence, as we find these reported in the Acts of the Apostles, are cited as a paradigm for the judicial mode. Indeed, how could the Middle Ages be expected to attach great importance to a branch of learning which no longer had any reason for its existence? Just as the orator was essential in antiquity, in virtue of the very substantial role which eloquence played in those days, so he was bound to appear redundant in these unsophisticated societies where there was no room for rhetorical jousts. Even if we stick to the definitions given by Alcuin himself, rhetoric allegedly has no utility value except with respect to political questions (*in civilibus quaestionibus*), and consequently would only be of use to those whose calling involved them in dealing with such matters. This is the reason which Charlemagne invokes at the beginning of the dialogue when he asks his teacher Alcuin to be initiated into this art, giving it as his view that it was foolish for anyone concerned with affairs of state to be ignorant of rhetoric (*Ut optime nosti, propter occupationes regni et curas palatii in hujuscemodi quaestionibus assidue nos versari solere, et ridiculum videtur ejus praecepta nescisse cujus occupatione involvi necesse est*). Here we have a remarkably limited view of the use of rhetoric. It is true that not all those who had theories about education at this time regarded it so narrowly. One of Alcuin's disciples, one of those who did most to revitalise academic life in Germany, Rabanus Maurus (who, however, was only taking up what St Augustine had taught in this matter) admitted that rhetoric could be made to serve pious aims. It is, he said, a necessary weapon for the defender of truth if he is to triumph over falsehood. Since the enemies of religion could have recourse to the devices of rhetoric in order to propagate error, why should the Christian be forbidden to use it in order to defend his faith? But it is only in this connection that it seems to him to have any use. Rhetoric is of interest to him only in as far as it can serve religious ends. Even then the services which it renders in this capacity seem to him of only secondary importance. Thus he thought that the Christian should not devote too much time to rhetoric: 'We do not esteem it to be of such great value that we should like to see men devoting themselves to it during their mature years. It is an occupation for quite young people (*satis est ut adolescentulorum cura sit*). It is not even necessary that all those whom we desire to bring up to serve the interests of the Church should cultivate it, but only those who are not yet taken up with more pressing and more important duties.'

Dialectic received only slightly more esteem. Of course it was already an important mark of progress that any place at all, however small, had been accorded to it within the curriculum. Indeed, we must not forget that of all the disciplines inherited from pagan culture dialectic was the one which the early fathers and the doctors of the Church regarded with the greatest suspicion. They thought in effect that true faith does not need to be proved; and, moreover, they felt that the appeal to reason and logic, as these had been understood by the ancients, had always benefited the heresiarchs. Aristotle is described by one of them as the Bishop of the Arians. But if in the ninth century there were some signs of a willingness to give up this prejudice, the fact remains that its influence was still felt. In as far as dialectic is valued, it is as a means of combating heresy; it is the existence of error which renders it necessary. On this point Alcuin and Rabanus Maurus are in agreement. An additional point is that, although Rabanus Maurus in principle recommended that the cleric devote himself seriously to the study of dialectic, it seems most probable that the subject was at that time very undeveloped. The best proof of this is Alcuin's own treatise. Not only is it extremely elementary but it is also put together in a manner which Prantl did not shrink from describing as 'monstrous'. It is easy to imagine the extent of the influence which dialectic would have when conceived of and taught in this way.

It was thus the teaching of grammar which overwhelmingly predominated in the curriculum. It was grammar that was considered as the supreme art. 'It is', says Rabanus Maurus, 'the origin and the basis of all the other arts (*Haec et origo et fundamentum est artium liberalium*).' It is grammar which teaches us how to understand texts, and all learning ultimately depends on the reading and the understanding of a text. This bookish conception of education for which the Scholastics have so often been reproached is in fact older than Scholasticism. Human civilisation is thought of as existing entirely in books, and consequently the science which initiates us into an understanding of books is the queen of the sciences, the key which is necessary in order to open all other doors. It is particularly necessary for the Christian since it alone can allow him to understand the Book which contains within itself all truth. This is why the period which runs from the ninth century to the twelfth can well be called, both from an academic and from an educational point of view, the age of grammar. It is the time when grammar constitutes the principal subject-matter of both academic and literary activity.

The numerous treatises on grammar which appeared at this period and which formed the basis for education were all constructed according to the same design and written in the same way. They did no more than reproduce the works of the Latin grammarians at the end of the Empire and in succeeding centuries. 'They were scrupulously followed,' says Thurot, 'and the only deviations were made out of respect for the sacred text of the

Vulgate.' Amongst the authors who were requisitioned in this way to serve as a model two in particular stand out; they are Priscian and Donatius. Their names stood as a symbol for the science of grammar almost throughout the whole of the Middle Ages. Donatius, in particular, was the Lhomond of the scholars of this period. To these two fundamental texts the teacher generally added nothing more than commentaries and glosses, following them slavishly and meticulously to the letter. For example, Donatius speaking of nouns says: '*qualitas nominum bipertita est* (the nature of nouns is twofold)', whereas when he comes to pronouns he uses a different expression and writes: '*omnia nomina quibus latina utitur eloquentia* (all the nouns used by Latin eloquence).' Immediately the grammarian begins to wonder why there is this change in phraseology. Priscian begins his treatise *De nomine et pronomine et verbo* with the following proposition: '*omnia nomina quibus latina utitur eloquentia.*' One of the principal grammarians of the ninth century, Remy d'Auxerre, ponders gravely upon the reason which led Priscian to write *eloquentia* and not *lingua* (language), and, of course he finds the reason. If one comes across a mistake or an inaccuracy one uses all the techniques of exegesis at one's disposal in order to show that the mistake is only apparent. One could not possibly admit that authors of such enormous authority could possibly have been wrong. It is clear that this method of interpretation, as Thurot has pointed out, is very reminiscent of that which was being applied to the Bible. What completes the resemblance is the fact that people frequently sought in the expressions, definitions and classifications of the grammarians a mystical significance like that which they discovered in the Bible with the help of the so-called 'anagogical' method of interpretation. Thus 'If the verbs have three persons,' says one of the grammarians, 'it is the result of divine inspiration (*quod credas divinitus esse inspiratum*).' In this way faith in the Holy Trinity finds its way even into our everyday speech. Similarly, according to the grammarian Smaragde, if there are eight parts of speech this is because the number eight is often represented in Holy Writ as a sacred number.

In any case ignorance went very deep. Thus we find somewhere in Donatius these two expressions: *Eunuchus comoedia, Orestes tragoedia*. The grammarians of the ninth century thought that Eunuchus and Orestes were poets of such illustriousness that their names had become synonymous with the words 'comedy' and 'tragedy'. In this kind of situation it is not difficult to imagine why quotations from pagan authors were rare. The few that we come across are almost all directly lifted from the two Latin grammarians who were being copied. As a matter of preference examples were drawn from the Holy Scriptures, in order to combine edification with instruction. However, it was not forbidden to follow up and to illustrate grammar by the study of poets. But Rabanus Maurus himself, although he was more liberal than Alcuin, advises that everything be disregarded in these authors which is not capable of serving the purposes of Christianity. After all, he adds, we must take great care not to shock our weaker brethren.

However flawed this curriculum might have been, it constituted an important advance when compared with what had gone before. The fact is that in the Dark Ages which followed the Frankish invasion the study of grammar had not completely vanished. It had survived but in a form which it is not without interest to examine, first of all because it is in itself curious and symptomatic of a state of mind which we may well find disconcerting, and also because it enables us the better to appreciate the work of the grammarians in the Carolingian period.

Towards the end of the sixth century or at the beginning of the seventh there lived in Toulouse a grammarian who took as his *nom de guerre* Virgil the Asiatic. And it is under this name that he is still known. The name of Virgil was very popular with the barbarians who had been converted to Christianity; and they adorned themselves with this name so eagerly that at the present time we know of a very large number of Virgils. 'For them,' says Ozanam, 'it was the name of a wise man, a prophet who, in the fourth eclogue, had predicted the coming of the Saviour. It is almost not too much to say that it was the name of a saint.' Several writings by this Virgil have survived, notably some 'Letters on different grammatical questions'. We are thus in a position to reconstruct the way in which grammar was taught at that period. For the method which Virgil followed was not exclusive to himself. We know indeed that this Virgil ran a school; and moreover he exercised considerable influence, and his school was not the only one. There were other teachers who, whilst not agreeing with him on certain matters of detail, must nevertheless have shared with him a very similar conception of grammar.

Now what is most immediately striking about these schools is the extent to which grammar was made the object of a cult. Virgil tells us that in his youth he was present at a gathering of thirty grammarians who had met to discuss their art. It was there decided that the most sublime object to which scholarly meditation could aspire was the conjugation of verbs. In these councils of grammarians two parties were constantly in evidence, endlessly engaged in dispute, and here are some of the subjects of their arguments. The two party leaders debated for fourteen days and fourteen nights the question of whether the pronoun *ego* has a vocative. Fifteen days and fifteen nights were necessary to decide whether all Latin verbs have a frequentive. What explains this fascination is the fact that Latin was for them a language of mystery and one which they themselves were at pains to enshroud in mystery; a meeting of grammarians was rather like a secret society which devoted itself in the shadows to the celebration of mystical rites. They were not content with co-ordinating the rules and teaching them as lucidly as possible; they subjected the language to a frenzied elaboration, torturing the meaning of words, the syntax and the spelling, in order to produce a system of symbols which would be inaccessible to the common people. It was at this time that they managed to establish the existence of twelve latinities superimposed upon one another in hierarchical order. The lowest was represented by the common language; the others moved ever further from this point of departure. Virgil gives us by way of example the twelve different names by which the word for 'fire' was known. The common people call it *ignis*, but the sages on the other hand call it *ardor* because it sets fire to itself, *spiridon* because it exhales a vapour, and so on. Entire treatises were written in this mystical gobbledygook, and we find passages from these treatises cited by people of no mean intelligence. This proves the authority which the school enjoyed. The very mystery with which it surrounded itself attracted the attention of the barbarians, for whom the scholar became once again a sort of magician and initiate. This is how the Ecole du Palais came to be a sort of secret society into which one could not enter without prior initiation and a new baptism involving a change of name. Hence also the taste which we find so surprising but which was so widespread for riddles, which even played an important part in academic exercises.

When one compares these pedantic lucubrations with the work of the grammarians in the Carolingian period, Alcuin's for example, it appears, despite its flaws and inadequacies, in a quite different light. It constituted a definite advance to have escaped from this fantastical magic and to have returned, over the heads of Virgil the Asiatic and his disciples to the tradition of the Latin grammarians, to Donatius and to Priscian. It was a re-awakening of common sense, of a sense of the need for clarity and consequently for the true spirit of scholarship, as opposed to all these mystical ideas and this taste for the obscure which bear witness to the total confusion which previously reigned in the minds of men. It is proof that the darkness in which human intelligence had been enveloped was beginning to be dissipated. This then is the first thing which we must not forget if we are to reach a fair assessment of this earliest curriculum.

Just the same, whatever its relative value may have been, we seem forced to conclude on the basis of everything that has been said that it had drastic failings. We have seen how, as a result of the overwhelming importance attributed to the sciences of the trivium, the school curriculum was entirely formal at that time. But there are degrees of formalism in education depending on whether the education is concentrated on forms which are more or less remote from things themselves. To say, as we have just done, that education began by being exclusively concerned with grammar is also to concede that it began with the most external sort of formalism possible, the most superficial and the most vacuous; namely, verbal formalism. Indeed grammatical forms are already a translation of the general forms of thought which are themselves an expression of the general forms of things. It is formalism at two stages removed. Thus what are we to think of a curriculum which took for its subject-matter a symbolic system so remote from reality?

We must undoubtedly admit that it was an inadequate diet for the mind; and we cannot possibly find fault with the numerous educationalists who in subsequent ages vigorously argued for placing things rather than words in the centre. But as against this, many of those who have fought most vehemently against this purely grammatical curriculum have also failed to recognise its considerable educational value. Far from its being necessarily vacuous, sterile and purely mechanical, it constituted when rightly understood an excellent and indeed irreplaceable means of developing a capacity for logical thought.

This is because language is not really, as has so often been said (using a metaphor which, for all that it is traditional, is nevertheless inaccurate) — language is not some sort of external garment in which thought is clothed from the outside, without any really satisfactory fit ever being possible. The truth is that language is a far more integrated element in human thought. It renders it possible no less than it presupposes it. Without language thought would remain at the lowest of levels: for none of the even remotely complex forms of mental life could have established themselves without the help of words. Thus with words, with language, we are dealing in some direct way with thought; and consequently the study of language is, if one knows how to set about it, to study thought itself. Now, is not to classify different types of words, or as we also say different parts of speech, is this not to classify the ultimate elements of thought, the most general categories within which we think, those which constitute the permanent canvas of our intellectual life, a canvas on which the concrete objects of experience come to display their changing shapes? The noun corresponds to the category or notion of substance, the adjective to the category of the attribute, the verb to the category of acting and being acted upon, the verbal noun to the abstract category of being, and so on. It is consequently impossible to treat of the most elementary questions in grammar without touching upon the most serious problems of logic. What is it that rules of agreement express unless it is the way in which ideas in certain circumstances harmonise with one another and, as it were, participate in and share a single life? What is it that the rules of syntax express unless it is the way in which the ultimate elements of the sentence are interrelated with one another to form a structure? To sum up, there is in every language an immanent logic, and it is the business of grammar to disinter this logic and to put it on display. Thus, although it is customary today to reiterate that grammar should have the smallest part to play in the curriculum, if it disappears it will leave a void, a very serious gap, in the education of the mind. At the same time, reflectiveness would also disappear from the study of languages. A great deal of their educational interest would be lost.

Although it is quite obvious that the humble attempts of the grammarians of the ninth and tenth centuries did not fulfil all the desired aims of grammar teaching as outlined above, nevertheless they were far from lacking interest in this conception of the subject. Alcuin's grammar, for example, is by no means a simple compilation of grammatical formulae; it clearly seeks to be also a work of scientific analysis. From the outset, the author connects words with objects and grammar with logic. 'Speech,' he says, 'is comprised of three elements. There are the objects which we receive from reasons, the ideas by means of which we are able to grasp things, and the words by means of which we objectify our ideas.' For each element of language, for each category of word, he seeks philosophical definitions which will express the function of the word and of the corresponding idea in intellectual life. Many of these definitions are even very abstract. In certain of the extracts which Thurot has published we even find metaphysical dissertation on the nature of the letter, on what really constitutes a species, and similar speculations. This is what we must constantly bear in mind if we wish to understand the very substantial role which this kind of education played in those days. It was much less concerned with teaching Latin to children who did not know it than with co-ordinating and rendering precise the ideas which could be left out of a preliminary and preparatory treatment of the language. This was not grammar for beginners; even adults like Charlemagne found value in it. It was not a question of learning rules, but rather of explaining them and systematising them in a logical way. These definitions, classifications and explanations may surprise us today by their excessive simplicity and naivety or alternatively by their obscurity; this in no wise lessens the witness they bear to the goal which was being pursued.

From this point of view education through the study of grammar appears in a quite different light; it takes on an importance which we would not have suspected at first. It is no longer a purely verbal study; it is an early form of the study of logic. It is a preliminary way in which the mind can reflect upon its own nature. Of course I am not claiming that the grammarians deliberately chose words and syntax as a convenient intermediary whereby it would be possible to gain access to, and to observe the life of, the mind. But their need to reflect and to analyse quite naturally took language as its subject-matter because it was the most immediate, the closest, the most easy to grasp for the human mind; and that is why the period we have been studying and which was the age of grammar prepared for the age which was to follow, that which we shall be entering in the next lecture and which was the age of Scholasticism, that is to say the age of logic and of dialectic. The fact is that mediaeval dialectic which played so substantial a role in the intellectual history of Europe was already contained in embryonic form in the grammatical researches which sufficed to occupy the intellectual activity of the Carolingian era.

Moreover, this is the only way of explaining the origin of that great problem which from the twelfth century onwards would be the sole subject of philosophical controversy and would suffice on its own, as it were, to feed the whole of mediaeval intellectual life. This is the problem of universals. It was a question of coming to understand the nature of abstract and general ideas. Do they express things, realities? Underlying the words 'white', 'good', 'diverse', 'profane', 'red', 'corporeal', etc., are there any external realities analogous to concrete individual beings? Whiteness, goodness, corporeality: do these exist in themselves, apart from the individual things which possess these qualities? Or are they not rather simple constructions of the mind, or perhaps they only enjoy a purely nominal existence. Such is the problem to which generation after generation men of rare intellectual acuteness applied all their powers of reflection. In order to explain how this question could have occupied people's minds so long and so obsessively, the influence of the philosophical systems of Plato, of Aristotle and of the Alexandrians has been invoked. The Middle Ages knew of these at least indirectly and it is true that this controversy certainly plays a great part in these systems. But there is more to it than that. For why of all the problems which are treated in these systems is this one alone in attracting the curiosity of thinkers? There must be some particular cause which inspired this particular slant in their meditation. Is it really likely that men who only yesterday were still barbarians and who were just beginning to initiate themselves into matters intellectual should suddenly become fascinated by so abstract a subject, one which is so remote from living reality and so devoid of all practical utility? Now, everything becomes clear once we have understood that thought in the Middle Ages began by applying itself to grammatical matters and that, additionally, the study of grammar paved the way for the raising of other questions. For, when all is said and done, the problem of the Scholastics can more or less be enunciated in grammatical terms and be formulated thus: what do the words mean which express abstract and general ideas? The substantive, as its name indicates, does it always correspond to substances? In that case to abstract and general substantives there correspond also abstract and general substances. Kinds have a real existence. The Realists are right.

Thus as a result of considering simple grammatical classifications, people were naturally led to ask questions about ontology. It is with reference to Alcuin that we should seek to explain the fact that Realism began to be the most widespread and the most widely believed philosophical doctrine. It wasn't simply because of matters to do with orthodoxy; it was rather the natural mode of thought for the human intellect as it then was, and as we have seen it becoming aware of itself in the works of the grammarians. Indeed we can see from the definition which Alcuin gives of the substantive that it was impossible for him to distinguish it from the adjective. For him *montanus* (mountainous) is a noun no less than is *mons* (mountain). The human mind was not yet sufficiently sophisticated with respect to intellectual analysis in order to be able to distinguish the object from the qualities which it might possess. In Alcuin's grammar the adjective is not a separate species of word. Now in order to be able to collate, within a single genus under a single heading, both the notion of concrete individual subjects as encountered in experience and as designated by concrete nouns, and the notion of the attributes which the subjects might possess, it is inevitably tempting to consider these attributes as if they were realities analogous to the subjects, and consequently constituting subjects in their own right and not predicates, and this is the fundamental tenet of Realism. If 'white' is a substantive like 'table' must it not be the case that white exists in its own right no less than the table? And it is precisely this principle which we find spelt out by another of the teachers at the

Ecole du Palais; namely, by Fridugise. 'All substantives', he says, 'express something particular (*Omne nomen finitum aliquid significat, ut homo, lupus, lignum*).' To every name there corresponds a specific reality. From this he concludes that to the word *nihil*, meaning nothing or nothingness, there also corresponds some reality, that is to say that nothingness itself is something positive, that the non-existent actually exists.

Moreover, in the period which we have been studying we find the seeds of that which was to ensue not only in its general orientation; there are also remarkable similarities of detail even with regard to the teaching techniques used. As we shall see, one of the most important exercises in the teaching of universities and the colleges during the scholastic era was debate, the *disputatio*, and we shall need to ascertain the meaning, the form and the educational significance of this particular teaching technique. We shall see that the causes from which it derives are very deep-rooted in the whole of the education system of the age. Alcuin's didactic treatises had already been presented in the form of the *disputatio*. Two pupils, in particular Alcuin himself and Charlemagne, argue about the subject-matter being treated, rather than having it presented *ex professo*. There are some which are expressly entitled *disputatio* (Migne, 101, p.975). Of course, these debates are not yet conducted in the style of the Scholastics, but they are nevertheless debates, and it is interesting to note that from this time on academic works were characteristically produced in this mode. This fact provides irrefutable evidence that this kind of exercise had its roots, in a very general way, in the spirit of the Middle Ages.

If I have felt it necessary to insist on the analogies between the education of the Carolingian period and that of the Scholastic period, it is first of all, of course, in order to make plain the link which exists between these two ages, but, more than this, it is because I wanted to explain how and why this grammar-centred education actually operated. Once one realises that it was preparing the way for Scholastic philosophy and how magnificently its academic system provided a framework for this philosophy, one is no longer inclined to make the mistake of regarding it with contempt. Its real significance lies in the future which it was carrying within itself. At the same time, seen in this light the whole intellectual development of the Middle Ages presents a unity of whose existence we are not normally aware. What is characteristic of it from its origins right up until the period of the Renaissance is an overwhelming pre-occupation with issues in logic. By the ninth century this pre-occupation has been aroused, albeit in only a vague and ill-defined way. By the eleventh century it has been thoroughly established and rendered precise, and is constantly being developed. We have here a characteristic which is wholly distinctive of the intellectual evolution of Christian societies. Whereas Greece begins by philosophising about nature and the universe and only, at a relatively late stage with Socrates and Plato, gets round to speculating about the human mind, the Middle Ages immediately set out by tackling head-on the problem of thought in its most formal and abstract aspect and made it the subject-matter of its own thinking and teaching. If we see this period as one in which the literary beauty of antiquity was set aside with apparent contempt the explanation is not to be found simply in iconoclastic enthusiasm or pure Philistinism. It is rather that the orientation of the whole period is quite different, since it is a period which experiences quite different kinds of need and which seeks to satisfy them. The remarkable continuity of this evolution in one and the same direction from the ninth century to the fifteenth can only be explained by the fact that it was deeply rooted in the intellectual structure of the nations of Europe, that is to say the nations of Christendom. This is what we shall have to bear constantly in mind when we come to assess the achievement of the Renaissance.

Up till now, however, we have studied this evolution only in its preparatory stages. We now come to the period in which these seeds were to develop and to bear fruit. With their flowering in Scholasticism we encounter for the first time the great institutions of public education such as we still have them today.

chapter 6

The origins of the universities

In the preceding chapters, we have seen what constituted the earliest established system of education in the societies of Europe. What is unquestionably characteristic of it is its extreme formalism. For all that it sought to be encyclopaedic in theory, in its practical application in academic life it consisted almost entirely of a handful of wholly formal disciplines which dealt with the general forms of thought and its expression: grammar, rhetoric and dialectic. Indeed of these disciplines the one which was regarded as being of primary importance and to which most attention was paid was the most formal of them all, the one which studies thought in its most exteriorised form and whose subject-matter is the most remote from things; I am referring to grammar. This is why we have been able to christen the Carolingian age, that period which extends from the ninth to the eleventh century, the age of grammar. But at the same time we have shown that, however meagre and inadequate this sort of education may legitimately appear, it nevertheless contained fertile seeds. Its object was not to teach beginners, more or less by using the techniques of rote-learning, the traditional rules of the language; rather it was concerned to co-ordinate these rules in a rational manner, to explain them, and to show the connections which existed between them and the laws of thought. Thus understood, grammar was, as it were, the womb of logic. And it is indeed beyond doubt that grammar was capable of being taught in such a way that it constituted a preliminary study to the study of logic. Just as words and combinations of words, considered on their own, are empty, lifeless, purely formal objects, so they become revitalised and fascinating as soon as they are considered as an externalising translation of the life of the mind. From this point of view, the age of grammar was nothing but a prelude for the age which was to follow, the age of Scholasticism, which we might very well characterise by describing it as the age of logic.

What constitutes the proof of this continuity between the two ages, what gives direction to all this grammatical education, what demonstrates the reality of the logical vitality with which it was imbued is not only the fact that, as I have shown, the great problem of Scholasticism, the problem which was to occupy the whole of the Middle Ages (namely, the problem of universals) is already very much in evidence in the works of Alcuin, but also the fact that one finds it posed in formal terms in the works of his immediate successors. Immediately after Alcuin his pupil, Rabanus Maurus, is speculating about the nature of genera. Are these realities or constructions of the human mind? Because, he asks himself, the word *ens* is used to designate everything that exists, does it follow that this singular substantive is the name of some unique substance which contains within itself all particular existing things? After Rabanus Maurus, it was Scotus Erigenus, that extraordinary genius who in the ninth century was already writing with a profundity which was not surpassed even by the greatest thinkers of the age of Scholasticism. Other successors of Rabanus Maurus are Heiric and Remi d'Auxerre, the former of whom propounded a thorough-going Nominalism, the latter of whom was the champion of extreme Realism. Of course, the words Realism and Nominalism were not yet in use. The two schools of thought had not yet established themselves in open competition, as they were to do later on. However, from this moment onwards the debate had been opened up, the question posed; all of which goes to show that this grammatical education by no means failed to be an intellectual stimulant of substantial potency. Nevertheless if it is true that from then onwards the few thinkers whose names I have mentioned elevated their thinking to the point where they could contemplate the great question of Scholasticism and if as a consequence, they intuitively foresaw the considerable importance which logic was to have in the schools, they nevertheless did not get around to making it the corner-stone of education. However interesting, however forceful certain of these attempts, especially that of Scotus, may have been, they still remained the enterprises of individuals, isolated and sporadic, which did not have the effect of generating a renewal in intellectual and academic life. The subject-matter and the methods of education remained approximately what they had always been, except that dialectic was accorded greater or lesser importance depending on the temperament of the teacher. How indeed could it be otherwise? The curriculum, founded by Charlemagne, could not develop and transform itself on its own and automatically, if nothing spurred it on to do so and it had received no vital charge overflowing from somewhere outside itself sufficient to set in train such transformations. Now, as soon as Charlemagne had disappeared from the scene education went into a period of decay and decline; gone were the days of that powerful concentration of all the intellectual forces of Europe whose instigator Charles had been. Intellectual life consequently could only become and in fact did become increasing decadent. In order for it to be revived, in order for it to be intensified to the necessary degree, it was therefore necessary that a new and forceful mind should come to set in motion the public intellect. It was necessary that new circumstances should appear which would somehow heighten the intellectual temperature of Europe in such a way that there would be a ripening and a blossoming of those seeds of the future which were already embedded in Carolingian education but which would have remained more or less buried if nothing new had appeared on the scene. It was in the eleventh century that these great changes took place. This was a period in which all historians see a veritable intellectual effervescence amongst all the peoples of Europe. It was a second renaissance which was taking place, which went much deeper than the first and which was by no means less important than the one which was to take place later in the sixteenth century. Once the millennium had been safely traversed it was as if a new inspiration was being breathed over the whole of Europe. Of course, we must be aware of attributing everything, as people have occasionally done, to the delight which men experienced at having survived the allegedly fatal date. If, at this time, the peoples of Christendom are reborn in hope and in confidence, it is not only because some dark misguided superstition has been dissipated; it is also because their lives were profoundly changed.

The tenth century which had gone before — the tenth century during which the Carolingian dynasty had finally died out — had been for Christendom an era of painful anguish and general anxiety. There were a thousand urgent problems which had to be endured. There were the Scandinavians who were once again ravaging the north. There were the Saracens who were invading the south, there were the Normans who threatened the entire coastline. In the interior the Carolingian Empire was crumbling into dust, shredded into different feudal groups, which, being badly co-ordinated, were seeking some sort of relatively stable mode of organisation in the face of all kinds of internal clashes and conflicts. It was a period of strife, of groping and of laborious adaptation. The peoples of Europe needed all their forces to defend themselves against enemies from without and to re-establish equilibrium within. Consequently they had neither the leisure nor the intellectual freedom necessary for cerebral achievements. Thus the tenth century was a century of intellectual stagnation some of whose tendencies were even retrograde. Education was carried on, of course, in the cathedrals and the monasteries, but without innovation and without progress; throughout this entire period it is impossible to pick out a single great name. By contrast, in the eleventh century the era of major problems was over. The Scandinavian pirates had become members of the great Christian communities, the Normans had become civilised and stable. The feudal system was fully organised.

Consequently all the forces, all the moral energy, which had been mobilised in order to confront this variety of problems found themselves, as it were, set free and rendered available. Since they no longer had any particular job to do they inevitably had to find some new employment. This caused a veritable rash of activity under which the whole of Europe laboured at that time, and whose most glaring examples are the Crusades. It is the only way we can explain the spontaneity and the suddenness of these great religious uprisings. If, from the moment that Pope Urban II, at Clermont, had indicated to Christendom the evils from which their brother Christians were suffering in the Holy Land, if in the twinkling of an eye not only the nobles but also the great masses of the people responded unanimously and ecstatically and made their way in a tumult towards these distant parts to which the Church had sent them, it was because there was at that time throughout Europe a genuine and intense need for action and movement, for a cause worthy of self-sacrifice. The Holy See did not create this movement artificially; it did no more than assign a specific goal to all this immobilised capacity for action which was seeking some goal to which it could devote itself. It is easy to see how this general effervescence easily came to take on an intellectual form. For, as far as civilisation is concerned, the creative ages are precisely those in which there has been amongst communities an accumulation of vitality which is only seeking an outlet, some means of expending itself, while at the same time there exists no vital necessity which can lay claim to it. Art, science, the intellectual life in general are all, in a sense, luxury occupations which presuppose a superfluity of energy in the community beyond that which is of immediate necessity for survival. In order to be able to devote oneself to the work of pure, objective thought, it is necessary to have a reserve of energy available, which is in surplus to that demanded by the difficulties of day-to-day existence. When such a reserve exists, because it is not compelled to put itself to use outside, it naturally turns to the inner life, to thought and to reflection.

But the Crusades reveal to us another characteristic of the society of that time, one which must have done at least as much to further extreme mobility of people from all classes and from all professions. In order for such extensive masses of men to be principal features of Europe at the time of Charlemagne. In the eleventh century the nations of Europe were no more firmly established than they had been at the end of the eighth. Even the large groupings which were then beginning to form or which had disappeared or which virtually only existed in name had been replaced by a mosaic of feudal groups too minute and too artificial to be able to take the place of a fatherland in the moral sense of that word. By contrast, Christendom had all the stronger sense of its own identity; the Crusades, then, were nothing but the popular nationalist war of Christendom against the infidels. Charlemagne's wars had been crusades, but they had been the will of a single man: the crusades of the eleventh century were a war which was the will of nations. This was, moreover, the moment when the Papacy and the Empire were fighting for supremacy in Europe; this meant that each one was trying, for his own advantage, to create the unification of Christian society. These conditions explain why people did not feel themselves strongly attached to their place of birth; why, despite very weak links beyond those of custom, they moved with a certain freedom over the whole surface of Europe, to say nothing of the fact that the insecurity of life at that time often made this a necessity. This sort of nomadicism combined with this effervescence, this general over-excitation of all the intellectual forces of Europe, could not fail to serve the interests of scholarship. Not only did the number of men wishing to become educated increase, but also, since there were no national barriers to stop them, they naturally travelled *en masse* to the points where they could best find this education which they felt they needed. Instead of scattering and disseminating themselves amongst a whole multitude of different schools, they were to take advantage of their freedom of movement by concentrating themselves around a handful of 'chairs', around those where they had the greatest chance of finding what they were looking for. This is indeed what happened. Whereas the schools of the tenth century languished in obscurity, in the following century we see large groupings of scholars become established which are more vigorous and more active because they are more extensive. And just as the function creates the organ, just as need procures for itself the means of its own satisfaction, so great names attach themselves to these great establishments. There was the Ecole de Reims, with its head, the illustrious Gerbert, one of the greatest intellects of the Middle Ages (Pope Sylvester II); there was the Ecole de

Chartres with Fulbert; there was the Ecole de Paris with Lambert, who had been Fulbert's pupil; there was the Ecole de Laon with the famous Anselme; there was the Ecole du Bec, with Lanfranc, and others. To each of these schools there thronged pupils from every country and every class.

If nothing else had happened there would certainly have been a large number of brilliant schools and brilliant teachers, but there would have been no real fundamental educational innovations. And indeed, education in the eleventh century, although it has more brilliance than in the preceding centuries, does not differ from them in essentials. The structures remain the same; they are still cathedral schools or monastic schools and the subject-matter taught has undergone no palpable change except in as far as dialectic tends to take on an ever-increasing importance. What differences there were were really only of secondary importance and were ultimately reducible to mere shifts in emphasis. But from the beginning of the twelfth century a great transformation was beginning to take place in France which was to have, not only for us but for the whole of academic Europe, extensive repercussions. The Capetian monarchy consolidated itself and became organised. The court, which had hitherto been peripatetic, moving from one place to another throughout the kingdom according to the whim of the king and the circumstances in general, now established itself definitely in Paris, which became the principal town and the capital of the kingdom. Henceforth France had a centre. Inevitably the Ecole de Paris shared increasingly in the prestige which the town itself was in the process of acquiring; for all the young scholars of the kingdom it had an attraction which was incomparably greater than that of the other schools in the kingdom and even in neighbouring countries.

The fact is, however, that this expression 'Ecole de Paris' had no very clearly defined meaning; for there had always been in Paris a variety of schools. Several monasteries had a school, notably the monastery of Sainte-Geneviève and the monastery of Saint-Victor. But amongst all these schools there was one which outshone all the others and which very quickly acquired a thorough-going domination; this was the one which was attached to Notre-Dame. It operated in a cloister quite close to the bishop's residence at the foot of the metropolitan church which was already called Notre-Dame, but which was not yet the magnificent monument which was only begun under Philippe-Auguste. This cloister was a precinct which began at the square in front of the church, ran alongside the northern nave of the church, and then joined the garden of the bishop's palace. This is where the students thronged who had come from every corner of Europe. The episcopal school thus acquired supremacy; we shall see that in relation to the others it even had some sort of legal pre-eminence. Henceforth academic life in France and also in the other societies of Europe had a fixed centre, clearly defined and immutable, owing its importance not to the authority and prestige of an illustrious teacher, an ephemeral personality who might go and teach somewhere else, who was bound to disappear sooner or later, and on whom the fortunes of the school depended. The pre-eminence of what was henceforth called the 'Ecole de Paris' derived above all from impersonal and durable causes, from its geographical situation and the place which it occupied at the very centre of the state. Consequently its status in the academic hierarchy no longer depended to the same extent on the personal quality of the teachers who taught there; and since the concentration of which it was the heart was thus more assured of enduring, it could have been expected that it was destined to produce a much more substantial effect than the transitory gatherings which formed themselves around an illustrious 'chair' occupied by some teacher of repute. It was about to become possible for the educational system to be organised in a new way which would be stable, regular, impersonal, and enjoying a continuous development, from which there would emerge a style of academic life hitherto unknown.

The forces — at least the impersonal forces — which produced these radical changes, and whose consequences we shall be investigating, can thus be reduced to two. In the first place, there was a general revitalisation of intellectual activity throughout Europe. This activity became concentrated in two ways: first in a handful of scattered situations, then in a single but stable location. And it is from the vitality which was generated in the environs of this single central and privileged location that the educational innovations were to emerge whose progress we shall be charting. It was from this womb that the organisation of university education was to emerge, in which mediaeval civilisation most truly developed and which, by transforming itself, was to ensure its survival right up until our own time. For it is a remarkable fact that of all the mediaeval institutions the one which, despite certain variations, still most closely resembles what it was in those days, is the university.

In addition to these impersonal forces, as chance would have it, a single individual appeared whose contribution to this phenomenon was substantial. What chance brought about was the presence in Paris of one of the most prestigious — perhaps the most prestigious — personalities of the whole of the Middle Ages. I am referring to Abelard. It is not necessary here to go into the many events of his turbulent life nor even to describe his curious physiognomy. Moreover, whatever part was played by the charm of his personality and his eloquence in his success, it seems to me impossible to explain the extent of his immense influence exclusively in terms of his talent. Few men have ever enjoyed so thoroughly all the delights of fame. The philosophers of antiquity, like those of modern times, have never been known and admired except by a limited circle of fellow intellectuals; Abelard was the idol of whole multitudes of people. 'Only Voltaire,' says Remusat, 'only Voltaire, perhaps, and his situation in the eighteenth century could give us some idea what the twelfth century thought of Abelard.' According to one chronicler, we have not seen his like since; earlier ages had not known his like. It was said of him that Gaul had never known a genius so great, that he was the greatest of the great, that his ability transcended all human measurement. He was put on a par with Plato, with Aristotle, and indeed with Cicero and Homer, no doubt on account of his literary talent. Now, the writer who has studied Abelard and his work in greatest depth, M. de Remusat, having acknowledged in him 'one of the noble ancestors of the liberators of the human mind', adds: 'Yet he was not a great man; rather he was a first-class mind of extraordinary subtlety and ingenuity, a critic whose penetration and gift for exposition bear witness to an amazing understanding.' His reputation was thus disproportionate to his personal qualities and must therefore, have derived from some other cause. If he enjoyed such fame he owed it not simply to his knowledge and to his eloquence; it was also the fact that he was one of those men that we characteristically find standing on the threshold of all great historical periods, one of those men in whom their contemporaries see themselves portrayed on a grand scale. Abelard was perhaps the most thoroughly representative figure of the whole mediaeval period. In him we still find personified everything which the Middle Ages loved: brilliant dialectic, faith grounded in reason, and that curious mixture of religious fervour and a passion for knowledge which was the distinguishing mark of this great era. Never had the problem which so fascinated the Middle Ages, the problem around which all mediaeval thought gravitated over several centuries, never had the problem of universals been posed more brilliantly and dealt with on such a large scale, with such eloquence and vigour. Every age has a tendency to exalt, even to deify, the men in whom it thinks it can recognise its own image and who offer an attractive incarnation of its own ideals. In admiring the person of Abelard the twelfth century was admiring itself, just as later on the eighteenth century was to admire itself in the figure of Voltaire.

Whatever its cause, his influence went beyond anything which we can conceive of. When he began to teach in Paris, this city became the focus of attention for the entire intellectual population of Europe. 'Everywhere he was talked about, from places as far removed from each other as conceivable, from Brittany and England to the Baltic and Teutonic countries, people flocked to hear him; even Rome sent people to listen to him. The crowds in the street, greedy to catch a glimpse of him, stopped him as he walked along; in order to see him the inhabitants of houses would go down and stand in their doorways and the women would pull back slightly the curtains of their narrow windows.' His pupils were to be numbered in thousands, and amongst them, many became illustrious teachers in their own right. It is said that his school produced one pope, nineteen cardinals, more than fifty bishops or archbishops in France, in England and in Germany; amongst them was the celebrated Pierre Lombard, the Bishop of Paris, whose book *Liber Sententiarum* was later to become the standard textbook for the teaching of theology in the University of Paris.

When one thinks that the heart of the curriculum consisted in a certain thesis about universals one finds it somewhat difficult to understand such enthusiasm. The question of whether genera are merely constructions of the human mind or whether they have some kind of objective reality over and above the particular thing in which the genus participates; the question, for example, of whether there exists or not over and above individual human beings some sort of abstract entity called 'humanity' or whether over and above animals there is some abstract principle called 'animality'; these questions seem to us to be too aridly theoretical to generate such passionate emotions.

In fact, in this famous controversy there were involved a host of other questions which went right to the heart of the most vital questions which the moral and religious consciousness of the time was capable of raising. Suppose we admit that there exists no other substance than individual substances and that this genus consists of nothing other than the individuals which compose it, that it is a word used to designate the agglomeration of these individuals or the collectivity of their common characteristics. In this case the most crucial teachings of the Church become unintelligible. How, for example, are we to conceive of the divine Trinity? If it is true that the individual by himself, taken in his totality and in his unity, is a substance, if the diverse elements of which he is made up have no substantial reality, then it follows that the three divine persons of the Trinity are three distinct and irreducible substances. Consequently we concede a thorough-going polytheism which is repugnant to the Christian mind; or alternatively we maintain that the three persons are really only one; and that they are different aspects of one and the same substance having no distinct individuality of their own. Then we wind up with a unitarianism which is no less contrary to the teachings of the Church. Similarly, given this problem, how are we to interpret the doctrine of the real presence in the Eucharist? If a morsel of bread is a single and indivisible substance, how do we explain the way in which this substance can disappear in order to be replaced by another which is quite different and which, nevertheless, retains all the outward appearances of the first one? Again, if individuals are irreducibly different from one another, if there is no substantial bond between them, if the class 'humanity', which they all express in different ways, has no independent existence, how are we to explain why the original sin of the first human being was not something which was strictly personal? How could it have communicated its effects to other men who had not committed it? The doctrine of original sin becomes self-contradictory.

Thus Realism which maintains that genera exist in reality, seemed to be logically implied by catholic orthodoxy, and indeed it already had itself something of the character of orthodox doctrine. Thus, for example, according to Realism, everything is made up of two elements; on the one hand, there is the generic principle which is the same in all the individuals belonging to the genus and which is the soul of these individuals, invisible, impalpable and purely spiritual; then there is the physical form by means of which this principle becomes individualised and which accounts for the fact that it appears in different forms in different locations. In this way we can see how in the act of consecration the generic and spiritual principle of the bread vanishes and is replaced by another, without having as a consequence changed in its material form. This is how the principle of divinity can be incarnated in morsels of bread. But if Realism had the advantage of rendering more easily intelligible certain articles of faith, what a vast amount of problems it raised! If the genus does exist as a reality in its own right, then it is the genus which is the true reality; everything which is individual about ourselves becomes nothing more than perceptible appearance, material form, pure accident. What is real is not what we possess in our own right, it is rather what we have in common with all the members of the genus to which we belong; the individual thus disappeared in the genus and one was led logically to take a pantheistic view of the universe.

What was at stake in this controversy were the beliefs which constituted the foundation for the moral and religious consciousness of the age; faith itself was at stake. In sum, underlying this apparently abstract speculative problem we find an early and powerful attempt to confront faith with reason. Certainly there was no question as yet of casting doubt on the truth of religion; but the need to examine it was being felt, to challenge the credentials which it claimed, and to find a form in which it could be rendered rational and intelligible. This need to understand faith was felt without the question even arising that it might be false, and this in itself constituted a substantial innovation. For the moment one introduces reason, criticism and the spirit of reflectiveness into a set of ideas which up to that time has appeared unchallengeable it is the beginning of the end; the enemy has gained foothold. If reason is not given its fair share, then from the moment that it has established a foothold somewhere it always ends up by casting down the artificial barriers within which attempts have been made to contain it. This was the achievement of Scholasticism. It confronted dogma with reason, even though it refused to deny the truth of the dogma. Between these two forces it sought to maintain an even balance; this was both its strength and its weakness.

There is something fascinating and even dramatic about the spectacle with which this period presents us, tormented as it was, lurching between respect for tradition and the attraction of free enquiry, between the desire to remain faithful to the Church and the increasing need to understand. These centuries which some have portrayed as slumbering in a kind of intellectual torpor knew no peace of mind. They were divided amongst themselves, pulled in two opposite directions; it is one of the periods of the greatest effervescence of the human mind in which innovations were fathered. The harvest was to be gathered in subsequent ages, but it was then that the seeds were sown. The full blossoming was to take place in blazing sunlight, joyfully, in the brilliance of the seventeenth and eighteenth centuries, but the seeds had been painfully sown and it was still the quality of the seeds which rendered the harvest so rich. This is what we must constantly bear in mind when we come to study the period we are about to embark upon. This is what explains the passion with which the men of the Middle Ages conducted their debates. It is the very interest that they hold for us which enables us to understand the interest which they held for the people of the time who lived through them.

Finally, this goes a long way towards explaining the origin of Abelard's influence. It is because he identified himself with his century. It is because he understood better than anyone the painful disharmony which caused both his fame and his suffering. Along with his age, indeed more than his own age, he knew both the passion for enquiry and, in the end, the sufferings of doubt.

We should neither deny the personal influence of Abelard nor should we exaggerate it. It has even been claimed at times that he was the founder of the University of Paris. This is thoroughly inaccurate. First of all, there did not exist at this period any organisation which might be accorded this title. Moreover, the intensity of the movement which is associated with his name is to a large extent the result of causes which transcend it. There was from his day onwards an intellectual anxiety, a thirst for knowledge and understanding which were the real moving forces behind the crowds which thronged around him. What is true is that thanks to his personal qualities he made a contribution in strengthening this movement and getting it established; and consequently he carved out the path which would lead to the foundation of the University. Indeed, the hosts of students which he had attracted to Paris rendered this city even more brilliant, and reinforced the movement which every year drew towards it the student population of Europe. When this happened the students became so numerous that the teachers themselves had to multiply. The Ecole de Notre Dame was no longer adequate; a large number of teachers began to teach in private houses, in their private residence, on the island or on the bridges of the Seine. This multiplicity of teachers, so grouped, was the material, but only the material, which was to give birth to the University of Paris. We need to show how it was to organise itself and to define the academic system which was accorded this name, a system which was entirely new and without parallel in antiquity.

chapter 7

The birth of the University

The *inceptio* and the *licentia docendi*

At the end of the last lecture we reached the threshold of one of the most important questions which we shall have to investigate in this course. It concerns the nature of that great academic movement which acquired, in the course of history, the name 'University of Paris'. What was the educational ideal of which it was the concrete expression? In order to ascertain the correct answer, the best method is to trace the genesis of the institution, investigating how it came to be formed, what caused it to come into existence, and what were the moral forces whose consequence it was. By examining the constitution of the original seed out of which it grew, by scrutinising the various elements of which it was made up and seeing how they were assembled and combined, we shall be able to specify the animating spirit which determined the orientation of the institution.

The question is of interest for manifold reasons. First of all, it is one of extreme importance and interest in educational theory. For the University of Paris was the matrix within which our entire educational system developed. In the beginning it embraced all the things which would later come to constitute our system of secondary education, and it was the womb from which our colleges would emerge. Our entire subsequent educational development would bear its imprint. Second, the question is of considerable historical interest; this, though it affects us less directly, will still not leave us indifferent. This is because there is no institution which gives better expression to the mediaeval mind. The university was not just a school in which a certain number of disciplines were taught. The university, perhaps even more than the Church and the feudal system, was the institution which most faithfully and representatively reflected this period. Never was the intellectual life of the European peoples equipped with an organ so accurate, so universally recognised, in short so well adapted to its function. Thus the influence of the universities was far greater than political historians lead us to suspect. The study which we shall undertake will enable us the better to understand this organisation from which our own is derived.

The problem of the origins of the University of Paris which we are about to tackle has already been the subject of numerous important works. Without seeking to offer here a complete bibliography, I must at least give a brief indication of the main sources to which reference should be made by anyone embarking on a study of the history of the University of Paris, as well as of the principal works which have made use of these sources. As far as the original documents are concerned, these will be found in the *Cartularium Universitatis Parisiensis* by Denifle and Chatelain, the first two volumes of which, published in 1889 and 1891, take us up to the year 1350. Another work which is very rich in material and which is also the first systematic history of the University is the *Historia Universitatis Parisiensis a Carolo Magno ad nostra tempora* by Du Boulay (Bulaeus; 6 folio volumes, 1665–1679). Unfortunately the author is wholly lacking in critical spirit; this account of the origins of the University is entirely mythical; it is legend posing as history. However, this did not prevent its remaining a classic for a very long time; it was more or less faithfully reproduced by a large number of writers whose names are not worth reciting since their works are valueless. There was at the Sorbonne itself a very ancient manuscript work whose object was precisely the refutation of Du Boulay. But this anonymous study entitled *Universitatis Parisiensis ejusque Facultatum quatuor origo vera* has not yet been published.

It was only in the second half of the nineteenth century that the history of the University of Paris entered the age of science. This movement was initiated by Charles Thurot, who, in his doctoral thesis entitled 'The organisation of teaching in the University of Paris during the Middle Ages' (Paris and Besançon, 1850), painted a most carefully researched picture of the educational system as it functioned in the mediaeval university; but he only touches upon the question of origins. This lack began to be filled in the great work of Father Denifle, *Die Universitaeten des Mittelalters bis 1 400*, which began to appear in 1885. Finally M. Rashdall, more recently, has produced an extensive study of the universities of Europe in the Middle Ages, *Universities of Europe in the Middle Ages* (Oxford, 1895, 11 vols) in which Paris inevitably plays a major role. Bearing in mind these sources, we can confront the problem for ourselves.

For a long time we used to have a penchant (and indeed evidence of this penchant still exists today) for accepting historical explanations which interpret social institutions with reference to some great figure who is supposed to have been their creator, and, so to speak, their inventor. It was in this spirit that people used to seek for someone with whom the foundation of the University of Paris could be associated. Now there is one such figure who appears at the beginning of the Middle Ages and who towers over it like a Colossus; namely, Charlemagne. It is for this reason that Du Boulay thought it possible to trace the origin of the University back to Charlemagne. The organisation of the University was thus seen as a simple development from the Ecole du Palais. We do not need to investigate here this truly mythological view. We need only to note that the University was born in Paris, as I have already indicated and as further evidence will shortly render indubitable. It was something essentially Parisian, whereas the Ecole du Palais, being attached to Charles's court, was peripatetic like this court itself. It is not even certain that this prince who visited so many towns, lived in so many palaces, spent even a few hours in the city of Paris. The only connection between Charlemagne and the University resides in the fact that Charles sponsored the resurrection of the cathedral schools and that the cathedral school of Paris, was, as we shall see shortly, at least in one sense the cradle of the University.

Few people today, and indeed for some time past, take this historical myth seriously. But there was another figure who succeeded Charlemagne in the role that had been attributed to him; this was Abelard. Even such eminent historians as Thurot have made out that he was the founder of the University. It appeared that the great intellectual vigour which was manifest at that time had created a wholly new era in education; and that a greater part of this enthusiasm for learning, which attracted to Paris the student population of Europe, was due to the personal influence attributed to Abelard. But whatever the true origins of this movement were (and we have seen every reason to believe that the essential causes for it transcended the personality of Abelard), it is quite certain that at the time when he found himself thronged by veritable armies of students there then existed in Paris nothing worthy of the name of 'university'. In fact, a university is not simply a more sophisticated version of a cathedral or abbey school, having a larger pupil population than normal; it is an entirely novel system of schooling whose distinctive features will emerge as we proceed with our investigation. Now, at the time of Abelard there simply did not exist any schools other than those which were attached to the churches and to the monasteries. He himself taught successively first in the cloister at Notre-Dame and then in the monastery of Sainte-Geneviève, situated on the peak of the mount which bears this name, at the spot where today we see the Pantheon; and the fact that thousands of scholars came to these schools in order to hear the word of the great teacher in no wise changed the nature of these institutions.

Yet at that time an important innovation occurred which was to carve out the path which would lead to the creation of the University and which was to render necessary its organisation. Because of the increasing intensification . of intellectual life, because of the prestige which Paris acquired in European public opinion, no less on account of its central situation in the kingdom of France than on account of the teachings of Abelard, the scholars became so numerous in the course of the twelfth century that the schools which had been established within religious institutions, whether churches or monasteries, no longer sufficed to provide the education which was being demanded by these masses who were so eager to be taught. Their inadequacy was soon to be exacerbated by the fact that the majority of these schools disappeared, with the single exception of the cathedral school of Notre-Dame. The school at Saint-Geneviève, where Abelard had taught with such brilliance, declined after his time; from the end of the twelfth century onwards, if it existed at all, it was as a shadow of its former self. The same thing happened with the school which was attached to the abbey of Saint-Victor. Thus the cloister of Notre-Dame became the only intellectual centre in Paris, the only educational centre which was open to lay people. Clearly it could not offer on its own to the ever-increasing multitude of students the education which they needed. It was therefore necessary to authorise individual teachers to open schools outside the cathedral. They taught in private houses which were their own homes; but they were required by diocesan authority to reside either on the island or on the bridges of the Seine. In particular, there were a number who had set up their schools on the little bridge (*rue du Petit Pont*). We know of a Jean du Petit Pont, an Adam du Petit Pont, and a Pierre du Petit Pont, who were teachers of repute during the twelfth century. The creation of these schools constituted a veritable revolution, which was itself the preparation for another revolution of even greater significance. As long as these schools were cloistered within the precinct or the dependencies whether of cathedrals or of monasteries, they had no need of any special sort of organisation; they were covered by the ecclesiastical organisation. They were an organ of the Church, and consequently subject to the rules and discipline of the Church. Now, however, we have a large population of both teachers and pupils operating henceforth outside this ecclesiastical atmosphere; although they remained and were obliged to remain in the vicinity of the cathedral, they were nevertheless to a large ex-

tent independent of it. They were lay people leading a secular existence; as far as the Church was concerned they were subject only
to indirect and remote regulation. Under such circumstances it
was inevitable that new ideas and new aspirations should see the
light of day, that a wholly new form of academic life should be
born, one which needed a special kind of organisation quite
different from anything that the Middle Ages had known up until
that time.

What was this organisation to be?

The period with which we are dealing was also the heyday of
corporate life in all spheres of public activity. On the one hand,
similarity of occupation inclined workers in the same profession
to band together, to establish more intimate relationships with
one another; and on the other hand, the very conditions of social
life made this banding together essential for them. For it was only
by uniting, by forming enduring associations, sufficiently powerful to command respect, that they managed to guarantee for
themselves the legal right to exist. Naturally this right virtually involved a monopoly; those who had obtained it kept it for themselves alone. But these monopolies also involved duties for those
who enjoyed them; for the association, in order to remain strong,
imposed obligations on its members, such that if they did not fulfil
them they were deprived of their privileges. The corporations of
the Middle Ages were characterised by being privileged groups
which were nevertheless subject to rigorous discipline. Now the
teachers who were teaching side by side on the *île de la cité* were in
an identical situation to the masters of some other craft or trade.
They too gained their livelihood by practising the same profession; they too had to struggle in order to ensure their right to
exist. It was therefore inevitable that they should organise
themselves in the same way, as a corporation.

An old professional custom provided, as it were, the crystallis-
ing centre around which the corporation of teachers became
organised. It was a custom of long standing that no one should
teach without having himself followed for some determinate
period — which seems to have varied between five and seven years
— the teaching of some other teacher who possessed due
authorisation and who had given to his pupil a sort of investiture.
Already at the time of Abelard this principle was recognised. Indeed at one moment in his career Abelard conceived the ambition
of teaching theology; he was obliged to conform to the custom
and to attend the school of a recognised teacher of theology before
he could teach the subject himself. The theologian by whom he
was instructed was Anselme de Laon. However, as a result of his
native impatience and his confidence in his genius, he cut short

the normal period of studentship and, without having received the authorisation of his teacher, started to give courses on his own. Such impropriety was judged very harshly and treated as a major misdemeanour. He was compelled to leave Laon, where he had in this way flouted the rules by giving instruction; and, when he was sent to trial at the Council of Soissons, this was one of the main charges against him; he was accused of running 'courses without a teacher, (*quod sine magistro ad magisterium...accedere praesumpsisset*).' These words clearly show that the presence of a teacher was necessary for at least the first lesson given by his pupil in order that the latter might be able to teach.

Nor was the role of the teacher restricted to listening passively to the lesson. It was up to him to pin on his pupil the badge of his new office, after which he kissed him and gave him his blessing. This ceremony, which was certainly very old, although it may not always have existed in the form which it later took, was, at a particular moment which we cannot establish, given the name *inceptio* (first appearance, inaugural attempt). Now it is clear that in the *inceptio* there was already inherent the idea that yesterday's pupil in order to become a teacher must be received into the society of existing teachers by one or more of them. It thus already provides evidence of certain feelings of professional solidarity and aspirations towards a total monopoly which is the first seed of all corporate life. There is indeed a very close connection between this custom and the organisation of corporate life in general; this is proved by the fact that there are hardly any corporations where the same kind of practice does not take place. We find it in the reception of the new companion into his trade after he has presented his masterpiece and had it accepted. We find it in the reception of the young novice by his elders into the chivalric orders. It has been noted that this latter ceremony resembles the *inceptio* in quite specific respects: it is almost as if the teacher was thought of as a kind of intellectual knight. Thus in certain parts it was customary to use a sword or a ring to invest the new teacher as well as the new knight. Similarly, a preliminary bath, intended no doubt to purify the candidate, seems to have been demanded in both cases.

The feeling of solidarity thus expressed is not difficult to understand. Authorised teachers had an interest in ensuring that no one could become a colleague of theirs against their will. It was one way of containing and restricting competition while at the same time maintaining respect for tradition. If this feeling was already alive and active in the time of Abelard, when no teaching took place outside the churches and the monasteries, at a time when consequently the number of teachers was regulated by the religious authorities, when there was nothing to threaten tradition, how much more intense and developed could this feeling be expected to become once teachers ceased to be enclosed within the precincts of the cathedral, when consequently they could expand their numbers and teach a much greater number of pupils. Practising teachers must naturally have felt, more than ever before, the need to organise themselves against the intrusion of newcomers who did not meet certain specific requirements. But in order to achieve that they had to form a group or association of a permanent kind. They had to elaborate a common code of discipline, in other words to develop that corporate life which was already germinating in the ceremony of the *inceptio*. This is how the corporation of teachers emerged by a kind of spontaneous evolution from the practice of the *inceptio* and from the ideas which it implied.

If this had been the only factor in the situation, this nascent corporation would probably have been a relatively lifeless affair; it would not have become one of the fundamental institutions of mediaeval society. In order for any social group, whether professional or otherwise, to acquire sufficient coherence and a sufficient awareness of itself and its own moral unity, it is not enough that there should exist a certain number of feelings and beliefs which are shared by its members. It is also necessary that it be provoked into opposing other groups which are restricting and resisting it. It is necessary that the demands of struggle force it to bind itself more firmly together and to generate a strong organisation. This is what happened in the case of the corporation whose formation we are currently studying. We have just seen what caused it to come into existence, but what gave it its characteristic features and forced it to make rapid advances was the war which it was waging against another very powerful body from which in a sense it derived: this body was the Church. For although teachers were now established outside the bounds of the cathedral they remained bound to it by strong links which they were only able to shake off after a struggle lasting several centuries.

In order to understand what this struggle consisted in and what its consequences were, we must first of all sketch, albeit briefly, the way in which education was organised in the cloister of Notre Dame, and in the cathedral schools in general for the matter of that.

Originally each of these schools was placed directly under the supervision of the bishop. He appointed the teachers; but more often than not he entrusted the supervision of education in the school to a particular teacher who was generally chosen from amongst the members of the chapter. This teacher was entitled *magister, magister scolarum, caput scolae*, or more briefly *scolasticus*, which was usually translated as 'écolâtre' (School Master). The School Master began by having no authority other than that which had been delegated to him by the bishop. But during the twelfth century his power increased. Since the schools had become more numerous and more important the bishop could no longer take responsibility for administering them; he consequently charged the schoolmaster with the task of choosing and appointing the teachers, in other words of conferring on whoever merited it the right to teach, the *licentia docendi*. It was a kind of certificate of virtue and ability which the schoolmaster had to bestow free of charge to any one who was worthy of it. Henceforth the function of the School Master took on an importance which it had not had before. He ceased being a simple teacher, and as a consequence he even entrusted the running of the episcopal school to someone else. His principal role henceforth was that of awarding or refusing a licence to candidates for the teaching profession throughout the whole of the region which was controlled by the church or the cathedral to which he was attached. This new and important function was generally fulfilled by the chancellor of the cathedral, as was most notably the case in Paris; this particular choice is to be explained by the fact that the chancellor was responsible for looking after the archives and was therefore necessarily someone relatively well educated. Whoever wished to open a school or to set up as a teacher was consequently obliged to obtain a licence from the chancellor of Notre-Dame, and it was only when he had done so that it was possible for him to be admitted to the *inceptio*, that is to say to make himself eligible for membership of the corporation. The licence and the *inceptio* (which was the earliest form of the doctoral degree) were thus two necessary stages, two degrees which the aspirant teacher needed to pass successively in order actually to become a practising teacher.

Hence arose conflict. The fact was that these two degrees were conferred by two different authorities which started from two quite different points of view. The teachers had no say in the way in which the chancellor performed his duties; he issued or refused to issue a licence in accordance with the way in which he himself understood things. It was thus possible for him to terminate the career of candidates adjudged to be highly meritorious by their teachers, and *vice versa*. It is not difficult to imagine the frustration which was provoked by this kind of intervention from a person who was not one of them and who did not possess in his own right the authority which is conferred by successful practice. This position of dependence was exacerbated for them by the fact that it was lifelong. At any time the chancellor could withdraw the licence, even after he had granted it, from anyone who, in his view, was no longer worthy of it. As a consequence he assumed for the whole academic community, both teachers and taught, the role of a kind of common-law judge, whose judgments were backed up by the redoubtable sanction of excommunication. In order to free themselves from this slavery the teachers became rapidly aware of the need to unite more closely together, to create an organisation of greater solidarity and of greater strength. And in proportion as they became more numerous, with the consequence that their moral influence was constantly increasing, the ecclesiastical authorities for their part realised that this opposition and these aspirations towards independence were not to be despised; that if they did not manage to crush this resistance the traditional influence of the Church was finished. The chancellor and the bishop whose representative he was, consequently, did all that was in their power to oppose the advance of the new corporation just as this latter strove strenuously to minimise diocesan control. These two adversaries embarked upon a long duel. The chancellor's weapon was excommunication; the principal weapon of the teachers was first of all the boycotting of those who held a licence without their consent; by refusing them admission to the corporation, by refusing to treat them as colleagues, and by refusing to go ahead with the *inceptio*, they effectively rendered null and void the right which had been granted to them. They had another weapon also, which consisted in the threat of refusing themselves to perform their teaching function; for given the importance of the student population and its permanent potential explosiveness, such systematic and widespread refusals to teach, induced periods of serious trouble and inspired chronic fear in the bishop himself. The historical interest of this struggle consists in the fact that two major moral forces were coming to grips with one another. On the one side lay the traditional power of the Church, which had hitherto been sovereign in the schools and moreover legitimately sovereign in the sense that the schools had been its creation. On the other side lay the new power, which was only just beginning to emerge and which was therefore still relatively feeble, but which nevertheless represented the power of the future and which was destined to channel schools in quite new directions. It was in the course of this struggle that the nascent corporation established and consolidated itself, becoming increasingly aware of itself and of its own personal identity.

During the period when it was only a weak and vulnerable organism it had been forced to rely on its own strength alone. But it inevitably developed to the point where it shattered the old episcopal organisation, for all the strength which it had accumulated from long tradition, from the respect which it enjoyed amongst the laity, and from the powerful political arsenal which it had at its disposal. In order to prevent the corporation of teachers from being crushed, so to speak, in its embryonic stage, it was essential for the corporation to ally itself to some other power which would provide aid and sustenance. On *a priori* grounds, one might have expected that it would inevitably turn to the power of the monarch, which was both closest at hand and also the natural defender of secular and temporal interests. However, nothing of the kind took place. The teachers sought the help they needed from a power which was both remote and essentially religious, which was indeed the supreme religious power; from the Papacy. And the Papacy supported, protected and defended the teachers against the cathedral with an intellectual consistency and a fidelity which were unswerving, at least during the first century of their corporate existence. Thus it came about that there was a series of papal bulls issued, solicited by the teachers, which increased their autonomy and by contrast increasingly restricted the powers of the chancellor. Already by about the year 1210 the society of teachers had acquired the right to choose for itself a principal who would represent it and who would act in its name as an intermediary and sue for justice on its behalf. It was thus rendered capable of more prompt action and its resistance became better organised, at the same time as the society itself was acquiring greater cohesion and unity. In 1212 new papal bulls made it obligatory for the chancellor to grant a licence to any candidate who had been adjudged worthy of this degree by a certain number of teachers, the number varying according to the type of teaching which the candidate was intending to undertake. In 1215 all these measures were collated in a code drawn up by the papal legate, Cardinal Robert de Courçon. This code granted recognition of the right of the society of teachers to legislate with respect to all matters which concerned their internal affairs, and to demand from its members an oath of obedience to the statutes of the company. Finally, around 1220, the most powerful weapon in the chancellor's hands was irreparably shattered. He was forbidden to excommunicate the corporation in its entirety without first receiving authorisation from the Holy See.

There is no need for us to follow every stage of this progressive emancipation; but what is still more interesting than the fact of this emancipation itself is the way in which it was obtained: the strange alliance of the Papacy and the teaching body despite the physical and moral distance which separated them. Here we have a phenomenon worthy of explanation since it resulted from causes which went very deep, inasmuch as it derived from one of the essential characteristics of the University which was in the process of becoming established. It was certainly no accident, no chance inspiration which led the teachers of Paris to turn towards the Pope and which decided the Pope to become their defender. It was rather in the nature of things that this relationship between these two moral forces should become established. It was ultimately, as we have seen, because the schools of the Middle Ages in general, but especially the Ecole de Paris, had an international character. It did not belong to any one nation in particular but rather to the whole of Christendom. It was made up of teachers and pupils from all over, irrespective of nationality. Moreover, in the early years of the thirteenth century the degrees which were conferred in Paris were recognised as valid in all the countries of Europe. A licence to teach obtained in Paris extended not only to France, but carried with it a right to teach anywhere at all (*jus* or *licentia ubique docendi*). A doctorate from the University of Paris was seen as a doctorate from the universal Church, *doctor universalis ecclesique*. It was then a natural consequence of the kind of cosmopolitanism which we have already noted as being one of the main characteristics of social life in the Middle Ages.

Nowhere is this cosmopolitanism more in evidence than in intellectual and academic life. Paris was regarded as the intellectual capital, not only of the kingdom but of the whole of Christendom. *Sacerdotium*, *imperium*, *studium*, priesthood, empire, and scholarship: these are the three pillars which support the Christian world, according to one mediaeval writer. The priesthood had its seat in Rome; temporal power (*imperium*) was in the hands of the emperor, *studium* or scholarship was centred in Paris. Under these circumstances the University of Paris, whose formation we are currently investigating, naturally appeared to be an institution not of some particular society but rather of the Christian community in its entirety; and consequently it was natural that it should ally itself to the supreme power which dominated the Christian world, the Papacy. Only the Papacy was sufficiently highly placed to be able to understand the relative value of things, and to see each of them in perspective so that it could prevent parochial and private interests, like those of a particular chapter or a particular bishop, from outweighing those general and universal interests which were vested in the institution of the University of Paris. This is how it came about that the University placed its still rudimentary organisation under the protection of the Holy See and why the Holy See took it under its wing. The close relationship which thus linked these two great moral forces conformed so closely to their nature that very soon in the Middle Ages, from the middle of the mediaeval period onwards, the principle was accepted that the

Pope alone was truly qualified to found a universal school (*studium generale*) similar to the University of Paris, with the right to confer the *jus ubique docendi*. The only power which also claimed and to some extent exercised this same right was the power of the emperor. If the emperor claimed an equal right to this prerogative it was because he saw himself also as being the head of Christendom, its temporal head. Thus we constantly revert to the same notion, that the schools like the one in Paris were something which Christendom held in common. In any case, the universities which emerged as a result of an imperial decree were vastly fewer in number than those whose existence resulted from a papal bull.

This feature of the university in its earliest days deserves notice not only for the light which it shed on what constituted the university in this remote period, but because it helps us to understand what a university is in its paradigmatic form and what a university should be even today. The fact is that it seems scarcely conceivable that an institution could in the course of its history rid itself totally of a characteristic which was so thoroughly inherent in it at the moment of its formation. Would this not indeed involve us in saying that this institution in the course of its development has totally changed its nature, that it has become a wholly different entity, that the only thing which it has in common with its former self is its name and that this name or label is misleading because it covers two entirely different sets of phenomena? If the university began by being an institution where institutional academic life prospered on an international basis it is fair to say that, even today, it cannot become narrowly nationalistic in character without betraying its own essential nature. Indeed hardly any of the universities of Europe have failed to retain something of this ancient internationalism; and indeed have we not seen in the renaissance of our own universities over the past twenty years an attempt to open themselves up to the outside, to attract foreign students and teachers, to multiply the opportunities for looking at the world from a different conceptual point of view to our own, while at the same time striving to extend their influence beyond national frontiers and, to sum it all up, to work gradually towards becoming centres of international civilisation? Modern universities must be for modern Europe what the mediaeval universities were for Christian Europe. Are they not the centres in which scientific investigation is carried out, a form of investigation which is far more independent of the accidents of nationality and consequently far more universal than the intellectual life of Christendom ever was? To conclude, we have seen in this lecture how the corporation of teachers was formed who populated the *cité* from the middle of the twelfth century, and what forces shaped and developed this corporation. It remains to us to investigate the internal organisation of this corporation, how the University was structured, before we study the methods and the contents of its curriculum; in other words, we must study the body before we study the mind.

chapter 8

The meaning of the word *universitas*

The half-ecclesiastical half-secular character of the
University
Internal organisation according to nations and
faculties

In the last lecture we witnessed the earliest manifestations of the
University of Paris. Far from its being possible, as has been attempted by certain historians, to attribute these to the personal
influence of a few men of genius, we saw that it was the result of
more general factors, the combination of a process of evolution
which continued so long without interruption that it is not possible to say at precisely what moment the University appeared, or to
establish the date on which it began its existence. Once schools
had been founded beyond the limits of the cathedral, a variety of
different factors combined to bring about a federation of the
teachers who were teaching there to organise them into an ever
more effective association with one another. At what point was a
degree of cohesion and unification reached, such that one can
legitimately see there something resembling what was subsequently to be called a university? This question has no clear-cut
answer. It was not until 1210 that the society of teachers produced
written statutes and regulations, but they quite certainly had
statutes which, albeit uncodified, were sanctioned by custom; they
had traditions if not a precise system of rules and regulations. Indeed, we know that round about 1170 or 1180, John de Cella, who
subsequently became the Abbot of Saint-Albert, being at the time
in Paris was received into the society of Parisian teachers (*ad elec-
torum consortium magistrorum meruit attingere*). On the other hand a
writer of the period, John of Salisbury, who was in France until
1149, makes not a single allusion to any grouping of this sort. We
must conclude therefore it was between the period of 1150 to 1180
(that is to say, towards the end of the twelfth century) that this
association began to make a sufficiently well-defined shape and to
exert a sufficiently palpable influence for observers to have noted
its existence.

The University began by being nothing more than a corporation of different teachers. Today we are accustomed to thinking of a university as an academic establishment which is clearly definable and specifically located, like a single school, and where different teachers teach the sum total of human knowledge. But there would have been no question in the Middle Ages of having the kind of establishment or group of common establishments which for us serves as the outward symbol, the physical manifestation of the University. There was no special building devoted to the common purposes of the University, whether academic or otherwise. The meetings took place in churches or in convents in which the teaching body enjoyed no rights and which, in any case, were not fixed once and for all but were chosen according to circumstances. It is only around the beginning of the fourteenth century that the situation begins to change. At this period we see the national groupings which made up the University beginning to hire schools collectively, and it is not until the fifteenth century that the faculties establish themselves as independent entities. Even at this period we know of no property which was common to the whole university. Even the *Pré-aux-Clercs*, which was situated on the present site of the *rue de l'Université*, belonged solely to the faculty of arts. The University of the Middle Ages was thus more or less completely bereft of patrimony. It had no roots in the ground. It was constituted exclusively by a group of people who held no property in common. This poverty gave the universities their moral strength and helped considerably in their development. Whenever the University of Paris found itself in conflict with either the ecclesiastical or the secular authority, the best weapon at its disposal in order to get the better of its adversaries was the strike. It suspended all lectures and moved somewhere else or else it dispersed. Several times it had recourse to this *ultima ratio*, which consequently never lost its power to inspire fear. In 1259, for example, not wishing to submit itself to a papal decree, it declared itself dissolved. It was able to take such extreme measures with relatively little difficulty because it did not own anything; it was simply a group of people who could disperse as easily as they had come together and as soon as they felt the need to do so. The teachers could easily liquidate and share out the meagre amount of common property which they did possess and go off to teach wherever they could find a locale which was suitable for use as a school. There was nothing to keep them in Paris. They were leaving behind them no material goods on which either the royal taxcollectors or the Church could get their hands. There are some circumstances in which poverty provides groups with power; it gives them mobility and increases their capacity to resist.

Just as we must abandon all idea of the *universitas* as a collective academic establishment, so we must beware of taking this word to imply that the teaching given by the associated teachers was necessarily encyclopaedic, embracing the totality of all the branches of human learning. In fact this term was borrowed from legal language and means no more than an association which has a certain unity, which is in fact a corporation. It is synonymous with *societas* and *consortium*, these different expressions are often used interchangeably. The same was originally true of the word *collegium*, although subsequently it came to be used to refer more specifically to a particular institution within the university whose formation we shall shortly be investigating. Nor is it only with reference to teachers that this word *universitas* means corporation; we find it used no less to refer to the industrial corporations and even to any grouping possessed of a certain degree of consistency and moral unity, such as the whole formed by the totality of Christians. Of its own this term had no academic or educational associations. For a long time when this special reference was intended it was necessary to specify it by the use of other expressions. Thus one said *universitas magistrorum et scolarum* or even *universitas studii*; the word *studium* was indeed the one which was most frequently used to refer to the educational life developing within the bosom of the corporation.

The *universitas* could still less refer to the universality of knowledge, the sum total of human learning, when it was frequently used to refer merely to a fraction of what was more properly described as the university. The same word applied both to the whole and to its parts. Thus, as we shall shortly see, the group of teachers who taught the liberal arts very soon formed within the totality of the corporation a special corporation, that of the arts teachers; this group was often referred to by the word *universitas*. One spoke of the university of the arts teachers (*universitas artistorum*). There were indeed very few universities to which the word *universitas* could have been applied even if it really did imply encyclopaedic teaching. More than one university limited itself to the teaching of a single subject: at Montpellier only medicine was taught; at Bologna, for a long time, only law was taught. Even in Paris, the mother of the other universities, at least for a long time, civil law was not taught at all. I could go on. Whereas for us the idea of the university implies above all the idea of a group of lecturers engaged in the same pedagogic task, there were in the Middle Ages universities which had no teachers at all, universities which consisted exclusively of students. This was the case at Bologna, for example: in Bologna only law was taught; the law students were men of middle age, frequently clerics who were already furnished with livings. Such students were not prepared to be dictated to. They therefore formed a corporation, a *universitas*, distinct from and independent of the college of the teachers; and it was their corporation which because of its powerful organisation made the rules and imposed its will on the teachers, who were obliged to do whatever their pupils wanted. However strange this type of academic organisation may seem to us, it existed in more than one instance.

Thus the University of Paris began by being a grouping of individuals and not a grouping of teaching subjects. It expressed at first the solidarity of the teachers far more than the solidarity of the subjects they taught; the latter was only eventually a spin-off from the former. It was the association of people which was to lead to the association of studies. The teachers were forced to come together and to unite ultimately as a result of chance factors (the particular circumstances of the society of the time, which made corporative life a necessity), particularly in the face of the need to defend themselves against the chancellor of Notre-Dame. This being so, one cannot but wonder whether this academic institution which exerted such a powerful influence on the Middle Ages and on all subsequent ages, was not itself the result of transitory and parochial factors which were in no way logically connected with the effect which they produced. This concentration of branches of learning and as far as possible of all the branches of human learning, which is what constitutes the truly valuable function of universities both in the past and in the present, seems to have been an unexpected, unforeseen and somewhat tardy reaction to historical accidents, particular contingent events which coincided in a single place at a specific time. It is unquestionable that this interpretation of the facts contains some part of the truth. As against this, when one realises that the University was not the institution of a particular time or a particular country but that it has perpetuated itself right down to our own day and that the organisation which characterises it spread throughout Europe adapting itself to very different social environments (for it is well known that the Universities of Paris and Bologna, but particularly the former, provided the two prototypes upon which all the others modelled themselves with a faithfulness and a respect which are truly extraordinary) — when one remembers all that it seems impossible that it was all really caused by mere accidents, so to speak, in the history of our nation and its capital.

The grouping of people, the grouping of the teachers is certainly the primary fact; this is what led on to the idea of grouping together and concentrating the subject-matters which were taught and learned. On the other hand, however, the idea would never have enjoyed such good fortune, it would never have become so rapidly generalised nor sustained itself with such consistency if it had not already been in the air, if it had not responded to the aspirations of the Middle Ages and of subsequent ages. And indeed, have we not already found this idea at the basis of all the educational systems of which we have had occasion to speak? Have we not in fact, established that, more or less consciously, it was inherent in the very notion of educative teaching which appears with Christianity and from which everything that followed was but a development? It is the idea that teaching must not be diffuse if it is to produce an educative effect; that all the branches of learning which are being taught ought to be narrowly grouped together with a single goal in view and informed by the one and the same spirit. It is precisely the same idea with which we are here dealing, albeit in a magnified form and one which has been developing over a considerably more extensive area than in the past. We are no longer dealing exclusively with a number of teachers whose association is contingent upon the fact that they are engaged in a common pedagogical enterprise, as was the case with the cathedral schools; rather, we are dealing with hundreds of teachers, making a concerted and communal attempt to organise an educational system designed to meet the needs of thousands of students. Of course, this idea would never have blossomed so dramatically if a variety of factors had not combined to bring together in a particular part of Europe a host of teachers, who were encouraged by circumstances to form themselves into groups. But on the other hand the mere existence of this association would not have sufficed on its own to generate the idea of an academic organism, as extensive as it was complex, if it had not already existed to some extent in the minds of men in a less ambitious form, but in one which was ready to expand extensively as soon as circumstances provoked it into doing so.

In some cases we can see this idea gaining ground despite the fact that circumstances at the time were not encouraging. We have shown how in the earliest conception of the *universitas* the need for an encyclopaedic curriculum was not necessarily implicit, and that the majority of the earliest universities were not characterised by this feature. But it is no less certain that they had a natural and spontaneous tendency to acquire this feature. If they indeed found themselves to include only one branch of learning they instinctively strove to become more comprehensive. This is recognised by one of the historians whose contribution has been greatest in showing the restricted meaning of the word *universitas*. 'The theory [of De Savigny],' he says, 'that the principal business of a university during the Middle Ages was not to embrace the totality of human learning, can lead to error. Although one cannot regard this encyclopaedic character as being of the essence of the university, nevertheless it was seen as a thoroughly desirable goal.' As early as 1224 Frederic the Second wanted there to be in the *studium generale* which he founded in Naples representatives from all the domains of human knowledge (*doctores et magistri in qualibet facultate*), and in the decrees and in the papal bulls which founded the universities we invariably come across the same phrase stating that the privileges thereby granted must apply *in quavis licet facultate*. The university was not imprisoned within well-defined limits; on the contrary it was encouraged to look beyond the farthest horizon. Thus was there a profound feeling from this time onwards that the university would never fulfil its true destiny, would never achieve its true identity except in so far as it comprised a plurality or even the totality of the branches of human learning. It was no more than an ideal which was rarely realised, but towards which the university strove and was expected to strive. This is what we must not overlook if we wish to understand accurately the formation and development of the university. Over and above the external factors which brought it into existence and however these contingent factors affected it, as they certainly did with respect to the organisation of the university, there was still an internal phenomenon without which they would have remained more or less sterile from an educational point of view. It is a *sui generis* view of education and teaching which is characteristic of Christian societies, a view which antedates the function which was performed by the corporation of teachers but which found there the means of realising itself in the most vigorous manner conceivable.

Having explained the factors which determined the formation of the universities, we must now try to get a closer look at what precisely the university corporation consisted in.

We have to begin with a question which has been passionately disputed and which we cannot pass over in silence; for, depending on the answer which one gives to it, one takes a quite different view of the university itself. Was the university a secular or an ecclesiastical body? This problem was much debated in the seventeenth century by lawyers because it touched on matters of law; but it is also of moral and historical significance.

The very way in which the University of Paris came into being scarcely supports the idea that it could have been a genuinely ecclesiastical body. Indeed it came into being outside the ambit of religion; it only became a possibility once schools had been established outside the cathedral precincts. From its beginning it found in the clergy, both secular and monastic, two implacable adversaries. First of all, there was the great struggle against the chancellor, which was, at least, finally crowned with success. It was somewhat later, around 1250, that another struggle took place which lasted less long, but whose outcome was less fortunate. This was waged against two monastic orders, the Franciscans and the Dominicans, who were surreptitiously seeking to monopolise theology teaching while claiming the right of immunity to the rules and customs of the University. The Papacy showed greater indulgence towards these two powerful orders than it had shown towards the authority of the bishop; it sided with the brothers, and the University had to give way on several points. The University retained, as a result of this struggle, not only an attitude of hostility towards the monastic clergy which had in any case existed before, but also a certain attitude of mistrust with respect to its former ally the Holy See, which had in this case gone over to the enemy. It is to this moment in time that we can trace back to its source the gallicanism which was always the mark of University theology. Not only was the cast of mind of the University not essentially clerical, but in addition it included a more or less substantial number — precise figures are difficult to establish — of laymen. Laymen were allowed to teach all the subjects except theology, and theology played a very small part in the totality of the university. At one time there were only eight teachers of theology. Nor is this all: there was at least one branch of learning from which all priests were excluded, whether secular or monastic; and two others (one of which was the most important in the whole University) from which the monastic clergy was excluded: these were law and the liberal arts. The teachers when they took their oath were obliged to swear that they would not admit any religious to any examination whatsoever (*Nullum religiosum cujuscumque fuerit professionis recipietis in aliqua examinatione*). On the other hand, although the University was in opposition to the Church, it had nevertheless emerged from it. It was ultimately due to a sort of exodus which had begun in the cloister of Notre Dame. Although it established itself outside the cathedral it nevertheless remained for a long time in its shadow; it was only at a fairly late date that it was bold enough to leave the site, to cross the bridges and to set itself up on the Left Bank of the Seine. It was therefore impossible that it should not remain profoundly imbued with the spirit which until that time had dominated academia exclusively. Even the struggle against the Canon of Notre-Dame, although it resulted in liberating the teachers from their most immediate religious bondage, from another point of view rendered them dependent on the Holy See. For by invoking the authority of the Papacy they implicitly gave it recognition; by the very fact of having relied on papal power to protect them they became subordi-

nated to it. Of course, the power upon which they found themselves dependent in this way was much more remote, the subordination was less restrictive and gave them a greater degree of
freedom; nevertheless they had become an institution of the
universal Church no less than the monastic orders, albeit for
different reasons and in a different way. The teachers no less than
the students had a vested interest in not completely breaking the
bonds which united them to the Church; for the Church and all
those who were a part of it, in whatever capacity, enjoyed certain
important privileges. Whoever belonged to the Church, provided
it was in the capacity of a servant, regardless of whether he was in
Holy Orders or not, was immune from secular justice, and could
only be tried by ecclesiastical tribunals. It is not difficult to imagine how reluctant the emergent corporation would have been
to give up such valuable immunities.

This explains the eagerness with which the corporation of
teachers sought to retain something from the ecclesiastical situation. Hence the use of academic dress and of the tonsure, *tonsura
clericalis*, which, however, in no wise implied that those who wore it
had been ordained to the minor orders. Hence above all the
obligatoriness of celibacy, which was at first absolute and universal within the University and which remained in force until the
middle of the fifteenth century; and even then it was only waived
in the case of members of the faculty of medicine. This was
because the lay servants or employees of the Church could only
continue to enjoy ecclesiastical immunities on condition that they
remained unmarried.

What was the outcome of all these conflicting phenomena?
This question is not susceptible of a simple one-word answer. The
University was neither an exclusively secular body, nor was it an
exclusively ecclesiastical one. It had characteristics of both at one
and the same time. It was made up of laymen who had to some extent retained the appearance of clerics, and of clerics who had
become secularised. Henceforth the body of the Church was confronted with a different body, but one which had shaped itself partially in its own image, and to which it was in opposition. This also
explains the diversity of the accounts which have been given of the
University and which, although they contradict one another, are
all equally true and equally false. This complexity in the organic
constitution of the University is a magnificent expression of the
system of ideas which was its soul. Indeed, we ought already to
have caught a glimpse of what we shall see more clearly in what
follows: that the University was the institution in which that particular philosophy flourished which has been called scholastic
philosophy. What is characteristic of scholastic philosophy is the

mutual interpenetration of reason and faith within a single system of ideas which renders them inseparable from one another. I used the word 'interpenetration', for it is this which enables us to distinguish very clearly between scholastic philosophy and the philosophy of the seventeenth century, which also undertook to bring together reason and faith, but in quite a different way. For the seventeenth century religion didn't exclude philosophy but was clearly distinct from it. Reason did not contradict faith, but the domain of the one was totally independent of the domain of the other. The former was a continuation of the latter, but there was no possibility of confusing them. For the philosophy which dominated the mediaeval university, for Scholastic philosophy by contrast, these two were but a single unity. It was not a question of juxtaposing reason and doctrine but rather of introducing reason into doctrine, of rendering faith rational. It is this inextricable mixture which reflects so accurately the parallel mixture of the secular and the ecclesiastical which we have found to be a mark of the external organisation of the University.

We must beware of seeing this mixed, and indeed one might say contradictory, state of affairs in the early University as a sign of inferiority. In time the character of the University was to become much more specific; of the two elements which went to make up the form which it took in the beginning, only one was to survive. From the sixteenth century onwards and above all in the seventeenth century it was to be considered as a purely secular body. One may well ask, however, whether by becoming a specifically lay institution, the University was not in fact impoverished; for this greater degree of specificity was only obtained at the cost of a lamentable restriction in the University's field of operations. If the University became purely secular it was because spiritual matters had been wholly removed from the province of its concern and taken over exclusively by the Church. Secular studies were liberated; but they became alienated from all the questions which were raised by religion and they took no interest in them. We shall have to investigate how this dissociation came about, which was a prelude to the thoroughly mediocre kind of eclecticism, whereby the seventeenth century, as I was saying a moment ago, thought that it could reconcile reason and faith simply by keeping them at a distance from one another, by establishing bulkheads between them which were intended to prevent any sort of communication between these two worlds. How much more interesting was the age which we are at present studying, when no one was yet trying to separate these two inseparable aspects of human life, when no one had yet attempted to channel and to build a dam between these two great intellectual and moral streams as if it were possible to prevent them from running into one another! How much more vital was this general, tumultuous *mêlée* of beliefs and feelings of every kind than the state of calm, which was artificial and only apparent, which was characteristic of succeeding centuries! In order to understand what constituted the University it is not enough to consider it in this way at a glance and as a whole, in such a way as to pick out only the most general features. It was a complex body made up of separate parts which were harmonised within a single organism. We must therefore seek out these parts and examine their nature and relationship with one another. In the course of such an analysis we shall encounter that part of the body of the University which is of most particular interest to us: I refer to that part which corresponds to secondary education. The University, as it appears to the observer at a period when it is an indubitably established institution, has a double organisational structure. On the one hand, students and teachers formed four distinct groups, enjoying a certain degree of autonomy depending upon the nature of their studies: these were the four faculties of theology, law, medicine and the liberal arts. Running concurrently with this division of the University population there was another which had a totally different basis. Teachers and students were grouped according to their nationality, according to their ethnic and linguistic affinities. They were known as the four nations whose names were 'the French'; by this was meant the inhabitants of the Ile de France and neighbouring provinces, the Picardians, the Normans and the English. Each one of these titles included a host of nationalities: amongst the French were numbered all those from countries where Romance languages were spoken; amongst the English were numbered all those from Germanic countries, so much so that towards the middle of the fifteenth century the word 'Germanie' had replaced that of 'Angleterre'; to Picardy were attached the peoples of the Low Countries. In the course of time each of these great divisions became subdivided into particular provinces, or, as was also said, into tribes; but there is no point in our entering into the details of the subdivisions, which hold no interest for us. What it is important for us to take note of is the fact that these two types of organisation did not completely overlap: the first, into faculties, covered the whole of the University; the second, into nations, applied only to the faculty of arts and thus excluded from its ranks the theological, the legal and the medical faculties.

For a long time it was thought that these two organisations corresponded to succeeding phases in the history of the University. Originally the faculty of arts was supposed to have existed on its own; that is to say, the '*maîtres ès arts*' were supposed to have been alone in forming themselves into a corporate group. It was said that they stood to suffer more than the others from the supremacy of the chancellor; they thus had a greater interest in uniting in order to resist. For another thing, they were very numerous; they formed by far the greater part of the teaching personnel; they were thus best equipped to organise resistance. On this view their corporation was the first to be established; but at the same time and as a result of its very vastness it was rapidly subdivided into groups according to the nationality of its members. Then, at a later date, the members of the other faculties (the teachers of the other subjects) are supposed to have followed the example which had been set them. They too formed associations and corporations (in law, in medicine, and in theology), which once they had become established entered into federation with the initial corporation of arts teachers. Thus the University as a whole allegedly resulted not from a massive concentration of people, which enveloped in one and the same system all the elements of the education which was given inside the *île*, all the specialisms which were taught there; but rather from the federation of distinct corporations which had been previously established.

Denifle has proved beyond doubt that this view of the matter is contradicted by the facts. First of all, it is quite certain that the faculties did not become established separately, only to federate later on. The word *facultas*, with the meaning of an academic group devoted towards the teaching of a particular subject-matter, does not appear before the thirteenth century; up till then *facultas* was simply a synonym for *scientia* and referred to any particular branch of learning. By contrast the *consortium magistrorum* (the corporation of teachers) dates from the second half of the twelfth century. On the occasions when this corporation is spoken of in its earliest days it is presented as a society of individuals and not as a federation of particular and distinct groups. What existed first was a vast society which included the entire teaching body, regardless of specialism. Then gradually, within the bosom of this association, more restrictive groups were formed on the basis of affinities resulting from a community of interest in particular studies. It is clear that theologians had ideas and interests which were different from those of the arts teachers or the lawyers. In the course of time these restricted groups increased in stability and acquired ever greater autonomy within the group as a whole; this is how the faculties were formed. They do not constitute a primary phenomenon, they result from a process of differentiation which took place within the primary community of teachers of every sort. Consequently there is no justification for making the faculty of arts the central nucleus around which the other faculties are supposed to have successively gathered. There was never a moment when the faculty of arts was the University itself; and this has the further corollary that the organisation into nations did not antedate the organisation into faculties. We know today that the division of the arts teachers into four nations only took place between the years 1219 and 1221, that is to say at a time when the University had already existed for more than half a century.

How then are we to explain this double organisation? Why this double structuring of the system? Are we to say that it was natural for the pupils and teachers in the faculty of arts, while remaining united in one and the same corporation by reason of the community of their studies, nevertheless to divide into distinct groups according to their nationality? In that case why did the same subdivisions not also take place in the other faculties? Why should the arts teachers be special from this point of view? After all, the same national affinities were just as strong amongst members of the faculties of law, medicine and theology. In addition, the faculty of arts and the body which was composed of the four nations, at least at the beginning, constituted two quite separate organisms, even though both were formed from the same ingredients. They were like two different personalities. Denifle cites a very revealing example of this duality: the faculty of arts had no seal of its own, whereas each of the nations had theirs. On one occasion when it was obliged to seal an act which it had drawn up independently of the rest of the University, it used the seals of the four nations; but only with their consent, *consensu earum*. To say that the faculty was obliged to ask for the seals from the four nations clearly involves a recognition that the two groups were not identical. They must each have had a separate function. This is what the difference consisted in: the faculty had established itself with a view to running strictly academic affairs, organising teaching and defending itself from the encroachments of Notre-Dame; but non-academic life was beyond its province. However, apart from his studies, a scholar's life needed a structure in which he could be sustained and watched over; he had to find a suitable lodging, he had to avoid being exploited. He had to be protected against all the risks of life in Paris. It was this need which was met by organising students into nations. So we can explain why it was peculiar to the faculty of arts. It was because this included, as we can see, some very young students, mere children who could not possibly be abandoned to themselves. The organisation of the nations bears witness, together with emergence of the University, to the fact that pupils were recruited from a considerably more extensive geographical area. As long as they had been grouped around the cathedral schools they lived for the most part in the vicinity; those who came from afar were certainly rare and constituted no difficulty. Now they were legion. They were to be numbered in hundreds. That is why they had to be organised into the nations: a novel solution and one which we shall see was only provisional.

chapter 9

The arts faculty

Internal organisation – The colleges

Of the four faculties which made up the university — theology, law, medicine, liberal arts — the arts faculty is the only one which we need to scrutinise in detail. Then as now theology, law, and medicine were special schools, professionally orientated towards preparing young people for specific careers. The arts faculty alone was an organ of general culture, with no special vested interest and fulfilling a function analogous to that which it fulfils in our secondary schools today. Indeed within the University it played a role which was identical to that which is now played by secondary education. It was in fact like the common vestibule through which everyone had to pass in order to enter the three other faculties. The student had to spend a certain amount of time there before going on to study courses in theology, medicine or law. It was a preparatory school where the student was expected to complete a sort of general education before devoting himself to specialist studies. The education given there was essentially introductory in character, just as is the one which students receive in our secondary schools today.

The entry requirements for admission to the faculty consisted in the ability to read and write, and a thorough knowledge of Latin. This knowledge was absolutely basic, and the child was taught it in little schools which were called 'grammar schools'. At least at first, these operated entirely outside the University, which only later on extended its authority to them. They were the remains of the previous system of education, that is to say of the cathedral, abbey, and college schools. The establishment of the University had usurped their position without fully absorbing them. During the great period of concentration and organisation from which it had itself resulted, it had attracted to itself all the most elevated aspects of education; but it had excluded all the inferior aspects which consequently retained the form they had had formerly. They remained in a position of dependence on religious authority. This is how it came about that there were within the *cité* teachers of grammar who did not join the University corporation and who continued to teach in the same conditions as previously. They received their *licentia docendi* and they were dependent, not on the chancellor of Notre-Dame (who was far too important to perform such petty functions) but on the precentor. Besides these schools there were other little schools of the same sort, attached to certain collegiate churches in Paris. The same was true in the provinces; it was in these schools that the children from the immediate neighbourhood came to acquire the instruction which would give them access to the faculty of arts and consequently to the University.

But if in order to get into the University one needed to possess a certain basic knowledge, this was of a thoroughly elementary sort. The grammatical knowledge demanded was very limited; consequently the teaching of grammar was continued at the faculty. As far as Latin studies were concerned, the level of learning was more or less comparable with that which existed in our grammar classes. This is why it has been possible to describe the arts faculty as corresponding to the senior classes in our secondary schools. The age of the pupils confirms everything which we have just been saying with regard to the preparatory nature of this education. The normal age for entry was only thirteen years. Indeed, it was quite often necessary to enter earlier, for it was permitted to take the 'baccalaureat' from the age of fourteen. The teachers themselves were not much older. It was possible to get a master's degree by the age of twenty. Thus the moral distance between pupils and teachers was considerably less than it was later to become. This is a question to which we shall return.

In these circumstances, and since the arts faculty was only a sort of inferior, more elementary faculty which served as an intermediary between the small schools and the University proper, one might expect that it would never play in the life of the University anything other than a secondary and somewhat subdued role. Since its principal function was to prepare pupils' minds so that they could be initiated into disciplines which it did not itself teach, it came to be considered as a means to ends which went beyond it, and consequently to occupy a relatively inferior position in the educational hierarchy. As far as the opinion of educated people was concerned the faculties of theology, law and medicine enjoyed, relative to the arts faculty, a kind of intellectual and moral superiority. As early as 1254 a pope, Alexander IV, officially recognised this pre-eminence in the case of theology (*praeest reliquis sicut superior*). Theology, the study of things divine; was it not indeed the ultimate object and true *raison d'être* of all studies and of all arts? Later law and medicine were promoted to the same rank; in ceremonies and in processions they took precedence over the arts faculty, as indeed they still do today. And yet, in spite of this traditional classification, in spite of its youth, in spite of its inferior status, the arts faculty, instead of becoming some sort of faculty of minor importance, instead of being kept in tutelage by the more elevated faculties, rapidly created for itself within the University a situation in which it predominated completely. It conquered important privileges and finally ended up by exercising a veritable hegemony over the rest of the corporation.

Thus, by special prerogative, it was allowed to expel, not only from its own bosom but from the University as a whole, any one of its members without having to submit the case to the assembly of the four faculties, whereas the allegedly superior faculties could not carry out an expulsion without the unanimous consent of the University as a whole. But what shows most clearly the superiority which the arts faculty finally acquired is the fact that the head of the University, from the moment when there was one, had to be from the arts faculty, chosen exclusively by its members and without members of other faculties having any say. I do not need here to go into the long story of how the power of the rector finally became established. In the early days the rector was only one principal among many, the head of the arts teachers; then he became, gradually gaining more and more ground, the executive organ for the collective resolutions of the University, the president as of right of general assemblies and finally the chief administrator of the whole community. Of course, we should not exaggerate his importance and the extent of his power; since he was only appointed for a very short time, he could not exercise a great deal of personal influence; but through him the spirit of the arts faculty dominated. Moreover, he it was who in the eyes of the public represented the university as a whole; and correspondence, whether from the laity or from the Church, which had to do with some matter affecting the University, was addressed to him. No doubt the higher faculties only recognised this superiority after vigorous bouts of resistance; the theology faculty in particular carried on the struggle for a very long time; but finally it was obliged to yield, and a papal bull gave sanction to the prerogatives of the arts faculty. We have here a phenomenon of exceptional strangeness, which deserves explanation. The faculty with the lowest status is the one which heads the whole University through the intermediary of its principal. Instead of trailing along behind the others it is their director. Nowhere was this contrast more striking than in the public ceremonies. The arts faculty came last after all the others;

but its representative the rector, on the other hand, walked at the head together with the highest dignitaries in the realm.

Two different reasons have been invoked in order to explain this peculiarity. First, it has been attributed to the numerical superiority of the arts faculty when compared with the others. We know that in 1348 there were 514 arts teachers as against 32 theology teachers, 18 in law and 46 in medicine; in other words the arts faculty represented five-sixths of the University (514 out of a total of 610 teachers). In 1362 the proportions remain not noticeably changed: 441 arts teachers as against 25 theologians, 11 lawyers, and 25 doctors of medicine. On this account then, the higher faculties are supposed to have been crushed beneath the sheer weight of numbers, their defeat was the result of a series of demonstrations of strength; and the explanation given for the fact that this victory was won only after a long struggle is that the arts faculty only gradually acquired this numerical preponderance. Indeed we know that in 1283 there were only 183 arts teachers, whereas we have records of 441 and 514 in the succeeding century. A second factor allegedly reinforced the effect of the preceding one. From the end of the thirteenth century (1289), candidates for the mastership in arts, before receiving the investiture for their new functions, had to swear in front of the rector an oath promising to defend the laws and customs of state and faculty wherever they were: (*Item stabitis cum magistris secularibus et deffendetis statum, statuta et privilegia corumdem ad quemcumque statum deveneritis...Item jurabitis quod libertates singulas facultatis et consuetudines facultatis honestas...deffendetis ad quemcumque statum deveneritis*). We know how sacrosanct the authority of the oath was regarded in those days. Anyone who broke it could be summoned before the ecclesiastical courts on charges of perjury. Thus the teachers who had committed themselves in the terms which we have just quoted found themselves, as a consequence, bound to the arts faculty for life; whatever their subsequent careers they were bound by a sort of special loyalty. The very vagueness of the terms used in the formula made it possible to charge with perjury anyone who refused to further the empire-building ambitions of the arts faculty. Together with this went the fact that the teachers in the higher faculties had all or almost all gone through the arts faculty, since this was treated as a preparatory introduction for the others. They had begun by acquiring their mastership in art before embarking on other degrees. Consequently, as a result of the oath which they had sworn, they continued to depend on this faculty; they were part of it even if they were not regular members but rather in their capacity as *jurati*; they were called *jurati facultatis artium*. They were consequently obliged to behave like good and loyal members of the arts faculty. We can thus explain how under these circumstances the faculties of theology, law and medicine gradually fell into a state of complete subordination to the arts faculty, despite the fact that the arts faculty was their inferior.

This explanation seems very simple and yet, as I see it, it does not stand up to close analysis. First of all, if the principle, once it had been established and recognised, does indeed provide an explanation of how the arts faculty was so easily able to make the others dependent upon it, it remains to be explained how the principle managed to become established and recognised. How did it come about that the University tolerated a practice which was bound to give to one of the bodies which made it up a supremacy which bore no relationship to the rank which was accorded to it in the hierarchy, and which was bound to diminish the autonomy of the other constituent bodies? It must have been the case that the arts faculty already enjoyed a considerable authority, that it was already dominant in the university as a whole; but how then are we to explain this dominance? The oath is symptomatic of it but it does not explain it. It may well have served to increase it but it could not have created it in the first place; and the only role which it could have played in this respect was necessarily that of an accessory.

There remains then, as a candidate for the primary cause, the numerical preponderance. By exploiting the power which their numbers gave them the arts teachers are supposed to have ended up by placing themselves at the head of the University. This explanation would be plausible if, in the University assemblies, the voting had been based upon a counting of heads; under these circumstances, one could indeed conceive of the arts faculty easily imposing its will and extending its empire by straightforward legal means. In fact, the method of voting was quite different: voting was by faculty. Even at the beginning, no proposal was passed unless it had obtained a majority in each of the faculties consulted separately. Later, during the fourteenth century they were content to take the majority produced by those voting in the greatest number of faculties. But in both cases each faculty, regardless of the political effectiveness of its members, was equal to every other faculty; each had one vote and one vote only. The weakest were thus protected from the sheer weight of numbers and, under these circumstances it is difficult to see how the arts faculty, despite its larger number of members, could have laid down the law for the others.

Does not this numerical superiority in the arts faculty itself need to be explained? Does it not indeed clearly presuppose that this faculty already enjoyed a quite special prestige, which was enough to justify the exceptional position it occupied in the University? If the young were thronging to the arts teachers, if for this reason the teachers had to increase in number, it is clearly because what they taught was taken to be the supreme form of teaching. And indeed, it was said of this teaching that it formed the basis, the fundamental principle, the source of all learning (*fundamentum, originem ac principium aliarum scientiarum*). This was because, as we shall see, the discipline which it taught almost to the exclusion of all others was dialectic, which was then regarded as the queen of the sciences, the key which opened all other doors. Anyone who understood its basic principles was adjudged also to possess implicitly the essentials of all the other branches of human learning. In any case, was it not the dialectical controversies which gave the University its brilliant reputation? Was it not they which attracted, first of all around Abelard, then around his successors, audiences too numerous to count? From that moment on, was it not quite natural that the faculty where these illustrious debates took place and where so refined a form of teaching was given should be regarded as having a quite exceptional importance? This provides a simple explanation of how this faculty came to acquire the chief rank. To this explanation it is objected that from the point of view of the thinkers of the time dialectic was simply a means whose final end was theology; and indeed there are numerous passages in which dialectic is presented as an instrument to be used in the cause of sacred learning. The trouble is that we need to add that with respect to this final goal little need was felt of actually reaching it. Teachers and students of theology were very thin on the ground; there was a time when the theology faculty included no more than eight teachers. The vast majority of students did not look beyond the profane learning which dialectic constituted. In as far as it was slanted towards theology, this slant was thoroughly Platonic and theoretical. Its pre-eminent worth was formally recognised, but as something only vaguely glimpsed in the misty distance. There was something else in the foreground; there was something else upon which attention was concentrated; life had its centre elsewhere and, consequently, authority was located elsewhere. In addition to this, the arts faculty was in a better position to defend the secular interests of the corporation against ecclesiastical power.

The conclusion which we have thus reached is of considerable interest with respect to the history of our educational thought and our educational system. The arts faculty, as we have said (and everything which follows will confirm this assertion), corresponded to what we call secondary education. Consequently in this complicated and confused system which was the University of

Paris at that time, which included within itself teaching of all types and at every level from the most modest (from the moment when the classes in grammar were attached to it) to the most elevated, it was secondary education which, through the arts faculty, was pre-eminent; it constituted the centre of academic life, it was the corner-stone of the whole system. It was the most vital, the one to which the crowds flocked in droves, the one on which the gaze of the world was fixed. It owed this position not to contingent and external circumstances but to its intrinsic character, to the fact that it met better than any other the needs of the student population. We thus find early confirmation for an observation which I made at the beginning of this book. There, as one of the peculiarities of our academic history, I pointed to the fact that in France secondary education, from times long past, has more or less completely dominated all the other levels of education and has made practically all the running. We can now see where this domination stems from. It appears as soon as we have an educational system which is somewhat developed. Now is not the time to investigate how it came about in the place where it came about. For the moment I am content to note the fact and to pose the question which we shall be trying to answer when we are in possession of more information, that is when we have seen this domination strengthening itself and becoming possibly more clear-cut in circumstances which were quite different.

We shall immediately be witnessing a new advance in this direction and a new manifestation of this same tendency. In the foregoing we have indeed seen secondary education acquire a central position within the University; but the structures within which it developed were not special to it, they were not related to its essential nature; on the contrary they were those within which higher education is developing today (the faculties). We shall now see how this same arts faculty created for itself new structures which have remained the distinctive structures of secondary education (namely, the colleges), and how they even attracted to them the best teaching resources available.

In order to understand this great transformation of which we shall be speaking we must first attempt to portray how the student's life was originally organised when he was at the arts faculty.

Let us imagine one of these quite young people, of thirteen or fourteen years of age, arriving in Paris to study during the first half of the thirteenth century. As we have seen, there did not exist in those days any great and renowned communal establishment such as the colleges were later to become, and to which the young man could be dispatched quite confidently by his parents. The arts faculty was only an association of teachers who were teaching concurrently in different locales, which they hired at their own expense and risk, originally within the *île* itself then later on in the *rue du Fouarre* on the Left Bank. The child was therefore going to have to choose himself a teacher from amongst the several hundreds who were all teaching at the same time, and to attach himself to him. He needed him not only to receive the instruction which he had come to seek, but also in order to have a sponsor with respect to the secular authorities. Indeed it was essential that, should he be arrested by the provost's men (which happened frequently), he could be claimed by one of the regular teachers of the University. This teacher would guarantee his status as a student, and by invoking the prerogatives which were attached to this status get him released from the clutches of the secular authorities. Then he had to choose a lodging for himself and also companions. For in those days it was impossible to live in isolation; and the same factors which elsewhere forced artisans, merchants and teachers to form themselves into an association produced the same effects amongst the student population and caused it to form itself into a group. Very probably it was this need which generated an organisation based on the 'nations'. It was indeed in the nature of things that students with the same origins should be mutually attracted and should form themselves into a group and share the same style of life. They would hire a place of some sort communally and live there as a kind of community, frequently with their teachers, eating at the same table as them and living the same kind of life. This was called a *hospitium*. Vincent de Beauvais portrays St Edmus tending to one of his sick pupils and every day taking them off with him to the *rue du Fouarre* to be taught: these would probably be members of the same *hospitium* as himself. What facilitated this intimacy was the fact that there was no great age difference between teachers and taught. The former frequently joined in the games of the latter and shared in the scandals with which they got involved.

We know very little about how these communities were organised because they had no kind of legal or official standing. However, the equality which reigned between members justifies us in thinking that they must have been very democratically administered. This is, after all, the character which they had and which they retained at Oxford; and it is known that Oxford University was modelled on the University of Paris. At their head was a principal elected by all the members of the group, who had only as much authority as the group delegated to him. No doubt it was often enough thought more fitting that the principal should be a teacher, but for a long time, at least, it was not a statutory rule. The custom only established itself over a long period of time and finally became legally binding.

This kind of organisation was by far the most common, but there were two categories of students for whom it was not suited. There were, first of all, the rich, who had a private apartment where they lived with an instructor. On the other hand, there were the poor who lacked the means necessary to defray the expenses of a *hospitium*. For all the social classes were represented in the universities of the Middle Ages: 'there were noblemen and there were plebeians, the sons of aristocrats rich enough to retain — out of pure ostentation — servants who would carry large books in front of them (see Rabelais), and sons of thieves who were so poor that they worked as servants and did all sorts of odd jobs, such as carry holy water to people's private houses, in order to pay for their studies.' Others used to beg; for in those days there was nothing dishonourable about begging since it had been rendered sacred by the example of the mendicant orders. In sum, the cancer of poverty with all its attendant evil which today is racking the universities of Russia also racked the universities of the Middle Ages. For the poor students it was extremely difficult to eat, to have a roof over one's head, to be able to buy candles and books (cheap, poor quality manuscripts, full of hieroglyphic abbreviations, which are still common in our libraries). In order to remedy these evils certain charitable people conceived the idea of founding establishments where a certain number of poor students could be lodged and supported for nothing, thanks to a permanent endowment made in favour of the institution. These houses did not really differ from the *hospitia* of the sort we have been discussing; that is to say, they were hostelries of a sort, but hostelries which were endowed, with places for a specific number of scholars. These endowed *hospitia* were the first colleges. They begin to appear from about the beginning of the thirteenth century onwards, but they are modest, humble and even wretched in form, so giving no hint of the fortunes which such institutions were subsequently to enjoy. Most often they were annexes to a hospital or a religious house. It was only towards the middle of the thirteenth and especially the fourteenth centuries that the great foundations appear. First of all, there is the college of the Sorbonne, founded around 1257 for sixteen theology students. Then, and above all, there was the college of Navarre which has a claim to be considered as the first great college of Paris. It was founded in order to take twenty theology students, twenty arts students, and finally twenty schoolchildren studying grammar. The pupils learning grammar (of whom we spoke at the beginning of this lecture and who until that time had lived in establishments which were separate from the arts students) now found themselves in close proximity to the latter; with these they had so many things in common that it was impossible to tell precisely where the one curriculum ended and the other began. After Collège de Navarre there was Harcourt, which was admittedly planned as early as 1280 but which was not in fact opened until 1311. Navarre and Harcourt can be regarded as the main proto-types of the kind of establishment which from the fourteenth century onwards was to proliferate.

They were so far modelled on the free *hospitia* (see Bouquet on the college of Harcourt) that they remained essentially democratic in character, although the democracy was somewhat attenuated. Today the notion of a college evokes the idea of a more or less authoritarian organisation where matters affecting the community are not dealt with by the people but by special functionaries who have exclusive charge over and responsibility for them. But the early colleges were quite different. No doubt the college principal, then known as the headmaster, was not simply a student who had been elected; he was a teacher who received his investiture from the University, who was dependent on it and, in some cases, simultaneously on certain ecclesiastical authorities to whom the founder had accorded the rights of control over the internal affairs of the establishment. However, it is far from being the case that the pupils had no role whatsoever to play in the administration of the house. Thus at the college of Harcourt the headmaster, before being officially invested with his charge, had to be elected by the assembly of the pupils. At Navarre for a very long time pupils who were not scholars could only be admitted (whether it was to study theology or the arts) with the unanimous consent of scholars. Only the pupils studying grammar did not have this right, but this was on account of their extreme youth.

That then is how the life of the arts student was originally organised. He went to be taught in particular parts of the *rue du Fouarre* by teachers whom he had chosen himself. There were only a certain number of places from which teachers operated. As for his non-academic life, he spent it either in *hospitia* or in charitably endowed *hospitia* or colleges which had been built, except for certain differences of detail, on the model of the former. Such at least was the way of life which was most common. There was a very clear boundary between education and the needs of daily living. We shall now be witnessing a veritable revolution which was to blur this boundary and eventually eradicate it, and by doing so radically transform the organisation of the University. It was the establishment and development of the charitable *hospitia* or colleges which originated this great transformation; its influence was to reverberate throughout the whole of our subsequent educational history.

The college scholar enjoyed certain important advantages by comparison with other students, whether external students (martinets), or the inhabitants of private *hospitia*. First, he was subject to a more regular code of discipline. Then, in addition to the public teacher who taught him in the *rue du Fouarre* he also had a sort of auxiliary teacher, a kind of private tutor, as the English say, in the person of his principal or headmaster. This latter had to attend the courses which were being followed by his pupils, answer the questions which they put to him, and offer them explanations when they asked for them. He would have to read with them some work on logic or grammar or mathematics, chosen by the majority of the scholars, and that in addition to those which were being expounded in the public schools. Exercises done communally were both easier and better directed. Then the colleges might have the means of providing libraries which an individual or a private community might not be able to furnish, and which constituted a valuable resource for students. These advantages were such that soon pupils who were rich or leisured sought admission to the colleges by paying out of their own pocket the expenses of boarding. These were known as guests of the college or 'scholar-lodgers' because they paid rent for their rooms and their share of the cost of food and drink. Once the custom had started it spread rapidly. Consequently the population of the colleges increased dramatically. Inevitably the teaching body responsible for the supervision of the pupils and for their studies increased proportionately. Supplementary and complementary teaching undertaken within the house became intensified. The teaching which was given there also took on greater importance; the teachers, instead of waiting for their pupils in the *rue du Fouarre*, came into the colleges to teach. Thus the centre of social life progressively shifted. From the *rue du Fouarre*, from the public schools, it moved to the interior of the colleges. By the fifteenth century the revolution was complete. The colleges became the sole structure within the University. In the colleges the pupils found, in addition to board and lodging, all the education which they asked for. Consequently there was no longer any need for them to go out; the principle of the boarding school had been established.

We shall have occasion to revert to this transformation and to appreciate its full extent. But before doing so we need to note one feature which this history of the University of Paris exhibits in a general sort of way. It is rare to find a great institution which has been formed so completely as the result of purely spontaneous evolutionary forces, as the result of organic growth analogous to that which produces living beings. Just as if it were a living creature, we have seen it grow from a tiny amorphous seed, developing, getting larger, making natural transformations under the pressure of general, impersonal, unconscious forces, so that nowhere can we see the work of a particular individual to whom the changes thus accomplished can be directly imputed. There is one fact which gives very concrete evidence of this feature. It is the fact that all the transformations which took place within this organisation, all the innovations which came about as the institution progressed, cannot be precisely dated. They result from an evolution so thoroughly continuous that we cannot precisely locate beginnings and endings. When did the teachers, having proliferated around the cathedral, cross over to the other side of the Seine? We simply do not know. When did the associations become an official and recognised corporation? No one can say for sure. When did the division take place amongst the faculties themselves; when did they recognise the authority of the rector? Gradually; this is the only answer which it is possible to give. When did the charitable *hospitia* which were the first colleges become also teaching establishments; when did they absorb the arts faculty? Precise dating is not possible here. All this proves that the University was a natural phenomenon, a product of the force of circumstance; that it sprang naturally from the loins of the society to which it gave expression perhaps better than any other institution. This is by no means the least interesting feature of the historical investigation which we have undertaken.

chapter 10

The colleges (concluded)

Today it is taken as self-evident, a truth recognised by everyone, that the structures within which academic life is developed ought to vary according to the age and the degree of intellectual development which the pupil has attained. When the pupil has become a young man, already furnished with a basic education, he has already developed a certain self-awareness in the course of a preliminary education in which he has got to know himself. The academic organisation which he enters in order to further his education needs to be sufficiently flexible to allow him to move within it with considerable freedom, to seek himself independently; courses must be offered to him, not imposed upon him; he must be able to choose according to the self-knowledge he has acquired and developed regarding his needs and his aspirations. The moment has come to render his apprenticeship to life even more direct; consequently it is no longer possible to subject him to an over-solicitous supervision, to a tutelage which is excessively restricted. It is this need which is met today in slightly different forms by the organisations of universities in all European countries. At an earlier age, when the pupil is still only a child or an adolescent, when he still lacks sufficient experience to be able to be left to his own devices amongst the world of people and things, when he is still very unsure of his emerging individuality, it is essential that he be subjected to a regime which is more impersonal, to a type of control which is more direct. The moral environment in which the child lives must enwrap him more closely in order to be able to sustain him effectively. It is on the basis of this principle that the organisation of secondary schools is founded. Now, especially in France, not only during the Middle Ages, but also during the succeeding centuries, it is remarkable that we nowhere meet these two different types of organisation, these two academic systems functioning side by side as they do today. The entire scene is always dominated by one or the other of them, as if they did not both have their special place and their special function. Originally the very young pupil of the arts faculty lived the free life of the University, despite his extreme youth. Later, by contrast, when the colleges appear, the reverse takes place and the student (in the strict sense of the term — the candidate for a master's degree no less than the child learning elementary grammar) comes to cloister himself and live in these new establishments which henceforth become the sole educational structure throughout the system from the most elementary level to the most elevated. At the end of the last lecture I had begun expounding this great revolution; but we must revert to it because of the repercussions which it has had on the whole of our history.

If we are to understand it properly, we must distinguish two successive but very different phases within it. In the first phase we see the formation and proliferation of a number of new types of establishment existing side by side with the University which they resemble. They are called colleges, and in them students find, in addition to board and lodging, supplementary and complementary teaching. This benefits them considerably in their studies at the arts faculty, but does not render the latter indispensable. The centre of University life remains located in the *rue du Fouarre* and in the public schools; from this point of view the colleges only act as adjuncts with an auxiliary role to play. Their immediate function consists in providing moral and material shelter for the pupils. We have seen that these colleges, which began as nothing more than communities of scholars created exclusively for poor students, gradually came to open their gates to an increasingly large number of pupils who were not scholars but were fee-payers; so much so that the scholars became a minority. Several factors combined to produce this result. First of all, as I have shown, there were the considerable advantages enjoyed by students who got themselves admitted to these establishments where they found all sorts of facilities, both human and material, not available elsewhere. The community for its part could only view with satisfaction an increase in the number of paying pupils because of the fees which they paid. But over and above these factors there is an additional one whose influence was certainly fundamental. This was the moral advantages which the new form of organisation offered; it was because of these that the University itself encouraged the colleges to develop.

It is impossible to overstress the depravity of the moral life of the student of those days. There was in any case inherent in mediaeval life a kind of natural and fundamental unruliness, just as there is in any civilisation which has not yet attained to a sufficient degree of development. The habitual avoidance of excess, a taste for moderation, a capacity for self-control and self-discipline: these are human characteristics which humanity exhibits only when it has been for centuries immersed in a culture and subject to a rigorous discipline. Mediaeval man was still too close to barbarism not to have an inclination towards violence in all its forms; his stormy, tumultuous passions were not such as could be easily tamed. All this, exacerbated by the immoderation of the age and by the extreme freedom which even the youngest of the students enjoyed, created a situation in which they spent their lives in debauchery and excess of every kind. Jacques de Vitry has depicted all this in a portrait which is well-known but which is too realistic to be reproduced here. It is true that Jacques de Vitry was a fearsome and fanatical monk who always painted the morals of his contemporaries in their darkest light. He may therefore be suspected of exaggeration. But Roger Bacon is no less severe. For his part, the chancellor, Prevostin, says that 'the arts student spends every night roaming the streets armed to the hilt, breaking open the doors of houses and filling the churchyards with the noise of his brawling. Every day *metriculae* [sic] come to lodge complaints against him, claiming that they have been struck, had their clothes torn to pieces, or their hair cut off.' Not did they restrict themselves to this kind of violent dissipation; they regularly committed veritable crimes. 'They associated with gangsters and crooks, stormed the streets at night fully armed, broke into houses and committed rape, murder and theft. The festivals which the nations celebrated in honour of their patron, instead of being edifying occasions, were merely an excuse for drunkenness and debauchery. The students ran through the streets of Paris carrying their weapons, yelling so loud that the peaceful burghers could not sleep, ill-treating innocent passers-by. In 1276 they even played dice on the church altars.' Their impunity increased their licentiousness. The students were effectively immune from the civil authority of the provost. Should one of them be arrested the University would claim him or go on strike unless he was set free, for it was keen above all to hold on to its prerogatives. Once the student had been handed over to the University he was sent for trial by the ecclesiastical courts under whose jurisdiction he fell; but these would treat him with their habitual indulgence. As Thurot says, 'the guilty would receive the lash when what they deserved was the rope.'

The people who lived in the colleges were exposed to involvement in such disorders. So the University, which was itself suffering from these excesses, especially from the time when it was no longer strong enough to defend its ancient prerogatives against the royal power, used all its authority to encourage the movement which impelled scholars to become boarders in the colleges. Indeed, it finally made boarding obligatory. In 1457 the nation of the French, then in 1463 the whole of the arts faculty, decided that no student could receive his academic qualifications unless he had resided in an establishment recognised by the University, or with his parents, or in the house of some noted member of the University for whom he acted as an unpaid servant. This ruling would have been ineffective if the paying pupils had retained their primal right to leave the college where they were whenever they wanted, and particularly when some punishment was inflicted upon them which they did not like. However, from 1452 onwards a ruling by Cardinal d'Estouville made it illegal for any head of an establishment to admit to his house any student who had left the one where he was simply in order to avoid a punishment (*ad evitandam disciplinam ac correctionem*). Henceforth, with relatively few exceptions, all the students in the arts faculty were boarders.

This phenomenon was certainly not the result of contingent local conditions, for there is no university which did not during the same period (that is to say, in the course of the fifteenth century) adopt more or less similar measures. Everywhere during this era war was being waged upon the martinets; everywhere it was felt necessary to place students under control whether by a community organised on a regular basis such as a college, or by an individual of unquestionable respectability such as a university teacher. Everywhere, in Oxford no less than in Paris, in Cambridge no less than in Oxford, in Vienna, in Prague, in Leipzig, the same need was felt and produced the same effects. We can thus be sure that this change in the organisation of academic life was the inevitable result of very profound general causes. If the University of Paris had stopped there, if it had restricted itself to stipulating that its students be resident whether in college or at the house of a teacher, the boarding system would have become established only in a moderate and mellowed form, in which it would have had all the advantages without any of the usual disadvantages. Education would have remained external to the colleges. The arts faculty, while retaining its links with these establishments, would nevertheless have remained distinct from them. The pupil would not have been utterly and inescapably immured; his life would have retained its former dual structure. In the lodging house he would have lived and worked under the direction of special teachers who, because they were more immediately in contact with him, would have been able to supervise him more intimately and to greater effect; but every day the gates of the house would have been thrown open in order to allow him to go and pursue his studies in the public schools. He would have retained his links with the outside. The system adopted could have been very similar to the English tutorial system, which was becoming established at the same time as a result of the same forces. But in France the movement which had led to a relatively modest residence requirement did not stop at this first stage; it rather continued until it finally culminated with colleges as institutions with full compulsory boarding even for the teachers, whose members received no teaching from outside. Originally such teaching as had gone on within the colleges had been purely supplementary; gradually it proliferated and increased in importance in proportion as that which took place in *rue du Fouarre* diminished. The teachers teaching in the public schools changed in character; they became special functionaries attached to the colleges; instead of allowing the pupils to come to them it was they who went to the pupils. Becoming redundant, the schools of the *rue du Fouarre* gradually closed down. They were no longer frequented except for official ceremonies which took place, for example, with respect to the conferring of degrees. Ramus informs us that he set eyes on the last teacher who taught there. But the time came when the teachers no less than the pupils were also obliged to reside in a college.

The full boarding system, the boarding system proper, is not the same as a system which makes use of halls of residence, it is a system whereby halls of residence are simultaneously schools. Only then is the boarding system complete. From then on, in effect, the pupil finds within the house which gives him shelter everything which is necessary to his material and also his spiritual life. He is thus definitively cut off from the rest of the world; the world ends for him with the walls of his dwelling, which he is no longer able to pass through. His horizon is limited to his precinct and everywhere else is out of bounds. He is cloistered.

In addition to this cloistering effect the full boarding system is seriously flawed by being a hybrid product created out of the fusion of two styles of life which are almost totally incompatible: on the one hand there is the school; on the other hand there is the hall of residence. The hall of residence, if it was to do its job properly (that is to say, to provide moral protection for the child, to sustain him and to look after him most effectively), needed to remain reasonably small in size. Indeed it was precisely because the teacher who was guiding them knew the children reasonably well that he was able to modify his conduct according to each of their individual natures. In addition and by contrast large agglomerations easily exert an evil influence from the moral point of view. The ideal constitution for a hall of residence is thus one whereby the pupils are dispersed amongst a large number of small establishments whose size, while not being equatable with that of the family nevertheless resembles it as closely as possible; and this is indeed what the first colleges were like, offering shelter to a fairly small number of scholars.

Education, by contrast, as we have already established, results from a process of concentration. As far as education is concerned dispersal means death. What is a school unless it is a gathering of a certain number of learned people who have associated with one another with a view to rendering others learned? It is a cluster of intellectual forces, and the quality of the education offered will be proportionately improved the richer this cluster is. If teachers are geographically concentrated then inevitably so will the pupils be; seats of learning have a power to attract proportionate to their importance, and it is an attraction which the student population is incapable of resisting. Besides, the process of concentration is so much a part of the nature of education that education tends towards it of its own accord, spontaneously, which is precisely the fact to which the history of our colleges bear witness. First of all a multitude of colleges were founded in Paris; then gradually education became concentrated in a very small number from amongst them ('fully practising colleges') and the others became dependent upon them, destined sooner or later to be absorbed into them. By the same process we have seen in our own time a tendency towards absorption of the colleges within the totality of public secondary education, with individual colleges escaping their fate only thanks to help supplied from outside the state which gave them an artificial ability to resist. It is by the same process that we still see small secondary schools lost in mergers with large ones; and the same is true of small universities with respect to the more important universities.

If this is correct, if, in order to fulfil their functions, the hall of residence and the school proper have such contrasting and conflicting needs, they cannot be merged into a single institution without sacrificing the legitimate interests of either the one or the other. If, in order that education might flourish, the structure of academic life was enlarged, the pupil, who was lost in his place of residence, received there no direct, personal education tailored to his individual needs. If, however, in order to meet this danger the school restricted itself to the size of the hall of residence, the education became unduly narrow and languished.

The two distinct phases which we have characterised in the academic revolution which took place in France during the fifteenth and sixteenth centuries are thus quite different from one another; and in order to be able to evaluate the total achievement it is necessary to keep them carefully apart. To precisely the same extent that the former was necessary and inevitable, as is proved by the fact that there is no country in Europe where we do not find it, the latter was contingent and due to a collection of local peculiarities, as is shown by the fact that it had nothing like the same degree of universality. The establishment of great centres of learning which appears with modern societies necessarily entails that the vast majority of children leave their families in order to collect around one of these intellectual centres and gain an education; consequently the necessity arose to create moral environments which as far as the youngest of them were concerned could take the place of the domestic environment. It was this need which the earliest colleges answered; their function was primarily residential, and education in the strict sense only played a secondary role. This is the first phase. But it was in no wise either necessary or even desirable that these colleges, these halls of residence should absorb into themselves the very schools for which they had originally fulfilled an auxiliary and complementary function. It was this process of absorption which took place during the second phase; it is this that has given our system of boarding education and consequently given our academic system its special features. What can have brought it about?

When speaking of this system, there is one word which springs readily to the lips in order to describe it: it is the word 'cloister'. Indeed there are undeniable similarities between boarding-school education understood in this way and the regime of a monastic order. Should we then not say that it was the latter which inspired the former? Was not the full boarding system simply an extension of the monastic idea which had expanded from the religious to the academic domain by a process of natural contagion? There is one fact which tends to lend plausibility to this hypothesis. The first, important colleges were colleges of theology (Sorbonne, Navarre). From the thirteenth century onwards, not only was theology taught in convents but it was there that it flourished at its most intellectual. In 1253 out of twelve chairs nine were located in convents; students indeed found in them all sorts of advantages which made them attractive. The first secular colleges of theology which were founded thus modelled their organisation on the prototype of the organisation of the convents. Is not full boarding the natural means of realising in an integrated way the Christian idea of education? We have noted that, because of what we saw as the goal of education (namely, the shaping of a person's entire humanity) Christianity inevitably had a tendency to envelop the child entirely within a system which would take control not only of his whole intellectual existence but also of his physical and moral life, in order to be able to penetrate more completely and more profoundly into his deepest nature, to prevent any part of it from escaping.

That this explanation is not sufficient by itself, that it only tells part of the story, is demonstrated by the fact that in Oxford as in Cambridge there existed universities and colleges in the thirteenth and fourteenth centuries, and yet, although England was still a Catholic country in those days, although the mendicant orders also played an important part there, the French system of full boarding education never took root there. This system cannot therefore be explained in terms of a general application of Christian ideas, but rather derives from some special peculiarity in our national make-up. What could this peculiarity have been?

Perhaps we shall begin to get at the truth by observing at the beginning that there was a fundamental difference between the English colleges and ours which became more, not less, exaggerated in the course of time. Whereas at Oxford the colleges were, to a large extent, independent of the University and always retained something of this independence, in Paris they collapsed immediately into a state of dependency upon the University, which, though relatively permissive to start with, eventually became very strict. Of course, as we have shown, the earliest colleges still had something of that democratic character which was originally exemplified in the private *hospitia*. However, even in those places where the headmaster had to be elected by the scholars, this function was reduced to a mere formality which, in order to take real effect, had to be sanctioned by the University authorities. Moreover this prerogative, which in any case had never been anything other than exceptional, was quick to disappear. From a very early date we see the arts faculty allocating itself the right of supervising the internal life of the colleges, of revising the regulations, of investigating the way in which principals, headmasters, and other officers were performing their functions and, if need be, removing them from office. The colleges became the University's colleges. In 1362, to quote but one example, the University forced the sale of the property of one college (the college of Constantinople) which had fallen into decline. Such intervention was not grounded in reality upon any legal right; indeed it frequently flouted the express dispositions which had been made by the founders who had not wanted the University to have such sovereign control over the destiny of their foundations. But the University possessed an all-powerful instrument for inducing obedience. Since the principals and their subordinates were members of the body of University, the University could expel the rebels among them. This threat was sufficiently powerful to ensure that its interference met with no resistance.

Such intervention by the University already had the inevitable consequence that it prevented the halls of residence from developing in accordance with their true nature. Since these two types of establishment have such profoundly different requirements, what should have happened is that, without relations being severed between them, each of them should have been allowed to pursue its own course independently. But once the University had started to intervene, and to intervene so directly, in the internal affairs of the colleges, amalgamation had already begun to take place; and as such intervention became more important so too did the amalgamation become more complete, with all the conflict and complications which it entailed. The hall of residence, in order to retain its identity, in order to fulfil its educative function, needs an organisation which is supple and flexible like that of a family so that it can change itself and diversify, according to circumstances, the place it occupies in time and space, the nature of the pupils, and other factors. It needs to be self-regulating in order to be sufficiently flexible to meet the varied demands of the situations which confronted it. By contrast, the pressure from the University was all directed towards subjecting all the colleges to a uniform regime. Just one piece of evidence: there is a regulation of 1452 which went so far as to regulate by statute the quality and the price of the victuals which were to be served to the members of the halls of residence and the way in which they were to be shared out.

But this is not all. When a body in authority, any body in authority, is fired by a love of regimentation, when it has a tendency to make everything conform to a single unique norm, it experiences an instinctive horror for everything which does not accord with the rules, for everything which is the result of whim and imagination. Anything which might disturb the established order takes on the appearance of a scandal which must be avoided; and since elective affinities are necessarily incompatible with programmes which have been decreed, since they easily become the occasion of a certain disorderliness, every effort is made to suppress them by restricting freedom. Hence the tendency to impose a style of life which is uniform and which leaves as little room as possible for irregularity. Now, pupils who have once moved out of college can no longer be so easily watched over and supervised as when they are still in college. It was impossible that life outside should be so contained, canalised and coerced into conformity with the norm. Once it was set free it could not but spread its wings freely. It was thus almost fatally inevitable that exeats should furnish opportunities for excesses, which doubtless appear venial in the extreme to those who are committed first and foremost to freedom and diversity in life but which seem shocking to people who prize uniformity so highly; every effort was therefore made to curb these excesses. Gradually every opportunity for an exeat was suppressed — public debates, processions, extra-mural athletics. Indeed the arts faculty frequently forbade heads from taking their pupils out on walks. The logical consequence of this development was the transfer of all teaching to the inside of the colleges and hence the establishment of a thoroughgoing system of boarding education.

Thus the French system of boarding derives from that excessive passion for uniform regimentation which imbued the university in the fifteenth century with an intensity which is matched nowhere else. But where did this passion itself come from? Clearly it must derive from some special feature of our history and, consequently, of our national character. Now, there is perhaps no feature which is more distinctive or which characterises us more completely than the extreme precociousness and intensity of our political centralisation. Well before any of the other countries of Europe, we had a firmly established central power. From the end of the fifteenth century, feudal institutions began to disappear; the plethora of small feudal states became merged into the unity which was the French nation; the monarchy began to concentrate all authority in its own hands. Of course, the same movement occurred more slowly and was less far-reaching. No European society at this time had such a powerful sense of its own political and moral unity, and it is this, moreover, which explains why it was in France two centuries later that revolution occurred. Remember as well that Paris became at this period the first great capital city in Europe. Now political centralisation necessarily presupposes the establishment of uniform government throughout the entire country and it tends of itself to reinforce this uniformity; indeed, the whole burden of the monarchy's endeavour was directed precisely towards levelling out the moral diversity of the country, towards imposing unity on the variety of local institutions and towards establishing a single code of laws and ethics throughout all strata of society. It was during the Middle Ages that life took on the appearance of a complex, irregular mosaic; came the monarchy and everything was unified, regulated and simplified.

Besides, social machinery of such size can obviously only function if all the cog-wheels of which it is comprised are moving in concert, according to a plan and under clearly defined control. But once the habit of regulation, the passion for order has been thus implanted in the very centre of the social organism, it will inevitably communicate itself from there to every organ, to every form of public activity, thereby becoming a feature of the national character. It is impossible that any institution in the state, even a private one, will avoid sharing in this same attitude of mind and

yielding to this same driving force, both because they have contributed to its manufacture and because they have subsequently
been subject to its influence, reinforced by collective momentum.
This is why we are, not without reason, regarded as an essentially
organising people who organise in situations which in reality do
not lend themselves naturally to systematic organisation. This is
because the disparate nature of life with its irregularities, the
capricious, flexible, unpredictable forms, which it assumes when
allowed to flow freely and not forced to pursue some predetermined course, all this the French mind finds disconcerting, so we
strive our utmost to classify people and things within specific
frameworks and clear-cut categories. And this has something to
do, moreover, with our taste for clarity, our love for distinctness;
for the need to impose order on the life of the mind does not differ
in essentials from the need to impose order upon the substance of
social life.

This then, to return to the particular question with which we
are concerned, provides the explanation of the university's attitude towards its colleges. We have focused on the fifteenth century for this was the period when, more than any other, education
became enclosed in the boarding system. At this period the
monarchy was on the point of achieving maximum unity and
power: in less than a hundred years it would reach its zenith. Consequently it is not surprising that this vast corporation which was
the university, being in frequent and direct contact with the state
and with roots that reached down to the very interiors of
mediaeval society, should have been animated with the spirit of
orderliness, of organisation, of regimentation which imbued all
the institutions of the era. Hence its reluctance to allow the colleges to develop each in its own way; hence its tendency to impose
upon all of them a single uniform regime, to prevent and correct
infringements of and deviations from the rules, no matter how
trivial; hence, finally, the absolute nature of the boarding system,
which was a precondition for this uniformity. If the universities of
other countries allowed greater independence to their halls of residence, if their boarding system developed in a less harsh form, it
was because they did not feel so compelling a need for logical and
systematic order; and by the same token, they did not feel this
need because their society had not attained the same degree of
centralisation.

That is how the boarding system took root in our society. On the
basis of memories which are still alive we have often wanted to attribute the boarding system to the First Empire. No doubt, the
system was reconsecrated at that period; perhaps it was even reinforced. This fact, however, only serves to confirm the explanation
we have been offering. Was not the First Empire the apotheosis of

political centralisation? Was it not the period when the French love of order, of administrative classifications reached its peak of intensity? However, it is not true that this was the period when the boarding system was introduced into the social organism. It had been in our blood for centuries. It was immanent in our social constitution from the day the latter achieved adulthood and took on the form which it has retained throughout the greater part of our history. And this is also why we find it so difficult to extirpate. Under the influence of the state of mind which I have been trying to describe and explain, the boarding system finally came to be seen by us as the natural framework for education. Consider that until very recently the special 'grandes écoles', which for so long fulfilled the function of higher education, replacing the university which had disappeared, were almost all boarding institutions and many of them still retain this character.

However, by showing the extent to which the boarding system is an integral part of our social organisation, I in no wise mean to claim that it is necessary or to justify it. On the contrary, it is quite definitely the product of a condition which is in part morbid. There is indeed every reason to believe that there was something excessive about the way in which our moral and political centralisation and unification took place. The state could have firmly established itself without engaging in such extensive levelling, without destroying all diversity in the secondary institutions of the nation, without becoming the only major form of social organisation; we could, in sum, have become a people morally and politically united without going as far as to make life the prisoner of such impersonal frameworks. All that I have sought to show is that the boarding system is no more than a particular symptom of a kind of constitutional state or condition. In order to transform it, it is not enough to rely on the will, however vigorous, of some legislator. It is our native temperament that needs to be modified. We must recover a taste for a life of freedom and variety with all the chance happenings and irregularities which that entails. The problem, though not insoluble, is of massive proportions. But we make progress simply by becoming aware of it. Nothing is more futile than seeking to solve it while trying to conceal the difficulties. The partial reforms being proposed in these circumstances can do no more than to conjure up transient illusions of progress which in reality serve only to reinforce and render inveterate the fundamental defect for which a remedy is being sought. For the failure which accompanies ill-executed attempts can only cause discouragement and give the impression that the disease is incurable.

chapter 11

Teaching at the arts faculty

Degrees. Courses of study

We have seen in the preceding lectures how the University and then the arts faculty were first organised; and we have seen how this organisation evolved from the thirteenth to the fifteenth century. Since there was no sharp divide between the time when the arts faculty was teaching in the schools of the *rue du Fouarre* and the time when it had been absorbed into the colleges, since this transformation took place gradually so that it is impossible to tell when it began and when it became an established fact, we have deemed it necessary to describe here the whole course of this evolution in its totality. But all we have gained so far is an understanding of the organ of academic life; now we must pass on from the organ and examine its function. We know what the structure of education was at different periods of the Middle Ages; we must now examine what this education consisted in throughout this same period of our history. There is a division within our subject here which we have already encountered and which we will encounter at every stage of our investigation. An academic system is defined by its academic institutions, by the way they are organised; and also by the nature of the subjects which are taught there and the way in which they are taught. We have tried to reconstruct the form of the mediaeval schools; we can now get inside them in order to see what is happening in them.

The entire life of the mediaeval student is dominated by a system of degrees and examinations which either open or close doors. At every stage of his academic career the pupil has his sights set on obtaining some qualification, and his studies are determined by the demands of the degree for which he is preparing. It is therefore natural to begin by trying to find out what this system consisted of and what caused it to be what it was. The problem is not one of pure scholarship. For the institution of University degrees still exists; we have inherited it. It has even retained the external form which it had in the Middle Ages, and the terms which we use today to designate different examinations are those which were already being used by people in the thirteenth and fourteenth centuries. What is interesting therefore is investigating their parentage, and the need which they met. It is true that they are so familiar to us that we have come to believe that this form of organisation is the natural one, that it must have been conceived of by men who saw it as self-evidently correct. But one of the most useful features of a historical study such as the one we are currently engaged in is precisely that it enables us to dissipate those prejudices which result from mere habit. Even the most cursory historical survey is enough to make us realise that degrees and examinations are of relatively recent origin; there was nothing equivalent in classical antiquity. Then one went to receive instruction from a particular teacher because of his reputation and not because his calibre was guaranteed and authenticated by a string of certificates. There doesn't even exist any Latin word which precisely expresses the concept of an examination any more than there is for that of a degree. The word and the thing only appear in the Middle Ages with the university. What was it that brought them into existence?

The ultimate in degrees, the final goal of all students, was the master's degree, which in certain faculties (law) was called the doctorate; the insignia of this degree was indeed the doctor's cap. Possession of a master's degree gave admission to the University corporation in the capacity of a teacher with all the rights and privileges which this status carried. The arts faculty thus appears to form a kind of vicious circle, since the ultimate goal of teachers is the creation of new teachers. Under such circumstances might one wonder why, in the course of time, there was not an excess of teaching personnel. The explanation here is that for many young people the master of arts degree was only a starting-point, an initial qualification which gave them access to other careers in theology, law, medicine, or the Church.

Although this was the highest degree in existence it appears that it was obtained without any kind of examination as we understand it. The candidate had only to present himself before the nation to which he belonged and then, without any kind of test, he would be given the *placet* or authorisation to give his inaugural lecture; this was called, as we have already had the opportunity of saying, by the name *inceptio*. There was nothing inherent in the nature of the *inceptio* which resembled an examination: it was a ritual ceremony such as one finds at entry to any corporation. Everywhere in order to gain access to some trade association, whatever it might be, it was necessary solemnly to perform some professional act in the presence of the masters of the corporation. The candidate for the master's degree performed such an act by teaching in the presence of his own masters.

If the master's degree was awarded without any proper examination, the same was not true of the degree which immediately preceded it and led up to it. This degree was the 'licence'. We know that originally the *licentia docendi* was not a University degree but an authorisation given by the chancellor of Notre-Dame, without any preliminary tests, without consultation with any teacher, awarded or refused entirely at his discretion and without its being possible for anybody to challenge his decisions. In these circumstances the conferring of the licence took place entirely outside the University. But the corporation, once it acquired a sense of its own power, refused to participate in a system which placed the interests of education, for which it was responsible and over which it had a monopoly, entirely in the hands of an alien functionary. In all its clashes with the chancellor what was essentially at stake was the issue of this licence. Initially it had been wholly within his gift, but the University demanded control over the award, the right to intervene, to play an increasingly important role, to exert its influence in such a way that it was stripped of its arbitrary character and converted into a University degree, taking its appointed place in the hierarchy of degrees. In this the University was successful. In fact it obtained a situation whereby the chancellor no longer had the right of turning down a candidate whose suitability had been sworn to under oath by six teachers. In order for such a declaration to be made some sort of examination was presupposed; after all, how could the six teachers conscientiously endorse the candidate's ability without having first satisfied themselves about it? This is the origin of the examination for the licence. In the course of time the role played by the faculty in this examination became increasingly important. Eventually the time came when the chancellor could award the licence only after an examination by a committee composed of four teachers whose judgment was binding upon him. A way was found for setting up another licence in opposition to that awarded by Notre-Dame and which was still more within the control of the faculty. The chancellor of the abbey of Sainte-Geneviève was granted by the Pope the right to award licences; henceforth there were two licences, the old one which was described as being *'d'en bas'* ('from down there') and the new one or the *'licence d'en haut'* ('from up there'). This new dispenser of the award was naturally much less demanding than the old one precisely because his rights were of more recent date; he was consequently much more willing to accommodate the claims of the teachers. The result was that the arts faculty gained the upper hand with respect to the 'licence d'en haut', which thus became the most important examination — in the modern sense of the word — of the age. So the licence took its place in the hierarchy of degrees; it came immediately below the master's degree, the award of which in any case followed very soon after, within six months. This no doubt explains why the candidate for the master's degree was not made to undergo any test; he had just taken one.

And yet, however great were the efforts made by the University to leave its imprint on the licence, the licence always stood out as something of an oddity amongst the other degrees. We have seen clearly that it did not come into existence as a result of the natural, spontaneous development of University life. First of all a figure who was an outsider to the University, the chancellor of Notre-Dame or the chancellor of Sainte-Geneviève, was involved with it to a greater or lesser extent. Most important of all, it did not correspond to anything in the academic life of the scholar; it did not mark the end of any specific stage of his career; nor was it the beginning of anything new. It was neither the master's degree itself nor an apprenticeship for the master's degree, since the title of master of arts was awarded almost immediately afterwards. It thus represented an indeterminate condition, which did not correspond to any change in the pattern of the student's studies. It is easy to see that if the University had developed normally according to the laws of its own nature, if it had not had to adapt to the demands of political necessity, the idea of the licence would never even have been conceived. The licence is an institution whose origins lie outside the University and which the University had to assimilate in the course of its struggles against Notre-Dame, but which was not its own natural progeny. Quite the opposite is true in the case of two other degrees which it remains for me to discuss. First and foremost amongst these is the *baccalaureat*, because it forms the foundation for all the others. This examination is the product of natural and spontaneous evolution and corresponds to a very clear division in the life of the student. In effect this life consisted of two successive and clearly distinguishable phases. In the first phase, which lasted until about the age of fifteen, the student was a pupil pure and simple and spent all his time doing exercises for pupils. In the second phase he became a candidate for the master's degree, and in that capacity he practised teaching while still continuing his studies with his own teachers. At the time when this change took place a ceremony was generally held which very closely resembled the *inceptio*; it was a sort of junior *inceptio*. Just as the candidate for the doctorate demonstrated the fact of his possession of the master's degree by teaching, so the young student who had completed the first part of his studies demonstrated his suitability for embarking upon the second part of his academic career by taking part in a public debate which was called a *determinance* from the word *determinare*, which means to posit a thesis. The *determinance*, which was only a faculty custom, gradually became compulsory; it was demanded from all candidates for the licence. At the same time the custom grew of preceding it with an examination which enabled the incompetent to be eliminated from the solemn business of the public debate. The 'determinance' thus became a third degree. In other areas, however, the word 'bachelor' was used in the different trades to describe young people who, while being in a position to practise the trade which they had learned, were not yet sworn masters of it. In the same way, in the language of feudalism, the word was applied to a young nobleman who, while not having the right to raise the standard himself, marched under someone else's; it was intermediate rank between squire and knight. So close is the parallel that it has even been suggested, albeit quite wrongly, that the word 'bachelor' derives from *'bas chevalier'*. According to Thurot, we cannot say at precisely what moment in the fifteenth century this expression, which already was being used in the guilds and by that corporation which constituted the chivalric order, was applied to the person who had successfully undergone his *determinance* and who occupied an intermediate position between scholar and teacher. At this point a barbarism came to the rescue, the expression *baccalaureat* (*bacchalariatus*, transformed into *bacca laurea*).

What emerges from this historical analysis is above all the fact that if one excludes the licence, which in any case as we have shown was imported from outside, the system of degrees and examinations is the result of the corporate organisation. It is an integral part of it; it derives from it. The supreme degree is the one which gives access to the corporation in the capacity of a master. The examination results from the fact that the corporation is a closed body which only allows in new members if they fulfil certain specific conditions; there is not one corporation which does not subject to preliminary tests anyone who asks to join it. The *dignus est entrare* is perhaps the formula which best summarises the fundamental principle underlying University examinations. If there is not a single degree but a series of degrees, hierarchically arranged, this was because of the corporation's resistance to the introduction of newcomers, with the consequence that one could not enter it at a single stroke and without further ado. There must always be a series of successive initiations. Think of the series of conditions through which the candidate for the chivalric order passed — page, squire, sometimes also bachelor — before being

fully and finally armed, that is to say, received into the corporation. It was indeed partly that a corporation has something of the
character of a secret society; it has its mysteries, you can only
become a member of it after having sworn a multitude of oaths; it
is consequently quite natural that it should be protected from the
outside by impregnable barriers which are only gradually lifted
one after the other. Hence the need to advance by stages before
being able to penetrate to the heart of the city. In the University
these stages consist of 'degrees' (*gradus*). We have seen how the
nature of the tests which precede entry to these degrees is
remarkably similar to the tests which precede entry into the corporations. The initial nucleus of both sorts of body was a solemn
ceremony in which the candidate, as it were, came into full possession of his trade. We can now see why examinations and degrees
remained unknown in antiquity and the early days of the Middle
Ages. It was because the concept could only emerge once the
teachers, instead of teaching separately, formed themselves into a
corporation with a sense of its own identity and governed by communal laws.

We must not exaggerate out of all proportion the value and the
scope of examinations in those days. We are still dealing with the
earliest beginnings of this institution. The ceremonies, the solem-
nities, the rituals played a far larger part than the tests which
enabled a genuine assessment to be made. This does not mean
that the candidates didn't have to take genuine examinations.
Robert de Sorbon, in a kind of satirical sermon ostensibly being
delivered to the pupils of his college, goes as far as making comparison between the examination of the arts faculty and the Last
Judgment, and even makes the claim that the University judges
are much stricter than their holy counterpart — a comparison
which would be inexplicable if all examinations had been simply
farcical. However, even allowing for crooked examination techniques (which were the product of patronage or even corruption,
and which were practices deserving to be explained in terms of the
morals of the age rather than in those of the institution itself), it
certainly seems that failure was relatively rare. There are universities, particularly in Germany, where the number of candidates
and the number of successful candidates is identical. In Paris the
faculty records do mention failure but these are more in the
nature of exceptions which prove a rule. For the only candidates
whose failure is recorded are those who have appealed against an
unfavourable judgment and are requesting to appear before a
new commission, or else that the faculty revokes its own decision:
in order for such extreme measures to be available it was clearly
the case that failure was regarded as a totally abnormal event. Was

it then possible to pass without giving evidence of a certain minimal knowledge? Certainly not; but only students who were virtually certain of success were allowed to reach the stage of the examination. Each candidate had to be presented by his teacher, who, given the considerable length of the course of studies, had had quite enough time to get to know him. It was possible to advise those who were not ready for it against taking the examination. This explains why, out of the total number of students registered, at most half sat the *baccalaureat* and much less than half of those who thus became 'bachelors' went on to take the master's degree. The elimination process was more or less self-regulating, taking place before the examination, which consequently performed no other function than that of confirming and hallowing results which had already been ascertained in advance.

This is the origin of the system of degrees and examinations which we still operate today; for it is remarkable to note that its essential contours have not changed. Of course, the knowledge demanded for each degree has changed; but the scale remains the same with the same number of degrees and each of the three stages which thus divide up a university career has approximately the same significance as formerly. The *baccalaureat* completes the first period of academic life, the doctorate is its culminating point, and the licence occupies an ill-defined, intermediate situation between these two extremes, just as it did before. When we realise that this system is derived from an archaic institution which has disappeared (namely, the mediaeval corporation), that one of the constituent elements (the licence) is the result of a simple historical accident, one cannot help wondering whether this persistence (with which fortune has favoured ourselves alone, for it is not in evidence to such a degree in other European countries) is entirely normal; whether this tripartite division in academic life which has been patently inherited from so distant a past is still, as the result of some miracle or other, the one which best meets contemporary needs. Until we have made further progress with this study, until we know what caused this persistence, we shall not be in a position to answer the question; but from now on at least we are committed to asking it.

But degrees and examinations are the most external feature of academic life; they mark the stages without enabling us to understand what these stages consisted in. Let us now try to reconstruct the entire course. To do this we must revert to the thought of the Latin Quarter at a time when the University was in its heyday, that is in the thirteenth and fourteenth centuries. It is winter, for this is the period — from the feast day of St Remi (1 October) until the first Sunday of Lent — that the University is fully active; this was when the most important teaching took place, and was called the 'grand ordinaire'. The Quarter awakes before daybreak and from all the *hospitia*, student hostels and colleges, which are crowded together in this part of Paris, the students make their way towards the *rue du Fouarre*. As soon as the Carmelite friars in the *Place Maubert* have rung out the first mass of the day at sunrise, the barriers, which at night deny entry to the less savoury element amongst the lay population (to prevent it, as was its wont, from dumping the most frightful filth), are lifted for the scholars, and they go to the halls where their respective teachers are teaching. Once they had entered the hall — which was called *scholae* in the plural, even when it consisted of a single room — the scholars sat down on the ground in the dust and dirt, for there were no seats. Only rarely, particularly in winter, the ground was strewn with straw, for which in any case the students had to pay a supplement. On two occasions, in 1366 and in 1452, the custom of allowing the audience to sit on benches threatened to establish itself; but Cardinals Saint-Cecile and D'Estouville suppressed this 'corrupting luxury' and the scholars had to continue sitting on the ground, *ut occasio superbiae a juvenibus secludatur* (in order to shelter youth from the temptation to pride). The only furniture was a single rostrum, a chair and a desk. It was here that the teacher came and sat down, wearing his black gown with its fine squirrel fur lining. Then the lesson began.

The teacher did not talk; he read and often he dictated. This wasn't because repeated statutes had not sought to impose different teaching methods. They had tried to get the teachers to improvise, or at least to talk instead of restricting themselves to a monotonous reading. Even the speed of the teacher's diction was regulated. He was supposed to speak not slowly (*tractim*) but quickly (*raptim*), 'by pronouncing the words as if there was no one in front of him who was writing (*ac si nullus scriberet coran, sese*).' His delivery should be like that of a preacher, so that the pupils would fix the ideas by using their memories and not by writing them down. Despite such legislative measures and the severe sanctions which backed them up, the custom, which was in any case a very ancient one — for we possess exercise books belonging to teachers which have clearly been dictated and which date back to the first half of the twelfth century, before the era of the universities — this custom of reading persisted. It is important to realise that this persistence wasn't simply due to tradition: there were sound reasons behind it. If one realises that the pupil in those days had no books by means of which he could refine and consolidate the memories which his lessons left behind, one is forced to ask what he could properly retain of them if he didn't take away written notes. In those days oral teaching was much more indispensable than it is today, for it had a *raison d'être* which it no longer possesses. It had to take the place of the books which did not exist; it was the only way in which knowledge could be transmitted. But in order to fulfil this function it was additionally necessary that it should not be reduced to mere fleeting words. So it is surprising to find the virulence with which people sought to build transitoriness into it.

This course which was read or dictated: what did it consist of? Whether the subject was grammar or logic or ethics or law or medicine, it had the same character throughout: it always consisted in a commentary on a specific book. As we see it nowadays, teaching a subject consists in expounding a certain number of general truths which, no doubt, were first discovered and expounded by particular scholars but which exist as truths independently of the works in which these scholars first set them down. We therefore expound them as they are and for their own sake, frequently without being at all familiar with the writings of those who discovered them in the first place. The thirteenth and fourteenth centuries had a quite different conception of knowledge and teaching. The Middle Ages never succeeded in rising above the belief that knowledge is not a question of knowing certain particular things but simply of knowing what certain authoritative writers ('authentic' was the word used to describe them in those days) said about these things. Teaching did not take place as part of the pursuit of truth for its own sake regardless of the authors who had dealt before with the subject-matter in question, as is our practice today; rather did teaching consist, in every branch of learning, in the exposition of a particular book which was alleged to be authoritative and dealt with this subject.

This is why the programmes of study which begin to appear at the beginning of the thirteenth century, and which set out the areas of knowledge which must be covered by candidates for the degrees, specify not lists of problems but lists of works. Studying logic consisted of learning how to expound Aristotle's *Organon*; the study of physics consisted in expounding the *Physics* and the *Parva Naturalia* by the same author, and so on. In order to extract the knowledge which these books contained they were subjected to the exegetic method. This was the fundamental principle of all mediaeval education. It was summed up by Roger Bacon as follows: 'When you have a thorough knowledge of the text, you have a thorough knowledge of everything about the branch of learning of which this text treats (*scito textu, sciuntur omnia quae pertinent ad facultatem propter quam textus sunt facti*).' This is why pursuing a course of study in the Middle Ages was known as 'reading a book' (*legere librum*) or 'listening to a book' (*audire librum*). Even in modern

German the verb 'to teach' can be translated by *lesen* or *vorlesen*; in English a 'lecturer' is a teacher; and in French the word *'lecteur'* (reader) has long carried the same meaning which it still retains in the terminology of the Collège de France. It is not only in the language of academia that this ancient notion survives to the present day; it is still very substantially with us. To ascertain this we need only inspect the prescribed curricula, whether at first degree or second degree level, even in history or philosophy, and we shall see the considerable place occupied in them by lists of authors who are to be expounded. We have here a whole collection of beliefs which may at first sight surprise us but which are still far from having completely disappeared. This makes it all the more important for us to succeed in understanding their origins and the causal factors which determined them. In order to do this we must first explain how the method of commentary and exegesis works, for it was by this method that the knowledge which was contained in the text was transmitted.

Two different methods were used. Sometimes the teacher expounded; he performed what was called an *expositio*. Even today we are able, as it were, to witness one of these expositions, for the *Commentaries* of St Thomas on Aristotle are simply his *expositiones* presented lecture by lecture. The purpose of these expositions or commentaries was not, as it is today with exercises of the same name, to translate the thought of the author by paraphasing it. It was an immense dialectical analysis of the work being studied. The starting-point was the idea that a book is simply a long piece of reasoned argumentation, a continuous syllogism. Indeed, what else could a learned book be, if it was not a series of propositions accompanied with their proofs, whether implicit or explicit? Consequently the problem presented itself as that of resolving this vast logical mass into its basic elements in such a way as to show the necessary connections between them. The teacher sets about this task as follows. He begins by explaining in a preamble the subject of a book, its aim and the way in which it relates to other works by the same author. Having thus given a preliminary idea of the whole, he then designates a first stage in the development of the argument and goes from the beginning to a point which he has determined and which seems to him to form a unit, in that it deals with one and the same thesis, which he enunciates. For example, the early chapters of Aristotle's *Politics*, according to St Thomas in his commentary on this work, are intended to establish this branch of learning as the queen of the sciences. How is this thesis demonstrated? By means of two pieces of reasoning: first of all, he proves the supreme dignity of the study of politics in an absolute fashion with reference to the intrinsic dignity of its subject-matter, political society; secondly, he proves the same conclusion by the method of comparison whereby he shows the superiority of politics over all those studies which deal with other human societies. We are thus confronted with two new theses supporting the initial thesis. The commentator takes the first of these two theses, shows that Aristotle is basing them on a third which in itself implies yet another, and so on until he reaches a proposition which he postulates as self-evident. Having done this he reverts to the second line of argument and treats it in the same way. When he has dealt with the first body of ideas he goes on to the next, which he specifies in the same way and elaborates along the same lines. Thus he progresses with indefatigable patience, breaking down the main arguments into secondary arguments, and then into others which are still more elementary, until these condensed and complex chains of reasoning have been resolved into their ultimate elements. The modern mind, which has over centuries become unaccustomed to any really thorough-going training in logic, gets lost in this labyrinth of divisions and subdivisions and analyses which the young arts student nevertheless had to understand simply as a result of listening and without, very often, having before him the text of the author who was being expounded. It needs to be noted that there was far less concern with the thought of the author, considered from the author's own subjective point of view, than with the objective truth which was, so to speak, enshrined in the book. Thus when reasons are not produced by the author they are eagerly sought for. When contradictions appear every effort is made to reconcile them. (See Thurot, *Les grammairiens au Moyen Age*, especially part II.)

This laborious method, demanding uninterrupted intellectual concentration, was not the only one which was used. There was another which was more lively and vigorous, and which appealed to the ever-tumultuous enthusiasms of this age of debate. Instead of slavishly following the text, all the controversial propositions which it contained were extracted from it; and these questions were subjected to direct examination for their own sake. People tried to make use of the clues to the subject under discussion in the works of the author being studied, but they were not restricted to this. Here the text was simply an opportunity, a pretext for starting an argument. This was the method of *quaestiones*. Thus, again with reference to Aristotle's *Politics*, which we have just seen subjected to commentary by means of the method of the *expositio* by St Thomas, this is how another scholastic teacher, Buridan, proceeds when he is employing the method of *quaestiones*. In the first book of his treatise Aristotle demonstrates that the power of a city exceeds that of individuals and consequently is different from theirs.

Buridan then asks himself the old question whether the common good is to be preferred to a particular good (*utrum bonum commune sit praeferendum bono particulari*). Aristotle says that the city exists as a natural phenomenon, *phusei*. Instead of enquiring into Aristotle's reasons for holding this thesis he treats it independently, merely allowing the ideas propounded in the text to emerge spontaneously in the course of the argument. As to his method of argument, this is what it consists of. First an examination is carried out (making them as convincing as possible) of all the reasons which militate in favour of a positive solution; then all those that might be advanced in favour of the contrary solution. This double exposition is carried out with such impartiality that it is impossible to guess at the private views of the teacher who is speaking. Then when he has confronted his audience with these two contradictory views he states his own position, justifies it, and refutes all the reasons which have been given in support of the view he is rejecting. All these debates are presented in the same form as the expository commentary which we were talking about earlier. All the reasons for or against, all the doubts raised, are established with the help of a syllogism; then each of the premises of the syllogism is taken up as the need arises and is demonstrated in its turn on the basis of another syllogism, which frequently implies yet another, until finally one arrives at a proposition which is intrinsically self-evident. Nothing is sacrificed for the sake of external form and interest; the sole concern is correctly to dissect the arguments, to show clearly all the links in the chain of reasoning. To achieve this, the person arguing does not hesitate to dot his i's and cross his t's. Each stage in the argument is labelled, classified, cross-referenced. Here is the major premise and the minor premise. This is the form which the major premise takes. Here are three objections. Here are the answers to the objections. This is a hypothetical proposition. This is the consequence which follows from it, and so on. This style of arguing may astonish us, but before we pass judgment on it we must understand what its object was and how it fitted in with the beliefs of the society in which it took place.

chapter 12

The teaching of dialectic in the universities

We saw in the last chapter how teaching was carried out in the universities of the Middle Ages, and particularly in the arts faculty. The branches of learning were not taught objectively, independently and for their own sake; teaching was limited to commenting upon one or a handful of books which dealt with this branch of learning. Sometimes the goal of this method of teaching was to retrace, in a positive way, the logical progression of the thought of some authoritative author; sometimes the book simply provided the opportunity for instituting a methodical controversy in front of the pupils on one of the problems dealt with in the work which was being analysed. In both forms the goal of the teaching was the same. It was a question above all of training the pupils in the practice of dialectic. In the former case they were confronted with the thought of a great master and the internal dialectic of his arguments was explained to them; this was why the teacher, so to speak, dismantled the arguments, broke them down into their simplest constituent elements; and in order that the logical framework might become more apparent all the argumentation was put in the form of a syllogism. What the pupil learned in this way was a passive form of dialectic whereby thought revealed and unfolded itself in conformity with itself and without concerning itself directly with objections and arguments which might be raised against it. In the second case, by contrast, it was a vital and vigorous form of dialectic into which the pupil was initiated through the method of controversy; he was shown the importance of setting one opinion against another, one argument against another; and how from the clash of contradictory arguments truth can emerge. The dialectic of peace-time and the dialect of war, the dialectic of exposition and the dialectic of debate; these more than anything else were what was taught, far more than any particular doctrine or set of doctrines.

This meant that the role of logic in education was absolutely overwhelming. And indeed this domination by logic reveals itself not only, as we have just seen, in the form which teaching took, but also in the choice of the subject-matter used. We know that the staple curriculum, the lectures which were in the main given from 1 October to 25 March, constituted the basics of education; it was these lessons which prepared pupils for the *baccalaureat*, thus corresponding roughly to the kind of teaching which goes on in our secondary schools. Now, these lectures were devoted almost exclusively to the exposition of treatises on logic. The following is a list of the authors who had to be read and commented upon in the thirteenth century; the introduction of Porphyry, the *Categories*, the treatises on interpretation, the treatises of Boethius on division, the first three books of his *Topics*, and the *Topics* and the *Elenchi* of Aristotle, the *Prior Analytics* and the *Proximate Analytics*, and finally Priscian's *Grammar*, which was later replaced by that of Alexandre de Villedieu. In sum, Aristotle's *Organon* remained even in later eras the virtually exclusive subject of basic education. In addition to logic, it is true, a place, but a very small place, was reserved for grammar. Far more than in the Carolingian epoch, grammar was at that period understood as a branch of learning very closely related to logic. The frontiers between these two disciplines were frequently ill-defined. Of course, the basics of Latin grammar were taught more or less by rote memory, in the little grammar schools and later on (when these schools were attached to the colleges) in classes of the same name. But when the pupil had ceased to be a 'grammarian', as he was called, when he had become an 'artist', when he had entered the second period of his academic life which lasted from twelve to fifteen years of age, grammar teaching took on a quite different character. At this stage the language was not studied independently and as if it were self-justifying, but only in as far as it related to the study of thought; it was not enough to ensure the memorising of a handful of rules; the rules had to be explained, and it was in terms of the laws of thought that the laws of language were explained. Because human thought is everywhere the same, because it is everywhere subject to the same essential laws, it was concluded that the same was true of its verbal manifestations; consequently there must exist some unique fundamental grammar, some human grammar corresponding to human thought, and of which national grammars are a particular and contingent manifestation. To quote one thirteenth-century grammarian: 'Since the nature of things and the way in which people are and think are identical in all men, it follows that the same must be true of the ways in which they express themselves. Thus the grammar which underlies one locution is identical with that which underlies another; they are both varieties of one and the same species which differ only because of the purely contingent fact of the form of words which they employ. Thus anyone who knows the grammar of one language knows, at least in essence, the grammar of the others.'

This unique and universal grammar is an abstract science, wholly similar to geometry. Its object is to discover the general laws of language. Robert Kilwardby says: 'Just as geometry does not deal with the size of particular lines or surfaces but treats of size in an absolute fashion (*simpliciter*), so grammar does not treat of constructions in Latin or Greek but rather of construction in general, abstracted from all the features which are peculiar to any particular language.' This universal grammar is clearly the logic of language. This does not mean that the science of language was taught in an abstract way without reference to any particular language, in the kind of way in which an expert philologist might set about teaching universal grammar today. In fact the particular subject-matter of grammatical science was Latin; but in studying Latin it was the general forms and laws of language which were being sought. And Latin, especially the Latin of the scholars and the clerks, seemed especially appropriate for this role; for it was it-self a sort of generic language, a universal language because its different popular forms, in the Latin of Gaul, of Germany and of Italy, were particular sub-species of it. It was thus the natural subject-matter for this geometry of language which people dreamed of constructing.

As for the disciplines other than logic in the strict sense and the logic of language, they were not completely excluded; but they were only taught in special lessons which were called 'extra-ordinary'. What was meant by this was that they did not form part of the regular curriculum; consequently they took place outside official academic hours on public holidays or perhaps on normal days in the afternoon, the morning being reserved for essential teaching. The summertime, from Easter to the Festival of St Remi, was more specifically allocated to them. It was in these lessons that metaphysics, morals, mathematics, natural history, astronomy, and such subjects were dealt with. Nor was there anything restric-tive about the list of permissible subjects; if a teacher wished to ex-pound some book which was not prescribed by the faculties, he only had to ask for their authority. But it is clear that these courses had the character of optional luxury extras; some of them were compulsory in order to gain the licence, but they were not designed for candidates for the *baccalaureat*. They were therefore not part of the cycle of studies with which we are particularly con-cerned, that which corresponds to our own secondary education.

They were branches of knowledge which the aspirant teacher must possess but which were not required by the young bachelor.

It may at first sight seem surprising that we do not find religious instruction mentioned amongst the basic compulsory subjects, even for adolescents; given the ecclesiastical character which we so readily attribute to the mediaeval universities one would have expected that religion would be specifically taught in them. However, the truth is that religion does not feature at all in the curriculum of the period. We have seen that it is possible to compare the colleges to the religious communities to which they were indeed similar in virtue of the fact that they were shut off from the outside world; but it would be a mistake to compare them to seminaries. For the whole concept of religious instruction did not exist in the Middle Ages. There were no courses in doctrine, or the significance of religious ceremonies. Religious education proper appears in the colleges only after the Reformation; it was one of the effects of the Counter-Reformation in as much as it was part of the movement which led the Church, in order to be able to combat the Reformation better, to borrow from the latter its own weapons. But until then it appears that ignorance with respect to religion, not only amongst pupils but also amongst the clergy, often went far beyond the bounds of imagination. One might well even wonder whether ordination was ever refused to a cleric on the grounds of his ignorance in matters of theology. All that was required was that he should know how to say mass.

Thus both the subject-matter and the form of education were closely related. On the one hand the teaching methods, even when they were being used to teach subjects other than logic, had as their supreme goal to provide a training in logic. On the other hand, logic itself more or less exclusively constituted the subject-matter of the education which the adolescent received until he had left school, as we would say today, that is until he had taken his *baccalaureat*. Thus the evolution of educational thought, whose beginnings we have already witnessed, continued. We have seen, in fact, how in the society of Europe, education, for all that it sought to be encyclopaedic, was from the outset thoroughly formal in character. For in the Carolingian schools its object was to inculcate understanding of the mind which grasped the world, and not of the world itself; the microcosm not the macrocosm. In this microcosm of the mind, in this miniature version of reality which constitutes consciousness, the world is only to be encountered in its most general forms. And that is why any education whose subject-matter is the mind is almost inevitably formal. Now we can see how with the universities and scholasticism the same movement developed; the only difference is that formalism in education has changed its nature; from being verbal and grammatical it has become logical. Education no longer limited itself to the outward form which consists in language, but sought to get beyond this and to reach the forms of thought itself.

But the word 'logic' is far too general, and is inadequate to characterise what was special about this education. In fact, the logic contained in it was of a quite special character because of the overwhelming role played by debate. It was far less a question of teaching people how to reason than of teaching them how to debate. What was taught above all was the art of arguing against another person, the art of refutation even more than the art of proof.

Of the two methods which were used in order to comment upon and interpret the authoritative books, one of them, the *expositio*, restricted itself to elucidating the arguments of the author under discussion. The other, by contrast, the method of the *quaestiones*, was a sort of debate. The teacher who practised it instituted a veritable argument. He debated with himself; he came into conflict with views contrary to his own, confronted and contrasted them, and it was this conflict which gave the exercise its interest. The first of these two methods soon fell into disrepute. In 1452 Cardinal D'Estouville reminds the teachers that they ought to expound Aristotle's text point by point, which itself proves that this kind of exposition was being neglected. The far more lively method of the *quaestiones* had replaced exhaustive and laborious analysis; it was far more suited to the needs and the tastes of the age. In addition to these exercises in which the teachers, as it were, debated with imaginary adversaries, they were obliged to debate amongst themselves in reality, at least once a week in the presence of students. Moreover, a solemn debate took place once a year in winter in the church of Saint-Julien-le-Pauvre. Four teachers, each elected by their nation, debated about questions which were related to all the liberal arts. This was called the *actus quodlibetarius*. It is true that this practice fell into desuetude during the Armagnac war. The weekly debates themselves were soon to be dropped by the teachers; but the teachers here were replaced by bachelors who, presided over by a teacher, would argue in the schools of their nation.

In addition to the debates between teachers or bachelors, in which the pupils were only spectators, there were also others between pupils. Indeed this was the only kind of exercise which was known to the schoolchildren of the Middle Ages. Written compositions were unheard of. The only active work which was demanded from the pupils was (apart from giving readings) weekly recapitulations of the lectures they had heard (*resumptiones*), and debates (*disputationes*). According to Robert de Sorbon: 'This exercise is even more useful than the readings because its effect is to illuminate all doubts. Nothing is perfectly known until it has been masticated in the jaws of debate.' Once the colleges had absorbed the life and functions of the University this practice of holding debates was developed further still. The scholars debated every Saturday, presided over by the head of the establishment; each of them was in turn proposer and opposer. And these weekly debates were certainly not the only ones which took place. Vivès, writing in 1531, says: 'They debate during dinner, they debate after dinner; they debate in public, in private, everywhere all the time.'

No practice was more violently attacked by the men of the Renaissance, and it is easy to make criticisms. Clearly, in these public debates the premium on brilliance must have encouraged people to vie with one another in empty subtleties. Controversies were aroused about the simplest of questions. Vivès and the humanists have handed down to us the memory of certain debates where dialectic degenerates into a game of wit involving plays on words, which are pretty mediocre in quality at that. One example is the debate described by one author, whose object was to decide whether the pig being taken to market is held by the rope or the person holding the rope. On other occasions the problem is posed in terms which are so rambling and sibylline that we have great difficulty in understanding it. From another point of view, a false sense of honour often encouraged the disputant not to back down even when this forced him into the extremes of absurdity, so that he might at least appear not to have given in. Finally, it is undeniable that the debates often degenerated into slanging matches, vulgarities, insults and threats: 'people even reached the point where they kicked, punched and bit one another'. Wounded and dead were left lying on the floor.

But all these facts, even if they were multiplied still further, would not suffice to justify the drastic opprobrium which the Renaissance succeeded in heaping on this exercise and on the entire system of education which revolved around it. We must not forget that nothing tends to become more easily stereotyped and prone to decay than any academic procedure whatsoever. The number of people who use it intelligently, constantly aware of the ends which it is serving and to which it ought to remain subordinate, is always very small. Once it has become a custom, once it has been invested with the authority of habit, it tends almost inevitably to function mechanically. It gets used without any awareness of the goal to which it is directed, as if it existed for its own sake and constituted its own justification. It becomes the object of a kind of fetishism which paves the way for all sorts of distortions and excesses. There is no educational practice which cannot be easily ridiculed on the basis of the way in which it operates from day to day. Does not the object lesson, which can be so fruitful, frequently degenerate into empty verbal exercises; and is it not easy to mock teachers who, like Pestalozzi (who was criticised on these grounds) waste their time getting their pupils to count the number of holes in an old tapestry or getting them either to name or to describe things with which they are fully familiar? Yet the way in which a principle may thus be abused in no wise proves that the principle is unsound, for the principle may be a very good one, capable of producing a beneficial effect even if some people operate it clumsily or to excess. If the debates served any purpose, if they met any need, all the excesses, all the ridicule which they might have occasioned will not suffice to condemn them utterly. The practice of the debate must be examined and evaluated according to its intrinsic merits. And the very fact that it played so important a role in European education for nearly three centuries scarcely justifies the historian in supposing that it was simply the monumental educational aberration which the pundits of the Renaissance believed it to be.

Indeed, it was far from being an accident which was the result of some outlandish but transient set of beliefs. In order to understand fully what this practice of debate consisted in and what its educational value was, our best method is to go back to Aristotle, who gave a clear analysis of the concept. It is, of course, not true that the Middle Ages practised the art of debate simply because they found it described in Aristotle. If the men of this era spent so much time in debate it was not simply out of fidelity to Aristotelian doctrines whose authority was respected; it was rather because the practice of debating answered certain needs and requirements of the age. The best way of understanding these needs and requirements is by looking to Aristotle himself, for he constructed a theory about the art of debate to which the Middle Ages added nothing of essential importance.

For Aristotle the role, the essence, the *raison d'être* of learning consists in demonstration, understood as the making explicit of the reasons for things. But if there can be no true learning without demonstration, it does not follow that all demonstrations lead to true learning. True learning only becomes worthy of this name when it is possible to establish necessary connections, that is to say connections of irresistible cogency such that no intelligent being can deny them without self-contradiction. The supreme example of such connections are those which are enunciated in the propositions of mathematics. But how is it possible to establish propositions of this sort? It is possible only if, when we analyse one of the terms which feature in the proposition, we find therein some property or constituent part which necessarily implies the other term and which forms a unity with it. For example, we are entitled to say that the sum of the angles of a triangle is necessarily equal to two right angles because, inherent in the concept of the sum of the three angles of a triangle, we find a property which allows them to be arranged so that they can be exactly superimposed upon a T-shape; and contrary-wise out of any T-shape it is possible to create a triangle. Similarly we can say that an eclipse is necessarily the product of an obscuring of the lunary disc if we know that the concept of an eclipse implies the passing of the solar disc over that of the moon. It is clear that for Aristotle mathematical demonstration provides the model for all scientific demonstration, and that no science is really worthy to be called such except in as far as it shares in the essence of mathematics. We shall see shortly what gave rise to so apparently exclusive a view.

It is by no means always possible to establish connections of this type. We can carry out demonstrations of this sort when we are dealing with concepts in mathematics because such concepts are simple, possess few properties and constituent elements, and moreover are constructs which we ourselves have made. We are thus thoroughly familiar with them; we know what they contain and consequently we can easily discover in one of these concepts the middle term which will serve as the link between itself and some other and which renders the second inextricably tied to the first. But the same is not true when we are dealing with matters which we know only through experience, matters which relate to either the empirical or the moral universe. Here the unifying connection can be established only by observation and induction; now, neither of these latter procedures can yield necessary connections. From the fact that we have always, in our experience, found A associated with B it by no means follows that A is necessarily associated with B. From the fact that all the swans with which we are familiar are white it by no means follows that swans are necessarily white, or that the concept of a black swan is self-contradictory. Does it follow that we can only note relationships of this kind, without having any understanding of why they are as they are and without our having any means of knowing whether they are indeed necessary or whether, despite their generality, they are merely a series of accidents which recur more or less frequently? Not at all. There is a form of demonstrative argument, whose nature and value are not the same as those of strict scientific proof, but which is by no means worthless as a means of furnishing us with serious reasons for ascertaining or denying the probability that the connection is necessary. The method is this.

Let the proposition be: 'Mules are infertile'. We can verify this proposition every day by observation. It is a question of knowing whether it is a necessary truth or not; consequently we must investigate whether there is anything about the nature of the mule which makes it necessarily infertile. In order to provide a strict proof we should have to seek the cause of infertility in the very concept of a mule; and since a mule is the offspring from the union of a horse and a donkey, we should need to start our proof by considering the specific property of horses and donkeys, by investigating their anatomical and physiological constitution. However, according to Aristotle, given the contemporary state of our knowledge such a strict demonstration is impossible. What we can do, however, is this. Instead of considering the mule in isolation, we can compare it with some other class of animal which it resembles in certain respects. We can try to discover whether we cannot find here some property which is also possessed by the mule and which might throw some light on our question. In a sense the mating of a male mule with a female mule is a mating of two parents of different species since in both there co-exists the two different species of the parents whose issue they are. Two parents of the same species cannot reproduce a species different from their own, and so it must be with a male mule and a female mule in as far as they are considered as being of the same species. On the other hand two parents of different species cannot engender an animal of the same species as themselves; and this law is applicable to the male and female mule, in as far as their mating is regarded as being similar to that of animals of different species. Thus the male mule and the female mule can neither produce offspring of their own species nor of any other species: consequently they are necessarily sterile. The same applies to politics. Suppose we are investigating how governments bring about their own destruction. Can we make no progress at all by setting out to analyse the concept of government and the concept of destruction? We already know how governments preserve themselves. Now, opposites produce opposites and preservation is the opposite of destruction. It follows then that the opposite of whatever it is that causes the preservation of governments is also that which causes their destruction. The principle underlying this method of arguing can thus be enunciated as follows: in place of the particular concept which we wish to analyse and which alone could furnish a watertight reason for determining the necessariness or the non-necessariness of the relationship, we must substitute one or several others which are related to the original concept and with respect to which we are in a position to verify propositions which we can then retrospectively apply to the original.

Can such a procedure yield absolute certainty? Not at all. On the contrary, it is clear that by thus extending to particular special cases propositions which have been established only with respect to more general cases we must allow for a wide margin of error. The best proof of this is to be found in the very argument which we have just recounted from Aristotle, and which is false because it is too general. It applies equally to all cross-breeds, and in fact there are cross-breeds which do reproduce themselves. All that we can derive from this kind of procedure are propositions which are plausible and probable but which intellectually are not absolutely compelling. So much is this so that the opposite of a plausible proposition can be just as plausible. Against the type of argument which we were exemplifying above, it is possible to mount contrary arguments which nevertheless are equally deserving of attention. Does this imply that such arguments are valueless? Of course, this would be the case if by saying that the proposition was plausible we meant that it only had the outward appearance of being true. But plausibility is to be understood in quite a different sense. A proposition is plausible if, while not being immediately self-evident, it nevertheless has a good chance of being true; it is one that there is good though not decisive reason to believe. Equally it is impossible that such probabilities don't contain any part of the truth. Thus they are not without value; everything depends on the use to which they are put.

Since there may be a variety of equally probable propositions some of which will be mutually incompatible, it is clear that we should not accept any of them simply on the basis of the reasoning which has been adduced in their support. Rather must one set out by confronting them with the conflicting views which other arguments appear to support; they must be set the one against the other, and the arguments on which they each rest must be compared: in a word, they must be debated. This is why whenever Aristotle confronts a problem he imposes upon himself as a strict methodological rule to assemble and examine the different solutions which his predecessors had given to this problem, so that he could set them beside his own, so that he could examine them simultaneously, in other words so that he could debate them. Indeed he often thinks up his own objections to his thesis. And he debates with imaginary adversaries. But would not such a confrontation yield better results if instead of being carried out in our own private speculations it took place outside in the open and in full view of the public; if instead of debating within ourselves against theoretical adversaries who can, after all, only speak with the voice which we give them and consequently are only capable of saying more or less what we want them to say according to our own enthusiasms and preferences, we set ourselves to argue resolutely against real flesh and blood adversaries; in other words, if, in a public debate, we came forward to champion our own view by crossing swords with the defenders of a differing opinion? Such a real-life debate, does it not constitute a much more appropriate method of revealing the true power of resistance of the opinions under discussion, and consequently their relative value? Within the sphere of things where we can only reach plausible opinions, debate and argument appear to be the right methodological procedure and an indispensable tool in the pursuit of truth. It is true that it is a delicate weapon which can be easily mishandled. It can be exploited simply in order to embarrass the opponent with specious arguments which only have the appearance of plausibility. In this case it is mere sophistry. But debate can be carried out in good faith with no other end in view than that of seeking the truth; in this case one is genuinely practising dialectic. For dialectic is precisely the art of arguing cogently for plausible propositions; and since debate forms an essential procedure in the practice of this art it is essentially the art of debate.

This view of dialectic and debate was also the view that was held in the Middle Ages. One must in fact beware of thinking that dialectic and logic are two synonymous terms, or that in the Middle Ages dialectic was regarded as the pathway to knowledge. On the contrary, dialectic only begins where knowledge in the strict sense is impossible; it is the method appropriate for matters which deal in propositions that are at best probable and plausible. It is this fact which enables us to begin to understand the role accorded by the Middle Ages to debate in academic and intellectual life. Not everything was the subject of debate, but only those matters where strict proof was impossible. There was no question of making debate a substitute for proof, but rather of setting debate beside proof in that area where strict proof had not as yet penetrated. Without going into the matter in depth it is not difficult to see that with respect to such matters discussion is indeed the only procedure which we have at our disposal for making distinctions between, and throwing light on the variety of views which might solicit our adherence. Thus we can understand why the art of debate and discussion was practised in the schools of the Middle Ages; and one must even anticipate that it is bound to have a place in any educational system.

The only question which remains to be examined is why the art of debate was practised in the schools so exclusively; why it was considered as the supreme educational technique for developing a capacity for logical thought; why, in a word, it was granted a more or less complete monopoly. The answer is clearly that the realm of the probable and the plausible in those days appeared infinitely greater than that which was governed by proof and strict demonstration. But why was that? Whence this quite disproportionate difference between these two realms, these two spheres of thought? If the answer to this question is elucidated and the disproportionate nature of the difference is shown to be legitimate and well-founded, we shall cease to regard the importance attributed to debate as exorbitant. It is a fact worthy of note at the outset that Aristotle himself made almost exclusive use of dialectical method and of the method of discussion which is its essential element. By his own admission he only applied the method of strict proof in constructing the theory of the syllogism. The domination of dialectic and debate does not thus depend on some contingent fact about mediaeval thought, on some momentary aberration, but rather must be the product of profound causal factors. What were they? It is only when we understand them that we shall be in a position to judge this teaching technique which has been so decried. We shall then appreciate its appropriateness, as well as the violent criticisms which the men of the Renaissance levelled against it; and can then examine the system of education which they substituted for the one which they challenged and fought against.

chapter 13

Dialectic and debate

The discipline in the arts faculty

If the men of the Renaissance were merciless towards scholastic education, if they thought that they must eradicate it completely in order to construct in its place an entirely new educational system, this was above all because of the predominance of dialectic and debate. These inspired such revulsion in them that it never even occurred to them that the arts which had been so enthusiastically practised over a whole series of generations must necessarily meet some intellectual need. All they could see in them was a monument to human stupidity. Consequently they did not stop to make a reasoned criticism of them; for the most part they contented themselves with railing against them, ridiculing them and heaping scorn upon them. No one had more fun at the expense of the dialectic than did Rabelais. It is dialectic personified that he portrays for us in the character of Dame Quintessence, Aristotle's god-daughter and queen of the kingdom of Entelechy. This old maid, 1,800 years old, surrounded by licensed abstractionists, eats nothing for dinner except a few categories, jecabots (a Hebrew word meaning abstraction), second intentions, antitheses, metempsychoses and transcendent prolepses. The courtiers are busy resolving the most abstract and tortuous questions. Some are milking he-goats, others are gathering thorns from grapes, and figs from thistles; others are 'creating large things out of nothing and causing large things to return to nothing'; others 'in a long room were carefully measuring flea-jumps, which act I was assured was more than necessary for the government of the kingdoms, the conduct of wars and the administration of republics'. It is not difficult to see how hard it was for dialectic to recover from such sarcasm and that an art personified by the wretched Janotus and his colleagues 'riff-raff, sophists, students, lecturers, lunatics, at the Sorbonne', should have been definitively discredited in public opinion. And yet, I believe, there are grounds

for appeal against a judgment which was as harsh as it was pre-
cipitate, and for reviewing this case which was dealt with in too
summary a fashion. It was such a review that we had already
begun to undertake in the foregoing chapter.

It is quite certain that there is no education in which the art of
discussion does not normally play a role. There is only one sort of
proposition which in a sense, can be regarded as being beyond
and above debate; that is those which are proved by science with
such rigour that any sort of doubt is excluded. However one con-
ceives of scientific proof, even if one has a completely different
idea of it from that which Aristotle had and which we have
described, there is no doubt that the rigorous procedures of scientific demonstration cannot be applied to all things. I do not mean
that one can assign to science specific limits which it will be eternally forbidden to surpass. It has consistently played havoc with
the barriers within which people have sought to enclose it, and has
invaded domains where it was thought to be incapable of
penetrating. Even so, science is not and will never be more than a
finite and provisional system, whereas reality is infinite in every
direction. In practice, therefore, scientific thought never could exhaust reality and, even if it could, this ultimate ideal point is still a
long way off and will always be at an infinite distance from us.
However, we cannot give up thinking and reasoning altogether
about those matters which are not susceptible to the infallible procedures followed by science. We cannot allow our intellects to ab-
dicate simply because we cannot guarantee them immunity from
error. So we continue to reason, even though our reasonings are
only to be rated as having probative value when they are strictly
scientific. Under these circumstances we must resign ourselves to
the fact that we should not ask of them more than they are capable
of giving: propositions which are probable and plausible and
which are supported by good reasons, even though they are not
intellectually incontrovertible in the way that necessary truths are.
Propositions which fall within the domain of the probable
are propositions which are debatable, which invite controversy.
Since none of them have the power to rule out absolutely
propositions which are different or antagonistic, there is
only one way we can choose between them: by bringing
them together and confronting them with one and another;
by making them compete against each other in order that the
one which is most fitted to survive may give evidence of its
superiority by triumphing over others. Such a confrontation is
the stuff of which arguments are made. This is why, with respect
to questions of this sort, argument must necessarily always have
the last word; and since dialectic is the art of reasoning plausibly,

argument and debate are necessarily an essential part of it.

If this shows that the aggressive, total and contemptuous rejection of dialectic and debate by the men of the Renaissance was by no means justified, we still need to enquire why in the Middle Ages this particular type of reasoning succeeded in developing to so prodigious a degree that it became virtually the only tool of investigation and overwhelmingly the most important academic exercise. The answer to this question is to be sought in the state of science at this time.

The only explanatory and demonstrative science established at this period was mathematics, which the Greeks had already developed to a considerable degree of sophistication. The result was, as we have demonstrated by pointing to the example of Aristotle, that scientific proof was conceivable only in as far as it conformed to mathematical proof. But the methodology of mathematics is not applicable to empirical reality, to the world of concrete facts which normally seems to be beyond the scope of scientific proof. Of course, the ancients and the men of the Middle Ages knew perfectly well what observation was; but they did not know that observation can be organised and transformed in such a way that it furnishes the elements of a rule-governed demonstrative proof. As far as they were concerned, observation could serve only to record the way in which phenomena had spontaneously appeared in a certain number of cases. Such records, even when they were correlated, could not give any guarantee that the relationships recorded would also obtain in cases hitherto unobserved. It thus seemed impossible to prove any kind of general proposition by observation. And indeed in order for observation to acquire probative power it was necessary that, instead of allowing it to result from chance encounters dependent upon contingent circumstances, it should eventually occur to people to provoke it, to set it up deliberately with a specific end in view, in order to be able to regulate it methodically and to organise it in conformity with certain rational principles; for it is only when observation is accompanied by theorisation that it is possible to transform it into a genuine logical operation.

This kind of concentrated, systematic observation is what we call experimentation or experimental reasoning. For experimentation is something quite different from observation; it depends on producing a combination of observations, such that a conclusion can be derived in the same way that the conclusion of a syllogism is derived from its premises. Whereas an observation is of scientific interest only if it is frequently repeated, the value and scope of experimental reasoning is to a large extent independent of the number of experiments on which it is based; what is important is not that the observations should be numerous but that they should be well-constructed, systematic and conclusive. Moreover, just as a theorem in geometry once it has been demonstrated is proved to be true for all time, so it is recognised today that by means of one experiment which has been well constructed and well carried out the scientist can demonstrate a law which is valid for all countries and all ages; vaccination against anthrax provides an example here. Experimentation is indeed a method of proof which plays the same role with regard to the study of nature as that which is played by mathematical reasoning in the study of numbers and quantities.

But in those days the idea of experimental reasoning was totally unknown. Today we take it for granted, but in fact it only emerged after a very long period of evolution. Its appearance was impossible, and did not in fact take place until the sixteenth century with Galileo and the scientific movement which is associated with his name; and it was only in the sixteenth century with Bacon that people began to realise that they were dealing with a *sui generis* logical operation, a new method of proof.

Herein lies the explanation of why dialectic and debate were so exclusively cultivated by the Middle Ages. With the sole exception of mathematical problems, argument inevitably appeared to be the only way in which the human mind could distinguish between truth and falsehood with the least possible chance of error. Everything was given over to public debate, because apart from special, restricted spheres of knowledge everything was within the domain of the controversial. The adage *Deus tradidit mundum hominum disputationi* was taken quite literally in those days: disputation in the strict sense of the word was considered as the queen of the sciences; it was the unique and universal instrument at our disposal for subjecting things to the scrutiny of the intellect. The inordinate trouble which was taken in those days to train young men in the practice of dialectic, therefore, should not be attributed to a sort of morbid dilettantism or severe over-development of the logical sense. It was rather because, given the state of contemporary science, there neither was nor could be any other way of reasoning applicable to the world of experience. It is consequently fair to say that at this moment of history learning how to think consisted of learning how to debate.

At the same time the bookish nature of this education no longer appears so astounding or outrageous. In order to be able to debate, to confront a variety of human opinions, one must begin by being familiar with them: it was to books that they had been consigned. From this point of view it was logically necessary, in order to know about things and the laws which govern them, to start by learning what people had said about them and written about them; for it was only from the conflict of views that the truth could blossom forth. Even the primordial importance attributed to certain authors of especial repute now seems quite natural. In order to understand it it is not necessary to introduce some theory or other about intellectual servility. The dialectical method allowed of no other means of proceeding. For if, in order to practise it, it was necessary to understand the variety of human opinion, it was particularly important to pay special attention to the opinions of the wise, of the most authoritative of the wise, because these had the greatest chance of being true. The frequently superstitious respect which during this period was shown towards those who were rightly or wrongly thought of as great thinkers was the effect not of the fact that people took it to be self-evident that truth must necessarily be encapsulated in its entirety within some particular book; it was caused rather by the fact that in this world where the intellect was groping simple-mindedly after probabilities people felt the need of a more reliable diet. I certainly do not wish to suggest that Catholic education was immune from deference to consecrated authorities; but what clearly shows that the essential cause must lie elsewhere (namely, in the concept of dialectic itself), is the fact that we find the principle enunciated in the works of that freest of thinkers, Aristotle. There are, he says, two signs whereby we can recognise a view as being plausible: either when it appears to be true to all or to the majority of men; or when it so appears to the sages, whether to all of them, to the majority of them, or to the most highly regarded amongst them. Thus the cult of the book was not a function of the fact that all sense of living reality had atrophied at this period, that the written word was the object of some kind of fetishism; it was rather the necessary consequence of a certain view of science which was forced upon the age.

We should be wary of thinking that a bookish education as such is somehow outrageous, and only to be explained in terms of some kind of aberration. On the contrary, it was precisely this concept of education which was, from the beginning, to appear most natural to the human mind once a system of education had begun to be organised. For what is education if it is not the transmission from one generation to another, in a particular civilisation, of a body of knowledge and belief which is at the time regarded as the essential part of that civilisation? Now, it is in books that the intellectual civilisation of different peoples is to be found preserved and condensed; it was thus quite natural that books were seen as the supreme medium for education. The opposite view, the view that books should be at least partially replaced by direct contact with the world of concrete realities, could only emerge at a relatively advanced stage. It presupposes a comparatively sophisticated degree of scientific development. Consequently, we can see it beginning to gain ground only in the course of the seventeenth century, and not fully flourishing until the second half of the eighteenth. We shall have occasion at the appropriate moment to investigate the sources which generated it. For the moment we need only note that it was not so self-evident and straightforward that we should be surprised that it did not receive instantaneous recognition. The question which it raises concerns how it finally emerged and not how it could have initially gone unrecognised.

Just as we can see the origin of the enormous importance of dialectic and debate in mediaeval education, so we can now understand why this importance, which was justified at the time, is no longer relevant to today in its original form. This is because we have evolved an awareness of the nature and value of experimental reasoning. Today we know that there is an alternative method of proof, a different mode of argument; and it is now no less essential that we inculcate this mode of argument in our children than it was necessary to teach the scholars of the Middle Ages the art of dialectic. Moreover, the fact that experimental reasoning should have taken the place of dialectic was an entirely natural development inasmuch as the former is itself a sort of dialectic, albeit of an objective kind. Just as dialectic consists in a systematic confrontation of opinions, so experimental reasoning consists in a systematic confrontation of facts.

If dialectic can nowadays no longer preserve all its ancient prestige, if we can see everything that is wrong with it more clearly than in former times, if we have recourse to it and should only have recourse to it with the greatest circumspection, this does not mean that henceforth we can have no further use for it and that we should uproot it and ban it completely from all education. However much progress the experimental sciences may have made they still do not cover and will never cover some more or less substantial portions of reality for the simple reason that they are incapable of exhausting it. In those areas where we cannot employ experimental reasoning we are nevertheless frequently obliged to take some side if only in order to be able to act where action will brook no delay. In order to behave intelligently we must be governed by reasoned reflection directed towards the relevant issues; since scientific reasoning cannot be applied, we must proceed as best we can by means of analogies, comparisons, generalisations, suppositions: in a word, by using dialectic. And since the conclusions which we reach by this kind of reasoning can at best be probable they necessarily raise the possibility of controversy.

Thus if legal, moral and political questions remain within the realm of the debatable this is because the experimental method is only just beginning to be applied to them. This is why, with respect to all subjects of this order, we must be familiar not only with things but also with books. In these controversial areas we cannot see the truth with absolute clarity; we need to meditate, to compare the views of our predecessors and the texts in which they are enshrined. The same is not true of the physical or natural sciences; but can one conceive of an education in philosophy, law, even in sociology which does not include a preliminary study of the most highly regarded thinkers in these fields? In this way we can justify the place accorded to a study of texts in certain of our examinations. To summarise, we may say that although science, as it progresses and arrives at results which are increasingly exact and demonstrable, forces back the frontiers of the controversial, it will nevertheless never be able to drive controversy completely off the surface of the earth. There will always be a place for argument in intellectual life, and for the art of argument in education.

Having described and explained the workings and the organ of academic life in the Middle Ages, we have attempted to reconstruct the nature of this life itself. But all academic life is composed of two different kinds of element: the matter and methods of the curriculum on one hand; the moral discipline, on the other. It remains to us to discuss the latter. The discipline of the Scholastics was no less vigorously attacked by the Renaissance writers than were dialectic and debate. Everyone is familiar with the violent polemics of Rabelais and Montaigne against the colleges of their day, against that 'dump of our college Montaigu', against those 'jails of captive youth', which they depict for us as reverberating with the noise of beatings and the screams of the tortured. On the evidence of these witnesses, a tradition has grown up according to which the Middle Ages was the era in which academic discipline attained its zenith in terms of harshness and even inhumanity. Moreover, it was thought that this barbarity accorded well with the coarseness of the morals of the age as well as with the bitter rigorousness of Scholastic education, which, bristling with philistinism and ignorant of the art of giving pleasure, was consequently better adapted to inculcating revulsion in the pupils rather than instilling enthusiasm in them, and looked as if it could command student attention only by means of brute force and external constraints. The truth is that this tradition is to a large extent based on a legend which it is important to expose.

It is quite true that from the beginning in the little schools where grammar was taught the whip was in use. The grammar teacher was always represented as being armed with rods; it was the symbolic insignia of his function. But he was always the only person who bore this insignia. On the façade of Chartres cathedral the seven liberal arts are represented by allegorical figures: grammar alone carries rods. In these elementary schools there were only children of less than twelve years of age. By contrast, once the schoolchildren had got beyond this age, once they had begun to study the liberal arts, once they had become students in the arts faculty, the discipline imposed upon them was extremely mild. Not until the fifteenth century do we find any trace of corporal punishment. Breaches of University regulations were punished either by excommunication or by straightforward fines. But these regulations did not interfere with the private life of the scholars unless their behaviour disturbed the public peace. A book entitled *De disciplina scolarium*, which has been wrongly attributed to Boethius but which dates from the thirteenth century at the latest, clearly shows the degree of indulgence with which pupils were treated at that time. It is indeed recommended that the teacher be firm (*rigidus*) but at the same time he should be indulgent (*mansuetus*); but it is also stated that he must sometimes know how to put up with *elationem discipulorum*, the arrogance of pupils. A little lower down, mention is made of a teacher who, unable to control his pupils, hanged himself in despair. He would have done better, says the anonymous author, to practise indulgence (*Sapientius egisset si mansuetudine usus fuisset*). It is only around 1450 that we see the University becoming more rigorous and repressive. At this period it was striving to prevent the continual battles which were the scholars' pastime, and which frequently caused the streets to run with blood. For this reason it forbade the bearing of arms on the feast of fools. Anyone who broke this rule was to be publicly flogged in the presence of delegates from the faculty. But it is clear that this was a far from ordinary measure whose very solemnity bears witness to its exceptional character.

From the moment when the colleges and hostels proliferated and the obligation for pupils to reside in them became stricter, the discipline tended to become harsher in the sense that actions which had hitherto been tolerated were henceforth forbidden. But the punishments remained very mild. We still possess the statutes of the college of Harcourt at the time of its foundation in the fourteenth century; punishments were restricted to fines, and for graver offences expulsion (see Bouquet). Several of the statutes only punished the introduction of women of doubtful virtue into the college in the case of a second offence. Frequently fines were replaced merely by an obligation to offer the community a certain number of bottles of wine. The reason for this leniency is that the earliest colleges were still democratically organised. The principal was elected by the scholars and to some extent the whole community had a say in the regulations. Democratic communities never have very harsh disciplinary systems; when both the judge and the judged feel that they are equals the law is mild for everyone, for the simple reason that he who is today judged may tomorrow become the judge, and *vice versa*. In order for the law to take a hard line it must be represented by one or several figures who appear to others and appear to themselves as being superior to the multitude whom they supervise and whose behaviour they judge, and who are not subject in the same way as everybody else to the regulations which it is their function to apply.

It was only in the sixteenth century, at the very moment when the Renaissance was dawning, that the whip became a regular part of college life. It was administered in the great hall in the presence of all the pupils, who had been summoned by the sound of the bell; hence this consecrated phrase used to refer to correction: *habuit aulam*. The expression *habuit dorsum* was also used, an expression which Mathurin Cordier, a writer of the time, comments upon in the following sententious fashion: *Omnino aliud est quam tergum; verum ubi agitur de poena, tergum dici solet*. It is this same *dorsum* which, in a piece of verse by Pierre du Pont, laments the tragedy and injustice of its fate since it is made to expiate all the wrongs committed by the other parts of the body:

Quidquid delirant alii crudeliter artus
Pectimur.

There was only one college in particular where the use of the whip seems to have developed to a quite excessive degree: this was the college de Montaigu, of which Rabelais, Montaigne, Erasmus (who was a pupil there) and Vivès speak with such horror and indignation. On this point all the evidence agrees. This was the field of operation of the celebrated Pierre Tempête, the great 'pupil-flogger' who features in the work of Rabelais. We must avoid the mistake made by the writers of the Renaissance of inordinate generalisation in assuming that what was true of Montaigu, which does indeed seem to have been an exceptional case, was also true of all the other colleges. Indeed this college, which dates from 1314, was at the beginning of the sixteenth century completely reformed by a sort of mystic and ascetic, Jean Slaudonc. As a protest against the excessively easy life which was led by pupils in the other colleges he took it upon himself to introduce an ultra-monastic disciplinary regime. Fasting and abstinence were part of the ordinary routine in this college. The pupils had next to nothing to eat. Their diet consisted of vegetable soup, an egg which was often mouldy, or half a herring, a few boiled potatoes or some prunes, all of it washed down with water from a well. The older pupils were allowed a whole herring or two eggs, a piece of cheese or some fruit, with heavily diluted wine. Meat was unheard of. Thus it was said that at Montaigu everything was 'aigu' ('sharp' or 'bitter'): its name, its domestic atmosphere, and the teeth of its starving pupils (*mens acutus, ingenium acutum, dentes acuti*).

But we know that this was not the case in the other colleges. According to Vivès himself, although one did not exactly find delicacies served in them, the food was adequately nourishing. It is thus reasonable to believe that the excesses in the regime for which this one college was rightly reproached were unique to it. This is proved by the fact that at the same period in the college De Tours, corporal punishment was only administered to pupils under the age of fifteen learning grammar; even then it was carried out with moderation and without brutality as stipulated in the wording of the statute (*modeste et non saeve*).

At all events it is clear that harsh disciplinary measures, the abuses of physical methods of correction, are in no way specifically characteristic of the Middle Ages and are certainly not connected with Scholastic education. On the contrary, the abuses begin to appear when Scholasticism has really begun to decline and the voices of the precursors of the Renaissance are already making themselves heard. One might almost say that they are the product of the modern era. In the thirteenth and fourteenth centuries the young student in the arts faculty, whose age was between twelve and fifteen years, was as Rashdall has said, a sort of gentleman who was subjected to no treatment that would be degrading, and who enjoyed a large degree of liberty that he both used and abused. At the end of the fifteenth century and at the beginning of the sixteenth, he became nothing more than a little schoolboy and he was treated as such. At this period a kind of fall from favour befell the student population: having lived up until that time a life which was similar to that of adults it suddenly had minority status inflicted upon it. The cause of the decline was the institution of the colleges, and in particular the reforms that were carried out in the cloisters erected extra-murally and organised on monastic principles. Once the heads of these establishments, instead of representing the pupils, represented the University; once they had been invested with a new dignity and consequently armed with substantial disciplinary powers; once (from a different point of view) the pupils were cut off and isolated from the outside world, they inevitably become rigidly dependent upon these teachers against whose despotism nothing could protect them any longer. By comparison with these personages of such substantial importance, dignitaries of the University, interpreters of the statutes, the young arts student appeared as a creature of little account; consequently any resistance or rebellion by him took on the appearance of an act of sacrilege and was suppressed accordingly. It was during this period that the transformation with respect to discipline took place. Indeed the new form which the colleges had taken was so profound a causal factor in the change in their style of discipline that, despite the attacks of the humanists, the new order perpetuated itself in varying degrees far beyond Scholasticism, far beyond the Renaissance right up to the end of the *ancien régime*. It took the young several centuries to reverse this process of demotion.

Academic discipline implies a system of rewards no less than a system of punishments. With respect to rewards the discipline of the Scholastics is of particular interest to us today.

We are so accustomed to believing that emulation is the essential motivating force in academic life, that we cannot easily imagine how a school could exist which did not have a carefully worked out system of graduated rewards in order to keep the enthusiasm of the pupils perpetually alive. Good marks, solemn statements of satisfactory performance, distinctions, competition essays, prize-givings: all these seem to us, in differing degrees, the necessary accompaniment to any sound educational system. The system which operated in France, and indeed in Europe, until the sixteenth century was characterised by the surprising fact that there were no rewards at all apart from success in examinations. What is more, any candidate who had assiduously and conscientiously followed the course of studies was certain of success. Of course, the desire to shine in debate had the power of firing the egotism of the pupils; but these jousts were supported by no clearly defined official statutes. The only thing which could be said to resemble official classification of more or less the same kind as those which have become an integral part of our academic mores was the custom of the period whereby the faculty ranked students by order of merit when it came to sending them to the chancellor so that he could solemnly confer on them their licence. As for prize-givings, these do not appear before the end of the sixteenth century. Under François I there came into being an annual ceremony in the course of which a sort of competition took place which was open to all the best pupils; a student cap was awarded to the winner. This still did not constitute a fully-fledged prize-giving in which the whole vast complex of competitions was venerated. But by this period Scholasticism is a thing of the past, and we are in the full flood of the Renaissance.

The experiment carried out in the Middle Ages is of lively topical interest for us today. We are still arguing about whether competitions and tests and periodical formal rewards do or do not constitute an essential part of the driving-force of any academic activity. Now, there existed in the past a system of education which endured several centuries, which excited intellectual life throughout Europe and maintained it at a particularly high level of intensity, and in which, nevertheless, such artificial educational devices were completely unknown. I am fully aware that the complete freedom which the young pupil in the arts faculty originally enjoyed, combined with the total absence of any immediate stimulus, probably had disadvantages. One can well imagine how so liberal a regime, while being excellent for the more intelligent and for young people who genuinely wanted to acquire knowledge, probably put mediocre students at a disadvantage. For since there was nothing to prompt them to react against their own mediocrity they were abandoned to it, and were scarcely capable of benefiting from the teaching that they were receiving, or were thought to be receiving. Also there was a large number of students who were students only in name. This explains why out of the total number of those matriculated only half reached the *baccalaureat*; and out of the total number of bachelors there was again only half who achieved success in higher degrees. The way to remedy such a state of affairs was not to institute a complicated system of rewards which would affect only the good students, since they were the only ones who would gain them. That would have been overstimulating the enthusiasm of the best, not improving the quality of the worst. What was needed was to establish a less relaxed style of discipline, one which was less indulgent towards the faults of young people; and it was this end which the colleges served. It is especially noteworthy that once the colleges had been founded and the pupils were treated as schoolchildren and no longer as students, it didn't occur to anyone to administer to them the luxury of those specious stimulants which are in use in our classrooms. I certainly do not mean that we must rid ourselves completely of all punishments and rewards and abolish at a stroke this whole piece of antique machinery. It cannot be destroyed unless it can be replaced, unless we can find other means of stimulating the enthusiasm of the pupils. But why should we fail where the Middle Ages succeeded? Why should the education that we offer be less capable of arousing and sustaining the interest and curiosity of the pupils than the stringent and crude dialectic of mediaeval Scholasticism?

chapter 14

Conclusions regarding the University

The Renaissance

We have completed the analysis of the educational system which operated in France from the twelfth to the sixteenth century. We are now about to enter a new era. But before we do so it seems worthwhile to return one last time to Scholastic education in order to conclude, by seeing it as a whole and drawing up a balance sheet of pros and cons. What I want to do is to ignore all matters of detail in order to bring out the features of this education which were essential; and then to distinguish those which should be regarded henceforth as organically embedded in our history, those which ought to become a fundamental part of our own national educational system, from those which, by contrast, were destined to disappear or to transform themselves. Since the men of the Renaissance set themselves the task of demolition, of radically revolutionising the work of their predecessors, we shall also need to make a thorough and accurate appraisal of the value of this project; only when we have done this shall we be able to understand and assess the work of those who came after them.

First of all it must be unconditionally admitted that the period we have just been exploring was one which was admirably fertile as far as the organisation of education was concerned. This was, indeed, the period which evolved virtually from scratch the most powerful and comprehensive academic organism which history has ever known. The humble schools of the cathedrals and the abbeys, which could never take in more than a very restricted number of pupils and which were without links with one another, were replaced by the establishment at a fixed point on the European continent of a vast teaching body which was anonymous, impersonal and self-perpetuating. It was comprised of hundreds of teachers and thousands of students, all engaged together in a single enterprise and all bound by the same rules. The organisation of this body was such that it was as far as possible representative of all the branches of human learning. Within this same system there were created organs for secondary education called faculties, which corresponded to the different academic specialisms. In the environment of the places of learning there were founded halls of residence, student hostels and colleges which provided moral shelter for the student population. Degrees were instituted which stratified academic life and mapped out its successive stages; examinations were instituted to control access to these degrees. Courses of study were laid down which clearly set out for the student what knowledge he needed to acquire at each of these stages, and for the teachers the subject-matter to be taught. These are the principal innovations which emerged in the space of two or three centuries.

All of these successive creations were the unique and original achievement of the mediaeval period, that is of this particular mediaeval period. Neither antiquity nor the Carolingian era offered anything on which they could have been modelled. Although all these institutions are closely linked with their origins, with the particular circumstances of mediaeval life, they were at this time, so to speak, struck in bronze, so much so that they have survived intact down to the present day. Of course, we do not interpret them in the same way as did our ancestors; we have animated them with a different spirit, but in their structure they have not substantially changed. A mediaeval student returning among us and hearing talk of universities, faculties, colleges, *the baccalaureat*, the licence, the doctorate, the course of studies, essential lectures and special lectures might well think nothing had changed except that the French words have replaced the Latin words formerly used. Only when he entered our lecture halls or our classrooms would he perceive the changes which have taken place. He would then see that academic life has been transformed; but it continues to flow in the same channels which the Middle Ages carved out for it.

As well as having this durability and resilience which enabled it to withstand the effect of time, this organisation was additionally magnificent in its flexibility. We have already had the opportunity of observing the ease with which in the course of the mediaeval period itself it transformed itself and manifested itself in the greatest variety of forms without, for all that, ever appearing to betray the fundamental principle on which it was based. What tremendous changes took place, took place during the era which spans its beginnings, when it was only a loose association without any official character, without binding statutes, without a fixed domicile, and the moment when it was simply a collection of colleges! And yet these changes took place without any drastic hiatus, without any shaking of the foundations, without any revolution, as the result of a slow process of day-to-day adaptation which responded to new needs in proportion as these made themselves felt.

It demonstrated this flexibility not only in the way in which it evolved through history but also in the way in which it diversified itself geographically. We have been studying it almost exclusively in Paris because it was there that the system was born, and moreover because the University of Paris was the main prototype which other universities strove to imitate. However, it is very striking to observe the extent to which these manifold universities, while reproducing the same essential features and despite being largely copies of the same model, nevertheless differed from one another. There were almost as many types of university as there were places where universities were sited. There were universities which covered the totality of human knowledge and others which were limited to a single specialism (Bologna, Montpellier); and between these two extremes there were all sorts of intermediate gradations. There were some, such as Paris or Oxford, where the faculty of arts played the dominant role; elsewhere it was another faculty which enjoyed supremacy. Paris was a university of teachers whose student population consisted overwhelmingly of relatively young people; Bologna was a university where the student population was composed mainly of adults. There were colleges in Oxford and in Paris, but the Oxford colleges differed from those of Paris.

It is rare to find an institution which is at once so uniform and so diverse; it is recognisable in all the guises which it takes, but in no one place is it identical with what it is in any other. This unity and diversity constitute the final proof of the extent to which the university was the spontaneous product of mediaeval life; for it is only living things which can in this way, while fully retaining their identity, bend and adapt themselves to a whole variety of circumstances and environments. Here, however, we encounter the dark side of the picture. These complex institutions which I have been trying to depict were ultimately founded upon, and derived their unity from, the concept of corporativeness. The University was essentially a corporation and it is with reference to its nature as a corporation that the main features of its organisation are to be explained. Besides, can it not still today be characterised in this way? We know that the mediaeval corporations or guilds, once they had established themselves, very rapidly began to manifest a marked tendency towards traditionalism and intransigence. On the one hand it is in effect harder for a body of individuals to change than it is for individuals acting in isolation, independently of one another; there is something about the sheer bulk of a corporation which aggravates the difficulties of movement and change. Moreover, the aim of the corporation was the exploitation of the monopoly and the elimination of all competition. Consequently, once its exclusive rights were established and uncontested it no longer had any reason to innovate or to change. It had nothing to gain from becoming preoccupied with, and trying to meet, the new needs which were emerging all around it. Isolated on its own, it lost contact with its environment. Because the University was a corporation it was exposed to the same danger. As we shall have more than one occasion to note, the evolution of education always lags very substantially behind the general evolution of society as a whole. We shall encounter new ideas spreading throughout the whole of society without palpably affecting the University corporation, without modifying either its course of study or its methods of teaching. To take just one example: a great scientific movement was to be born in the sixteenth century and to be developed throughout the seventeenth and eighteenth centuries without making the slightest impact on the University before the beginning of the nineteenth.

However, despite this disadvantage, this constitutional deficiency, it is difficult to exaggerate the magnitude of the mediaeval achievement with respect to academic organisation. With respect to curriculum content and teaching methods its contribution was less substantial and, in particular, less original. This is because education can never do more than reflect in miniature the state of human knowledge in each era of history. Now the Middle Ages contributed nothing to the creation of new knowledge; it simply took over what had been achieved by the end of the Roman Empire or rather, since the Romans themselves had not added anything very significant to what the Greeks had achieved, by the end of Greek civilisation. But the Middle Ages saw only one limited aspect of Greek civilisation: its cultivation of logic; and out of this it constructed its entire educational system. Indeed there has never been a time when logic has occupied so exclusive a place in the intellectual education of a people. This accounts for the prestige which was accorded to Aristotle at that time. This prestige did not result from a mere accident, from the fortuitous fact that people did not know the works of Plato, nor is it to be explained in terms of a kind of philistinism which would show that the men of this period were incapable of appreciating the thought or the poetry of Plato. The point is that their attention was focussed elsewhere. Above all they felt the need to subject themselves to a rigorous discipline; and it was not without reason that they turned for this to the works of Aristotle. As for the causes which determined this the absolute pre-eminence of the develop-

ment of the logical faculty, these derive from the most profound
characteristic of the mediaeval mind. The fact is that all intellectual activity in the Middle Ages was directed towards a single goal:
to create a body of knowledge which could serve as a base for faith.
By that I do not mean that theology took upon itself at this period
to become the guardian of philosophy; but rather that faith was
experiencing a need to appeal to reason, while simultaneously
reason had gained in self-confidence and was ready to embark
upon an explanation of faith. How was this science which was felt
so necessary to be constructed? By synthesising observations of
empirical phenomena and interpreting them? We have already
seen that as far as this period was concerned, upon observation
alone no valid argument could be based; and it was therefore
epistemologically worthless. Human experience at that time was
still too brief, too lacking in positive data, for it to be possible to
derive from it any conclusions of significant scope. Reasoning and
reasoning alone was therefore all that remained. It was by the
powers of reasoning that this new science must be constructed
which was destined simultaneously both to strengthen and to
vindicate doctrine. The only way of achieving this was by accustoming people's minds to the art of reasoning, by practising and
exploring all the exercises of which the machinery of logic is
capable. This accounts for the kind of intellectual colour-
blindness which caused the men of the period to see nothing in the
whole of Greek civilisation except this discipline of logic, which
the subtle genius of Greece had developed to a very high degree of
sophistication.

Besides, it was inevitable, given the end to which it was subordinated, that the dialectic of the pagans, once it had been
transported into Christian times, should take on a new character
which it never had or could have had in antiquity. Formerly it was
an entirely worldly activity, a straightforward game played by
sophists, and a method of proceeding with respect to secular
knowledge as Plato and Aristotle conceived it. Now that it was
narrowly linked with doctrine, it shared in the feelings which
doctrine inspired. It was no longer something outside, an alien to
moral and religious education; it was a preparation for this. As a
pre-condition of the highest sanctity it also took on an aura of
sanctity. There has perhaps never been a time when men have
held learning and its moral value in such high esteem. This is what
gave rise to that intellectual enthusiasm which every year resulted
in those enormous migrations of students who, despite the exhausting and dangerous nature of the journey, transported themselves from one point in Europe to another in pursuit of the truth.
Thus if it is true that the Middle Ages borrowed from antiquity the

materials for its education, it nevertheless animated them with a new spirit and in doing so transformed them. When we today examine this training in logic from the outside it appears thoroughly arid, cold and grim; the truth is, however, that for the men of this time it was a part of moral training. There can be no doubt that this view is a far more fruitful one than the contrary doctrine which advocates a more or less complete separation of these two aspects of human life. It is particularly important to realise this because we have arrived at the eve of the period in which this divorce was to take place.

However sublime the mediaeval conception of training in logic may have been, it cannot by itself constitute a complete education of the human mind. A man does not consist simply of pure intellect alone; and in order to educate the whole man it is not enough to engender understanding of how the formal mechanism of human thought is constituted and how it normally works. He must be initiated into an understanding of his human nature in its totality, and, since a man at one time and in one country does not constitute the whole of mankind, he must be shown the multiple and diverse forms which human nature has taken, which have developed in the course of history and which are manifested in the whole variety of arts and literatures, systems of ethics and religions. And since man is only one part of the universe, in order that he should really understand himself he must learn to understand things which are different from himself. Instead of concentrating exclusively on himself he must look around him, he must strive to understand the universe which surrounds him and of which he is an integral part, he must appreciate its richness and complexity which are infinitely too great to be bounded within the narrow confines of pure logic. If then the educational theories of the Middle Ages were grounded in the intellectual needs of the period, it is also clear how one-sided and incomplete they were. It was natural that in view of its vital importance all efforts should be concentrated on this one limited objective at the outset; but it was up to later ages to expand this early ideal, to enrich it with new ingredients in proportion as man's understanding of himself became more and more comprehensive. This was the task which fell to the men of the sixteenth century. We are now in a position to investigate how they interpreted this task and how they acquitted themselves of it.

Educational transformations are always the result and the symptom of the social transformations in terms of which they are to be explained. In order for a people to feel at any particular moment in time the need to change its educational system, it is necessary that new ideas and needs have emerged for which the

former system is no longer adequate. These needs and ideas themselves are not born of nothing; if they are suddenly to come to the
forefront of human consciousness after having been ignored for
centuries, it is necessary that in the intervening period there has
been a change and that it is this change of which they are an expression. Thus in order to understand the educational achievement of the sixteenth century we need as a preliminary to know
what, in a general way, constituted this great social movement
which historians call the Renaissance and whose educational
theory was but one of its manifestations.

The essence of the Renaissance has often been identified with a
return to the spirit of classical times; and indeed this is precisely
the meaning of the word normally used to designate this period of
European history. The sixteenth century is supposed to be a
period when man, abandoning the gloomy ideals of the Middle
Ages, reverted to the gayer and more self-confident view of life
which prevailed in the ancient pagan world. As to the cause of this
change of direction, it allegedly consists in the rediscovery of
classical literature, the principal masterpieces of which were, at
this period, rescued from the oblivion in which they had been
vegetating for centuries. On this view it was the discovery of the
great works of classical literature which brought about this new
change of outlook in the western European mind. But to speak of
the Renaissance in this way is only to point in the most superficial
way to its exterior façade. If it were indeed true that the sixteenth
century simply took up the classical tradition at the point it had
reached when the Dark Ages arrived and temporarily blotted it
from view, the Renaissance would emerge as a movement of
moral and intellectual reaction which would be hard to account
for. We would have to assume that humanity strayed from its
natural path for fifteen centuries, since it had to retrace its steps
back over a period of such length in order to embark afresh upon
a whole new stage in its career. Certainly progress doesn't proceed
in a straight line; it makes turnings and detours; advances are
followed by recessions; but that this kind of aberration should be
prolonged over a period of fifteen hundred years is historically incredible. It is true that this view of the Renaissance accords with
the way in which the eighteenth-century writers spoke of it. But
just because they felt a kind of admiration for the simple life of
primitive societies, are we supposed to say that their social philosophy was an attempt to restore prehistoric civilisation? Because the
men of the revolution thought that they were imitating the actions
of the ancient Romans, are we supposed to view the society which
resulted from the revolution as an imitation of the ancient city?
People involved in action are least well placed to see the causes

which underly their actions; and the way in which they represent to themselves the social movement of which they are a part should always be regarded as suspect, and by no means thought of as having any special claim to credibility.

Besides, it is simply not true that classical literature was unknown during the centuries which we have just been studying, that it was discovered only towards the beginning of the sixteenth century, and that it was this revelation which suddenly expanded the intellectual horizons of Europe. There was not a single period during the whole of the Middle Ages when these literary masterpieces were not known; in every generation we find a few people sufficiently intelligent and sensitive to be able to appreciate their work. Abelard, the hero of dialectic, was at the same time a literary scholar: Virgil, Seneca, Cicero and Ovid were just as familiar to him as were Boethius and Augustine. During the twelfth century there was a famous school at Chartres which, inspired by its founder, Bernard de Chartres, offered a classical education which makes one think of the education which would later be organised by the Jesuits. One could multiply examples of this type. It is true that these attempts to introduce literature into education remained isolated cases; they never succeeded in capturing the imagination of the Scholastics, who cast them back into obscurity. But they are nonetheless real for all that; and they are sufficient to prove that if classical literature was not appreciated in the Middle Ages, if it did not play any part in education, this was not because people did not know of its existence. Briefly, the situation is that the scholars of the Middle Ages knew about all the main aspects of classical civilisation, but only retained what they regarded as important, what answered to their own personal needs. Their entire attention was caught by logic, and this eclipsed everything else. Thus if everything changed in the sixteenth century, if suddenly Greek and Latin art and literature were recognised as being of incomparable educational value, this must clearly have been because at that moment in history, as a consequence of a change which had taken place in the public mind, logic lost its former prestige, whereas, by contrast, for the first time an urgent need was felt for a kind of culture which would be more refined, more elegant, more literary. The taste was not acquired because antiquity had just been discovered; rather people demanded from the classical antiquity which they knew the means of satisfying this new taste which they had just acquired. What we must seek, therefore, is an account of this change of direction in the intellectual and moral outlook of the European peoples, if we wish to understand the nature of the Renaissance in as far as it affected educational thought no less than scientific and literary thought.

Peoples modify their mental outlook to such an enormous extent only when very fundamental features of social life have themselves been modified. We can therefore be certain in advance that the Renaissance derives not, I repeat, from the fortuitous fact that certain classical works were exhumed at this time, but rather from profound changes in the organisation of European societies. I cannot attempt here to paint a complete and detailed picture of the transformation; but I should like, at least, to point out its most important features so that I shall be able to relate the educational movement we shall be exploring to its social roots.

In the first place, there was a whole complex of changes in the economic sphere. People had finally got away from the paltry lifestyle of the Middle Ages, where the general insecurity of relations paralysed the spirit of enterprise, where the limited number of markets stifled great ambition, where only the extreme simplicity of their tastes and needs enabled men to live in harmony with their environment. Gradually order had been established; better government and more efficient administration had rallied confidence. Towns had proliferated and become more populous. Finally and most important of all, the discovery of America and the trade route via the Indies had galvanised economic activity by opening up new worlds in which it could operate. Consequently the general welfare had been increased; vast fortunes had been amassed and the acquisition of wealth stimulated and developed a taste for the easy, elegant life of luxury. Already in the reign of Louis XII internal peace had rendered this movement sufficiently marked to be noticed by observers. One contemporary says: 'Everywhere in the whole kingdom you can see great buildings being erected both public and private which are gilded throughout, not just the flooring and the front walls, but also the window-frames, the roofing, the towers and the exterior decorations; also the houses have the most sumptuous of furnishings that the world has ever known. And people in every walk of life make use of silver table-services of incomparable extravagance, so much so that it has been necessary to correct these excesses by law.' Indeed, several edicts relating to private expenditure on luxuries were promulgated at this period; from 1543 until the time of the 'League', we have records of twelve of them. Naturally, none of these presented measures had any effect other than that of furnishing us with proof of the change which had taken place in people's way of life. The Italian wars contributed substantially to this result. For in Italy luxury had for a long time been carried to a degree of sophistication which was unknown to the people of the north, especially in the great merchant cities such as Venice, Genoa and Florence. Velvets, silks and cloths of gold and silver which were made in Venice and Genoa; the pottery of Bologna, of Castel-Durant and Urbino; the products of the goldsmiths and the jewellers of Florence and Rome; the laces of Venice: all these elegant luxuries made Italy appear as an enchanted world. Once the aristocracy had been transported thither in the reign of Charles VIII, they were completely dazzled; and when they left this magic land they wanted to imitate what they had so much admired. They assembled a higgledy-piggledy army of 'architects, painters, sculptors, scholars as well as perfumers, jewellers, embroiderers, fashion designers, carpenters, gardeners, organ-makers, and alabaster workers'. The expeditions of Louis XII and François I completed the process which those of Charles VIII had begun, and within half a century France had been transformed.

If this transformation had been limited to the world of the aristocracy, it probably would not have had such extensive social consequences. But at the same time one of the effects of increased wealth was to produce a narrowing of the divides between all the social classes. Up till then the *bourgeoisie* had not even dared raise its eyes to look at the aristocracy across what it felt to be a great, fixed gulf. It found it quite natural to lead a quite different existence. But now that the *bourgeoisie* had become richer and consequently more powerful, it also became more ambitious and sought to narrow the gap. Its expectations had increased with its resources, making the life it had led up till then appear intolerable. Consequently it was no longer afraid to cast its gaze upwards and it wanted also to live the life of the noblemen, to imitate their style, their manners, their luxury. As one writer puts it: 'Pride was reaching ever higher peaks in every section of the community. The *bourgeoisie* in the towns have started wanting to dress in the same way as the aristocracy... and the people from the villages in the same way as the *bourgeoisie* in the towns.' According to another author, the *bourgeois* ladies grew bored of their life of obscurity; they now wanted to copy the great ladies. 'One can scarcely distinguish any longer between a noble lady, and a plebeian....One sees women who are worse than plebeian dressing in flowing robes embroidered in gold and silver....Their fingers are loaded with emeralds and other precious stones....In the old days the practice of kissing a lady's hand in greeting was restricted to aristocrats; and noble ladies did not offer their hand to the first comer, let alone to any one at all. Today men smelling of leather rush to kiss the hand of a woman whose escutcheon is exclusively aristocratic. Patrician ladies marry plebeian men, plebeian ladies marry patrician men: thus we are breeding hybrid creatures.' It is easy to guess that so considerable a change in the way in which life was understood would inevitably be accompanied by a change in the way in which education was understood, that instruction designed to produce a good bachelor of arts initiated into all the secrets of syllogism and of argument would be quite unsuited to the enterprise of producing an elegant and fluent nobleman who was capable of holding his own in a salon and who possessed all the social graces.

In addition to this transformation, there was another one which was no less important and which took place directly in the world of ideas.

By the sixteenth century the great nation states of Europe had been in large measure established. Whereas in the Middle Ages there had been but one Europe, one Christendom which was united and homogeneous, there now existed great individual collectivities with their own intellectual and moral characters. England found its identity and its unity with the Tudors, Spain with Ferdinand of Castille and his successors, Germany with the Hapsburgs (albeit more vaguely); and France did so before any of the others under the Capetians. The old unity of Christendom had been shattered for ever. However much people continued to profess respect for the fundamental doctrines, each of the groups which had been formed had its own special mode of thought and feeling, its own national temperament whose particular emphasis tended to affect the system of beliefs which had until that time been accepted by the vast majority of the faithful. Since the great moral forces which had thus been generated could only develop their individual natures, since they could only organise their thoughts and beliefs according to their own likes provided they were granted the right to deviate from accepted beliefs, they claimed this right; and in claiming it they proclaimed it. That is to say, they claimed the rights of schism and of free inquiry — albeit only to a limited extent and not as absolute rights, since such a thing would have been inconceivable at the time. It is here that we find the root cause of the Reformation, that other aspect of the Renaissance which was the natural result of the movement towards individualism and differentiation which was taking place at that time amongst the homogeneous mass of Europe. In one sense Scholasticism had paved the way for it. Scholasticism had taught reason to be more self-confident by confronting it with monumental questions and equipping it with a rigorous logical training so that it might make fresh conquests. However, between the audacities of Scholasticism, especially at the end of the fifteenth century, which were always moderate, between the more or less bold claims made by a few thinkers whose voices were scarcely heard outside the schools, and the sudden explosion which was the Reformation and which shook the whole of Europe, there is clearly a radical break which bears witness of the fact that new forces had come into play.

Thus we have here a new causal factor which was to bring about a change in the theory and practice of education. The Christian faith had played too large a part in mediaeval education for the educational system not to be affected by the variations which that faith was undergoing. Moreover there were ways in which the economic factor exercised a parallel influence. It is clear that the ascetic ideal of the Middle Ages was quite unsuited for pupils who had acquired a taste for luxury and a life of leisure. And since this ascetic ideal was the ideal of Christianity, Christianity itself was affected by the same phenomenon. For it was not possible that the aversion felt henceforth for this view of life should not be extended to the whole system of beliefs upon which this view of life was grounded. If, as we have argued, Christianity was accepted so readily by the barbarians this was precisely because of its starkness, its indifference towards the products of civilisation, its disdain for the joys of existence. But the same reasons which accounted for its triumph then were now to diminish i·; authority over people's minds. Societies which had learned to savour the joy of living could no longer put up with a doctrine which rendered sacrifice, self-denial, abstinence and suffering in general the supreme object of desire. Individuals, sensing that this system ran counter to their deepest feelings and opposed the satisfaction of needs which they regarded as quite natural, could not but be disposed to cast doubt upon it or at least to cast doubt upon the way it had been interpreted up to that time; for it is impossible to accept uncritically, unreservedly and without a reasoned account a doctrine which in certain respects seems to go against nature. Without renouncing it completely people came to feel the need to revise it, to interpret it afresh, in such a way that it would harmonise with the aspirations of the age. Any such revision and reinterpretation presuppose the right to revise, to inspect and to interpret; in sum, the right to examine, which, however one looks at it, implies a diminution of faith.

We can now see more clearly how far the Renaissance was from being merely the result of a few happy discoveries. What distinguishes the Renaissance is a crisis of belief in the history of European societies. The Middle Ages was the period of childhood. Just as the child possesses only enough strength arduously to survive, so the peoples of Europe still had only the necessary resources to cope with the most immediate and pressing requirements of their existence. By contrast, in the sixteenth century they had entered into the fullness of youth. A richer and more abundant blood flowed in their veins; they were possessed of a surplus of vital energy and they sought to make use of it. They could no longer be satisfied with the harsh and precarious existence which had characterised the beginning of their history; the vigour they had accumulated stood in need of wider horizons and larger aspirations, so that it could deploy itself in freedom. The old structures were no longer able to contain this vital exuberance, were no longer able to maintain themselves; and this is why the educational ideal itself was necessarily to be revolutionised. Peoples possessed of all the strength of youth could not be brought up according to the same educational principles and practices as peoples in their infancy who were weak and unsure of the future. It now remains for us to investigate the nature of these transformations.

part two

chapter 15

The Renaissance (I)

Rabelais or the encyclopaedic movement

The principal characteristic of the period that we have just studied is, as we have seen, its admirable richness in matters of academic organisation: it is to that period that we owe the principal organs of our educational system. The contribution of the new epoch which we are now going to enter is of a completely different nature. The Renaissance is the era during which was elaborated the educational ideal by which France lived, to the exclusion of all others, from the sixteenth to the end of the eighteenth century, and which, in more moderate form, still survives today alongside the new kind of academic system which has been struggling for some fifty years to get itself established. It was in schools informed by this ideal that were formed the basic traits of our national mentality as these emerged from the seventeenth century onwards, in other words, of our classical mentality. There is thus no need to point out the interest of the problem. It is the still controversial question of classical education with which we shall be dealing. Only, instead of treating it dialectically and analysing the totally subjective idea that each one of us may have of it, we shall begin by investigating objectively how this system of education was formed, what causes brought it into being, what was its nature, what influence it had on our intellectual evolution, all of which research is indispensable if one is to judge, with a full knowledge of the causes, what it was destined to become in the future.

The ideal whose beginnings we shall be attempting to trace presents itself, from the time of its first appearance in history, in a very definite form which is worthy of note. It is not the continuation and development of the various ideals pursued in preceding centuries, but quite the opposite: from the first it stresses dramatically its antagonism to them. The Renaissance in terms of educational theory marks a hiatus in our mental evolution, a break with the past. In one sense, it is the beginning of something completely new. This is ingeniously expressed by Rabelais in an allegory from Pantagruel. When Gargantua, having been for some time brought up according to the doctrine of the teachers from the Sorbonne, was finally entrusted to the guidance of Panocrates, who to Rabelais represented the spirit of the Renaissance, his new master's first concern was to purge his pupil's mind 'canonically' in order to cleanse him of 'all corruption and perverse habits of the mind'. By this means 'Panocrates made him forget everything he had learned under his former instructors, as did Timothy with his disciples who had been taught by other musicians.' So it was that, according to Rabelais, there was nothing of the former ideal of educational theory worth keeping, that a revolution was necessary, one which would totally destroy the old educational system and put in its place one that was totally new. One cannot build anything until one has cleared a space. One must begin by overthrowing once and for all the worm-eaten structure, and by clearing the ground of its useless ruins. There must remain no trace of Scholasticism in the mind in order that true reason may gain entry. Rabelais was not alone in adopting this intransigent and revolutionary attitude towards Scholastic education. It was that of all the great thinkers of the time. They saw in it a furore of unreason, a plague, a scourge: *'Pestis publica tanta quanta in republica non queat ulla major existere,'* as Erasmus says (a public plague of the worst possible kind that could exist in a state).

This attitude explains an important new development presented by the period which we are entering, by which I mean the appearance of great doctrines of educational theory.

Up till now we have not actually come across any. From the moment when Charlemagne roused studies and schools from the state of semi-inertia in which they were languishing, great changes were certainly brought about, but in a spontaneous and unpremeditated way. They were the product of a movement that was anonymous, impersonal, unaware of the direction which it was following and of the causes which determined it. At no time have we encountered on our way either a Comenius or a Rousseau or a Pestalozzi who, using what knowledge he had, consciously and deliberately undertook the methodical construction of a plan of education, totally or partially different from that which was in operation at the time. The constitution of the University, the function of the colleges, the variations through which passed the ideal of education, all came about of their own accord, so to speak, without any theorist intervening to indicate in advance what path was to be followed and giving reasons for his affirmations and his preferences.

The fact is that all this part of our academic history was merely the very slow, very gradual development of one single idea. We have seen, indeed, how the grammatical formalism of the Carolingian period gradually became the logical formalism of the following epoch that it already contained in origin; how the cathedral school gathered to itself private schools who then united, and how, by progressively tightening the bonds that linked them, they became the University, without there ever having been a sudden shift or change of direction. Such continuous changes, spread over such long periods of time, and consequently fragmented to such a great extent, are naturally imperceptible. Thus all these transformations took place without contemporaries being aware of them. The idea progressed slowly, spontaneously, unconsciously and in awareness of newly emerging needs determined, on a day-to-day basis, the modifications which were immediately necessary. At no point did anyone think of anticipating what was to come, of formulating a general plan, and consequently of directing the course of events. Under such conditions, all educational theory was impossible.

This is no longer the case in the sixteenth century. At this point the academic tradition ceases to develop along the lines followed hitherto; a revolution is in preparation. Instead of the movement continuing to follow, peacefully and silently, the path of the preceding seven centuries, it suddenly branches away in a completely new direction. Under these circumstances it was no longer possible to allow things spontaneously to follow their normal course, since, on the contrary, it was necessary to resist them, to block their path, to make them retrace their steps. It was necessary to set up an opposing force against instinct and acquired habit and this force could only be that of thought. Since the new system to which they aspired could not be brought about simply by a major transformation of the prevailing one, it was obviously necessary to begin by constructing it mentally, in all its aspects, before being able to attempt to make it a reality; and, furthermore, in order to lend to it an authority which would ensure its acceptance by thinking minds, it was not sufficient merely to announce it with enthusiasm: it must be accompanied by proof, that is to say reasons which seemed to justify it. In a word, there had to be established a theory. This is why we suddenly see, in the sixteenth century, the blossoming of a whole literature on educational theory, and this for the first time in our academic history. There is Rabelais, there is Erasmus, there is Ramus, there is Budé, Vivès and Montaigne, to mention only those who are of particular interest to France. To find another example of such abundant production, we have to look ahead to the eighteenth century, in other words, to the period of our second great revolution in educational theory. The appearance of this multitude of doctrines is no coincidence and it was no accident which gave birth at this time to a 'Pléiade' of thinkers. Rather was it the consequence of the violent crisis that our educational system underwent at this time, which awakened thought and created thinkers.

Thus, in combining the history of education in the sixteenth century, we find at our disposal some very precious information which was lacking until now. Up till now, indeed, the immediate object of our research was the academic or educational institutions as they appeared, when they were formed, or at the very least when they had already acquired their first tangible forms, when they were something other than projects, when they had already begun to function in daily life; for it is only at that moment that one can grasp them. As to the movements of ideas, the hopes, the trends, from which these institutions originate and which they interpret, of which they are the visible consequence, these we cannot observe directly, since, for reasons which we have given, all this happened unconsciously, without conscious awareness on the part of the people involved. At these we can only guess retrospectively according to the effects they produced; that is to say, according to the academic institutions and the educational methods which they engendered.

In the sixteenth century, on the other hand, the observer finds himself in very much more favourable conditions. For these mental processes which escaped us until now can now be observed directly, since they are manifestly apparent, on the surface, so to speak, in the writings of the educational theorists. The educational theories, indeed, are nothing more than the expression of the various schools of thought on this matter current in the social milieu where they originate. The educational theorist is a man of broader, more sensitive, more enlightened awareness than average, one to whom the prevalent aspirations come home with greater force and clarity. We can therefore pursue our analysis further than has been possible until now, and beyond the educational institutions and established educational practices; we can penetrate the depths of that state of the social conscience from which everything else derives, and which hitherto has remained hidden. Let us therefore try to explore in this spirit the great Renaissance doctrines of educational theory which have come down to us. It is not a question of studying each one separately, in all the details of its inner workings, and of making thereof a summary monograph; but, on the contrary, of comparing them, of throwing light on one by the study of the others, of seeing the points where they overlap and the points where they diverge. Thus one can sift out the major currents of opinion which they interpret; these are themselves the root of the educational reforms with which we shall subsequently be concerned.

I say 'the major currents of opinion'. This is because the Renaissance was the product of factors too complex for very different schools of thought not to have appeared at the same moment. One can predict in advance that, without being aware of it, people must have been influenced by divergent concepts and trends. There are two in particular to which it seems to us very important to draw attention. Not, indeed, that they are mutually exclusive or radically opposed one to the other; there are points where they overlap; and consequently there is perhaps not a single great Renaissance thinker who did not feel and express both one and the other to some degree. But, on the other hand, they are too different for one mind easily to espouse them both, let alone both to the same degree. Depending on the educational theorist, their personal inclinations and the environment in which they lived, now one and now the other was more strongly felt and was hence given more adequate expression. So it is relatively easy to dissociate the two, even if one investigates their relationship and their points of contact. Of these trends the first is that which is most completely and most powerfully embodied in Rabelais. To define it briefly is not easy, so let us examine closely what it consists in.

The dominant idea in all of Rabelais' works is a horror of everything which means regulation or discipline, or which creates obstacles to the free generation of activity. Everything which hampers, everything which restricts the desires, the needs, the passions of man is an evil. His ideal is a society where nature, liberated from all restraint, can develop in complete freedom. This perfect society is achieved in the famous Abbey of Thélème whose rules are entirely based on this very simple formula: do as you wish. The entire life of the Thelemites, says Rabelais, 'was directed not by laws, statutes or rules, but by their own desires and free-will'. They ate, drank and slept when they liked, how they liked and as much as they liked. There was no outer wall to this monastery, which was built in complete contrast to ordinary ones. No vows, of course, since the aim of vows is to fetter and curb the will. Not even any bells or clocks to divide the day into definite sections or prescribed periods devoted to predetermined occupations. Hours are like limits placed on time; time also must flow easily and freely, without any self-awareness, so to speak. At the root of this entire theory is the fundamental postulate of the whole of Rabelaisian philosophy, that nature is good, completely and without reservation or restriction. Even needs generally regarded as the lowest are no exception; in spite of prejudice, they are good because they are natural. As we see, it is this conviction of the

fundamental goodness of nature which forms the basis of Rabelais'
realism. If this is so, why make rules? To legislate on nature is to
impose limits on it, to restrict it, and, consequently, to mutilate it.
All rules are therefore an evil, since they constitute gratuitous and
irrational destruction.

Underlying this outlook is an impatience with all limitations, all
restrictions, everything which causes hold-ups; and a need for
unlimited space where man can freely develop every aspect of his
nature. We have here the idea that humanity, as formed by traditional education, is stunted, incomplete and diminished, and the
conviction that there lie within us almost unlimited reserves of
unusual energy, which seeks only to burst forth, but which a
deplorable system discourages and represses, when, on the contrary, it should be creating openings by which it can escape and
expand. Over and above the mediocre, narrow and artificial life
led by most of mankind, Rabelais imagines another where all the
forces of our nature would be used without exception, while at the
same time they would have been developed to a degree of which
humanity does not even suspect itself to be capable; and it is that
life which seems to him to be the true life. This is no doubt why the
Rabelaisian ideal is incarnated in giants. It is because giants alone
are capable of achieving it. The giant is the popular concept of the
superman, of the man superior to ordinary men. The important
thing is to go beyond the ordinary human condition. It is
therefore quite natural that this elevated form of humanity should
readily be imagined as being of gigantic shape and proportions.

Let us apply this principle to education; what are the consequences that ensue? Obviously a child must be made to exercise
all the functions of his body and mind without distinction and,
furthermore, each one must be developed to the highest degree of
which it is capable. He must be a stranger to none of the acquisitions of civilisation. Thus first Gargantua, then Pantagruel
become complete men, in whom nothing is lacking; they are
universal men. Physical strength, manual dexterity, artistic ac-
complishments, practical as well as theoretical knowledge of all
kinds; nothing must be omitted; and, in each subject, all sources
of knowledge must be exhausted. Gargantua is not limited to
learning music; he can play every instrument, he knows every
trade, he is acquainted with all forms of industry. As Rabelais says,
he went 'to see the mining of metals, or the casting of artillery;
the work of stone-carvers as well as that of goldsmiths, of cutters
of precious stones, of alchemists, of coiners of money, of
upholsterers, of weavers, of workers in velvet, of watchmakers, of
makers of mirrors, of printers, of organists and of dyers.' He
visited 'the shops of druggists, herbalists, and apothecaries; and

diligently studied fruits, roots, leaves, gums, seeds and grease, as also how they were blended'. He went to see 'the jugglers, tumblers and mountebanks, and considered their movements, their tricks, their somersaults and their smooth talk.' The same excess and abundance is found in all matters of physical education. Games of skill and gymnastics play a large part in his day. He indulges in a veritable orgy of physical exercise. 'Then, changing his clothes, he rode a courser, a cob, a jennet, a barded or trapped steed, then a light fleet horse whereon he went for one handed gallops and whom he made perform the high jump, bound in the air, clear a ditch, leap over a stile and run in a circle both to the right and left. With his strong lance he would force a door, pierce a harness, beat down a tree, and carry away a ring...then he would toss the pike, play with the two-handed sword, with the back sword, with the Spanish tuck, the dagger, the dirk...then he would hunt the hart, the roebuck, the bear, the fallow deer...he would play with a large ball...he would wrestle, run and jump', and so on. No doubt, as Sainte-Beuve says, Rabelais is here having fun. These gigantic fantasies are not, however, mere amusement. All the excess and exuberance of this programme is not due solely to the overflowing of an unbridled imagination; it is closely linked to Rabelais' own concept of man and life, that is to say to the nature of his ideal.

But that with which a teacher must above all concern himself is knowledge. Indeed, according to Rabelais, it is by knowledge and by knowledge alone that man can achieve the full development of his nature; thus it is the *sine qua non* of bliss. All other forms of human activity are merely inferior stages on the path to this supreme state. This is well illustrated in the allegorical story which forms the last pages of the book. Frère Jean des Entommeures, the first Abbot of Thélème, has taken ship along with Panurge and travels through fabulous countries in search of the recipe for happiness. They arrive at a distant island, where there is a strange temple consecrated to the divine bottle; it is of this mystical bottle that our travellers come to enquire the secret of happiness. And thus, questioned by Panurge it replies in one word and one only: 'Drink.' Drink is the intoxication which brings bliss.

There can be no doubt that this reply has an allegorical meaning. It was not to be initiated into the joys of vulgar drunkenness that Panurge made this long journey: for of these joys he had already, by himself, gained quite sufficient experience. Rabelais himself warns us that, in the church of the divine bottle, nothing must be taken literally: everything there is symbolic and has 'mystic reasons'. One is admitted there only if one has given evidence beforehand, by a symbolic action, that one 'despises wine';

only if, in imitation 'of the pontiffs and all people who give and devote themselves to the contemplation of things divine', one has succeeded in keeping one's mind 'free of all confusion of the senses, which is more manifest in drunkenness than in any other condition whatsoever'. The most elevated of thoughts, the highest of moral maxims are engraved on the walls, in order to inspire a suitable state of meditation in the faithful. Finally, and perhaps more significantly, there issues from the divine bottle, not wine, but water, 'good fresh fountain water, clear and silvery'. Thus, as Monsieur Gerhardt very rightly says, 'the drunkenness of which man will experience the delight when he achieves his true end, is nothing other than the delight of the mind, the heroic ecstasy of the mind when it is steeped in truth'. The thirst with which we are dealing here is the unquenchable thirst for knowledge, and it is thus that Bacbuc, the temple's priestess, interprets it: 'For you must know, my friends,' she said to Frère Jean and Panurge, 'that by wine we become divine, nor is there any argument more sure nor means of discovery less fallacious...for it has the power to fill the soul with all truth, all knowledge and philosophy.' And what solemnity there is in her words as she gives to the two friends three bottles of this marvellous water: 'Go, friends, with the protection of that intellectual sphere whose centre is everywhere and whose circumference is nowhere, and which we call God: and, on your return to your own country, may you testify that under the earth lie great treasures and things worthy of admiration...That which you see in the sky and that which the earth reveals to you...cannot be compared to what is hidden under the earth.'

Thus supreme happiness must be sought in that state in which the soul finds itself when it plunges enthusiastically into the river of knowledge. When one has such an elevated idea of knowledge, when one loves it with such absolute, such unbridled passion, it is natural that one should demand that the teacher steep his pupil therein, unsparingly, without moderation or discretion of any kind. Only total command of human knowledge can permit him to satisfy this fundamental need of his nature. He must be taught not selected branches of knowledge, but knowledge in its entirety; he must be initiated into the joys of the drunkenness of knowledge. I have no 'other treasure,' writes Gargantua to Pantagruel, 'than, once in my life, to see you absolute and perfect...in all liberal and noble knowledge. In short, let me see in you a bottomless pit of knowledge.' Already, from the extensiveness of this concept, one has the impression of drawing away from the mediaeval ideal. Yet the Middle Ages too loved knowledge; at that time, perhaps more so than at any other, there was great intellectual enthusiasm. But to complete the picture of where Rabelais

and the new movement which he represented differ, one has but
to examine his concept of this knowledge by which he was so passionately and so desperately smitten.

In the Middle Ages knowledge was reduced to the formal art of
suitably combining the propositions of dialectical syllogisms. For
Rabelais, by contrast, one must first of all know facts, and acquire
positive learning. Pantagruel, if he is to follow the advice of his
father as laid out in the admirable letter in the second book, will
not limit himself to learning arithmetic, geometry, and civil law,
which are still formal disciplines; 'I wish you wholeheartedly to
devote your curiosity...to understanding the facts of nature in such
a way that you will know the fishes of every sea, river and fountain, all the birds of the air, all the trees, bushes and fruits of the
forest, all the grasses of the earth, all the metals hidden in the
depths of the earth, the precious stones of all Eastern and
Southern countries; in short may you remain ignorant of
nothing.' And then, 'by frequent anatomical studies, acquire a
perfect knowledge of the other world which is man'.

Yet natural sciences and the study of external objects do not
constitute, for Rabelais, a complete education; far from it. There
is also the study of languages, and to them, indeed, he expressly
gives first priority. 'I intend and desire that you learn languages
perfectly. First of all Greek, as Quintillian will have it; secondly
Latin; and then Hebrew for the study of the Holy Scriptures; and
then Chaldean and Arabic likewise.' But what is the purpose of
these philological studies? Is it a question of moulding the pupil's
taste, of initiating him into the beauties of classical literature and
of teaching him to imitate them? Such concerns are almost entirely foreign to Rabelais. At most it is as if Gargantua recommends to his son in passing to 'model his style in Greek on Plato,
and in Latin on Cicero'. It is hard to see in this very brief piece of
advice, thrown out as an aside, any great enthusiasm for
literature. But what proves definitely that for Rabelais the educational interest of these studies lies elsewhere is the nature of the
authors whom he particularly recommends for reading. If his goal
had been above all to make his pupil a literary sophisticate he
should have restricted himself to making him study the masterpieces of classical literature. By contrast, we in fact see him constructing his curriculum with a complete disregard for the literary
value of the writers. Gargantua tells us that he takes equal delight
in reading 'Plutarch on morals, the fine dialogues of Plato,
Pausanius on historic buildings, and the *Antiquities* of Atheneus'. It
is a peculiar sort of eclecticism which puts on a par Plato and
Atheneus, Plutarch and Pausanias. In another passage (1, 24), we
see the *Rustics* of Politian, an obscure author of the fifteenth

century set beside the *Works* of Hesiod and the *Georgics* of Virgil. Clearly his favourite authors are not the great writers, the great poets and the great orators but those whose work contains the richest variety of information of all sorts. They are Pliny, Atheneus, Dioscorides, Julius Pollux, Galen, Porphyry, Oppian, and similar writers. Many of these names are only known to scholars. If Virgil is mentioned, it is as the author of the *Georgics* because the *Georgics* contain curious details about the agricultural practices of the ancients. Thus for Rabelais antiquity is not a means of providing an education in the arts, a paradigm of style and literary elegance; rather is it a mine of concrete pieces of knowledge. It is as a man of learning that he appreciates it, and it is as a man of learning that he wishes it to be studied. If he gains knowledge about it, it is because he is curious to know what the ancients thought and said about nature and about themselves, about things and about their own lives; briefly, and reverting to Rabelais' own views, it is because if one does not know this, 'it is a scandal if a person claims to be a scholar'.

Thus everything centres round knowledge. Even literature is only a means of satisfying, of partially appeasing this burning thirst for knowledge which Rabelais feels, and which he would like to communicate to the young by means of education. There are thus, as it were, two sorts of science: on the one hand, direct knowledge about things, about the universe, about nature; on the other, there is the knowledge of men (especially the men of antiquity), of their opinions, of their ethics, of their beliefs, of their customs, of their doctrines. But if for the sake of clarity I have felt it necessary to distinguish these two forms of knowledge in expounding Rabelais' views, it is certain that for Rabelais himself they were not really separable from one another. As far as he was concerned, to know about things was to a large extent to know what the ancients had said about these things.

Certainly it would be inaccurate to say that Rabelais himself lacked a feeling for the real world and for the educational potential which it possessed in its own right; he didn't fail to notice the usefulness of placing the child in direct contact with reality. Some of the lessons which Gargantua receives in some respects resemble what we today would call 'learning from experience'. When he is at table Gargantua is told 'of the virtue, property, effect, and nature of everything that is served: bread, wine, water, salt, various kinds of meat, fish, fruits and herbs'. But the other point of view immediately reappears: for when he is told of these things and their properties it is via the classical texts which deal with them. 'By doing this, there will be learned, in a very short time, all the passages on this subjects in Pliny, Atheneus, Dioscorides, Julius

Pollux, and others'. When he goes for a walk in the country he encounters 'trees and plants', but how does he encounter them?
Rabelais' answer is 'by consulting the books which the ancients
have written about them such as Theophrastus, Dioscorides, Mar-
cinus and Pliny'. When he is playing at dibs with his teacher 'they
go over the passages in the classical authors in which mention is
made of some metaphor taken from this particular game'. Here
we have a feature which is wholly characteristic of the Renaissance
concept of science, even that of men who had the most elevated
ideas about it. The direct, objective study of nature and purely
bookish erudition are inextricably muddled, and it is certainly the
second which constitutes the most important part of knowledge.
What attracts Rabelais and all the men of his day, what they are
burning to know is not so much things in themselves and for
themselves, but rather the texts in which they are spoken of. Between reality and the mind the text intervenes and very often it is
the text which is the immediate object of study and of education.
This is a measure of how difficult it has been for man to rid himself of all intermediaries and to make direct contact and commu-
nion with the universe which surrounds him, and which appears
so close but is in fact so remote.

We can see now the link which binds Rabelais and his age to the
Middle Ages and Scholasticism. In spite of everything the book remains the object of a superstitious cult, albeit one of quite a
different kind; the text remains something sacrosanct. But as
against this, what a transformation, what a revolution has taken
place! Something quite different is being sought for in the book:
beyond the book, behind it, one can just see emerging, however
timidly and uncertainly, the Thing. Up till now European societies
have only known a curriculum which was purely formal; they
have passed from grammatical formalism to dialectical formalism. Here at last there appears for the first time the idea of a new
kind of curriculum whose object will be not to train the mind in
formal intellectual acrobatics, but rather to nourish it, to enrich it,
to give it some substance. Instead of these arguments in which it
exercised itself in the void, in which it could only stretch out
nervously without being able to feed itself, here a rich treasure of
subject-matter is placed within its reach and it is invited to take it
all. Knowledge proper becomes the supreme object worthy of desire;
the price put upon it is so great, so infatuated with it are they, that
people think of it and experience it as some kind of absolute
which is an end in itself. It doesn't even occur to them that it exists
for some purpose extrinsic to itself, that it is a means to an end,
and that it is from the end that it derives its value. On the contrary,
it seems to be something which is intrinsically good in all its forms

and in any degree. What is wanted is not to know what is useful for this purpose or that, for the development of intelligence for example or for the conduct of life; what is desired is knowledge pure and simple, but as much knowledge as is possible. All ignorance is bad; all knowledge is good; even those pieces of knowledge which are totally useless are passionately sought after and joyfully collected. This is why Rabelais is just as interested in the peculiarities of polygraphs, in the most puerile tales of storytellers, in the most insignificant details of mythology as he is in the doctrines of the great philosophers or in the social institutions of the peoples. He knew all the oracles, all the authors, all the prophetic imaginings of the ancient world, all the maenads which surround the chariot of Bacchus. He pays no more attention to the theories of Plato about immortality than to some weird idea of Hippocrates, or some strange problem like that which was propounded by Alexander Aphrodiseus: 'Why does the lion who simply by his roar terrifies all animals himself only fear and revere the white cock?'

It is easy to see how this insatiable thirst for knowledge is but a consequence of the need for infinitude which we have found at the root of Rabelais' thought. Since it is through learning that man most fully realises his own nature, it is natural that intellectual activity, still more than any other kind, should easily become excessive. And this need for infinitude itself is only the translation into the moral order of that feature by which, in the foregoing chapter, we have thought it possible to characterise the Renaissance. The Renaissance, we have argued, is the period when European societies entered into the fullness of youth. It is in the nature of youth to take no notice of any boundaries or limitations. Because it feels within itself a plethora of life which is only seeking an outlet, it thinks that there cannot be too much empty space in front of it in which it can deploy its energy. It aspires to the infinite. The idea that the moment might come when it must stop is intolerable to it and it denies it. It is only with time that man learns the need for boundaries and moderation. It is only by experience that he discovers the impenetrable limitations of his nature and that he learns to respect them. Peoples are subject to this generous illusion of youth no less than individuals, and that helps us to understand Rabelais' educational thought; on this subject he is only the spokesman of his age. Indeed we shall see that these aspirations are by no means peculiar to him, and that the Renaissance strove to realise this unrealisable ideal.

chapter 16

The Renaissance (II)

The Humanist Movement. Erasmus

In the last lecture we singled out one of the two great strains of educational thought which developed during the Renaissance: this is the one which finds its most characteristic expression in the work of Rabelais. What distinguishes him from everyone else is the gigantic nature of the ideal to which he is aspiring. He communicates a lust for life which is both intense and varied, he seems to aspire to a sort of humanity whose powers — all of whose powers — would be developed to a degree which seems inconceivable when we contemplate the spectacle of the average man. It is a question of liberating human nature which an artificial education has confined within narrow limits, and which needs to be extended in all directions. But there is one particular faculty which we must strive to exercise and to exalt above all others because this faculty pre-eminently expresses what we are in ourselves: this is our cognitive faculty, the capacity for knowledge in all its forms. Man does not truly realise his nature unless he extends the empire of his knowledge as far as possible, unless he expands his consciousness so that it embraces the whole universe. He is only truly absolutely happy in that state of exultation whereby the intellect finds itself in possession of the truth; and it is in the delight of intoxication with knowledge that he should seek the supreme state of blessedness. This is a notion, it is true, that we might be tempted at first sight to regard as purely fanciful, a sort of poetic reverie in which Rabelais' imagination took pleasure. But what proves that we are dealing here with something quite different from what a single individual might have made up, is the multiplicity of the men of the Renaissance who yearned for this ideal and who strove to realise it. As we shall shortly be seeing, this was not the only ideal which preoccupied men's minds at that time; but it does hover over the whole era and certainly reflects a major feature of it.

If there was anyone who really lived this ethic and who applied to himself this educational theory, it is Rabelais himself. Far from his having constructed it like some kind of fiction, the theory is but a summary of the education which he had given himself. All the languages which he recommends through the mouth of Gargantua that Pantagruel should study, he knew himself; he was passionate in his erudition, he knew everything there was to know about antiquity down to the smallest detail; he was a doctor, a legal consultant, an archaeologist, a theologian; and, in addition to all this, he was one of the first to attempt anatomical experiments; finally, in the way in which he speaks of the arts of his times, of the various trades, of gymnastics, he clearly shows that none of these techniques was foreign to him. Nor was he the only one to have displayed such prodigious activity. There is Ramus, for example: there is not a single branch of human learning with which he was not only familiar but which he also wrote about with a substantial degree of scholarship. Although an eminent Humanist, he was at the same time a dialectician who ventured to substitute a new form of dialectic for that of Scholasticism. As a grammarian he himself wrote a Latin grammar, a Greek grammar and a French grammar; and his Greek grammar was still being applauded one century later by Lancelot. He undertook to rationalise and reform spelling; he was one of the foremost mathematicians of his time. He wrote about optics and the astronomy of the *scolae physicae*, in which he attempted to replace the abstract speculations of the Middle Ages with a science of nature, even though he was ignorant of the experimental method. He composed a work on military tactics, *De militia Caesaris*, which was regarded as being of major importance for a considerable time. Although he was not a specialist in law and medicine he nevertheless concerned himself with them. Finally, he attempted to reform theology.

But it was above all in Italy that these intellectual giants, these universal men were to be found, who are most characteristic of one aspect of the Renaissance. It is no accident that as early as Dante, he was being called by some a poet, by others a philosopher, by still others a theologian, according to the account given by Boccaccio. Anyone who has read *The Divine Comedy* is bound to agree 'that there is scarcely any object of importance either in the world of bodies or in the world of spirits, into which he has not given us a deeper insight and about which he has not pronounced with a sovereign authority, even when his opinion is summarised in a few words'. Additionally, we know that he was a magnificent draughtsman, that he was a great lover of music; his poem includes comments on the arts of his time which could only have been made by a man of considerable competency. Do we need to mention the names of Pico della Mirandola, of Leonardo da Vinci, of Cellini's father, who was at the same time an architect, a musician, a draughtsman and a poet?

The most remarkable of these genii was Leone-Battista Alberti, who died at the end of the fifteenth century and who appeared to have transformed the Rabelaisian ideal into a literal reality: 'From his childhood Alberti excelled in everything that men admire. Incredible feats of strength and skill are told about him: it is said that he used to jump over people's shoulders with his feet together; that in the cathedral he threw a silver coin right up to the vault of the building; that he made even the wildest of horses shudder and tremble beneath him.' So much for physical strength and manual ability. 'Constrained by need, he studied law for many years until he fell ill with exhaustion; when at an advanced age he realised that his memory had deteriorated but that his capacity for the exact sciences remained intact he devoted himself to physics and mathematics, investigating without prejudice the most diverse of practical methodologies, for he questioned artists, scientists and artisans of every type about their secrets and their experiments.' He built an optical chamber which earned him the admiration of his contemporaries. So much for science. Finally, 'he taught himself music and reached a standard where his work was acknowledged by the professionals...Moreover he engaged in painting and in modelling, and even produced from memory portraits and busts which were striking in their resemblance to their models....Then, in addition, there was his huge literary activity: his writings about art in general furnish the reader with an important source of evidence in the study of form at the time of the Renaissance, especially in the field of architecture. Then there are his Latin prose compositions, his novellas, several of which were mistaken for works of classical antiquity, his delightful table talk, his elegies, his eclogues,...his treatises on ethics, on philosophy, on history, his discourses, his poetry, even a funeral oration in honour of his Duke'. That accounts for the level of his educatedness in matters artistic and literary. Is he not the veritable prototype of Pantagruel and Gargantua?

It is quite certain that the Rabelaisian ideal was also, at least in part, the ideal of its age. The man whom he sought to create by means of education was the man that he himself, along with many of his contemporaries, had sought to be. His work does not, therefore, express a personal point of view but gives voice to one of the major aspirations of his whole century. It was not, however, the only ideal which was seeking recognition at that time. There was another which was simultaneously coming to the fore. Although from certain points of view it is related to the first ideal, it is nevertheless very different from it; it reflects a quite different orientation in the intellectual life of the time. We should not be surprised to find running through one and the same society, at the same moment, divergent and even conflicting currents. Is it not constantly happening that individuals are divided against themselves; that one part of themselves is drawn in one direction whereas all the rest is attracted elsewhere? Now these divergences, contradictions even, are, if anything, perhaps even more common amongst peoples than amongst individuals. They are particularly inevitable during crucial eras of transition; it is therefore quite natural that the sixteenth century was unable to hold consistently to a single philosophy peculiar to itself.

This second tendency which we shall now seek to delineate is the one which finds its most sublime expression in the work of Erasmus, and it is here that we can study it. It is true that Erasmus was not a Frenchman, and that our primary concern here is with education as it was in our own country. But apart from the fact that Erasmus lived in France, most notably during his youth when he was a pupil at the college of Montaigu, it would have been impossible for his influence to have been exercised parochially in some particular country. He was first and foremost a European; his influence was equally great here as in his native country. We can be sure therefore that his beliefs and aspirations with respect to education were also those of French society, that they had their champions in all the great societies of Europe. They are mainly expounded in three consecutive works: *Anti barbaros*, which is a violent diatribe against Scholastic education; *Declamatio de pueris ad virtutem ac litteras statim et liberaliter instituendis, idque protinus a nativitate* (on the need to teach boys virtue and literature right from their birth), and, finally, a treatise *De ratione studii* or 'On the curriculum'.

When one reads the first pages of the *Plan d'études* one might well think that, at first sight, Erasmus is pursuing an ideal identical with that of Rabelais. For Erasmus also lays claim to the same ideal of an understanding of the totality of human knowledge. Indeed Erasmus, in effect, demands also that teachers be polymathic. According to him, they must be knowledgeable about everything (*omnia sciat necesse est*). He adds: 'As far as I am concerned, it is not enough that he be an expert with respect to ten or a dozen authors; rather, I demand that he has investigated the entire orbit of human doctrine, *orbem doctrinae*; I wish that he should be ignorant of nothing even if he is only proposing to teach at an elementary level. He should still have studied everything that writers have had to say about every topic and every specialism; let him read the best, first of all, but let him ignore none of them, even the most mediocre, whose work he has not yet enquired into'. Thus he will study philosophy, preferably via Plato and Aristotle, theology via St Augustine, St John of Chrysostom, St Basil, St Ambrose and St Jerome, mythology at the hands of Homer and Ovid, cosmography (understood as geography) in the writings of Pomponius Mela, Ptolemy and Pliny; additionally, there were astrology, history and the various natural sciences. If his talent is insufficient to bring him to an understanding of all these encyclopaedic branches of knowledge he must at least have a command of what is essential in each of these disciplines (and we know that Erasmus applied to himself the rule of conduct which he prescribed for others). On the face of it, it seems that he was imbued with the same thirst for knowledge, the same enthusiasm for learning, the same craving to understand simply for the sake of understanding, which we have already come across in Rabelais. The truth is, however, that the resemblance between the two doctrines is, at best, superficial, for the sources of their inspiration are entirely different.

In the first place, if the teacher is required to possess this immense breadth of knowledge, it is not so that he can progressively transmit it to his pupils; but rather so that he can to some extent spare him the necessity of it. Erasmus says, 'I fully realise that having enumerated all the branches of knowledge which the teacher needs to be familiar with, you will frown and accuse me of having imposed too heavy a burden upon the schoolteacher; this is fair comment. However if I lay so great a burden on a single man, it is only in order to lighten the load of the great majority. My aim is that a single individual should read everything in order that not everyone should need to read everything'. As for the pupil, he will certainly not need to be familiar with all the authors but only with some of them who have been chosen amongst the best; and the list of these which Erasmus draws up is not particularly long: Lucian, Demosthenes and Herodotus; Aristophanes, Homer and Euripides, — so much for the Greeks: Terence, some of the plays of Plautus, Virgil, Horace, Cicero, Caesar, Sallust — that will do at a pinch as far as Latin writers are concerned. This restraint, this extreme eclecticism in the construction of the academic curriculum, is in marked contrast with the unbridled demands made by Rabelais. Clearly for Erasmus knowledge was not something which was a good thing in its own right, the supreme good in which man should seek to share as far as possible; for if this were the case then there would be no way of exempting the pupil. Instead of being the goal of education knowledge becomes merely a tool in the hands of the teacher, an instrument of which he needs to make use in order to attain the goal after which he ought to be striving. But this goal is located elsewhere. So where is it and in what does it consist?

Most characteristically Erasmus describes this goal in the following terms: *orationis facultatem parare*. It was a question of developing in the child the discursive faculty, the ability to understand a discourse whether it was delivered orally or written down. What he calls *orationis facultas* was not simply the art of developing an idea by the correct use of language; the language had to be elegant, rich, and suitable to the subject-matter. This is the art of intellectual analysis, of organising the elements of thought in the best possible way and above all of rendering the form of its expression ideal; in a word, it is the art of speaking or writing. This is the supreme art for Erasmus, the one which we must inculcate in children before all else. 'There is nothing', he says, 'more magnificent and more worthy to be admired than discourse (*oratio*), which, when it contains a wealth of words and phrases, flows in abundance like a river of gold.' In other words the faculty which we need to practise and to develop before all others is the ability to use words; this is what Erasmus specifically states at the beginning of his *On the Curriculum*: 'Knowledge', he says, 'can take two forms, that of ideas and that of words (*rerum ac verborum*). And it is with words that we must begin (*verborum prior*).' It is true that he adds that ideas have greater value (*rerum potior*), but we shall see later what he means by this; at all events, what is certain is that verbal education, as far as he was concerned, must occupy the whole period of youth. Vivès, who nevertheless takes a more moderate line than Erasmus on this point, considers that up to the age of fifteen education should be restricted to the exclusive study of languages. Language-teaching thus becomes for Erasmus, as well as with Vivès, the principal subject-matter, the main intellectual discipline in education.

Once this goal has been posited — and we shall see later on how it is to be explained — a whole new theory of education ensues.

The only way of teaching the young to write in a style which is both pure and elegant is to immerse them as intimately as possible in the great literary works which can serve as a model to them, and which will develop their taste as a result of constant contact. In the sixteenth century the only languages which met these conditions were the classical languages. Hence the overriding importance attached to Latin and Greek by Erasmus, Vivès and so many others, who saw in these languages the supreme form of intellectual nourishment.

It is very important to realise that this constituted a substantial innovation. Of course, for the Middle Ages too Latin had been the language of academia, perhaps even to a more exclusive degree than in the subsequent period. Indeed the national language was completely banned from the universities and the colleges; the pupils were not even allowed to use it in their private conversations, whereas, by contrast, certain Renaissance educationists allow it to be used even when texts were being expounded. The crucial difference is, however, that it did not occur to the Scholastics to attribute to it any educational value; they used it as a living language which was convenient for use amongst people of widely differing nationalities but which was not fundamentally different from colloquial speech. For them it was quite natural that, like any living language, it should continue to evolve in such a way as to be able to express new ideas and to meet new needs. So they had no inhibitions about deforming it when this was necessary, about introducing neologisms which were more or less barbarous but which in no way shocked them. For Erasmus and Vivès, by contrast, these deformations almost amounted to acts of sacrilege and vandalism. This was because, for them, Latin was not simply a convenient international language. They saw it as a teaching tool of incomparable value. And since Latin owed this role which was thus attributed to it to the fact that it was a literary language, the only language which, on these terms, had the right to appear in classes was that which exemplified this literary characteristic to the highest degree, in other words the Latin of the classical era. This alone could provide the services which were expected of it. Consequently it could certainly not be allowed to mingle with ordinary life and to evolve with it. It must, on the contrary, be extracted from it, rendered immune to change, purified of all the distortions and corruptions which had been introduced into it and maintained in that state of purity and perfection which it had attained around the time of Augustus; congealed in this immutable form was how Latin must henceforth be taught. We are really dealing with a quite different sort of Latin from mediaeval Latin; for the first time Latin entered education as a dead language. Yet it was this dead language which was supposed to provide a model for the intellectual development of living people.

This explains why the pupil does not need to be familiar with all the authors, why a well-constructed anthology is sufficient. The point was that the important thing was not to instil in him a wide and varied range of knowledge, but simply to develop his taste. To achieve this, what is important is not that he should be familiar with a whole host of authors; it is rather that he should be assiduously versed in the best of them, all those who can serve him as a model. They must therefore be selected, and selected with discrimination. The very method of their selection indicates the vast difference which exists between the educational principles of

Erasmus and those of Rabelais. There is no place for those men of erudition, those compilers of pieces of knowledge of every description who were Rabelais' favourite authors: the writers now prescribed for special study are those which are to be recommended because of their literary worth: Virgil, Horace, Homer, Euripides. It is true that the teacher himself must possess greater erudition. But this erudition was not thought to be a good thing for its own sake, possessing some kind of intrinsic value; it was simply that the teacher needed it in order to be able to get his pupils to appreciate the works which he was expounding to them. For in order that they should respond to the literary value of the books they must understand them; and in order that they should be made to understand them it was essential for the teacher to be knowledgeable about the whole of ancient civilisation. If the teacher had to understand mythology this was not because it was conducive to an understanding of how the religions of former times were constructed; it was solely in order to be able to interpret the poets in whose works the myths played such a large part. If he needed to have studied geography it was in order to be able to read the historians; and if he needed to read the historians it was because there are hardly any writers who do not deal at some point with historical events. The same reason determined his need to be familiar with the arts of war and of farming, to know about the culinary arts, the architecture and the music of antiquity. Thus erudition, far from being an end in itself, is pressed into service as a means to another educational end: as an aid to the exposition of literature. Erasmus even goes as far as saying that if we have to study things in nature and their properties this is not in order to understand them but in order to understand the metaphors, comparisons and stylistic figures of every kind which have been drawn from them.

Already we can begin to feel how close this new educational theory is to that which, in a somewhat attenuated form and somewhat adjusted, is still put into practice in our secondary schools. But if we go into detail resemblances are perhaps even more self-evident and important. For the fact is that it was with Erasmus and his contemporaries that the academic exercises appear, some of which still form the basis of our curriculum. First of all there is the exposition of texts from a literary point of view. Instead of the *expositio* of the Scholastics, whose principal object was to reconstruct the logical development of the thought, what is now recommended is a commentary which brings out the aesthetic merits or the literary oddities of the work under examination. The teacher is supposed to bring out the points of stylistic elegance, to point out archaisms or neologisms; he indicates the passages which are obscure or open to criticism; he sets the passage under examination against passages by the same author, or by another who resembles the former. Is this not how our teachers of rhetoric have proceeded for centuries? If the pupil follows the advice of Erasmus he will even note carefully the felicitous turns of phrase, the idioms and the structuring of the passage when these appear particularly worthy of imitation. It is the earliest form of the vocabulary book which the teachers of rhetoric were still using less than twenty years ago. Erasmus even went as far as writing, under the title *Commentarius de verborum copia*, a treatise which is nothing more than a vast vocabulary book for use by future teachers of rhetoric.

In order to learn to write it is not enough to read; one must try to write oneself. The pen, says Erasmus, is the finest teacher of the art of writing. Hence a new type of exercise: the exercise in style, the written composition, which makes its appearance for the first time. Up till now nothing similar had existed. In the university and colleges of the Middle Ages the active work of the pupils was restricted to recitation by rote memory and to debate. Since importance was attached exclusively to the content and not at all to the form, since ideas themselves were believed to flow in the impersonal forms of the syllogism, it could not have occurred to them to institute exercises in style. Everything was transacted orally. We know what progress this new idea made, since very soon it had taken over everywhere, leaving virtually no place for oral exercises. What is still more curious is that, in the overwhelming majority of cases, these exercises had the form which they retained almost until the present day. To say nothing of exercises in translation and in versification, we see the appearance of the composition in the strict sense of that term, of narration, the exposition of some theme in morals, the discourse, the letter. For example: the discourse of Agamemnon to Menelaus in order to persuade him to renounce his quest for vengeance; the discourse of Menelaus to the Trojans to persuade them to give up Helen; the letter by a friend of Cicero's to persuade him to refuse Antony's conditions; and so on. Just as today, the proposed theme had to be accompanied by a more or less substantial body of argument showing how the main ideas could be developed. Erasmus did not invent this kind of exercise all by himself; he borrowed the idea from the rhetoricians of antiquity such as Libanius or Seneca. The sixteenth century roused them from the long slumber in which they had slept so long, infused them with new life, and gave them the form in which they have come down to our own times.

All this is a far cry both from Scholasticism and from Rabelais. For the Middle Ages and for Rabelais it was knowledge which was the supreme tool in education. Certainly, they both had very different ideas about what counted as knowledge. For the Middle Ages it was a tourney, an intellectual fencing match; for Rabelais it was a vast luxurious banquet at which even the most robust appetites could find satisfaction. But for both of them it was the intelligence — whether this was conceived of as a capacity for knowledge, for understanding, for familiarity or for reasoning — which needed to be exercised and developed. For Erasmus it is the art of self-expression, the literary faculty. Of course, he does not completely exclude scientific knowledge but he accords it at best a secondary place; he only mentions it in passing as an accessory to teaching. He does indeed say in a letter to Vivès, that the knowledge of languages is a preparation for higher studies (*graviores disciplinae*). But what do these higher studies boil down to? He dare not completely proscribe reading of the *Organon*; he allows that a pupil who has received a thorough-going literary education might turn to it; but he recommends that he does not dwell on it for too long. Dialectic only interested him in as far as it could be used as an auxiliary to rhetoric. The same goes for mathematics: it is only necessary to have tasted it (*degustate sat erit*). When it comes to physics he is no less mealy-mouthed; he is content that the pupil should have a smattering of knowledge in this field (*nonnullus gustus*). And from the way in which he talks about physics in two of his *Family conversations* it is clear that, as far as he is concerned, this knowledge is of little interest except in so far as it serves to further literary studies. He amuses himself by recounting all sorts of fabulous legends or examining questions such as the following: 'Why is it that the antipodes which are under our feet do not fall into the sky?'

We are thus dealing here with a concept of education which is very different from the one which we have been studying hitherto. What is characteristic about it is the fact that literature is considered in it as the most highly educative of all the disciplines. It is above all in literature that the means of moulding the pupil's mind is sought. How are we to explain then the staggering importance and educational efficacy which was thus attributed to it, and which it has retained in people's opinion for such a long time? One of the causes which generated the great moral and intellectual revolution of the Renaissance was, as we have said, the increase in public wealth and public well-being. A people which grows rich discovers new needs. The luxury which develops renders character more delicate, more gentle and less brutally aggressive. Men give up their crude ways and consequently morals and manners to whose coarseness they had been hitherto insensible become intolerable to them. Then gradually there grows in them a taste for polite society with its elegant rituals, its more delicate pleasures, its more mannered delights. For a polite society is an environment in which the asperity of individual egoism becomes at least cloaked beneath a sort of general mutual sympathy; in which one lives a somewhat imaginary and idealised life remote from the realities of existence from which for a moment one deflects one's gaze, with the result that the mind can refurbish itself and relax.

The evidence of the extent to which Erasmus felt this need is a book which he wrote: *De civilitate morum puerilium*, with the specific aim of teaching politeness to children. He attached so much importance to politeness that he made it one of the indispensable aims of education. It was the first time that the question had been treated methodically and extensively as a special topic in its own right; and this is the proof that the taste for polite society had just been born. On the other hand, the extraordinary success which this little book had shows how general was this tendency at this time and that it answered aspirations of which people were only aware in a confused way. Only two years after the work first appeared in Basle in 1530 it was already being reprinted in London. But it was above all in France that it was appreciated. There it very soon became a standard school textbook. From 1537 onwards translations and imitations follow one another in an unending succession.

Rabelais also shared this sentiment. Why, after all, does he reproach the teachers of the Sorbonne who had originally been entrusted with Gargantua's education? Because they have made a sort of lout out of him, a social ignoramus, who does not know how to take his place in society: 'Although his father realised that he was working very hard at his studies...they were nevertheless doing him no good and the worst of it was that he was becoming a thoroughly clottish, dozy simpleton'. When he is in society 'all he can do is moo like a cow', to 'hide his face under his hat'; one is unable to 'get a single word out of him however hard one tries'. In contrast to this clodhopper, this bumpkin, who is the product of the old education, Rabelais places the sophistication, the perfect decorum, the perfect manners of Eudémon, a young page 'who is so well dressed, so spotlessly turned out, so elegant, so noble in his bearing that he bore more resemblance to a young angel than to a man'. On being invited to greet Gargantua, 'Eudémon..., hat in hand, open-faced, red-lipped, eyes assured, and with his gaze resting on Gargantua with youthful modesty, remained standing and began to praise him and exalt him...with gestures which were so fitting, pronouncing his words with such distinction, in a voice so eloquent and such good and ornate Latin that he resembled rather a Gracchus, a Cicero or an Emilion from times past rather than a youth of this century.' What is the abbey at Thélème if it is not the most polite society, the most elegant and the most refined which has ever been imagined? The happiness which is enjoyed there derives entirely from the delights which different minds experience on encountering one another, in conversing with one another, in holding social intercourse.

What gave flesh to these aspirations, what both gave them direction and intensified them, was the fact that this polite society, the need of which people confusedly felt, did not need to be constructed or imagined from scratch. Henceforth there existed a relatively well-formed example of it before people's very eyes: this was the world of the aristocracy. Indeed, the young knight was brought up quite differently from the young cleric, from the future *bachelier ès arts*. He was not taught dialectic but rather horse-riding, fencing, gymnastics, dancing, singing, music, good manners, deportment, polite speech, and the art of conversation. He was not necessarily taught to write; but he usually knew several foreign languages and all the forms of heroic literature starting with those which antiquity has bequeathed to us. From the Middle Ages onwards, the castles and courts of the nobles constituted centres of elegant life, where the role played by the young was of preponderant importance. Now that, as a result of changes in the distribution of public wealth, the distance between the different classes had diminished, now that the leisured classes felt themselves closer to the nobility, it was quite natural that they should experience a desire to reproduce for themselves, to imitate on their own account this model of refined life which they had admired and envied from afar for centuries without ever dreaming that one day it might be their own.

There can be no doubt that this aristocratic ideal haunted the minds of the educational theorists of the time, or at least of certain from amongst them. It is the polite ways of the courts which Erasmus proposes to popularise in his *De civilitate*; he warns us of this right at the beginning of his treatise. The young Eudémon, this product of the new education, is presented to us as a young page; and the abbey at Thélème is a society, not of noblemen and noblewomen, but one in which intellectual nobility is placed on the same footing as that which depends on birth. It is not too much to say, when one thinks of the role which is played by conversations relating to affairs of the heart, that it is veritably a lovers' court.

How was this desired goal to be reached? How were men to be made to rid themselves of their crudity and their coarseness? How were they to be made to acquire the sophistication of taste and delicacy necessary to this more noble existence to which they ambitiously aspired, unless it was by living in intimate association with those literatures in which the genius of the most literate, the most refined, the most civilised peoples then known to history had found expression, and in which we can still today encounter this genius? Seen from this point of view, it appeared quite natural that the ancients, and particularly their great writers, should be charged with the responsibility for education. This must be our starting-point if we wish to evaluate this educational theory, which we shall be doing in the next chapter.

chapter 17

Educational theory in the sixteenth century

A comparison between the humanist and the scholarly movements

We have successively traced the two great educational movements which emerged in the sixteenth century. The first, represented by Rabelais, is characterised by a need to extend human nature in every direction but also and above all by an inordinate taste for erudition, by a thirst for knowledge which nothing can slake. The second movement, exemplified by Erasmus, lacks this scope and is not possessed of such lofty ambitions: on the contrary it reduces the whole principle of human culture to literary culture alone, and it makes the study of classical antiquity virtually the sole instrument of this culture. The art of speaking and writing here occupies the place reserved for knowledge in Rabelais' educational thought. The essential goal of education was to be to train the pupil to appreciate the masterpieces of Greece and Rome and to imitate them intelligently. Thus the educational formalism, from which we seem about to be delivered with Rabelais and the great men of learning of the sixteenth century, with Erasmus reasserts its dominion over us in a new form. The grammatical formalism of the Carolingian era and the dialectical formalism of Scholasticism are now followed by a new kind of formalism: a literary formalism.

Having thus characterised this second movement we needed to try to explain it. The question is all the more important because there are clear connections between these educational viewpoints, in appearance so far removed from one another, and those which still today form the basis of our classical education. It is thus of the greatest interest to know whence they derived and what needs they met.

At precisely the same moment as these new educational tendencies appear, there occurred a change in manners the importance of which it is hard to exaggerate: this was the development of polite society. It is true, as we have said, that the world of the aristocracy, the world of the *châteaux*, had always constituted a special environment in which, predominantly under the influence of women, morals and manners were stamped with an elegance and a courtliness which was not to be found elsewhere. But in the sixteenth century this need for sophistication and refinement, this taste for the more delicate pleasures of society, became simultaneously more intense and more generalised. In the book *Les Moeurs polies et la littérature de cour sous Henri II* by M. Bourciez, we can read how at this period the tourneys, the great horse races, the long hunts, which had furnished diversion for the chivalric orders in time of peace, were succeeded by the clubs and the salons in which the principal role was again played by women.

The intensity of this need is proved by the fact that when the means of its satisfaction through normal channels was absent great ingenuity was devoted to artificial substitutes. The literate population, which was dispersed all over the surface of Europe and which could not hold intercourse by means of the spoken word, substituted for the pleasures of conversation those of correspondence. Being unable to talk, they wrote to one another. At this period epistolary literature developed and grew in importance to a quite exceptional extent. Petrarch tells us that he had spent a good part of his life writing letters. These letters were not mere common-or-garden communications like those which we write today, and whose aim is to give information to someone absent about what we are doing and what is happening to us. They were literary pieces in which subjects of general interest, literary and moral problems, were dealt with just as they might have been dealt with in a salon. Besides, they were not addressed to a single recipient but, at least in the form of copies, were circulated from one person to another. The company of the literate in Europe thus formed a kind of society of intellectuals which, despite being scattered to all points of the Continent, from Naples to Rotterdam, from Paris to Leipzig, was not lacking in unity thanks to the great trouble to which its members went in order to keep in touch with one another, and to maintain intercourse in spite of the distances which separated them.

It is clear that there was nothing in Scholasticism which could have satisfied these new tastes: on the contrary, it was bound to be repugnant to them. Since it attached no importance to form, it did not hesitate to twist language savagely to satisfy all the needs of thought without regard to considerations of purity or harmony. As a result of the very great place which it accorded to debate it developed a taste not for ideas which were delicate, subtle or measured, but rather for opinions which were dogmatic, clear-cut, and whose features stood out in such a way that conflicting opinions could be clearly contrasted. Moreover, the violent arguments which were born of such polarisations could only encourage a coarseness in manners similar to that which tourneys and other such practices had for so long fostered among the knights of the nobility. The student of the Middle Ages was primarily concerned with crushing his opponent beneath the weight of his arguments, and did not care in the least whether his presentation was attractive. His unkempt and rustic deportment and manners were an expression of this same state of mind.

Here we have the reason why the men of the new generation were quite literally horrified by Scholasticism and its methods. The virulence of their polemics at first sight seemed, in its extremeness, to be out of place in a purely educational quarrel. But the fact is that the issue was really more wide-ranging. The sixteenth century did not simply accuse Scholasticism of having engaged in certain debatable or regrettable academic practices, but rather of having constituted a school of barbarousness and coarseness. Hence the frequency with which the words *barbarus*, *stoliditas*, *rusticitas*, recur in the writings of Erasmus. To these refined minds a Scholastic is quite literally a barbarian (remember the title of Erasmus' book *Antibarbaros*), who speaks a language which is scarcely human, crude-sounding, formally inelegant, delighting only in arguments, in deafening yells, in verbal and other battles; ignorant, in sum, of all the benefits of civilisation, of everything which contributes to the charm of life. We can readily conceive of the feeling which such an educational system would be capable of arousing amongst men whose aim was to render humanity more tender, more elegant, more cultivated.

The only way in which this goal of ridding the human intellect of its coarseness, of polishing it, of refining it, could be attained was by introducing it to, and placing it in a relationship of intimacy with, an elegant and refined civilisation, so that it might become imbued with this spirit. The only civilisation which at that period could satisfy this condition was that of the classical peoples as it had been expressed and preserved in the works of their great writers, poets and orators. It was thus quite natural that these should be seen as providing the schoolteachers needed by the young. 'What then,' says Erasmus, 'what then could have guided these coarse men of the Stone Age towards a more human life, towards being more gentle of character and more civilised in morals? Was it not literature? It is literature which moulds the mind, which mollifies passions, which checks the untamed outbursts of natural temperament.' For this purpose there existed no other established and developed literature apart from those of Rome and Greece.

With this in view, the moral environment in which the child was to be moulded had to be made up of all the extant elements of these literatures. Hence the enormous attention accorded by the public at this time to the masterpieces of Greco-Latin civilisation. If people esteemed and admired them, if they sought to imitate them, this was not because they were exhumed at this moment in history and, by being discovered, suddenly inculcated in people a taste for literature. Quite the reverse: it was because a taste for literature, a new kind of civilisation, had just been acquired that they suddenly became objects of enthusiastic veneration; for they appeared, and quite rightly so, as the only means available of satisfying this new need. If this vast body of literature had been hitherto neglected this was not because nothing was known of it (we have already seen that the major works were known), but rather its virtues were not appreciated because they did not meet any contemporary need. If, by contrast, they were now regarded in the eyes of public opinion, or at least of a certain section of it, as being of incomparable value, this was because a new attitude of mind was in the process of developing and could only be fully realised in the school of the classics.

One may even wonder whether the greater frequency of the finds and exhumations which occurred at this period was not a result of the fact that since, henceforth, the value of these discoveries was fully appreciated people devoted more of their ingenuity to the making of them. To find one must seek, and one only seeks in earnest when one attaches importance to what one hopes to find.

Thus the educational ideas of the Humanists were not the result of simple accidents; they derived rather from a fact whose influence on the moral history of our country it is difficult to exaggerate; I refer to the establishment of polite society. If France did indeed become from the sixteenth century onwards a centre of literary life and intellectual activity this was because, at this same period, there had developed amongst us a select society, a society of intellectually cultivated people to whom our writers addressed themselves. It was the ideas and the tastes of this society which they communicated, and it was for this society that they wrote and for it that they thought. It was here in this particular environment that the driving force of our civilisation from the sixteenth century to the middle of the eighteenth century was generated. The object of education as Erasmus conceived of it was to prepare men for this special and restricted society.

Here too we can see the essential character and at the same time the radical flaw of this educational theory. It is essentially aristocratic in nature. The kind of society which it seeks to fashion is always centred around a court, and its members are always drawn from the ranks of the aristocracy or at least from the leisured classes. And it was indeed here and here alone that the fine flowering of elegance and culture could take place, the nurturing and development of which was regarded as more important than anything else. Neither Erasmus nor Vivès had any awareness that beyond this small world, which for all its brilliance was very limited, there were vast masses who should not have been neglected, and for whom education should have raised their intellectual and moral standards and improved their material condition.

When such a thought does occur to them it disappears again very quickly without their thinking it is necessary to examine it at length. Since he realises that this expensive education is not suitable for everyone Erasmus wonders what the poor will do; the answer which he gives to this objection is utterly simple: 'You ask,' he says, 'what the poor will be able to do. How will those who can scarcely feed their children be able to give them over a sustained period of time the right kind of education? To this I can only reply by quoting the words of the comic writer: "You can't ask that what we are capable of achieving should be as great as what we would like to achieve". We are expounding the best way of bringing up a child, we cannot produce the means of realising this ideal.' He restricts himself to expressing the wish that the rich will come to the help of those who are well-endowed intellectually but who would be prevented by poverty from developing their aptitudes. He does not even seem to realise that even if this education was made available to everybody the difficulty would not be resolved; for this generalised education would not meet the needs of the majority. For the majority the supreme need is survival; and what is needed in order to survive is not the art of subtle speech, it is the art of sound thinking so that one knows how to act. In order to struggle effectively in the world of persons and the world of things, more substantial weapons are needed than those glittering decorations with which the Humanist educationalists were concerned to adorn the mind to the exclusion of anything else.

Think now how much more Scholasticism, for all its abstractness, was imbued with a more practical, more realistic and more social spirit. The fact is that dialectic answered real needs. Intellectual conflict and competition between ideas constitutes a genuinely important part of life. The strength and virility which was acquired by thought as a result of such arduous gymnastics were capable of being used in the service of socially useful ends. Thus we must beware of thinking that the mediaeval schools served only to produce dreamers, seekers after quintessences, and useless pettifogging quibblers. The truth is quite the opposite. It was there that the statesmen, the ecclesiastical dignitaries, and the administrators of the day were brought up. This training which has been so denigrated created men of action. It was the education recommended by Erasmus which forms a totally inadequate preparation for life. Rhetoric supplants dialectic. Now, if rhetoric had good reason for featuring in the education of the classical world, where the practice of eloquence constituted not only a career but the most important career, this was by no means the case in the sixteenth century when it played only a very small part in the serious business of life. A theory of education which made rhetoric the principal academic discipline could thus only develop qualities related to the luxuries of existence and not at all to its necessities.

This initial fault implies another. If this education is an education for a life of luxury, this is because it cultivates only literary and aesthetic qualities. Any culture which is exclusively or essentially aesthetic contains within itself a germ of immorality, or at least of inferior morality. Indeed, art by definition moves in the realm of the unreal and the imaginary. Even when the subjects represented by the artist are borrowed from reality, it is not the reality which is the cause of their beauty. It matters little to me whether the character whom the poet brings to life in his verses actually existed historically; my admiration for him is occasioned by his beauty, and it would be in no wise diminished if he had been entirely a product of the artist's imagination. Indeed, when the illusion is too thoroughly effective and causes us to see the scene being portrayed to us as being real, the pleasure of beauty vanishes. We can appreciate it only when we are aware that the events which we are witnessing are incapable truly of affecting the fate of human beings, of causing suffering to people like ourselves, whether physical or spiritual; if we can see the things described to us in a quite different light to that in which they appear to us in real life. In brief, we can only fully succumb to the aesthetic experience if we lose sight of reality.

Ethics, by contrast, operate in the realm of action, which either gets to grips with real objects or else loses itself in the void. To act morally is to do good to creatures of flesh and blood, to change some feature of reality. In order to experience the need to change it, to transform it and to improve it, it is necessary not to abstract oneself from it; one must rather stay with it and love it despite its ugliness, its pettiness and its meanness. One must not avert one's gaze from it in order to contemplate an imaginary world, but on the contrary keep one's gaze directed steadily towards it. This is why a culture which concentrates to an excessive extent on aesthetic values tends to create slackness in the moral sphere, because it turns us away from the real world. It is not by collating ideas or harmoniously manipulating phrases, sounds or colours, that we learn how to do our duty. In this respect the evil of which art is capable is exaggerated by its capacity for disguising its own inadequacies even from itself. For it may choose as the subject-matter of its creations morality itself, and by presenting us with an idealised portrait of moral sublimeness it causes us to live in imagination a life which possesses the external appearances of the truly moral life, the only difference being that in this case it is entirely fictitious. We are only too willing to take seriously this simple trick of the mind. People are quite ready to believe themselves pious because they are capable of praising piety in an eloquent way or because they enjoy hearing it praised in this way; they think they are men of high principles because they know how to talk about moral principles in the appropriate fashion or because they appreciate well-conducted arguments of which they form the subject-matter. There is no need to spell out the falsity of this belief. For true virtue is essentially a matter of acting and behaving in such a way that one externalises some inner part of oneself; and it has nothing to do with the silent intellectual construction and the private contemplation of noble spectacles and moving characters. Virtue as it is exemplified in the most literate people exists only too often in the imagination alone.

If this flaw is inherent in any culture which is exclusively literary and aesthetic, there was in the particular culture whose specifications were drawn up by the sixteenth-century Humanists a special element which aggravated the danger of the situation. What, after all, did the education which it generated consist in? Presenting the child with classical civilisation not just so that he could familiarise himself with it as a scholar and understand how it was constituted, but so that he could become saturated by it, so that he could 'imbibe its spirit', as Montaigne was later to say, since it was this which was to serve to mould him. He had to experience this civilisation as if it were his own and since the principal exercises consisted, as it were, in causing the ancients to speak again, he needed himself to assimilate their way of thinking. Is there not something truly monstrous from a historical and educational point of view about trying to mould a sixteenth-century man in the image of a civilisation which had reached its zenith fifteen centuries earlier? Are we then to explain the morality which the sixteenth century sought to embody, that which was best adapted to its real needs, as really nothing more than pagan ethics restored and revitalised? In that case we should have to regard Christianity as a sort of historical side-dash, a detour pursued by humanity laboriously but fruitlessly, since it finally led back to the original point of departure. There is no need to demonstrate the complete untenability of this thesis. The truth is that the long process of evolution which had been taking place from the end of the Roman Empire throughout the whole of the Middle Ages had finally resulted in the elucidation of a certain number of moral beliefs, which had been hitherto unknown and which for all that they themselves were destined to evolve and to be transformed (for there is nothing immutable even in ethics) could nevertheless now be regarded as an established feature of human nature. Amongst these the principal one, and the one which can be regarded as the most characteristic of this new ethic which became part of our cultural heritage, has to do with the concept of duty.

This concept was unknown to the moralists of Greece and Rome or, at any rate, they only had a very vague and flimsy notion of it; for there is no term or locution either in Greek or in Latin which corresponds to the concept of duty. They conceived of morality not as a categorical law which commands and which must be obeyed simply because it does command, but rather as a seductive ideal which is inherently attractive and which spontaneously gives direction to the will of anyone who has managed to see it clearly. For them the problem of morality presented itself in the following terms: what is the sovereign good, the object supremely worthy to be desired? They had different ideas about where the road to happiness lay; but they conceived of virtue as being inseparable from a state of blessedness. This is why all their doctrines, even the most sublime, even those of the Stoics, were derived from the eudaemonic ethics which they were never able to shake off.

In this respect they provide the most marked contrast with the ethic which was born of Christianity, but which was destined to survive its progenitor, according to which all considerations of personal happiness were banished from the whole moral sphere, as they could only serve to corrode and diminish the moral value of our actions. The ideal of the Christian way of life is to do one's duty because it is one's duty, to obey the rules because they are the rules; it depends on the idea of man rising above his nature and freeing himself from it by taming it and subjecting it to the spiritual laws whose object is, in a word, sanctity. By contrast, the ideal of antiquity is harmony with nature; nature is regarded as the source of information about the laws of human life. *Sequere naturam: zēn homologoumenōs tē phusei*, Stoics and Epicureans are agreed in making of this principle the foundation of their systems.

If it is true that throughout the unsophisticated period of the Middle Ages the Christian ideal was excessively possessed by a spirit of harsh asceticism, and if it can be justly accused of having carried too far its contempt for the flesh and the senses; if, to say the least of it, this lack of sophistication became redundant now that times themselves had become less hard, it is nevertheless equally clear that our modern secular morality, by becoming more humane, more gentle and less austere towards men in their frailty and wretchedness, was and is in no wise inescapably obliged to sell short this lofty ideal. For us too, morality only has a purchase in the domain of striving, struggle, sacrifice and unselfishness. For us too, the moral life is not simply a matter of embarking upon the easy downward slope which is empirically prescribed for us by our physical nature: it is rather a question of building with our own hands upon this foundation a natural structure which is more special and more sublime, which is truly and uniquely characteristic of humanity, which is entirely spiritual, which we alone are capable of creating but whose laborious construction is so arduous that it would never even have been attempted, had we not felt morally and socially obliged to undertake it.

We have here two quite different and even mutually contradictory moral systems. It follows that by making the child live in an environment which was saturated with classical education and which was the inevitable product of the academic organisations described by Erasmus, the only result could be a troubling of the child's moral consciousness. He was bound to emerge as a moral hybrid, divided against himself, torn between the present and the past and enfeebled by the conflict. This was precisely what had been intuitively foreseen more or less clearly by the doctors of the Church who denounced the dangers of an education which was exclusively pagan. Allowed to grow side by side in the hearts of the pupils, these conflicting views of life could serve only to debilitate each other and to leave the moral agent in a state of veritable disarray.

Indeed it is beyond dispute that at this period we can see a kind of general enfeeblement of moral feeling. I will only adduce one piece of evidence which can be closely derived from the aesthetic nature of education. What provided the main driving force of the Humanists? What drove them to read, to learn, and to create? Was it patriotism or a love of humanity, or a feeling that man has a duty to cultivate his intellect? Was it some generous enthusiasm? Absolutely not. Their motive was an entirely pagan one, one which had been all-powerful in classical culture but which was wholly amoral and whose overwhelming influence Christianity consequently strove to diminish: for them the supreme goal was to possess a name which was upon everybody's lips. Already in Petrarch we find the admission that it is a thirst for glory which has driven him out of the family nest and prompted him to seek success in a literary career:

Implumem tepido praeceps me gloria nido
Expulit et coelo jussit volitare remoto;

and after he has been crowned as the prince of poets he glories in his fame:

est mihi fama
Immortalis honos et gloria sueta laborum.

Similarly, in the preface to the *Antibarbaros*, Erasmus records his veneration for all those who have succeeded in making a name for themselves in literature: *Qui in his (litteris) aliquid opinionis sibi parassent, eos ceu numina quaedam venerabar ac suspiciebam.* He regarded them as gods and it was his dream to follow in their footsteps. Such illustriousness alone, he thought, could compensate for and explain the labours which the writer was forced to take upon himself (*Quis tantas tamque diuturnas vigilias adiret, si nihil magni sibi promitteret*). This passion was even more so intense, and at the same time so alien to all moral considerations, that on occasion it led to the most heinous of acts, 'More than once,' says Burckhardt, 'when they are recounting some terrible enterprise, serious historians pick out as the motive a burning desire to do something memorable.' This was the case with Lorenzino di Medici who, when pilloried in a pamphlet by Molza for having mutilated certain ancient statutes in Rome, resolved to eradicate the memory of this defamatory chastisement by performing some dazzling deed which would perpetuate his name for ever, and so he assassinated his relative and his sovereign. The same historian cites several examples of the same kind.

I have thought it necessary to stress this feature of morality not just because it illuminates and throws into vivid relief the spirit of the age, but also because it had an important and direct repercussion in educational thought. School life cannot differ in its nature from the life of adults, of which it must always be a miniature version; consequently the motive of action, the mainspring of human conduct, cannot be different in the one case and the other. If it was a thirst for glory which generated action amongst men, it was bound to seem natural to have recourse to this same source of motivation in order to generate activity amongst children. This in effect is what Erasmus recommends. He postulates a discipline which is in sharp contrast to that of the Scholastic schools and which was supposed to appeal solely to the child's self-esteem, to his sense of honour, to his taste for praise. 'The philosopher Lycon,' he says, 'believes that there are two powerful ways of generating activity amongst children: appealing to their sense of honour and appealing to their love of praise . . . praise is the mother of all the arts. Let us therefore make use of these two goads.' Since praise is only valuable when it is comparative one must not shrink from differentiating, from graduating it, so that it will engender a desire to emulate. The teacher must 'by comparing the progress made by different pupils provoke or excite them to a certain spirit of rivalry (*aemulatione quadam inter eos excitata*). It is even a good idea to translate praise into material and tangible forms by means of prizes which are promised in advance to successful competitors (*praepositis praemiolis*).' Here we see the emergence of the system of prizes, of competitions, of discipline based on the spirit of emulation which was, as we have seen, unknown in the Middle Ages. It has been important to note its appearance, while at the same time specifying the social and moral conditions of which this system was an integral part.

Set beside this literary and aristocratic view of education, Rabelais' doctrine seems to be inspired by a breath of morality which is altogether more sublime and powerful. The humanist, the man of letters, thinks of little else other than being brilliant, being attractive, having his talents enjoyed and admired. He rarely loses sight of himself. Before all else he is athirst for praise, and the love of praise is a narrowly egotistical sentiment. How much more generous is the thirst for knowledge which Rabelais feels and which he wishes to awaken in his pupils! The absolute polymathy whose realisation is the ultimate goal constitutes a sublime ideal which no one can attain and which, since it hovers far above them, forces men to look further and higher than themselves. In his pursuit of knowledge the scholar becomes absorbed to the point where he completely forgets himself. Is it not this complete self-forgetfulness, this estrangement from one's own personality, which is symbolised by the mystical intoxication which for Rabelais constitutes the supreme state of blessedness? Besides, in order to succeed in understanding things one must necessarily step outside oneself and out of the internal world of images in which the pure man of letters delights; it is necessary to make contact with the real world which surrounds us, and to live in it on terms of intimate familiarity; one must thus be enthusiastic about it, one must love it and love it in its entirety, despising no part of it. We must remain indifferent to nothing which is contained within it. Remember Gargantua's exhortation to his son Pantagruel: 'Let there be neither sea nor stream nor fountain with whose fish you are not familiar . . .. Let there be nothing, neither all the birds in the air, all the trees, bushes and fruitful shrubs of the forests, all the plants of the earth, nothing of which you are ignorant.' By the very fact that in this way man gains a more accurate idea, forms a more precise conception of what the universe is, he also realises better the place which he occupies within it; by comparing himself with the immense universe surrounding him he understands that he is not the whole of it but only a small part. He no longer runs the risk of thinking of himself as the centre to which everything must be related; rather he perceives that he belongs to a system which goes infinitely beyond him and which has its centre outside him.

Is it not this the sentiment expressed by Rabelais in a celebrated passage which Pascal, as we know, was to pick up again later, and which confronts man with the infinite, with 'that intellectual sphere whose centre is everywhere and whose circumference is nowhere'? Does this not also explain the significance of the endless invocations which one is constantly surprised to encounter in this humorous and apparently licentious novel? 'May God grant,' says one of his heroes somewhere, 'that we may never do anything before we have first praised His most sacred name.' This piety is evident in every possible form. Now it is the simple gratitude of the stomach: 'Undoubtedly we should praise Almighty God, our creator, who serves and sustains us and who by means of this good bread, this good cool wine and all this good meat cures us of all perturbation, whether of the body or of the soul, with the exception of the pleasure and delight which we derive from drinking and eating.' Now it is a sense of the greatness and the omnipotence of God which finds expression in terms of sublime eloquence: 'Devote your whole mind to God,' says Pantagruel to a prisoner-of-war whom he is setting free, 'and he will not desert you. For even myself, although I am powerful as you can see . . . I do not base my hopes on my own strength or on my own diligence, rather is all my trust in God, my protector, who never deserts those who let their hopes and their thoughts dwell in him . . .. Go in the peace of the living God.' It does not, I believe, detract from the passages from Rabelais, to say that for him God is nothing other than a name given to nature in its immensity and infinitude, to nature as something pure and good which nourishes us and upon which we depend. Does he not go so far as to have the priestess Bacbuc say that this immense sphere whose centre is everywhere and whose circumference is nowhere is what we call God? This piety, this sense of the greatness of the divinity, is only another manifestation of the sense of dependency with which we are inspired when we compare ourselves to the whole great universe which surrounds us, which envelops us, which dominates us, but which at the same time provides the source and sustenance of our lives.

Here we are indubitably far removed from the frivolous vanity of the Humanist, who is wholly preoccupied with being attractive and getting himself applauded. The sense of moral dependence, in whatever form it expresses itself in our consciousness, provides a solid bastion against egotism. And yet, because Rabelais belongs to the sixteenth century, we find in his work, albeit in a more veiled form, certain of the tendencies which we have encountered in Erasmus. However great the contrast may be from certain points of view between this educational system and that of the pure men of letters, there are nevertheless similarities between them of which it is important to take cognisance for they clearly derive not from the attitude of mind of one particular individual or another but rather from the very spirit of the sixteenth century, and consequently they will help us to understand it better.

chapter 18

The educational thought of the Renaissance

At the end of the last chapter we began to compare the two great educational movements of the sixteenth century. They are to be contrasted not only because of the fact that the one accords to knowledge and learning a place which the other reserves almost exclusively for literature; the moral inspiration from which they issue is also quite different. Their different ways of approaching the education of the intellect help us to understand their conceptions of moral education. A scientific education, indeed, has the very great advantage of forcing man to step outside himself in order that he may have dealings with things; and this fact alone causes him to take cognisance of his dependent position in relation to the world which surrounds him. It is impossible that we should form any conception, however imperfect and confused, of what the universe is, of its immensity, without immediately perceiving that we are not at the centre of it. Now, at the very root of the moral life is the sense that man does not belong entirely to himself. Everything which makes us aware of what there is in us which is impersonal opens up a path for the spirit of sacrifice and devotion; for in order for man to give himself, to sacrifice himself for something other than himself, it is essential that he be dependent upon something other than himself and that he should feel this dependence.

We have seen how vigorously present is this feeling in the work of Rabelais. By contrast, the man of letters, the pure Humanist, in his intellectual explorations, never comes into collision with anything which is resistant, upon which he can gain a purchase and of which he can feel himself a part; for he is moving in a fictive world of images which he has created out of nothing, which are as he wants them to be, which arrange themselves in his mind according to the pattern which he likes to impose upon them: all of which throws wide open the gates to a more or less elegant dilettantism and leaves man to himself with nothing to link him to any external reality or any non-subjective enterprise. This danger was still more aggravated by the Humanists of the sixteenth century because of their intimate and sustained intercourse with classical ethics; and this could only act as a bastion for the sense of independence, for the tendency towards isolation and egotism, since it makes all human happiness conditional upon this kind of independence. When Epicurus advises us to examine what, as individuals, gives us pleasure, when the Stoics prescribe for us the extirpation of those passions which bind us to the diverse beings which surround us, they are both equally in different ways ultimately recommending that we free ourselves from the environment and shut ourselves up alone within ourselves.

However real is the contrast between the two doctrines from this point of view, they still display similarities which bear witness to the fact that fundamentally they share a common origin, that they emerge from one and the same social environment, to different aspects of which they give expression.

We have pointed out how in the Humanist ethic the sense of duty became enfeebled. What motivates the Humanist is not any disinterested respect for the rule of law but an egotistical passion (even when this derives its inspiration from things of greatness): this is the taste for praise and the love of fame. The consequence of this in the realm of education was to make the spirit of emulation the fundamental mainspring of the disciplinary structure. The sense of duty is just as lacking in the ethics and the educational theory of Rabelais. We have already noted the horror in which Rabelais holds everything which is regulated: we recall that in the abbey at Thélème there was no regimentation of any kind: 'They spent their whole lives not following laws, statutes or rules, but according to the dictates of their wishes and their free will.' The Thélémites do not act out of a sense of duty, for duty is regulation in its supreme and archetypal form. How then does it come about that these wills, which are thus free each to go its own way, do not collide with one another? The abbey at Thélème is a society, and a society cannot function without a certain moral order. If this moral order does not result from a common discipline which has jurisdiction over the egotism of individuals, how can these latter live together in an orderly and harmonious fashion? This apparent miracle is accounted for by a sentiment of which each Thélémite is naturally possessed and which Rabelais calls honour: 'Liberated people,' he says, 'well-born, well-educated, conversant with cultivated society, have a natural instinct and impulse which always drives them to virtuous deeds and restrains them from vice; this they call honour.' Now, as a sentiment, honour is a very

close relation of the love of praise and of fame which were so important to the Humanists.

Honour is constituted by the esteem and the regard in which we
are held, it is the opinion which other people have of us; illustriousness is also a matter of other people's opinion. Honour is
the same as fame on a small scale. Fame and glory are grounded in
the opinion which all men in their generality have of us, regardless of the society or the social condition to which they belong;
honour concerns rather the opinion of those who form a part of
our immediate environment. We have lost our honour when we
are ill-regarded in the eyes of those close to us, of our peers, of our
equals, of those of our class or of our profession. Similarly the pursuit of honour, no less than the pursuit of glory, places people in a
relationship of competitiveness. For anyone who craves to be
honoured wishes to be honoured no less than his peers;
he therefore makes an effort to ensure that others do not get
ahead of him, and if necessary, to get ahead of them himself.
This is just how things happened at Thélème, according to
Rabelais: 'Granted this liberty [the Thélémites] sought laudably to
emulate one another by all of them doing whatever they saw one
of them choosing to do.' Thus the mainspring of action is the
same in both Rabelais and Erasmus: it is fundamentally the spirit
of emulation.

At the same time the nature of this motive shows us that from
yet another point of view the two educational theories are similar.
Indeed we do not need to show that honour is a sentiment which
of its very nature is to some extent aristocratic. As Montesquieu
said, 'it is the nature of honour to seek preferment and distinctions', and if he makes it the fundamental principle of monarchi-
cal government this is precisely because such government
'presupposes positions of pre-eminence, of rank and even of noble origin'. Was it not in the very bosom of the feudal aristocracy
that the point of honour was suckled? If it seemed so natural to
Rabelais to attribute such power over the souls of the Thélémites
to this sentiment, this was ultimately because Thélème was for
him the ideal model, the paradigm case of noble society. The fact
is that honour is above all a matter of class; each class has its own
code of honour and the higher the rank occupied by any particular class in the social scale the greater the importance attached to
honour. The nobleman was much more sensitive about everything which concerned his honour than was the simple labourer;
thus it is in aristocratic circles that this particular moral stimulus
has always been maximally effective. Rabelais' educational theory
also is orientated in the direction of the aristocracy. This emerges
from the very conception which he has of educational ideals. He

wishes first and foremost to make his pupil a scholar, a man of learning. But to what end? Is it because knowledge can be of use in the conduct of life, because by getting to understand things we enable ourselves the better to adapt to them? It is clear, at least in a large number of cases, that the scholarship he prescribes is wholly lacking in practical utility. In order for us to know the best way of living our lives it is not necessary to know what has been said about things by Pliny and Atheneus and Dioscorides and Julius Pollux and Galen and Porphyry and so many others. Is it then that learning serves as an intellectual discipline to inform the mind, to exercise and to develop in a general way our faculties of judgment and reasoning? Rabelais does not even seem to suspect that learning might be used as an instrument for logical training. Clearly for him the value of knowledge resides in knowledge itself, and not in the effects which it may have. He believes in the necessity of knowledge for its own sake, because understanding anything is a good thing even when the product of our learning serves no useful purpose whatsoever. Its value is intrinsic; it is an absolute, an end in itself and not a means to some other end. This explains the very considerable place which he accords to memory-exercises in his curriculum. At every instant Gargantua is engaged in learning, in reciting, in revising, in recapitulating the lessons he has learned; there are up to eight pieces of revision or recapitulation in his school day. Learning thus understood has no bearing upon any utilitarian goal whatsoever. It is thus, as it were, a luxury article just like the elegance and sophistication of the Humanist. Just as Erasmus finds inelegance of speech repugnant, so for Rabelais ignorance is repugnant. For him knowledge fulfils a role precisely analogous to that which is played by the art of writing amongst the humanists: it is not a tool for action designed to be of use in the serious business of living, but an ornament which renders beautiful the mind which it decorates. A scholarly education is thus understood as a kind of aesthetic education.

Having noted the points of contrast between these two educational movements, we can now see where it is that they meet and whence it is· that they bifurcate. In both cases the child and so the man is considered as a work of art to be adorned and embellished, rather than as a valuable source of power which needs to be developed with a view to action. In both cases the aim of education is taken to be not the generation of productive energies in the pupil, not the arming of his mind for the struggle, but rather its decoration, whether with a lush abundance of pieces of knowledge, whether with those attractive graces which literature bestows. In both cases the immediate necessities of life, as well as the urgent need to prepare the child in advance to confront them, seem to have been lost sight of.

It seems then, in a general way, that in the sixteenth century, at least throughout that part of cultivated society whose ideas and sentiments have come down to us through literature – for we know nothing of what the rest of the country was thinking and feeling — a style of life was thought to be realisable and to be in the process of being realised which would be liberated from all preoccupation, unencumbered by any constraint and servitude, a kind of life in which activity would not be forced to submit itself to narrowly utilitarian ends, to canalise itself, to regulate itself so that it could adapt to reality; but it would rather be expended for the sheer pleasure of the expenditure, for the glory and the beauty of the spectacle which it performs to itself when it can be employed in complete freedom, without having to take into account reality and its exigencies. We have just emerged from the Middle Ages; we have just traversed the long centuries during which individuals and societies struggled so painfully to replace the chaotic, convulsive and precarious condition, to which the dissolution of the Carolingian Empire had given rise, with a more stable and harmonious organisation. Now that men felt the soil more solid beneath their feet, now that social functions had been regularised, now that material existence had become easier and more abundant, it is as if, by contrast with the preceding sombre period of toil, humanity was overcome with a sense of cheerfulness and ease. The atmosphere weighs less heavily on people's shoulders, they can breathe more freely; the environment in which they move seems more amenable, less hostile to human desires. Hence the sense of power, of autonomy, of independence, of leisurely, unfettered activity which needs only to be abandoned to its own momentum.

It is with this kind of existence in mind — easy, free, wholly unencumbered and unfettered — an existence, moreover, which was thought to be not only possible but actual, that people proposed to set about educating children. This is what gave rise to the different educational systems, all of which were aimed at the sons of a privileged aristocracy for whom the difficulties of serious living did not exist.

Starting from this common point of departure different minds took different directions; and we have seen what these directions were. This free existence was sought by some in intercourse with the finest minds of both the present and the past; others, as a matter of preference (for the two were not mutually exclusive), sought it in learning and scholarship. For the former the crucial thing was to satisfy the demands of refined taste; for the latter of being able, without let, to quench the burning curiosity which consumed them. These differences in orientation are not just trivial matters of secondary importance; it makes a difference whether one seeks the subject-matter of education in learning or in literature. Indeed, whatever one does, even when knowledge is considered merely as a luxury article to be explored without any expectation that it should be specifically useful, in spite of everything, whether one will or no, it is very rare that it serves no useful purpose at all, if for no other reason than that it concerns itself with reality. It is rare, in spite of everything, that there should be no benefit to be derived from knowledge concerning things which are real; and science, simply because it forces us to have dealings with such things, arms us more effectively for the struggle and renders us much more easily and more naturally disposed to respond to the serious side of life. Thus even when knowledge is considered merely as a noble decoration it contains something which resists this aristocratic and aesthetic characterisation, which acts as a corrective to it and attenuates its consequences.

This accounts for the higher moral inspiration which informs Rabelais' doctrine. There is something more sublime and more fertile in devoting the life of luxury, towards which people aspire, to knowledge rather than to the art of writing. Yet there was still a grave danger in the fact that scientific education was understood in this way and brought down to the level of aesthetic education; for nothing runs more counter to its true nature. Science can be appreciated by public opinion only if, either directly or indirectly, it serves to illuminate action and if people are aware of this. When it is diverted from its true goal there is a serious risk that once it has gone beyond the first enthusiastic and intoxicated moment when people are revelling in free enquiry, in satisfying their curiosity, their recently acquired thirst for knowledge, they will look no further; there is a serious risk that once this moment has passed, reflection will not be aroused, will not question the scope of this learning which glories in its own uselessness and luxuriousness; and that consequently no one will come forward to question its *raison d'être* and its educative value. There is a serious risk that we have here a way of preparing the path for a kind of educational scepticism. And what proves that this danger is in no wise imaginary is the existence in this self-same sixteenth century of an educational theory which is neither that of Rabelais, nor that of Erasmus, neither that of the men of learning, nor that of the Humanists, but which candidly displays the characteristics I have just mentioned: this is the educational theory of Montaigne.

Montaigne wrote approximately fifty years after Erasmus and

Rabelais. He was familiar with their ideas; he had even seen them applied at the College of Guyenne where he completed his childhood and where the educational doctrines of the Renaissance were beginning to be translated into practice. But towards both of them he exhibits an equal indifference.

Montaigne, with his practical mind and his common sense, is fully aware that literary education is not self-sufficient and is more trouble than it is worth. It is not that he is unmindful of the delights of fine style, but he refuses to turn this into the basic principle of education: 'This is not to say,' he writes, 'that it is not a fine good thing to talk well, but it is not as good as has been made out.' He regrets all the time which is devoted to it: 'I am disgusted that for so much of our lives we are bothered with all that.' Language is the garment of thought, but it is a garment whose function it is to render transparent that which it covers. Its principal quality, the only one which is truly valuable, is transparency. Words are useless, and do their job only when they allow ideas to appear clearly. They run counter to their ends when they seek to dazzle with a profusion of brilliance which attracts attention to themselves: 'Eloquence does injury to things when it diverts their attention to itself....I would like things so to overpower and fill the imagination of whoever is listening that he does not care about the words.' Since the essential thing is the idea, it is the idea which must be striking; the word is but an extension of it. There is consequently no case for subjecting the verbal faculty, the faculty of self-expression, to a special training. Let thought be rigorous and clear, and words will follow suit: 'It is the place of words to serve and to follow, and where French will not suffice let us use Gascon.' 'If our disciple is well-provided with things (i.e. ideas), words will follow in abundance, he will drag them after himself if they are unwilling to follow.' One can readily imagine that under these circumstances Montaigne will not attach any great importance to the study of classical languages. Of course, his was a mind which was far from being revolutionary, and he does not go as far as to pour scorn on them; but the way in which he speaks about them bears witness to no great enthusiasm: 'They are doubtless splendid gadgets, Greek and Latin, but they are too expensive.' At the very least he would like to see less time devoted to them. He even regards the native tongue and modern foreign languages as far more worth knowing. It is with them, in his view, that one should start: 'First of all I should like to have a thorough knowledge of my own language and of that of my neighbours with whom I most ordinarily have intercourse.'

In that case, literary education having been set aside, it will doubtless be replaced by scientific education? Not at all. Starting with the very conception which contemporary educators (by whom I mean those who were most sympathetic) had of science, he draws the conclusion which is logically implicit in it, that it is educationally useless.

It never even occurs to Montaigne that science might serve to ameliorate the human condition, to prevent or to attenuate the miseries inherent within it. Indeed, if science consists above all in knowing what the ancients said about things, about health and disease, how could this empty erudition, whatever it consisted in, diminish the suffering of the world by one iota? 'What profit can we claim to have derived from the understanding of so many things which we owe to Varro and to Aristotle? Have they lightened the porter's load with their accidence? Has logic furnished any consolation for the sufferings of gout? Because they knew how this humour is located in the joints did they feel it any the less? Is there any evidence that the delights of sensuality and good health are any greater for those who know astrology and grammar?...In my time I have seen a hundred artisans, a hundred labourers who were wiser and happier than university rectors.' The only thing that matters is to know how to endure these inevitable sufferings and how to appreciate fully the joys which nature grants us by way of compensation. This cannot be learned. A peasant knows how to die no less courageously than a philosopher: 'Would I have died any less light-heartedly before reading the *Disputatio Tusculani?*' This is roughly the kind of language used by modern detractors of knowledge when they accuse it of being no more than a useless description of reality, which can indeed give us information about the way things are but which can teach us nothing about what we ought to strive after, about the goals which we should seek to realise; in other words, about the things that it is most important for us to know.

If it has no practical value, does science then at least have an educational value? If it is virtually useless as a guide in life, can it at least fashion the intelligence? Again, no. Like Rabelais, Montaigne sees science as merely an accumulation of pieces of information which can be readily deposited in the child but which remain external to him. There are numerous famous passages where Montaigne compares the mind to a vase into which science is poured. Just as the shape of a vase does not depend on the liquid which it contains, so the shape of the mind is equally independent of the knowledge which it happens to possess. Knowledge cannot mould it. Learning is not what produces right judgment and similarly it is possible to possess rightness of judgment without any kind of learning: 'We can possess learning and truth without possessing judgment, and *vice versa.*' This is the true meaning of those famous aphorisms in which, in different ways, Montaigne recommends that we always prefer 'a well-constructed head to a well-filled one'. This and other similar precepts are often held up as models of perfect educational wisdom. People do not realise that, first and foremost, they express a profound indifference towards learning, a strong sense of its educational uselessness. If Montaigne sets instruction and judgment in such formal contrast to one another, this is because he does not see that the right use of instruction provides a way, and the best way at that, of cultivating judgment. He is not aware that science possesses not only a wealth of accumulated information but also ways of thinking which we cannot learn elsewhere; consequently by initiating the mind of the child into science we are not only furnishing it, we are moulding it. Scholasticism, for its part, had a much more accurate sense of the educational value of the scholarly disciplines. It is true that the only science with which the Scholastics were acquainted was the science of dialectic; but by means of dialectic they thought to give the mind a rigorous logical training. In the sixteenth century dialectic was discredited and relegated to the realm of educational curiosities; but nothing replaced it.

If science serves neither to guide our conduct nor to mould our intelligence, must we then exclude it completely from education? Montaigne would easily make this sacrifice without any great difficulty; he even goes as far as to praise those who systematically renounce science: 'I have been delighted to see in some places men who out of devoutness have made a vow of ignorance in the same way that vows of chastity, of poverty or of penitence are made; by blunting the lust which addicts us to the study of books and by depriving the soul of the titillating, sensual pleasure which we derive from knowledge we also curb our unbridled appetites; and when the vow of poverty includes poverty of mind, it is indeed richly fulfilled.' However, Montaigne's mind is too conservative and too moderate to carry matters to such a degree of rigour. He doesn't go so far as to claim that children should be systematically sustained in a state of ignorance. It is just that, since science serves no useful purpose, it can only be an intellectual decoration; and it follows that it should only be sought after as such; we should not devote more time and trouble to it than is merited by something which is pleasant but superfluous: 'Learning (that is, science) takes its place amongst the things necessary to life in the same way as do glory, nobleness, dignity, or, for the most part, beauty, wealth and suchlike, which are valuable in life but only remotely so, and more as a result of human imagination than of nature.' Scientific knowledge is an external decoration of speech, which it enriches and renders more varied and more interesting. But it does not derive from fundamental realities: 'Most of what science has to teach us is more spectacular than substantial, more decorative than productive.' It is easy to imagine how little benefit could be derived from science conceived of and taught in this frame of mind.

Montaigne is generally taken to be a classical author and is represented as such in all our courses of study. One is recommended to read him as if he were an educational theorist whose thought could not be pondered too deeply by future educators. But it is doubtful whether his doctrine has the fortifying virtues which are so liberally attributed to it. Few doctrines are more discouraging. If, as we have just seen, neither literature nor science serve any useful purpose, where can we then turn in order to seek the subject-matter of a serious education? Nothing significant remains to be taught. In sum, Montaigne finally comes close to reaching a more or less consistent kind of educational nihilism. The fact is that in his view the educator can make no difference to that which constitutes the fundamental part of our nature. This part is incapable of being profoundly influenced from the outside: 'Nature can do all,' he says 'and nature does all.' This is what is important. He is constantly repeating that at birth we innately possess all the science which we need in order to live: 'We scarcely need learning in order to live comfortably, and Socrates teaches us that learning inheres within us as does the means of acquiring it and profiting from it.' All the products of civilisation, whatever they may be, science, moral education, religion, all manner of customs, are for Montaigne only a kind of external garment in which the mind wraps itself with a greater or lesser degree of elegance, but which does not impinge upon the substance of our souls. What kind of education can it be which attaches so little importance to the acquisition of human civilisation, the transmission of which is precisely what constitutes the function of education? The only kind of education possible according to this thesis is an entirely practical education. Children must be taught how to apply this natural sense, this innate judgment, to their relations with men and with things; they must practise using it so that they can discriminate between what is valuable and what is not, more or less like those animals who, without any scientific knowledge, are fully cognisant as to what is good for them. Children must acquire what is called experience or practice, and those responsible for them must help them in this as much as is possible. But of education which is intellectual in the strict sense, of education whose object is the development of the intelligence as such, there can be no question. How could there be? There is absolutely no subject-matter to provide it with nourishment. Besides, practice is enough to guide our conduct. Such practical education, since it demands the aiding by experience of natural reason, is not really the kind which can take place in school; this kind of education is acquired above all from life itself and it continues throughout our entire existence. The role of the teacher and consequently of the educator in the strict sense is reduced to something very trivial.

If I have been concerned to delineate the spirit of this doctrine it is not on account of its inherent interest, but rather because it so vividly exposes the congenital vice inherent in the educational thought of the sixteenth century. We have just seen that it finally leads to a kind of educational nihilism. From another point of view, it is only the logical development of the principles postulated by the great educational thinkers of the period. Indeed it is based on a certain number of premises which Montaigne did not invent but which he borrowed from his contemporaries. It is contained in its entirety in Montaigne's conception of literature and science and their educational role. These views were not exclusively personal to him; he acquired them from Erasmus, from Rabelais, and from others. However, he extracted the conclusions which were implicit in them and which his immediate predecessors, in their ardent enthusiasm, had not noticed. If the study of literature serves only to teach people how to write, if the sciences are reduced to futile erudition, then education can necessarily impinge only upon the external surface of the mind and cannot penetrate to its foundations. It is concerned only with façades, and we may well wonder whether it is worth what it costs. As a result there is no longer any room for any educational faith; and what are we to say of an educational theory which is incapable of arousing any faith in those whom it is supposed to inspire?

Thus the sixteenth century is a period of educational and moral crisis. Changes of economic and social organisation had rendered a new kind of education necessary. But the thinkers of the time conceived of this new education only in the form of an aristocratic education and one which was, directly or indirectly, aesthetic; and we have just seen all the dangers of this. Although a scientific education as Rabelais envisages it was certainly superior to the purely literary education recommended by Erasmus, it too was nevertheless seriously flawed by remaining remote from serious life and by occupying people's minds in a mere aristocratic game. The question thus arises as to whether, when these ideas which were still purely theoretical came into contact with reality, when practitioners set about translating them into facts, they would discover through experience what was fundamentally defective and would strive to correct it; or whether, rather, we should see the establishment of an academic system which would merely constitute the realisation of this vicious idea. Such is the serious practical problem which the sixteenth century had to resolve, and upon whose resolution the intellectual and moral future of our country was to depend. For it is clear that depending upon the path that was taken the French mind would inevitably become orientated in quite different directions. The responsibilities for the ways in which this resolution came about belong less to the University (whose academic role was to cease to be predominant) than to a new teaching corporation which very shortly would become all-powerful: these were the Jesuits. To determining the nature of their influence and the conditions of their success we shall devote the following chapter.

chapter 19

The Jesuits (I)

In the preceding chapters we saw how, at the time of the Renaissance and as a consequence of changes in economic and political organisation, all the peoples of Europe came to feel the need of a new educational system. This resulted in an awakening of educational thought which was hitherto without precedent. The most enlightened minds of the age, in order to meet the needs which public opinion experienced as pressing and which they themselves had been the first to feel, posed the problem of education in all its generality and undertook to solve it, using all the methods and the whole corpus of knowledge available at the time. Hence arose the great educational doctrines whose principal features we have tried to delineate and which, all of them, set themselves the goal of determining those principles according to which the educational system should be reorganised so that it could enter into harmony with the demands of the age.

As we find them expounded in the works of Erasmus, Rabelais, Vivès and Ramus, these doctrines are still only systems of ideals, conceptions which are purely theoretical, schemes and plans for reconstruction. We must now investigate what happened to them in practice, how these theories fared when, emerging from the world of the ideal, they sought to enter that of reality.

If it was the rule that educational doctrines become fully realised in the self-same form in which they have been conceived by the thinkers who propounded them, if academic reality did no more than faithfully to reflect them, the question would only be of secondary interest. But I do not know of a single historical case where the ideal proposed by an educational theorist has passed in its entirety and without essential modifications into practice. Have Rousseau's theories ever been literally applied? However great Pestalozzi's influence may have been, he is virtually the only person whose practice was in strict conformity with the method to which he gave his name; and the failures which he encountered in his endeavours show clearly enough that his method needed to be transformed before it could become practicable. This is, in fact, because great educational theorists are most commonly extremists by temperament. They are vividly aware of what is lacking, of recently evolved needs which have not yet been satisfied. As for those needs which have long been receiving satisfaction, precisely because they make no demands, the theorists are only dimly aware of them and consequently they scarcely take them into account at all in constructing their systems. As a result the systems become one-sided and exclusive, needing, in order to become viable, to become more broadly based, to moderate their essentially simplistic tendencies, to open themselves up to concerns quite different from those which in the beginning provided almost their only source of inspiration. Educational ideas shed their initial intransigence when they make contact with reality, when they seek to become actualised. In order to understand what happens to them once they have entered the domain of practice we need to be familiar with them in the form in which they were conceived by the educational revolutionaries; for it was this that fermented the evolutionary process which brought them into being. But as against this, when this evolutionary process does not restrict itself to giving them an outer covering, a material and visible body, but rather transforms them as it actualises them, then it forms part of their internal history and on this account deserves quite special attention.

In the present case the question is all the more important because the educational theory of the Renaissance had posed a problem which it had left unanswered and which was to be resolved by actual practice alone. We have noted the existence of two different educational movements. For some, enamoured above all by knowledge, the principal aim of education was the fashioning of encyclopaedic intellects. Others, by contrast, delighting more in fine speech than in genuine learning, aimed first and foremost to mould the mind so that it would be polished, cultivated, sensible of the charms of fine language, of the refined pleasures to be enjoyed in intercourse with cultivated minds, and capable of taking an honourable part in it. Certainly these two movements never came into complete conflict with one another so that they were mutually exclusive; indeed there is not one from amongst the great geniuses of the Renaissance who did not, to a greater or lesser extent, come under the influence of both of them simultaneously. But at the same time the difference between them was too great for any one mind to be equally responsive to both of them. We have even seen that the educational value of the two viewpoints was very different. Rabelais is capable of appreciating the skill involved in a discourse constructed according to the rules since Eudémon, with whose gracefulness he contrasts the heavy clumsiness of Gargantua, is a past master of this art; however, there is no doubt that literary preoccupations do not have over-whelming importance for him. Erasmus, for his part, is far from being contemptuous of learning, since he demands that the teacher possess extensive knowledge; but this knowledge for him is only a way of more effectively initiating the pupil into classical literature, of getting him to understand its beauties better and of teaching him to imitate them. Which of these two movements, with their rival claims for dominion over the minds of man, will triumph and leave its stamp on our system of schooling? The seriousness of the problem is apparent. Our national cast of mind had two paths open before it; depending on the one upon which it embarked it would emerge transformed in one of two quite different ways.

Nor is this all. We have seen that these two movements, in spite of the differences which separate them, nevertheless have one feature in common; this is that they are both the product of an aristocratic mentality. In both cases the qualities which it is impor-tant for the pupil to acquire are luxuries wholly lacking in utility value. If, as Erasmus claims, we must study classical literature, this is in order to become intellectually elegant, sophisticated in con-versation and attractive as a writer. If Rabelais recommends an extensive education in the sciences it is not because, and in as far as, the sciences are useful; it is because in his view knowledge for its own sake is a fine thing. In both cases nobody seems to suspect that the function of education is first and foremost social, in-tegrally bound up with other social functions, and that conse-quently it must prepare the child to take his place in society, play a useful part in life. To judge from the concept of education com-mon to both movements we might well think that children are destined to a life spent entirely in the company of lords and ladies, just as the inhabitants of Thélème did, conversing learnedly or tenderly, exchanging well-turned observations or noble ideas, but never having to use their powers in the execution of specific tasks. We would not guess that at the same time there were men oc-cupied in fulfilling specific social functions as artisans and merchants, as soldiers and priests, as magistrates and statesmen. But if education is not to prepare the child for any of these particu-lar professions it must nevertheless equip him so that he can profitably take up whichever of them he chooses when the time comes.

Now, *a priori*, it would not seem rash to suppose that when these two educational theories passed from the realm of theory into that of practice they would necessarily divest themselves of this aristocratic character which so flawed them. When one is speculating in the quiet of one's study one can allow one's thoughts to roam in an ideal world where they encounter no resistance, and thus lose sight of the most immediate necessities of existence. But when one seeks to translate these speculations into actualities it is very difficult to avoid being awoken out of this kind of reverie; it is very difficult not to become aware that the serious business of living does not consist exclusively in the noble employment of leisure, that man is not just a work of art to be polished and sculpted. From this it would be reasonable to expect that the educational theory of the Renaissance, when it attempted to penetrate actual academic practice, would have been impelled to correct and transform itself. We might, for example, imagine that instead of demanding from the child useless erudition people would have realised the necessity of making a choice, and of teaching him only those subjects which were best suited either to developing his judgment or to guiding him in the conduct of his life; that instead of introducing him to classical civilisation solely in order to teach him to write and speak elegantly, they would have used it as a means of expanding his experience of men and of things, of acquainting him with a kind of humanity which was different from that which he saw around him and whose beliefs, practices and ways of thinking differed from those to which he was accustomed. I only cite these possible changes by way of example in order to show how the theories of the sixteenth century, without even modifying their essential principles, could nevertheless have acquired a novel aspect in response to an awareness of the necessities of life.

As we shall see, the way in which the problem was in fact resolved is almost the exact opposite of what, by analogy, we might have most reasonably expected. We were saying earlier that generally when an educational doctrine comes to be put into practice it is corrected and attenuated and sheds its original simplistic character. In direct contrast, the educational ideal of the Renaissance, as it became realised in practice, grew more exclusive, more extreme, more one-sided. The aristocratic and aesthetic character for which we have criticised it, far from moderating itself, only became more pronounced. Education became more foreign to the needs of real life. But let us not anticipate events; let us see how they unfolded.

Although the colleges of the University of Paris had been for centuries the refuge of Scholasticism, they opened up relatively quickly to the new thinking. At the time when Erasmus, Vivès and

Rabelais were schoolchildren, around the year 1500, the old kind
of education was still in force, since that was the education which
they received; thirty years later, under François I, the reformation
had been, if not completed, at least set on the road to completion.
Everywhere or nearly everywhere classical literature and scholarship were taking the place which had hitherto been occupied by
dialectic. Everyone remembers the enthusiasm with which
Rabelais greets the dawn of the new era: 'In my youth', he says, 'it
was a dark age which reeked of the wretchedness and calamitous-
ness of the Goths who had wrought the destruction of all fine
literature...but by God's gracious mercy, in my maturity, light and
dignity have been returned to literature....Now all the disciplines
have been reinstated, languages instituted; Greek, without a
knowledge of which only the shameless would call themselves
learned, Hebrew, Chaldee, Latin....The whole world is full of
scholars, of learned teachers, of full libraries, and it is my opinion
that neither in the time of Plato nor in that of Cicero was there
such an abundance of opportunity for study as that which we see
today'. It is with equal confidence that Etienne Dolet speaks of the
revolution which has taken place before his very eyes: 'Was I not
right', he exclaims, 'to do homage to literature and to their
triumph? They have regained their ancient illustriousness and at
the same time rediscovered their true mission, which is to make
for human happiness and to fill man's life with all things good. It
will render great the youth which at this very moment is receiving
fine, liberal instruction; and with the young will grow public
esteem for literature. It will bring down the enemies of learning
from their seats; it will hold public office; it will enter into the
counsels of the King; it will administer the affairs of state, and will
bring wisdom thereunto.'

In order to know what became of the educational theories of the
Renaissance when they were translated into practice it would thus
seem that we have only to investigate how the University understood them and applied them. But what makes such a procedure
impossible, what makes the whole question more complicated, is
the great change which took place at this very moment in our
academic organisation. Up till that time the University had a complete monopoly and sole responsibility for education, and consequently the future of any educational reforms was dependent
upon the University and upon the University alone. However,
towards the middle of the sixteenth century, over and against the
University corporation there was established a new teaching corporation which was to break the University's monopoly, and was
even to achieve with quite remarkable rapidity a kind of
hegemony in academic life. This was the corporation of the

Jesuits.

The order of the Jesuits was generated by the need felt by the Catholic Church to check the increasingly threatening progress of Protestantism. With extraordinary speed the doctrines of Luther and Calvin had won over England, almost the whole of Germany, Switzerland, the Low Countries, Sweden, and a notable part of France. In spite of all the rigorous measures taken, the Church felt itself impotent and began to fear that its dominion in the world was collapsing completely. It was then that Ignatius Loyola had the idea of raising a wholly new kind of religious militia the better to combat heresy and if possible to crush it. He realised that the days were over when people's souls could be governed from the depths of a cloister. Now that people, carried by their own momentum, were tending to elude the Church it was essential that the Church should move closer to them so as to be able to influence them. Now that particular personalities were beginning to stand out from the homogeneous moral and intellectual mass which had been the rule in preceding centuries, it was essential to be close to individuals, in order to be able to exercise an influence over them which could be accommodated to intellectual and temperamental diversities. In short, the vast monastic masses familiar to the Middle Ages which, stationary at their post, had restricted themselves to repulsing such attacks as occurred, without knowing how to take the offensive themselves, had to be replaced by the establishment of an army of light troops who would be in constant contact with the enemy and consequently well-informed about all his movements. They would at the same time be sufficiently alert and mobile to be able to betake themselves anywhere where there was danger, at the slightest signal, while remaining sufficiently flexible to be able to vary their tactics in accordance with the diversity of people and circumstances. Moreover, they would do all this while always and everywhere pursuing the same goal and co-operating in the same grand design. This army was the Society of Jesus.

What was distinctive about it, in fact, was that it was able to contain within itself two characteristics which the Middle Ages had adjudged irreconcilable and contradictory. On the one hand, the Jesuits belong to a religious order in the same way as the Dominicans or the Franciscans; they have a head, they are all subject to one and the same rule, to a communal discipline; indeed passive obedience and unity of thought and action have never been carried to such an extreme degree in any militia, whether secular or religious. The Jesuit is thus a regular priest. But, on the other hand, he simultaneously possesses all the characteristics of the secular priest; he wears his habit; he fulfils his functions, he preaches, he hears confessions, he catechises; he does not live in the shadow of a monastery, he mingles rather in the life of the world. For him duty consists not in the mortification of the flesh, in fasting, in abstinence, but in action, in the realisation of the goal of the Society. 'Let us leave the religious orders', Ignatius Loyola used to say, 'to outdo us in fasts, in watches, in the austerity of the regime and habit which, out of piety, they impose upon themselves....I believe that it is more valuable, for the glory of Our Lord, to preserve and to fortify the stomach and the other natural faculties rather than enfeebling them....You should not assault your own physical nature, because if you exhaust it your intellectual nature will no longer be able to act with the same energy.'

Not only must the Jesuit mingle with the world, he must also open himself up to the ideas which are dominant within it. In order the better to be able to guide his age he must speak its language, he must assimilate its spirit. Ignatius Loyola sensed that a profound change had taken place in manners and that there was no going back on this; that a taste for well-being, for a less harsh, easier, sunnier existence had been acquired which could not conceivably be stifled or fobbed off; that man had developed a greater degree of pity for his own sufferings and for those of his fellow-men; he was more thrifty about pain, and consequently the old ideal of absolute renunciation was finished. To prevent the faithful from drifting away from religion the Jesuits devoted their ingenuity to divesting religion of its former austerity; they made it pleasant and devised all kinds of accommodating arrangements to make it easy to observe. It is true that in order to remain faithful to the mission which they had assigned themselves, to avoid seeming to encourage the innovators against whom they were struggling by their own example, they had at the same time to stick to the letter of immutable dogma. It is well known how they extricated themselves from this difficulty and were able to reconcile conflicting demands thanks to their casuistry, whose excessive flexibility and over-ingenious refinements have frequently been pointed out. While maintaining in their sacred form the traditional prescriptions of Roman Christianity, they were still able to place these within the scope not only of human weakness in general — there is no religion which has ever managed to escape this necessity — but even of the elegant frivolousness of the leisured classes of the sixteenth century, the leisured classes amongst whom it was so important to triumph against heresy and to preserve in the faith. This is how, while they became essentially men of the past, the defenders of the Catholic tradition, they were able to exhibit towards the ideas, the tastes and even the defects of the time an attitude of indulgence for which they have often been reproached, and not without reason. They thus had a dual identity as conservatives, reactionaries even, on the one hand, and as liberals on the other; a complex policy the nature and origins of which we needed to show here, for we shall encounter it again in the foundations of their educational theory.

They very quickly came to realise that in order to achieve their end it was not enough to preach, to hear confession, to catechise: the really important instrument in the struggle for mastery of the human soul was the education of the young. Thus they resolved to seize hold of it. One fact in particular made them acutely aware of the urgent need for this. One would have had to be blind to all the evidence not to see that the new methods which were showing a strong tendency to take root in the schools could only have the effect of opening up the road to heresy. The greatest minds of the time, the most illustrious of the Humanists, had been seen openly to become converted to the new religion; this was the case with Dolet, with Ramus, with Mathurin Cordier, with the majority of the teachers in the Collège de France, recently founded by François I. Thus it was a fact that Humanism of its very nature constituted a threat to the faith. It is clear that an inordinate taste for paganism was bound to cause people's minds to dwell in a moral environment which had absolutely nothing Christian about it. If this evil was to be attacked at source it would be necessary, instead of abandoning the Humanist movement to its own devices, to gain control of it and to direct it.

In itself this endeavour constituted a step backwards, a retrograde movement which was to put back the organisation of our schools by several centuries. From the beginning of our history we have seen education becoming progressively and consistently more secular. Born in the shadows of the churches and the monasteries, it gradually freed itself from them, and with the universities established itself as a special organ which was distinct from the Church and which, although it retained certain features reminiscent of its earliest origins, nevertheless in part retained a secular character. With the Jesuits we see the centre of academic life once again transported back to where it had been three or four centuries earlier, to the very bosom of the sanctuary. Just as in the days of St Colomba or St Benedict, albeit in different forms and under novel conditions, education was once again to be in the hands of a religious order.

Precisely because such an undertaking ran counter to the general direction of our academic evolution, it generated formidable resistance. The Jesuits had ranged against them all the great powers of the state, clergy, university and parliament, and yet they triumphed over all the obstacles which were strewn in their path.

In order to be able to teach they needed to be able to open a college. One of their protectors, Guillaume Duprat, the Bishop of Clermont, secured for them the means of doing so; in his will he left them a considerable sum for the creation of an academic institution. But the Jesuit order was not recognised in France and consequently had no legal entitlement to take possession of the wealth which had been bequeathed to it. To do that they needed letters patent from the King. They finally got them from Henri II in 1551. Parliament refused to register these letters, and in its resistance it was supported by the Bishop of Paris and by the theology faculty, which declared the new society 'dangerous in matters concerning the faith, inimical to the peace of the Church, and fatal for monasticism'. The reason for this opposition was that everybody was keenly aware that the passive obedience to Rome to which the Jesuits had committed themselves spelled ruination for the Gallic Church with which the Bishops and the theology faculty were closely associated. In vain the King reiterated his wishes; parliament persisted in its refusal, and it was only ten years later that the Jesuits obtained from the assembly of clergy which was held at Poissy (on the occasion of the colloquy) the right to found a college, not in their capacity as a religious order but simply as a society of teachers. Since, in memory of their benefactor, they called their college, the College de Clermont (our modern *lycée* Louis-le-Grand), they were officially designated the Society of the Collège de Clermont. They were forbidden to use the title of 'Jesuits' or 'Society of Jesus'.

No sooner had they regularised their position with the clergy and the theologians than they were confronted by a new adversary, the arts faculty. Indeed, in order to be able to teach in Paris it was necessary to obtain letters of academic entitlement from the University which, as we have seen, until that time enjoyed an undisputed monopoly. In particular, in order to be able to teach the liberal arts from grammar to philosophy it was necessary to be a member of the relevant faculty, which was the arts faculty. Now, a statute which was as old as the University itself strictly excluded all regular clergy from the arts faculty. Nevertheless the Jesuits managed to exploit the good faith of a rector who, without even consulting the faculty and consequently exceeding his powers, granted them the right which they were seeking. Hardly had this illegal concession been made than the University recovered itself, protested against the abuse of power by the rector, and called upon the Jesuits to close their college. This led to a court case, which came before parliament. What is interesting about this case is the fact that even at that time the University was fully aware of the general question involved.

What was at stake was the issue of secular education, and the issue had been posed in the most explicit terms. This is how Pasquier, the advocate for the University, put it: 'This maxim (the maxim distinguishing the two kinds of education) was full well recognised by those who first drafted the policy and the statutes of this University. For, being aware that peace amongst all subjects depends upon the indoctrination of children, while at the same time realising that there are two foundations upon which any well-ordered state is established, namely religion and justice, they established two kinds of people to teach the young; one kind who were secular, the other who were religious and who frankly belonged to a religious order. The former were intended to mould children who would be able one day to take up a vocation in the administration of affairs and of justice, the latter to prepare them for preaching and for the exhortation of the people to Christianity. Verily, in this their policy was of such piety that in order to contain all things in their appointed place they refused to allow the religious to roam and rush about the town in order to hear the teaching of laymen; nor, by the same token, were they allowed themselves to teach laymen; rather they commanded . . . that laymen should have charge of the laymen, and the regular clergy should be responsible for those of their own order.' Incidentally, Pasquier pointed out the danger inherent in entrusting responsibility for the education of the kingdom's youth to an order which was subject to a foreign authority.

The Jesuits, he said, vow 'to recognise the Pope as being above all other dignitaries . . .. They are new vassals who claim that the Pope has such authority and power over everyone that he can do anything he likes: without any kind of check he can overrule the authority not only of all other prelates but also of emperors, kings and monarchs. Has any more dangerous proposition ever been propounded?' From a legal point of view the whole debate centred upon the question of whether the Jesuits were regular or secular clergy. The interrogation in the course of which they were called upon to state clearly what manner of men they were is a model of the art of making nice distinctions and skilful evasions. The question was embarrassing. If they declared themselves to be secular, they were betraying their vows and they ran the risk of losing the bequest of the Bishop of Clermont, in which the legatees were designated as the religious of the Society of Jesus. If they admitted that they were regular clergy they would lose their case. We are, they said, what parliament has pronounced us to be (*sumus tales quales nos nominavit Curia*); in other words, members of the society of the Collège of Clermont; and it proved impossible to get any other answer out of them.

We do not need to trace the labyrinthine intricacies of this interminable case, which on three separate occasions rose up again out of its own ashes. Finally (and despite the fact that in the meantime the Jesuits had been for eight years banished from the kingdom, after an assassination attempt upon Henri IV for which, not perhaps without an element of party spirit, they were held morally responsible) their cause was successful, and they established themselves in France until 1762, when they were again the subject of an edict of banishment. Scarcely had they set foot on our soil than the population of the University colleges went off, as if spellbound, to fill the Jesuit colleges. From the beginning of the seventeenth century (1628), the College de Clermont had 2,000 pupils on its role, and the number went as high as 3,000. At the same time Jesuit colleges were founded more or less throughout the provinces; at the time of their second banishment they had no less than ninety-two establishments, some of which, such as, for example, the College de La Flèche, where Descartes was brought up, had a population which fluctuated between 1,000 and 1,400. Such was their vogue that the University had to take measures to prevent its own principals from sending their pupils to follow courses in the Jesuit colleges. The University virtually only retained, says Quicherat, 'candidates for degrees in the higher faculties, the poor about whom the Jesuits cared little, and the children of those rich people who, as a matter of principle, did not wish to have recourse to the good offices of the Reverend Fathers'; and the number of these was, of course, not very substantial. Even the decree of banishment which, as we have just said, was issued against them under Henri IV did not suffice to check the progress of the movement. The Jesuits, dispossessed of their colleges in the large towns, remained in the small ones as masters in boarding-houses, and everywhere as private tutors. Large numbers of families even sent their children to the establishments which they had close to the frontiers such as those at Douai, at Pont-à-Mousson, and at Chambéry. This emigration, as it were, was so significant that it upset the University authorities, who complained about it to the King.

To what was this extraordinary success due? It has sometimes been attributed simply to the fact that the Jesuits offered education entirely free of charge. The boarders only had to pay the cost of board and lodging, which was minimal thanks to the donations which the Company received from all quarters. 'For the same amount needed to maintain one child in a college one could have two educated by the Jesuits.' This is the explanation of their earth-shaking success given by Du Boulay: *Jesuitae docere incipiunt idque gratis! Quod vehementer placuit pluribus. Hinc frequentantur eorum scolae et academicae depopulantur.* (The Jesuits began to teach for free! Which massively delighted many people. Consequently their own schools were much frequented and the academies became depopulated.) But we have just seen that at the time of the first banishment of the order in 1595, families, rather than entrusting their children once again to the University, preferred to send them far and wide to continue their education under the direction of the Jesuits. Thus the predilection did not derive exclusively from economic considerations. Moreover, reasons of this kind could only have a decisive effect amongst the less well-off, and it was certainly from other quarters that at least the greater part of the Jesuits' academic clientele was recruited. We must therefore seek the explanation elsewhere. If the education offered by the Jesuits was so sought after this must have been because it was appreciated, because it was thought preferable to all others, because it was responsive to the tastes and the needs of the age. It is undoubtedly this which explains the fact that in spite of so many adversaries and obstacles they were nevertheless successful in implanting themselves in our country. However clever they might have been it would not have been sufficient to protect them against such a coalition of hostile forces if they had not themselves derived powerful support from public opinion.

In studying the methods practised by the Jesuits and by comparing them with those which were synchronously being used by the University we shall be able to understand their extraordinary academic success. In the course of this study the Jesuits will naturally have to receive a disinterested hearing such as they have not always been granted and which, we must realise, one may be very tempted to deny them. This is because the physiognomy of the Jesuit possesses nothing in its own right which spontaneously evokes sympathy. Dominated, obsessed by a single idea, that of ensuring the triumph of the cause to which he has given himself wholly, body and soul (I refer to the cause of the Catholic Church), the Jesuit is, as it were, trained and drilled to the point of being completely insensitive to anything which does not concern the mission of his order. He walks straight ahead of himself, allowing nothing to distract him from the goal at which he is aiming. And there is something about this rigidity, this silent impassiveness, which is reminiscent of the forces of nature and which inspires mistrust and terror rather than affection. Add to this the appalling contrast between this inflexibility in the pursuit of the goal and the extreme flexibility apparent in the choice of means, and we have more than enough to explain why Jesuits are the object of hostile prejudice of the sort which we ourselves must guard against closely. In order to appreciate their academic achievement we must rid our mind of all such emotive impressions. We shall succeed in this if we recall that all the great names of the seventeenth and eighteenth centuries were pupils of the Jesuits: that in a general kind of way, Jesuit education played the major part in the formation of our national genius, and gave it the distinctive features which it exhibits in the period of its full maturity. This is the conclusion which emerges from such a study. If we hold that the French national temperament suffers from some serious flaws which it contracted in part at the school of the Jesuits and which it owes to their methods, nevertheless it is now equally beyond doubt that it has figured with considerable prominence in the general history of thought. This is what we must bear in mind if we wish to be fair to those who fashioned it.

chapter 20

The Jesuits (II)

The external organisation of the education

Before we expound the Jesuits' educational system it is worth at least mentioning the main sources upon which such an exposition depends.

First, we have the official programmes of the Company. An early and succinct programme of study was inserted as early as 1558 by Ignatius Loyola himself in the Statutes of the Institute of which it constitutes Part Four under the title: *De iis qui in Societate retinentur instruendis in litteris, et aliis quae ad proximos juvandos conferunt*, (on that manner of instructing those entrusted to the Society in literature and other matters of value to one's fellow-men). In 1584, when these earliest instructions had already been put into practice for close on thirty years, Father Aquaviva who was at that time the general of the order conceived the plan of collating, co-ordinating and setting down the results of experience so far acquired by issuing a ruling which would be binding on all the colleges of the Society. This work of investigation and co-ordination was embarked upon with meticulous carefulness. A committee was formed in Rome which included one representative from each of the countries in which the Company was established: France, Germany, Austria, Italy, Spain and Portugal. From these confabulations there emerged a project which, after having been revised by twelve fathers of the Roman college, tried out in the colleges for several years, adjusted in the light of the observations made in the course of this experiment, was finally and definitively adopted, though not without fresh modifications, by the fifth Congregation of the Order in 1599 under the henceforth renowned title of *Ratio atque institutio studiorum Societatis Jesus*. Once it had been promulgated this code was uniformly observed in all the provinces of the Company without any important variations being made right up until 1832. Then it was reworked in order to bring it into line with the progress of human learning. In 1858 fresh modifications were added, but only in the area of philosophy.

The *Ratio studiorum* was much more concerned with the pupil and the knowledge which he should acquire in his various classes than with the teacher and the instruction which he should receive, and the methods which he should employ in order to transmit his knowledge to children. The fourteenth Congregation of the Order was sensible of this deficiency and charged one of its fathers, Father Jouvency, with the task of remedying it. To this end he wrote a treatise entitled *De ratione discendi et docendi* (on how to learn and to teach, translated into French by Ferté in 1892 and published by Hachette). This work has been for the Jesuits what Rollin's treatise for so long remained with respect to university education.

Finally, if you wish to familiarise yourselves with the methods of the Company, not simply in terms of abstract regulations but rather as these methods were actually employed in real life, you would do well to consult from amongst the numerous monographs devoted to Jesuit colleges the great work of Father de Rochemonteix on *Le collège de La Flèche* (Le Mans, 1889, 4 vols). Of course, this work is apologetic in tone; it is concerned to defend the Jesuits against certain of their contemporary detractors. But the apologetics are grounded on very elaborate and methodical documentation and, ultimately, there is no other work which gives one a better idea of what a Jesuit college was like during the seventeenth and eighteenth centuries.

Having mentioned these sources, let us now embark upon an analysis of the facts. Proceeding from the exterior to the interior, let us look first of all at the outward organisation of a Jesuit college.

The analogies between the regimes of boarding schools and of cloisters naturally inclines us to believe that our French boarding system — so enclosed, so hermetic, so strictly regulated — was formed under the influence of the monastic ideal. It is indeed probable that the idea of cloistering the student population would never have emerged in a country where monasticism was an unknown phenomenon. However, already when we were investigating what caused the French colleges of the sixteenth century to close themselves to the outside world and to immure their pupils, we had occasion to point out that there is at least one fact which this hypothesis cannot accommodate: this is the existence of a system of boarding which bore no trace of monasticism in a country which at that period was no less Catholic than was France: in England, the homeland of the tutorial system. The history of the Jesuit colleges completes the proof of the inadequacy of the explanation: if our system of boarding has been but an extension of monastic ideas within our academic life it ought to have established itself and to have developed nowhere more easily than in the academic establishments founded and administered by religious orders. Nowhere could it have found a more favourable terrain. Yet first the Jesuits and later the Oratorians showed more hostility than sympathy towards the system of boarding.

Originally the Jesuit colleges admitted as boarders only future members of the order: they were called *scolastici*. The other pupils lived out. Thus the boarding system (*convictus*) is only mentioned incidentally, and that only three or four times, in the *Ratio studiorum*. It was only gradually, on the grounds of tolerance, that other pupils were admitted as boarders, and even then this was manifestly distasteful to the Company. According to a canon which was deliberated in the fourth General Congregation (1581), it would have been entirely desirable if the Society could have been relieved of the burden of looking after its boarders. The gates of the colleges were opened to boarders in the strict sense only at the insistence of sovereigns or cities. Boarding establishments remained far less numerous than those where pupils lived out; in the eighteenth century, out of a total of ninety-two colleges, they numbered only some fifteen. Even in those places where boarding was established, by far the greater part of the student population consisted of non-residents. Thus at La Flèche, there were initially only 60 boarders as against 200 non-residents; and eventually the figure was 300 against between 800 and 1,100. At Louis-le-Grand the figures for 1620 are 300 as against 1,700, and whereas the former figure never topped 550 the total pupil population reached 3,000.

The boarding system within the college functioned as a distinct institution whose head, although he was subordinated to the authority of the rector, still enjoyed a large measure of independence. He not only supervised the material organisation of life, but also directed all the work done outside classes. The boarders were divided into two categories. The first, known as *chambristes*, were lodged in private rooms. They were allowed private tutors and servants attached to their person, and these resided with them. But they were the exception. The other boarders were lodged in communal bedrooms; and there were as many of these as there were classes. In these dormitories each occupant had his own cell, which was separated from the neighbouring cells by a partition two metres high and closed off at the front by a curtain. The cells extended in two parallel rows along the walls. Between these two rows there was a corridor which was used as a meeting place for prayers and also for recitations of work which, as we shall see, played a large part in the life of the schoolboy. The boarding system in the colleges of the Jesuits had at least this advantage over our present boarding system in that it ruled out loathsome promiscuity associated with communal dormitories.

As for those who were not boarders, they came for the most part from outside the vicinity: clearly the little country town of La Flèche in the seventeenth century could not have provided the 800 or 1,000 non-resident pupils of the college. When they were not rich enough to be placed in the care of a private tutor for both their work and their conduct, they were placed in either private halls of residence or boarding houses outside the college, or with private families. Sometimes a single family would give shelter to several pupils who lived in common, just as in the old *hospitia* of the University of Paris which we have already had occasion to describe. Marmontel, who was a pupil of the Jesuits, has portrayed for us, in his 'Memoirs of a father intended for the instruction of his children', one of these little communities of pupils in which everyone worked round the table, took his meals at the same time, slept in the same room and made use of the same candles. If he is to be believed there were no difficulties connected with the establishment of orderliness. This was no doubt facilitated by the strict supervision carried out by the Jesuits. No non-resident could settle except in a house authorised by the rector of the college; and at unspecified times the director of studies would come to find out what was going on, what the pupils needed, how they were behaving, how their work was progressing. In sum, if we compare this view of non-residential education to the disfavour with which the Jesuits regarded the boarding system, we can see that their sympathies in fact lay with a regime which approximated to the tutorial system, a system which dispersed the pupils into a multitude of separate groups. If, on the other hand, one thinks that the religious of Port-Royal also preferred this system to any other, we can see that if it did not come to prevail amongst us this was not because of the influence of religious ideas, it was not because of the prestige in which the monastic ethic was supposedly held by our educators. The true cause of the evil of the boarding system was much more that our passion for centralisation and for regimentation was transplanted into a domain which cannot sustain it.

Now that we are familiar with the external framework of academic life let us look more closely at what this comprised; that is to say, at what the teaching consisted in and how it was understood.

A Christian teacher, says Father Jouvency, must teach two things: piety and literature. If we disregard piety, which strictly speaking cannot be taught and which in any case is not specific to any particular intellectual discipline, the sole remaining subject-matter of education, properly speaking, is literature. Dialectic and philosophy which, in the Middle Ages, took up the entire life of the pupil from the moment when he emerged from the classes in grammar, that is to say from about twelve onwards, have thus relinquished that very substantial position which they used to occupy. They have not completely disappeared, but they have been compressed into three years of study whose principal function was to introduce, to prepare the mind for, the study of theology. Thus philosophy initiated a special cycle of study which, while it was not barred to simple laymen, was more specifically designed for future Jesuits, for the *scolastici*: it was the cycle of the *studia superiora*. The remaining classes, which were six in number, formed what were called the *studia inferiora*. It was in these classes which spanned the grades from the sixth to the 'rhetoric' that the teaching was given designed for the majority of pupils; this was what really constituted secondary education. Literary culture, that is to say languages and literatures, had a complete monopoly here.

But which languages, which literatures, were taught? Exclusively those of Greece and Rome. As for French, which at the time when the Jesuits attained their greatest popularity, in the seventeenth century, was itself becoming a literary language, it was entirely excluded. There were no commentaries carried out in French, no analysis and no discourses. No French author was read and expounded in class; Latin grammar was taught in Latin (Despautère), and it was in Latin that the classical authors were expounded except in the grammar classes (from the sixth to the fourth), where French was permitted. There was no teaching of French grammar. It was even forbidden to pupils to speak French amongst themselves not only in class but also in their living quarters. Thus the Jesuit fathers, who could handle Latin with remarkable dexterity, were almost completely ignorant with respect to their mother tongue: 'The majority had no inkling of either the essential mechanism or of recent advances, and whenever they had to venture to use it they displayed incredible clumsiness' (Doucieux: 'A Jesuit man of letters in the seventeenth century'). This ignorance is ingenuously admitted by the author of the first grammar which was composed by a Jesuit father (Father Laurent Cheflet): 'If you study this work well you will enable yourself to distinguish between those who write nicely from those whose language is ill-tutored...you will also see that there are few writers who don't make no mistakes.' The author himself admits that before he composed his grammar he made as many mistakes as other people in the works which he offered to the public. Indeed the grammar was not wholly French, we are told in the memoirs of Trevoux, since the author was born and brought up in Franche-Comté.

This ignorance of French placed them in a position of very marked inferiority when it came to the struggle which they had to wage against the Jansenists: they could not find any from their number who was capable of replying to Pascal and to the other attacks which were made upon them. With time, it is true, under pressure from public opinion, things changed somewhat. In some colleges a class was created at the seventh grade in which French grammar was taught; in the course of the eighteenth century Latin grammars appeared which had been written in French. But the place accorded to French still remained insignificant in the extreme. In the whole of Father Jouvency's treatise only one little page is devoted to its teaching and that page begins as follows: 'Although the teachers of the Society of Jesus should strive above all to gain a thorough knowledge of Greek and Latin they should nevertheless not neglect the mother tongue (*non est negligenda tamen lingua vernacula*)'. No particular exercise is specified for this subject; the worthy father limits himself to recommending that attention be paid to correctness and elegance whenever French is used in class. And, as if he feared that he had made excessive concessions, he concludes with this warning: the young teacher 'must be persuaded that he is seriously sinning if, beguiled by the charm of the French language or revolted by the hard work involved in more serious study, he uses the time which the Society has set aside for the learning of more difficult but necessary languages in any way other than according to the rules which have been established with strictness and wisdom.'

Why then this exclusion of French? Many of the educationalists of the Renaissance would not have approved of it. Rabelais ridiculed the use of Latin in everyday conversation, and Montaigne wanted people to learn French before they learned classical languages. Of course one can readily conceive that the Jesuits would have accorded a certain primacy to Latin because it was the language of the Church and even to Greek because, as Father Jouvency incidentally points out, some major works of the Catholic faith were written in this language. But why this ban on French?

Clearly, even in the eighteenth century, French literature was regarded with mistrust by the Jesuit educators; they feared its influence: 'a young teacher,' says Father Jouvency, 'must above all be on his guard against becoming too enthusiastic about works written in his mother tongue, especially poetry, which would make him waste the greater part of his time and even of his virtue'. And at least as far as poets are concerned, he tells us in another passage, one of the reasons why he thought them a bad influence was because of the exorbitant importance of the sentiment of love in their work. In tragedies, he says, and he is dealing with tragedies written by the Jesuit fathers themselves, 'there should be no place for profane love even when it is chaste and, similarly, no parts for women no matter how they are dressed. One must remember that the fire which smoulders beneath the ashes cannot be handled with impunity and that the cinder, even when it is extinct, even though it does not burn, it still at least sullies.' On this point, moreover, Jouvency is doing no more than to recall and comment upon a formal defence in the *Ratio studiorum*. Then he adds: 'This precaution will for the religious teacher have the advantage of making it unnecessary for him to read certain French poets who have devoted themselves to making tender love the centrepiece of their plays; nothing is more diabolical than such reading.' The fact is that this preponderant role accorded to love in literature, especially poetry and drama, is a recent phenomenon characteristic of our modern literature. The poets of antiquity sang of many other passions. This privileged position which love holds no doubt results from the very special circumstances which surrounded the development of our polite and elegant society which was, as it were, the womb of our literary life. We have seen that it centred round the woman; and consequently it was natural that feelings which have women for their object should take on in the eyes of our writers an importance which they had not previously had. Thus we have had a real peculiarity in our literature; and since, additionally, amorous passion has always appeared to the Church to be somehow contaminated by a kind of congenital immorality, we can easily see why the same mistrust should be extended to literary works in which this same sentiment was glorified and celebrated.

This explanation is satisfactory only in part; for if French poets, in particular, were held at arm's length, the writers of prose were not regarded with much greater favour. The ban must have some more general reason. I am inclined to see it in the logical consequence of a principle which has for a long time remained fundamental to our education and which, moreover, if it is interpreted wisely and with moderation, has a certain justification even though in the forms in which it has usually appeared, and especially in present circumstances, it is unreasonable. I am referring to the principle which dictates that the academic environment must be to a very large extent foreign to the spirit of the age, non-contemporary and hostile to the dominant ideas of the time which are stirring men's passions. Even recently nineteenth-century literature, and to some extent that of the eighteenth century, was taboo in our secondary schools, just as that of the seventeenth century was in the colleges of the Jesuits. It is a kind of axiom that a civilisation can produce nothing of educational value unless it distances itself somewhat in time and, to some extent, adopts an archaic character. The present was regarded with suspicion; the educator should strive to avert the eyes of children from it; it was implicitly admitted that present reality is uglier, more mediocre, more defiled, simply because it is present, and that humanity idealises itself in proportion as it returns into the past. We shall see later on how this principle became effectively established amongst the Jesuits, and that it derives from one of the most essential features of their educational theory.

These then are the reasons that classical literature, to the virtually complete exclusion of the national literature, constituted the entire subject-matter of the Jesuits' education. But Greek and Latin can be studied from widely different points of view. One can, as we glimpsed in the last chapter, use the works of antiquity as a means of initiating the child into classical civilisation. One of the principal aims of all education is indeed to give children an idea of the nature of man. If it is necessary for us to know something about the physical world it is undoubtedly far more important still that we should not be ignorant of the human world to which we are bound by much closer ties. If the human sciences were more advanced it would be to them that we should turn in order to ask for an explanation of human nature, in exactly the same way as we turn to the physical sciences (from physics in the narrow sense to biology) when we are seeking an explanation of the nature of things. Unfortunately, even today the scientific study of man (psychology and sociology) is still in a very rudimentary state. Thus we can only come to know what the nature of man consists in by direct experience, that is to say by making contact with other men, by living with them and holding intercourse with them. In order for this experience to be genuinely instructive, it is essential to range over as wide a variety of types of people as possible. For the man of one specific time or place expresses only one aspect of humanity and embodies only certain distinctive features of human nature. In order to have an even remotely complete understanding of man in general it is necessary for us to be familiar with a wide variety of human exemplars as different as possible from one another. In this respect the classical civilisations are particularly valuable. For because they are remote from us in time they differ palpably from our own cultures; consequently the men whose work they are, the men who were nurtured within and expressed through them, the men whom we see in them living, acting and thinking, are very different from the men that we are or that we can see around us. So they may serve to reveal to us aspects and properties of human nature whose existence we would not otherwise have even suspected. They enrich to an incalculable extent our knowledge of man. Was it in this frame of mind that the Jesuits used to teach classical letters to their pupils?

When such is one's goal what one strives for above all is to multiply the points of contact between the pupil and the civilisation with which one wishes to familiarise him. From this point of view, what is important is that he should have read many and various classical authors so that he can form as complete a picture as possible of this world of ideas and feelings into which he is being initiated. For this the exposition of reading is at least as valuable as written assignments, if not more so. They are what should constitute the essential basis of academic exercises. But the Jesuits proceeded in a quite different fashion.

It is true that expositions had their place in the life of the scholars, but it was not a very great one. Normally a portion of the class time was devoted to it, but the exposition was conducted by the teacher; the pupil was restricted to repeating it after him. He was not trained to penetrate for himself into the minds of the classical authors. The active exercise which was required of him was, in addition to the memory lesson, the written assignment. Unknown in the age of Scholasticism, in the hands of the Jesuits the written exercise exacted drastic compensation. It was with the Jesuits that the educational system was born whereby the written assignment becomes the paradigm for academic exercises, the system which the university inherited, and which has been perpetuated until recent times. Even in the lowest classes the pupil was required to do at least two assignments in Latin, to say nothing of any work that might be set for Greek. But the number and importance of the assignments steadily increased as one ascended the hierarchy of the classes. In the 'rhetoric', one did at least one composition every day whether in prose or in verse. Moreover, from time to time, the principal would dictate the subject of a long discourse or a vast poem which pupils would spend a week or a fortnight composing.

During classes, while recitation was going on, those pupils who were not being heard were not supposed to remain inactive; they did assignments. The same was true while corrections were taking place. These corrections consisted in a sort of whispered dialogue between the teacher and the pupil involved who had been called up to the 'chair'. During this time the other pupils, says the *Ratio studiorum*, 'will practise imitating a passage from a poet or an orator, composing a description of a garden, a temple, a storm and other similar things. They will compose a sentence in several different ways; they will translate a speech from Greek into Latin or *vice versa*; they will put Greek or Latin verse into prose; they will compose epigrams, inscriptions, epitaphs; they will do summaries ... they will practise certain rhetorical figures on particular subjects.' Nor was this all. Every occasion was exploited which might stimulate the pupils into doing exercises: a peace treaty, a victory, the canonisation of a new saint, the arrival of a governor, and so on. We shall see, when we come to speak of discipline, how the Jesuits managed to extract this additional work from their pupils. These composition exercises, moreover, were intensely diverse: 'In prose they are analogies, speeches, theses, pleas, panegyrics, dissertations, letters, imitations of a masterpiece; in verse they are eclogues, pastoral scenes, descriptions, allegories, metamorphoses, choruses, elegies, idylls; in prose and in verse they are epigrams, dramatic scenes, fables and even mottoes, riddles and all manner of verbal puzzle.' If the Jesuits wanted the pupils to be occupied constantly and occupied in writing, they are equally keen that diversity of the exercises should prevent satiation. However, there was one literary genre which enjoyed a veritable pre-eminence in their eyes: this was the oratorical genre. Eloquence was the supreme art, and its acquisition should represent the pinnacle of all study. This is why the 'rhetoric' class was the pinnacle of school life. Poetry only came second. All teaching was orientated towards oratory. Consequently there was one author who absolutely dominated the school curriculum, namely Cicero. His works were perpetually on the lecterns. He was read, expounded, learned by heart, imitated, worked over and reworked from every possible point of view. In every class from the sixth upwards it was his works which provided the principal subject-matter for expositions. He was a supreme model: *Stilus ex uno fere Cicerone sumendus*, said the *Ratio studiorum* (as far as style is concerned it must be more or less exclusively borrowed from Cicero).

The aim of the Jesuits had nothing to do with getting the pupil acquainted with and able to understand classical civilisations, but exclusively with teaching them to speak and write in Greek and Latin. This explains the importance attributed to written assignments and the nature of these assignments. This is why in the grammar classes prose composition was predominant; it was far more important than translations from Latin, which were hardly practised at all. This is why stylistic exercises were so numerous and so varied. This attitude even influenced the way the expositions were carried out. Father Jouvency has left us model expositions of Latin authors; one only has to read them in order to see that their main aim is to get the pupils to appreciate the Latin of the author and his literary style, and to encourage them to imitate these same qualities.

Far from seeking to get their pupils to think again the thoughts of antiquity, far from wishing to steep them in the spirit of classical times, one may say that the Jesuits selected for themselves precisely the opposite aim. This was because they could see no other way of extricating themselves from the contradictory situation in which they had quite deliberately placed themselves. Because the fashion was for Humanism, because classical letters were the object of a veritable cult, the Jesuits, always sensitive to the spirit of their age, professed, as we have just seen, a form of Humanism which was even quite uncompromising, since Greek and Latin alone were permitted entry into their colleges. But from another point of view, as we have said, they realised full well that Humanism constituted a threat to faith, that there was a real danger in wishing to fashion Christian souls in the school of paganism. How could these two contradictory needs be reconciled? How could the faith be defended and safeguarded as was required by the self-imposed mission of the Jesuits, while they simultaneously made themselves the apologists and exegetes of pagan literature?

There was only one way of resolving the antinomy: this was, in the very words used by Father Jouvency, to expound the classical authors in such a way 'that they became, although pagan and profane, the eulogists of the faith'. To make paganism serve the glorification and the propagation of the Christian ethic was a daring undertaking and, it would appear, remarkably difficult; and yet, the Jesuits had enough confidence in their ability to attempt it and to succeed in it. Only in order to do this they had deliberately to denature the ancient world; they had to show the authors of antiquity, the men they were and the men they portray for us, in such a way as to leave in the shadows everything which was genuinely pagan about them, everything which makes them men of a particular city at a particular time, in order to highlight only those respects in which they are simply men, men as they are at all times and in all places. All the legends, all the traditions, all the religious ideas of Rome and Greece were interpreted in this spirit, to give them a meaning which any good Christian could accept.

Thus the Greco-Roman environment in which they made their children live was emptied of everything specifically Greek or Roman. It became a kind of unreal, idealised environment peopled by personalities who had no doubt historically existed but who were presented in such a way that they had, so to speak, nothing historical about them. They were now simply figures betokening certain virtues and vices, and all the great passions of humanity. Achilles is courage; Ulysses is wily prudence; Numa is the archetype of the pious king; Caesar, the man of ambition; Augustus, powerful monarch and lover of learning. Such general and unspecific types could easily be used to exemplify the precepts of Christian morality.

This kind of disinheriting of antiquity was made easier for the Jesuits by the fact that, at least for a long time, all teaching of history was more or less completely absent from their colleges. Even literary history was unknown in them. The works of the writers were expounded without anyone bothering to notice the character of the author, his manner, the way he related to his age, to his environment, to his predecessors. His historical personality mattered so little that it was normal to study not an author, not even a work, but selected passages and extracts. How was it possible to form a picture of a specific man out of such sparse and disjointed fragments, amongst which his individuality was somehow dispersed and dissolved? Each of these pieces could scarcely appear to be anything other than an isolated model of literary style, as a sort of fair copy of exceptional authority.

We can now understand better how it came about that the Jesuits, and perhaps to a lesser extent so many other educators, tended to attribute to the past, and to the distant past, an educational value greater than that which they attributed to the present. This was because the past, at least at a time when the historical sciences had not advanced sufficiently to render it precise and specific almost to the same extent as is the present, the past, because we see it from afar, naturally appears to us in vague, fluid, unstable forms which it is all the more easy to mould according to our will. It constitutes a more malleable and plastic substance which we can even transform and present according to what suits us. It is thus easier to bend it for educational purposes. These people, these things from former times, we embellish without realising we are deceiving ourselves in order to turn them into models which we can offer for the imitation of youth. The present, because it is before our very eyes, forces itself upon our attention and does not lend itself to this kind of reworking. It is virtually impossible for us to see it other than as it is with its ugliness, its mediocrity, its vices and its failings; and this is why it seems to us ill-adapted to serve our educational ends. It was in this way that antiquity in the hands of the Jesuits could become an instrument for Christian education; they would not have been able to use the literature of their own age in the same way, imbued as it was with the spirit of rebellion against the Church. In order to attain their goal they had a powerful vested interest in fleeing from the moderns and taking refuge in antiquity.

chapter 21

The Jesuits' system and that of the University

In the last chapter we saw how one of the general principles of Jesuit policy consisted in deferring to the tastes and ideas of the age in order the better to guide their development. This is the same principle which we found to be basic to their educational theory. Because classical literature enjoyed the favour of the cultivated public they turned themselves into devotees of it; but they only expounded Humanism in order to be able to contain it, to channel it, to prevent it from issuing in its natural consequences. Humanism, unfettered, was in the process of bringing about a revival of the pagan spirit; the Jesuits undertook to transform it into an instrument of Christian education. To do this, however, they had to expunge virtually all positive content from the works of the classical authors; they had to rid them of their paganism and to retain only their form so that this form might be inspired by the spirit of Christianity. Their humanism was thus doomed to the most absolute formalism imaginable. In short, all that they asked of antiquity was not its ideas or its special way of looking at the world, but rather words, verbal combinations, stylistic models. They studied it not in order to understand it and to get others to understand it but in order to be able to speak its language, a language which was no longer spoken.

If then we can say of the Jesuits that they, in one sense, realised the educational ideal of the Renaissance, they did not achieve this until they had mutilated and impoverished it. In their hands it lost one of the essential elements in its make-up: the love of learning. I do not mean only that thirst for omniscience which Rabelais and the great encyclopaedists of the age experienced; it is only too plain that there is no trace of this in the educational system of the Jesuits. The sumptuous banquet to which Pantagruel sat down in order to satisfy his insatiable appetite for knowledge had been cleared away. But even the educationalists from whom the Jesuits seem to draw a more direct inspiration, even Erasmus, did not conceive of Humanism as being devoid of extensive substantive knowledge. For in order to be able to understand and expound classical authors one must be familiar with the classical civilisation in which they are steeped; and indeed we recall the many and diverse kinds of learning which Erasmus demands from the future teacher.

The fact is that the great Humanists of the sixteenth century loved antiquity unreservedly; they loved it for its own sake and in its entirety because they found realised in it that ideal of polite culture and elegant erudition to which they were aspiring. Without recognising it, without admitting it to themselves, they had developed a soul which was in part pagan; and, as a consequence, they were curious about everything to do with this ancient world in which they lived out in imagination the best part of their lives and in which they felt themselves to enjoy, as it were, the rights of citizenship. The history of civilisation of Rome and Greece was in reality their civilisation and their history.

Nothing of this kind was true of the Jesuits who, while introducing the child to this same environment, regarded it as their duty to see that he remained there as a stranger from the moral point of view. It is enough for them if he has a thorough knowledge of the mechanism of the languages which were spoken there. In order to achieve this, the learning and science of antiquity were superfluous. Consequently for the Jesuits their role was quite secondary. We have already had occasion to point out that history was not taught by them. It is true, that, in the course of his exposition, the teacher had to transmit in passing certain pieces of historical or archaeological information. If a question arose concerning the great gods he would explain how the Romans regarded the higher divinities; if they came across the word *clipeus* (buckler), he would describe the different sorts of buckler, their shapes and their uses. But teachers were exhorted to accord only a limited place to erudition. According to the *Ratio*, it was an exercise which was a kind of treat, more suitable for recreation and consequently reserved for academic holidays. 'On holidays,' says paragraph five of the statute which deals with the teaching of rhetoric, 'one will from time to time be able to treat of learned matters in connection with a historian or a poet . . .. This will only be indulged in in moderation.' Here we have the only concrete studies which feature in this education as it was originally conceived.

We can now see that, as we had expected, the educational theory of the Renaissance, instead of following the usual pattern and growing broader and more complex as it realised itself in academic practice, on the contrary became narrower, more restricted, more exclusive and, in the strict sense, more extreme. We have already accused Humanism of being stained with a kind of formalism; with the Jesuits this formalism became more pronounced still; with them antiquity ceased to be something which one studies with love, out of sympathy and curiosity, and becomes merely a school for the study of style. At the same time the aristocratic nature of education, as it had been conceived by the Renaissance, only became more marked. What useful ends could be served by an education whose sole aim was to teach a language which was not even that employed in ordinary life? One aspect of the education of the Jesuits, it is true, was profoundly realistic: for they sought before all else to make their pupils into faithful Catholics who respected tradition. Thus the culture which, for the educationalists of the Renaissance, was to be valued in and of itself and which they celebrated because it seemed to them to be the finest which had ever been known, was henceforth made to serve a practical end. But it served this end in spite of itself; it was subordinated to it by skilful coercion. Humanism, by its very nature, found repugnant the use which was made of it; the result was that, in every direction, it went beyond and swamped the goal which had been assigned to it. It is only too clear that in order to become a good Catholic it is in no wise necessary to become a skilful imitator of Virgil and Cicero, to be an initiate in all the secrets of the oratorical period or Latin versification. The qualities developed by the education of the Jesuits were of no more use to the faith than they were in civil life. In brief, this was because Humanism was for them a kind of curtain behind which they proceeded to their goal, much more than it was itself a means of reaching this goal.

In that case, whence came the success of this education? How can we explain its so rapid triumph over that which was available alongside it in the colleges of the University?

Comparison between these two types of education is facilitated by the fact that at the very moment when the Jesuits were feeling the need to set down the principles of their educational theory in a detailed set of regulations, the *Ratio studiorum*, the University for its part instituted the same kind of codification. Henri IV, sensing that the new age called for a complete reworking of the old University courses, in 1595 charged a committee composed partly of teachers, partly of magistrates and secular ecclesiastics, with the task of drawing up new statutes; these were finally promulgated in the year 1600. When one compares this new set of regulations, which remained the charter of the University until the end of the *ancien régime*, with that contained in the *Ratio studiorum*, one notices that the two views do not differ in anything essential. The principal aim of education is to teach people how to write; the method consists in the exercises of composition and exposition of classical authors. Out of six hours in the academic day one is to be devoted to exposition, the recitation of the rules (of grammar or rhetoric); all the others to readings, expositions or stylistic exercises. Just as with the Jesuits the only authors expounded are either Latin or Greek, so here no French authors are mentioned; as with the Jesuits too, Latin is the only language tolerated inside the colleges. Even the division of the classes is effectively the same. Originally, it is true, the Jesuits had only five classes; but in the course of time the fifth was split into two.

What differences there are are only of minor importance. We have seen that the Jesuits' pupils lived amidst a flurry of written assignments. The University was less exacting in this respect. The scholars were obliged to submit to the principal of the college only three pieces of Greek or Latin prose per week. The result was that more time would be spent on expositions; and indeed they took up the greater part of the classroom time. Moreover, contrary to the practice of the Jesuits, the texts had to be expounded in their entirety. One of the University reformers, the one who perhaps did most to prevent the University from being completely swamped by the new corporation, Edouard Richer, protests against the practice of 'castrating books', which he says, 'results in the young people learning nothing coherent or completed, nothing which forms a perfect and finished whole'. This shows that the University teachers did not look to the classical authors exclusively for isolated passages for study — as it were, fair copies of exceptional authority — but were aware that a work has a unity for which the pupils must be given a feeling.

A more important difference derives from the state of mind in which the University confronts the study of antiquity. The Jesuits, as we have seen, exposed their pupils to it anxiously and mistrustfully; they strove to conceal from them certain aspects of it, including the most important. The University teachers were closer to the thought of the great Humanists of the Renaissance. Paganism did not frighten them; they studied it confidently and without ulterior motive. They in no wise felt obliged to denature it in order to render it inoffensive. This confidence came primarily from a historical illusion which the more clean-sighted Jesuits did not share. The Jesuits had a very sharp sense of the distance which exists between these two civilisations, the one thoroughly impregnated with the eudaemonistic ethic, the other steeped in the contrary principle; the one regarding happiness as another aspect of virtue, however this might be conceived, the other sanctifying and glorifying suffering. The University teachers, by contrast, while they were not pagans, nevertheless had a view of Christian morality which was more simple, straightforward and down to earth; for this reason, they sincerely believed that they were rediscovering it in antiquity which, consequently, they had no reason to mistrust.

Nothing is more indicative in this respect than the terms in which Rollin writes who, however, was writing at the beginning of the eighteenth century, at a time when the historical sciences had already made some progress. With Horace, he thinks that there is in Homer 'a purer and more rigorous ethic than in the books of the most excellent philosophers'; he shows us how we can learn from Homer how one must respect the divinity, kings or the family. He recognises full well that in the description which the poet gives us of the gods of paganism there are errors which no good Christian could accept: 'One must admit,' he says, 'that he gives us a strange idea of them. They quarrel amongst themselves, they reproach one another, they exchange insults. Adultery, incest, and the most loathsome of crimes lose their blackness in heaven and are even held in honour there.' But at the same time he adds that it is not difficult to see something else here. There are, he says, fundamental religious truths 'which nature has engraved in the heart of man and which a constant and universal tradition has preserved there'. In this way he thinks to discern in Homeric religion the belief in one supreme god who is unique and all-powerful, whose decrees determine the destiny of the world; also the ideas of providence and of the immortality of the soul; and, says he, 'it is upon these fundamental maxims of religion that we must take care to direct the attention of young people'. Thus basically Rollin and the University were doing, unconsciously and sincerely, what the Jesuits were doing as a matter of skilful policy. They too portrayed the people of antiquity to their pupils not as they really were but stripped of all local colour, of all their main special features, as if they were some kind of Christian existing before the event. What they were seeking in classical civilisation was that which seemed to them to constitute the common basis of all human civilisation. The only difference between themselves and the Jesuits was that they portrayed things as they really saw them and in no wise thought that they were resorting to artificial embellishment; whereas the Jesuits to some extent deliberately watered down the true facts in order to present them in guise which they deemed more fitting.

We have here a difference of a point of view upon which the future would be able to build. But these differences are, after all, matters of degree and emphasis, not matters of principle. In both cases classical languages and literatures are regarded as the best possible tools for the cultivation of the mind; in both cases the art of writing is assigned the same dominant role in education. And if the university had more real sympathy for the men of Rome and Greece this was in part because they considered them from the point of view of their general humanity rather than from the point of view of what made them specifically Greek or Roman.

That there was no fundamental divergence between the two systems is shown more clearly by the way in which Rollin speaks of Father Jouvency, whose treatise he admires unreservedly: 'This book,' he says, 'is written with such purity and elegance, such soundness of judgment and such thoughtfulness, with such passionate piety, it leaves nothing to be desired unless it is that the work might be longer and its subject-matter treated in greater depth; but that was not the author's plan.'

Yet, at this period, one cannot assimilate completely the methods of the Jesuits to those of the University. The real difference was not so much in the nature of the goal being pursued or of the means being employed, but rather in the way these means were handled in order to attain this goal. The Jesuits' education was extraordinarily intensive and crammed. One feels that an immense effort is being made in order almost violently to drive the mind to a kind of apparent and artificial precociousness. Hence this plethora of written assignments, forcing the pupils incessantly to stretch their active resources, to produce work prematurely and without genuine thoughtfulness. Hence these innumerable stylistic exercises designed to initiate the pupils into all the secrets of the classical languages. The general tempo of University education was less hurried, less urgent, less vertiginous. In sum, the goal was the same and even the road which one travelled to reach it was effectively the same; but the journey was undertaken at a slower, more hesitant pace.

This moderation was the result of a wide variety of causes. First of all, we must take into account a kind of general relaxation which manifested itself in University activity at the end of the sixteenth and at the beginning of the seventeenth centuries. The University had been violently shaken by the wars of religion and had difficulty in recovering from the shock. Moreover, in this period it was changing its character. From being the free and independent corporation which it had been throughout the entire period of the Middle Ages, it was becoming a public body, a state institution, subject to control by the royal power. Henri IV's reform initiated this new policy, which the University did not accept without resistance. Hence a period of strife and turmoil, during which the former ardour of the profession became enfeebled. Richer complained of the casualness of the teachers, 'who go to their classes at a snail's pace, yawning and not until nine o'clock'.

It is clear that so leisurely a tempo is quite different from that of the Jesuits. But it is more than probable that other reasons, less transient and more to do with education, combined to produce this result. It does indeed seem that the University was aware of the complexity of the problem. However much importance it attached to the art of writing, it did not remain insensible of the fact that antiquity could be used for purposes other than as a school for style; the evidence for this is the greater importance it attached to expositions and the more substantial place which it gave to them in classes. The University man was thus restrained by a sense of the varied needs which required to be satisfied and so he did not move single-mindedly in one direction only. The Jesuit by contrast has a single and simple goal which leaves no room for hesitation and half measures. Indifferent or rather hostile to what constitutes the basis of classical civilisation, he can teach only its form; it is with this that he concerns himself exclusively; and his concern exhibits that single-mindedness which, as we have seen, is one of the traits of his character. Thoroughly imbued with the belief which he was serving, he sees nothing else, knows nothing else; and consequently, when it comes to ensuring its triumph, he cannot permit himself any restraint. Since his educational mission is a function of his religious mission it is natural that he should consider the former in the same light as the latter, and that he should engage in it with the same unyielding extremism. This is why when he is charged with teaching children how to manipulate classical languages with dexterity he will call upon all his own energies and all of theirs. Such intensive methods yield results which are brilliant, palpable, and which everyone can see to be spectacular. The slow maturation of a mind which is developing normally is not something which can easily be perceived from the outside; its fruits will only be really visible later. By contrast, one can see here and now a well-turned piece of verse or a well-composed letter in Latin; these are physical phenomena which command the attention of families and which consequently inspire confidence in them. Here we have an initial reason explaining the favour which the Jesuit colleges so quickly acquired in the eyes of public opinion.

So far we have only studied the Jesuits' teaching. We must now consider their disciplinary structures. It was perhaps in this area that they showed the most art and originality, and it was their superiority in this respect which best explains their success.

Their entire discipline was founded upon two principles.

The first was that there could be no good education without contact which was at once continuous and personal between the pupil and the educator. This principle served a double end. It ensured that the pupil was never left to his own devices. In order to mould him he had to be subjected to pressure which never let up or flagged; for the spirit of evil is constantly watchful. This is why the Jesuits' pupil was never alone: 'A supervisor would follow him everywhere, to church, to class, to the refectory, to his recreation; in the living quarters and sleeping quarters he was always there, examining everything.' But his supervision was not intended only to prevent misconduct. It was also to enable the Jesuit to study at his ease 'character and habits, so that he might manage to discover the most suitable method of directing each individual child'. In other words, this direct and constant intercourse was supposed not only to render the educational process more sustained in its effect but also to make it more personal and better suited to the personality of each pupil. Father Jouvency never stops recommending teachers not to limit themselves to exerting a general and impersonal influence on the anonymous crowd of pupils but to graduate his influence and to vary it according to age, intelligence and situation. If he is conversing with a child in private, 'let him examine the child's character so that he can mould what he says in accordance with it and, as they say, "hook" his interlocutor with the appropriate bait'. In order the better to get the pupils to open their minds to him, he will need to get them to open their hearts by making himself loved. Indeed there can be no doubt that in the course of the relationships which were thus cemented between teachers and pupils there frequently formed bonds of friendship which survived school life. Thus Descartes remained very sincerely attached to his former teachers at La Flèche.

One can readily imagine how effective this system of continuous immersion must have been. The child's environment followed him wherever he went; all around him he heard the same ideas and the same sentiments being expressed with the same authority. He could never lose sight of them. He knew of no others. And in addition to the fact that this influence never ceased to make itself felt, it was also all the more powerful because it knew how best to adapt to the diversity of individual personalities, because it was most familiar with the openings through which it could slip in and insinuate itself in the pupil's heart. By comparison with the disciplinary style which had been practised in the Middle Ages it represented a major revolution. The mediaeval teacher addressed himself to large and impersonal audiences, amongst which each individual, that is to say each student, was lost, drowned and consequently abandoned to his own devices. Now education is essentially an individual matter. As long as it was dealing with vast masses it could yield only very crude results. Hence the rowdy discipline of the students of the Middle Ages, in an attempt to counter which the residential colleges were instituted even though they were never fully successful. For the colleges did not have at their disposal a staff of teachers and supervisors who were sufficiently numerous or perhaps sufficiently committed to the task of supervision to be able to exercise the necessary control and influence over each individual.

In order to train pupils in intensive formal work which was, however, pretty lacking in substance, it was not enough to surround them, to envelop them at close quarters with solicitude and vigilance; it was not enough to be constantly concerned to contain and to sustain them: it was also necessary to stimulate them. The goad which the Jesuits employed consisted exclusively in competition. Not only were they the first to organise the competitive system in the colleges, but they also developed it to a point of greater intensity than it has ever subsequently known.

Although today in our classrooms this system still has considerable importance, nevertheless it no longer functions without interruption. It is fair to say that with the Jesuits it was never suspended for a single moment. The entire class was organised to promote this end. The pupils were divided into two camps, the Romans on the one hand and the Carthaginians on the other, who lived, so to speak, on the brink of war, each striving to outstrip the other. Each camp had its own dignitaries. At the head of the camp there was an *imperator* also known as dictator or consul, then came a *praetor*, a tribune and some senators. These honours, which were naturally coveted and contested, were distributed as the outcome of a competition which was held monthly. From another point of view, each camp was divided into groups consisting of ten pupils (*decuries*) each, commanded by a captain (called the *decurion*) who was selected from amongst the worthies we have just mentioned. These groups were not recruited at random. There was a hierarchy amongst them. The first groups were composed of the best pupils, the last groups of the weakest and least industrious of the scholars. Just as the camp as a whole was in competition with the opposite camp, so in each camp each group had its own immediate rival in the other camp at the equivalent level. Finally, individuals themselves were matched, and each soldier in a group had his opposite number in the opposing group. Thus academic work involved a kind of perpetual hand-to-hand combat. Camp challenged camp, group struggled with group, supervised one another, corrected one another, and took one another to task. On some occasions the teacher was not supposed to be afraid of pitting together two pupils of unequal ability. For example a pupil would have his work corrected by a less able pupil, says Father Jouvency, 'so that those who have made mistakes may be more ashamed and the more mortified about them'. It was even possible for any individual to do battle with a pupil from a higher group and, if victorious, to take his place.

It is interesting to note that these various ennoblements carried with them not only honorific titles but also active functions; and indeed it was these that constituted the prize. The captain enjoyed extensive powers. Seated opposite his group he was responsible for ensuring silence and attentiveness amongst his ten scholars; he noted down absences, made them recite their lessons, and ensured that assignments had been done with care and completed. The consuls exercised the same authority over the captains in their camp as did these over their own group members. Everyone was thus kept constantly in suspense. Never has the idea that the class is a small organised society been realised so systematically. It was a city state where every pupil was a functionary. It was, moreover, thanks to this division of labour between the teacher and the pupils that one teacher was able without too much difficulty to run classes which sometimes numbered as many as two or three hundred pupils.

In addition to such methods of chronically recurring competition there were intermittent competitions too numerous to enumerate. From time to time the best pieces of work were affixed to the classroom doors; the most noteworthy were read publicly in either the refectory or the 'Salle des Actes'. Leaving aside the annual prize-giving, which solemnly took place to the sound of trumpets, prizes were given out spasmodically in the course of the year for a good piece of declamation, for a meritorious literary work, for a well-executed dance, or other achievements. From the second form onwards there was in each grade an academy to which only the best pupils belonged. Then there were all kinds of public meetings in which the most brilliant pupils appeared and to which the families came to hear and applaud them. Thus an infinite wealth of devices maintained the self-esteem of the pupils in a constant state of extreme excitation.

Here again the Jesuits were effecting a revolution compared with what had gone before. We have seen that in the University and the colleges of the Middle Ages the system of competition was completely unknown. In those days there were no rewards to recompense merit and induce effort. Examinations were organised in such a way that for conscientious pupils they were little more than a formality. Then here we have, quite suddenly, a totally different system, which not only establishes itself but which instantaneously develops to the point of super-abundancè. It is easier to understand now how the training given by the Jesuits managed to acquire the intensive character which we were recently remarking upon. Their entire system of discipline was organised towards this goal. The state of constant competition in which the pupils lived incited them to strain all the resources of their intelligence and will-power and even rendered this essential. At the same time the careful supervision to which they were subjected diminished the possibility of lapses. They felt themselves guided, sustained, encouraged. Everything was inducing them to exert themselves. As a result within the colleges there was genuinely intensive activity, which was no doubt flawed by being expended on the superficial rather than on the profound, but whose existence was incontestable.

Now that we have noted the transformations which the Jesuits initiated in the realm of school discipline, we must seek for the causes. Where did these two new principles come from? Did they derive exclusively from the particular aim which the Jesuits were pursuing, from the very nature of their institution, from the mission which they had assigned themselves; or were they not, by contrast, rather the effect of more general causes, were they not a response to some change which had occurred in public thought and ethics?

What must immediately rule out the first hypothesis is the fact that if the Jesuits were the first to realise these principles in academic practice, they had nevertheless been already recognised and proclaimed by the educational thinkers of the Renaissance. We remember Montaigne's protests against teachers unintelligent enough to wish to regiment the minds of all individuals in identical fashion. He too wants teachers to study the temperament of the pupil, to test him in order to understand him better, to make him, as he says, 'run in front of himself' in order to be able to guide him in an enlightened way. From another point of view, we have seen that the love of glory, the thirst for praise, the sentiment of honour were for Rabelais and for Erasmus as for the major thinkers of the sixteenth century the essential motive for all intellectual activity and consequently for all academic activity. The Jesuits were thus on these two points, at least in principle, in agreement with their time. It is even interesting to note that we know of at least one college where, before the time of the Jesuits, the competitive system was organised and practised and, moreover, in a form which in more than one respect resembled the one which we have just described. This is the college at Guyenne where Montaigne spent several years. The pupils in any one class were divided according to their varying ability into sections which bore considerable resemblance to the Jesuits' groups of ten. Examinations took place frequently in which the pupils of one class were questioned by the pupils from a higher class or section. Similarly, we again encounter here competitions in public speaking which took place before the assembly of all the classes.

It was the fact that a great change had taken place in the moral constitution of society, which rendered necessary this double change in the system of academic discipline. In the seventeenth century the individual played a much greater part in social life than that which had been accorded to him hitherto. If, in the Middle Ages, teaching was impersonal, if it could be addressed diffusely to the indistinct crowd of pupils without any disadvantage being experienced, this was because at that time the notion of individual personality was still relatively undeveloped. The movements which occur in the Middle Ages are mass movements which carry along large groupings of human beings in the same direction, and in the midst of which individuals become lost. It was Europe in its entirety which rose up at the time of the Crusades; it was the whole of cultivated European society which soon afterwards, under the influence of a veritable collective urge, flooded towards Paris to receive instruction. The didactic style of the time thus accorded with the moral condition of society.

With the Renaissance, by contrast, the individual began to acquire self-consciousness. He was no longer, at least in enlightened circles, merely an undifferentiated fraction of the whole; he was himself already, in a sense, a whole, he was a person with his own physiognomy who had and who experienced at least the need to fashion for himself his own way of thinking and feeling. We know that at this period there occurred, as it were, a sudden blossoming of great personalities. Now, it is quite clear that in proportion as people's consciousness becomes individualised education itself must become individualised. From the moment it is required to exert its influence on distinct and heterogeneous individuals it cannot continue to develop in blanket fashion, homogeneously and uniformly. It had to diversify; and this was possible only if the educator, instead of remaining distant from the pupil, came close to him in order to get to know him better and to be able to vary his actions according to the diverse natures of individuals.

From another point of view, it is equally clear that an individual possessed of self-awareness, with his own set of beliefs and interests, cannot be motivated or trained to act by the same methods as an amorphous crowd. For the latter there are needed grand passionate shakings of the foundations, powerful collective impressions of a rather vague and general kind such as those which, on the Montagne Sainte-Geneviève, sent tremors through the multitudes gathered around Abelard. By contrast, in proportion as each individual has his own particular moral life he must be moved by considerations which are specifically appropriate to him. Thus one must appeal to self-esteem, to the sense of personal dignity, to what the Germans call *Selbstgefühl*. It is no accident that competition becomes more lively and plays a more substantial role in society as the movement towards individualisation becomes more advanced. Since the moral organisation of the school must reflect that of civil society, since the methods which are applied to the child cannot differ in essence from those which, later on, will be applied to the man, it is clear that the processes of the mediaeval disciplinary system could not survive; it is clear that discipline had to become more personal and take greater account of individual feelings, and consequently allow for a degree of competitiveness.

There was thus nothing intrinsically arbitrary about the two innovations which the Jesuits introduced into the disciplinary system: the principle, at least, was well-grounded in the nature of things, that is to say the condition of society in the sixteenth century. But if the principle was right, if it was to be retained, if it deserved to survive, the Jesuits applied it in a spirit of extremism which is one of the features of their academic policy and, in simply doing this, they denatured it. It was good to keep close to the child in order to be able to guide him confidently; the Jesuits came so close to him that they inhibited all his freedom of movement. In this way the method worked against the end which it should have been serving. It was wise to get to know the child well in order to be able to help in the development of his nascent personality. The Jesuits studied him rather in order to stifle more effectively his sense of himself; and this was a potential source of schism. At least, once they had recognised the value of rivalry and competitiveness, they made such immoderate use of them that the pupils lived in relationship to one another on a veritable war footing. How can we fail to consider immoral an academic organisation which appealed only to egotistical sentiments? Was there then no means of keeping the pupils active other than by tempting them with such paltry bait?

chapter 22

Conclusion on classical education

The conclusion which emerged from the last chapter was that Jesuits gave evidence of no originality except in the domain of the education of the will. This was because, on this point, they were pursuing a goal which was special to them and which could not have been that of the University teachers. Before all else they wished to make their pupils faithful servants of the Church, devoted subjects of the Holy See.

The University teachers themselves were good Christians and good Catholics, and regarded it as part of their professional duty to work for the maintenance and development of religious awareness. But because of the way they viewed religion, religious education did not strike them as being a complicated task; they regarded it as the natural and logical crowning achievement of classical education properly understood. No doubt they realised that the ancients had not been so favoured that they might see in all its glory the truth of the Christ; but the best of them were thought to have had, as it were, an obscure anticipation of this; they were on the road to discovering it. Given this view, in order to set the child's will in the right direction, in order to reveal to him and to cause him to love Christ, it did not seem necessary to institute a whole special training programme. All that was needed was to push a little farther the ideas of antiquity, to render them clearer and more exact, to develop the seeds which they contained. Without trauma and without any violent effort it was possible to pass from a purely intellectual training, from study of the classical literatures, to religious and moral training and to Christianity.

The case was quite different with Jesuits. They were acutely aware of the distance which separates these two civilisations, that they imply different orientations of the will and that it is impossible to rise from the one to the other without making a dramatic break. For them, the study of antiquity could only be a preliminary, a valid preparation for the Christian life. Of course they made use of antiquity; but they used it as a wind-break behind which they could shelter in order to construct a highly sophisticated piece of machinery designed to master the pupil's will and to instil in him the attitude of mind which the interests of the faith seemed to them to demand. This is why their system of discipline was much more personal than their system of teaching. It is because discipline provides the ideal basis for the nurturing of the will. They were thus bound to conceive of it and to administer it in a particular way which accorded with the particular goal which they were pursuing. They did not invent from scratch the principles on which it had hitherto reposed; we have seen how these principles are linked with the ideas of the age; but in the systematic and extreme way in which the Jesuits developed these principles they made them their own. What is particularly characteristic of them are the skilful methods of insinuation and envelopment by means of which they shape the soul of the child without the child's being able to resist the slow, imperceptible influence to which he is being subjected.

If we disregard the education of the will and consider only the education of the intelligence, that is teaching in the narrow sense, we can see how the differences between the two competing systems were ultimately of only secondary importance. Both corporations were pursuing roughly the same ideal, the Jesuits with more stringency, vigour and single-mindedness, the University teachers with a greater degree of moderation, a more lively awareness of the complexity of the problem; and also perhaps with less professional ardour. In both cases the important thing was to teach the art of writing by imitation of the ancients. In both cases in order to be able exploit antiquity in this way it had to be uprooted, detached from its historical setting so that the Greeks and the Romans were portrayed as impersonal models belonging to all ages and all nations.

The similarity between these two types of education was finally completed when the University teachers, confronted by the success of their rivals, finally came to adopt their methods. We have said that the reform of 1600 required the University pupils to produce only three pieces of work per week. There is every reason to believe that, in fact, this minimum was quickly exceeded; it suffices to recall that, only some twenty years ago, written assignments were scarcely less numerous in our *lycées* than they had been in the seventeenth century in the colleges of the Jesuits. Similarly, the competitive system created by the Jesuits with its endless compositions, its public recitations, its prize-givings, was imported virtually in its entirety into the University. Even the prize-givings in the University developed in the prodigious manner of which Geoffroy complains at the beginning of the nineteenth century. 'Work', he says, 'has slackened off a great deal in the schools but the rewards for work, the prizes have been multiplied: they are distributed in vast quantities.'

The *ancien régime* up to the second half of the eighteenth century, when new ideas were coming to light, thus really knew only one intellectual ideal, and it was on the basis of this ideal that French youth was moulded for more than two hundred years. In all this long period of time there emerged only one innovation of importance and even then, as we shall see, this limited innovation did not have the effect of altering in any essential way the view of education which we have just described.

Towards the middle of the seventeenth century there was founded, independently of the University and of the Jesuits, a new academic institution which was in no way tied to the two rival corporations. This was a modest institution, however, whose existence was extremely short-lived, but which still succeeded in exercising a certain influence on the development of our secondary education: these were the Small Schools which the 'Gentlemen of Port-Royal', as they were known at the time, opened in the environs of Port-Royal-des-Champs in 1643, but which they transferred three years later (at the end of 1646 or the beginning of 1647) to Paris, to the cul-de-sac in the *rue Saint-Dominique-d'Enfer*. These schools were still flourishing in 1650. At this date the events of the Civil War and of all manner of tribulation forced them to emigrate to the country; finally in 1660, as a result of Jesuitical intrigue, they were closed. Thus they only lasted for some fifteen years. If, moreover, we remember that in Sainte-Beuve's estimation they could barely take more than fifty children at a time, we will realise that they were scarcely able to exert their influence except over a very small number of pupils. Yet it was in these Small Schools that the innovation occurred which we have still to examine. For it was in these schools that for the very first time French was allowed to play a part in secondary education.

We must remember that both the Jesuits and the University taught Latin grammar in Latin. Port-Royal broke with this absurd practice. 'Where is the man,' writes Lancelot, 'who has sought to present a grammar written in Hebrew versicles in order to teach Hebrew? ... Does this not presuppose an already existing knowledge of the subject-matter to be learned and that what one is seeking to do one has already done?' In 1644 he published in French a 'Method for learning the Latin language easily and in a short period of time'. At the same time Lancelot thought he had succeeded in facilitating and elucidating the teaching of grammar, which he thought was obscure and pointlessly complex in the work of Despautère which was used by all the children of the time. He boasted that he had transformed something obscure and boring into something pleasant and illuminating, of getting children to pluck flowers where previously they had found only thorns. On this point the good Lancelot was deluded, for his rules in barbarous French verse were no more to delight the pupils of that period than they would delight the pupils of today. Here is one of his rhymed mnemonics:

'Feminins sont les noms en x,
Hors hic *calix, calyx, fornix,*
Et *spadix, varix, urpix, grex.*
Joins le dissyllabe en ax, ex:
Fornax, carex, forfex pourtant,
Au seul feminin se rendant;
Laissent douteux *tradux, silex:*
Joins-y *cortex, pumex, imbres*
Et *clax* (talon), mie ux masculins,
Sandix, onyx, mieux feminins.'

At the same time the teaching of French was becoming established. It was not that the rules of the language were taught methodically. There was no French grammar at Port-Royal. This was certainly not because they failed to recognise its value. Lancelot had had on more than one occasion decided to attempt this task; unfortunately, he had always found it fraught with such great difficulties that they appeared insuperable and he was forced to abandon the project. But even if it did not entail any theoretical teaching, French was at least the object of practical exercises. Before children were made to write in Latin, they were given little dialogues to compose, little narratives or stories, little letters, in which they were allowed to choose their subject-matter from what they remembered from their reading. At the same time the exercise of translation into French, which had been neglected up to that point, now outstripped prose composition. It was thought that by this means French would be saved from the Latinisation which was thought to be invading it, 'The Latin way', says Lancelot, 'has, as it were, enshrouded the French language with Latin thoughts and expressions; if we wish to set French free and to establish it in its full originality, Latin must cease to make all the running and instruction must begin with French. Excessive Latinisation is debilitating and crippling the French language.'

If the idea had been able to develop normally and yield all the results which were implicit in it, it would perhaps in the long run have resulted in a genuine educational revolution. Be it noted, indeed, that Port-Royal did not stop at protesting against the absolute ban imposed upon French but challenged the supremacy which had been unanimously attributed until that time to Latin and Greek at least since the Renaissance. Thus it was the very principle of Humanist education which was being attacked. Once it had been shaken and shattered, people would most probably have felt the need to replace it with another, and consequently to reconstruct the academic system along different lines. Indeed, there can be no doubt that the Jansenists were questing after innovation. Their discipline was wholly dissimilar to that practised by the Jesuits, indeed it conflicted with it : competition had no role to play. Anything which might excite the self-regard of the children was strictly prohibited. But the attempt did not last long enough to bear fruit. We know indeed that the powerful hostilities generated by Port-Royal prematurely put an end to the existence of the Small Schools.

The idea did not founder completely, but it only survived in a stunted form. It was a different corporation of teachers which, alongside the Jesuits and the University, was not without its own very honourable role to play in the history of our education : it was the Oratory which took over the idea. The Oratory, which was not without a certain secret sympathy for the doctrines of Jansen, finally guaranteed for French a place in its classes. However, being more timid than the 'Gentlemen of Port-Royal', the Oratorians, while still affording a modest part to this new subject, continued to make Latin and Greek the fundamental basis of intellectual training. The main stylistic exercises were conducted in Latin and Greek. Equally it was in this attenuated form that the University finally adopted the reform, and that only after more than sixty years of resistance. In 1716 its deputies, gathered together in the Collège du Plessis, decided henceforth to use in its classes the grammar and the other classical works of Gaullien, all of which were published in French. And Rollin tells us that in his day, at least in the college which he was running, French grammar was taught and some French authors were expounded.

But if it was impossible to pass over this innovation in silence we can see that it in no way modified the general physiognomy of education. This remained essentially literary. To the two classical languages another was added which, moreover, occupied the least important place; but languages and literatures continued to constitute the supreme subject-matter of education. The sciences, despite the very considerable progress they had made since the fifteenth century, were, so to speak, denied entry to the colleges. It was only very slowly and very tardily that a few scraps of science managed to filter their way into the second year of philosophy. This literary education continued to be carried on essentially through the medium of the languages and literatures of antiquity. One fact amongst others demonstrates how pronounced this domination still was in the eighteenth century. Rollin advises teachers to teach history, but he speaks only of ancient history. As for that of his own country, he admits that he himself knows very little about it. Thus it remains true that the educational system of France – at least that which was designed for the leisured classes – endured without perceptible change from the sixteenth century until the eve of the Revolution.

Having established that, the time has come to seek for the historical consequences of the system. We can safely anticipate that they were of the most considerable importance, both because of the very great length of time during which the system functioned and also because the period in which it was moulded immediately preceded that in which the principal features of our national cast of mind became established. In the investigation upon which we are going to embark it will not be necessary to distinguish in particular between the University teachers and the Jesuits, since they both had the same conception of education. If, however, it is the Jesuits that I seem to have particularly in mind, this is because, thanks to the dominant role which they played throughout this period as well as to the intensive nature of this intellectual regime as carried out by them, they are more especially responsible for the consequences whether good or evil which resulted from it.

First we need to dismiss one charge which has often been levelled against this system. It has been said that because of the very considerable place given to Latin and Greek the educational thought of the Humanists must have had the effect of delaying the blossoming of our national language, and that it was to ward off this danger that Lancelot and the teachers at Port-Royal strove to strip Latin of its ancient supremacy. There is one fact which it is extremely difficult to reconcile with this charge. It was in the sixteenth century that this Greco-Latin education was being organised; never was it so exclusive in form; never was the elimination of French more complete. And yet the age which immediately followed it was the one in which our language reached the fullness of maturity; it was then that French literature became itself a classical literature comparable to that of Rome and of Athens. Certainly I am not claiming that the writers of the seventeenth century owed their genius to the renaissance of classical letters and to the way in which these were taught; the development of polite society, the importance which it had acquired since the Italian wars, the refinement of taste which had emerged, are sufficient causes to explain the spectacular richness of the literary output of the age of Louis XIV. But it is none the less true that the development of the language seemed in no wise to have been inhibited by contemplation of the masterpieces of antiquity. Was this not the moment when French took on its own physiognomy, acquired its qualities of clarity and almost mathematical exactness, as well as that logical orderliness which distinguishes it from other languages whether ancient or modern? This observation has an educational corollary which it is interesting to pick out. Is it not strange that the men who contributed the most to making French what it was to become, to giving it its originality, should have spent their entire youth doing Latin prose compositions, reciting in Latin, and writing Latin poetry? Does this not prove that in order to teach children how to manipulate their native tongue it is not necessary to inflict upon them repetitive exercises in composition in that language, piling discourses upon narratives and dissertations upon discourses? What was essential was to teach them the art of analysing and dissecting their thought. Ideas present themselves to us in global, synthetic, confused form: to distinguish the different elements of which our thought is composed and the relationships whereby ideas are linked, that is the secret of style and that is what it is important to know about. Of course, prose composition can serve this end; for in order to translate our thought into words we are forced to become conscious of it, not to leave it in that indetermined and confused state which is its natural habitat. But lots of other exercises can be used to this end: prose translation work from and into no matter what language, analyses of the thought of masters — that exercise which is so badly neglected and which could be so profitable. Let us beware of overloading our pupils prematurely with a multiplicity of composition exercises. The effort of producing is valuable only when the mind of the child has already been nourished, when he has reached a certain maturity. With too much stretching or too much repetition he grows weary and sterile. Let us not forget that the greatest craftsmen of the French language were educated in classes where no French was written; and let this fact be a lesson to us.

There is more. Far from its being the case that the Latinism of the colleges had the effect of turning us into Latins or Greeks, as we shall see, certain of the most distinctive peculiarities of our national spirit derived from it.

It is well known that one of the essential characteristics of French literature of the seventeenth century is its pronounced and

exclusive taste for generalised and impersonal types. The characters which the dramatic poets place on stage are not specific
individuals bearing the stamp of a particular social and ethnic
environment, a special education and a special universe; they
represent simple facets of man in general. It is the eternal failings of
the human race, as these can be seen everywhere, which the comic
poet mocks; it is the great sentiments which have always ennobled
human nature which the tragic poet sets in motion. Andromaque
is no more a pagan than she is a lady at the court of Louis XIV; she
is the essential mother, maternal love incarnate. Similarly
Celimène is the embodiment of flirtatiousness, Harpagon of
avarice, and so on. Anything which might particularise these
characters, anything that might turn them into concrete individuals from a particular time and place, is systematically excluded. When they have not been directly taken from history we
do not know whence they came, where they were born, whether
they belonged to the nobility or the bourgeoisie, were from Paris
or from the provinces. Very often the names they have are not
really genuine names but generic denominations denoting
abstract types: there are names for the valets (Scapin), others for
cuckolded husbands, others for young girls in love. Hence the dis-
daining of local colour, whether in the matter of costume or of
decor. The events portrayed take place in a kind of abstract ideal
environment which is outside space and time because it belongs,
as it were, to all time and to all places. This way of looking at
things has become so deeply engrained in us that despite our recent efforts to liberate ourselves from it our literature still bears its
imprint, even if this is becoming fainter.

How did this come about? Was it the result of some inherent
tendency in the French mentality? If so, we have to face the fact
that at the beginning of the Renaissance men saw people and
things quite differently. How far distant are the heroes of Rabelais
from the heroes of Corneille, the former with their extreme complexity, the latter with their abstract simplicity. What then can
have happened in the interval?

If you examine the mentality of our classical era in education, as
this had been administered in the colleges of the Jesuits and the
University for close on a hundred years when the great century
began, it will cease to strike you as some kind of inexplicable idiosyncrasy. Taking only the Jesuits' pupil, his was a life of sustained
intercourse with the people of antiquity; however, he was trained
not to notice that which was specifically Greek or Roman about
them; he was shown them only in those aspects in which they appeared simply as men scarcely different (except in the matter of
religious faith) from those he saw around him. The same general

sentiments seemed to motivate both the ancients and the moderns, and they both seemed to be guided by the same habits of thought. If, then, this remote species of humanity differed so little from that which he could see with his own eyes how could he ever acquire the idea that humanity varies in different periods, that it is diverse, and that its diversity is real and profound; that, depending on time and place, it thinks, argues, feels and acts in different ways and is governed by different moralities and other kinds of logic?

By contrast, everything tended to sustain young people in the belief that man is always and everywhere the same; that the changes manifested in the course of history can be reduced to superficial external modifications; that man might well wear different costumes, live in different kinds of house, speak different languages, observe different customs, but fundamentally his intellectual life remains always and everywhere identical without any essential variations. It was impossible to leave school without a conception of human nature as some kind of eternal reality, immutable, unchanging, independent of time and space, since it is not affected by the diverse conditions obtaining in different times and in different places.

Is it not obvious that minds which had been educated in this way, and were consequently flawed by an inability to perceive the changing and changeable element in history, would not be able to depict man except as they had been taught to view him, that is in his most general, most abstract and most impersonal form? As for the multiple and complex features which make up the peculiar nature of each one of us, which cause a man in one country and in one situation to be different in a different situation and country, these were regarded as mere supplementary details which could be harmlessly ignored and which, indeed, it was best to render abstract so as to get at what was essential, invariable and universal. That is how the cultivation of the intellect which was the product of Humanism inevitably gave birth to the attitude of mind which has remained one of the distinctive characteristics of our national literature. Even the terminology which I have used to describe the unreal, artificial environment in which the Jesuits immersed their pupils can equally serve to define the no less ideal, no less abstract environment in which seventeenth-century literature immerses us.

This character trait has not only affected our literary life; it has also left its mark on our entire intellectual and moral temperament.

First of all, it is manifestly in this that our constitutional cosmopolitanism originates. When a society has been trained in this way to conceive of man without regard to any of his national and historical contingent features, in his most general and abstract embodiment, it is capable of subscribing only to an ideal which seems valid for the human race in its entirety. Consequently, in this respect, the Frenchman can only avoid going against his intellectual nature by posing moral and political problems in terms that are not narrowly national. When he legislates he thinks that he is legislating for the whole of humanity, since humanity is the only genuine reality; the superficial forms which it assumes and which particularise it at different moments of history no more deserve the serious attention of the philosopher and the statesman than they do that of the poet. That is why, when the authors of the Constitution set about drawing up the list of what they regarded as essential liberties, they claim them not for themselves as Frenchmen living in the eighteenth century but for all men in all times and in all places. What shows clearly that there is a connection between this kind of universalism, of intellectual cosmopolitanism, and Greco-Latin culture is the fact that an awareness of national idiosyncrasies is much more acute amongst peoples in whom Humanism has become less deeply rooted than it is here, amongst the Anglo-Saxon and Germanic peoples where the influence of Humanism was very rapidly curbed by the progress of Protestantism. I do not mean that England or Germany is more collectively self-interested than France: we have our own variety of egotism. I only mean that they have a keener awareness than we have of the real differences which exist between different national types, differences of which the statesman should take account.

This is the reverse side of the coin. Man himself, man in general, is man reduced to his most general characteristics, those which are to be found wherever men are to be found; he is an abstraction made from the particular forms in which men may manifest themselves according to circumstances. Such a notion is inevitably one of extreme simpleness, since it has been systematically stripped of anything which might make it complex. Complexity resides in the living, concrete individual who belongs to such a country, such and such a class, and who is the product of a particular heredity and social condition. A multitude of all kinds of characteristics cross and recross within him and, depending upon the way in which they are combined, these create what is truly personal in his nature, for in reality his complexity is infinite. By contrast, the more generalised a type becomes the fewer qualities he possesses, for only thus can the type be made to fit a large number of different individuals.

It is clear that an education such as that which was to be found in France in the colleges of the sixteenth, seventeenth and even the eighteenth centuries, which acquainted the child only with the human world (since the world of the physical and natural sciences was excluded), but which also acquainted him only with the most general features of humanity, was to imprison the mind permanently in an environment inhabited exclusively by abstractions, simple types and generic entities, with the result that people became incapable of thinking in any way other than in abstractions, in generalisations and in simplifications. For in order that the intelligence be persuaded to conceive of complexities as they really are, in order that it should go to work to give itself some adequate idea of them, it is essential for it to be aware of the reality of their existence. If, on the other hand, it has been trained from infancy to conceive of all complexity as something that is merely apparent, it will inevitably turn away and pass on without noticing it. The mind takes on the shape of the things which it thinks about. In order for it to expand it must be confronted with a rich and abundant subject-matter which it must feel the need to understand. By contrast, it shrinks and becomes narrow if long habit has accustomed it to conceive only of things which are elementary, simple and tenuous, and which it requires no great effort to grasp. This is why an exclusively mathematical education is so dangerous intellectually, since it renders the mind unfit to think about anything other than abstraction. The education of the Humanists could not avoid having the same effect.

From this is derived one of the constitutional defects in our national genius: I refer to the spirit of extreme over-simplification, the mathematical mentality which inculcates in us a kind of natural tendency to deny all reality to anything which is too complex to be contained within the meagre categories of our understanding. Clear evidence of the connection between the simplistic quality and Humanist education is furnished by the fact that the latter reached its apogee in the seventeenth century, that is one century after this kind of education had been instituted in our colleges; thus it follows it immediately. Indeed it is generally agreed today that we see in Descartes (that former pupil of La Flèche) the supreme expression of the spirit of the 'Grand Siècle'; and in Cartesian philosophy, that universal mathematics, the systematic elaboration of the French urge for simplification. We know how for Descartes there was nothing real about physical bodies apart from uniform, homogeneous, geometrical extension. As for the innumerable properties of which life is composed, the individuality of things, he sees them as mere appearances, tricks of light and shade, lacking in consistency and in reality, just as he makes the whole of consciousness consist in abstract and impersonal thought alone. I do not wish to suggest that the education given in the colleges was the unique cause of the evil; but it certainly contributed substantially to this result. How could a sense of diversity and complexity fail to be eradicated from these schools where nothing was designed to stimulate it? How could intellectual anaemia be avoided when, without being nourished by any solid sustenance, the pupils were still forced to produce too much too early?

We can now see the full extent of the influence which this system of education exercised over our national temperament and, consequently, over our history. For a state of mind which caused us to see things from a particular point of view, which inflicted on us a kind of intellectual blindness with regard to one whole area of reality, naturally had an effect upon our practice. In particular, the abstract individualism of the men of the nineteenth century derives from this, their atomic conception of society, their contempt for history. Does this mean that the evil produced no compensating benefits? Indubitably not. A simplistic frame of mind, almost as a matter of necessity, leads to rationalism; and the power of reasoning is in itself a power indeed. When one is thoroughly imbued with the belief that things are simple or reducible to simple components, one also believes that everything is clear or can be translated into clear terms. Thus reason is sheltered from bouts of despair, and refuses to concede that reality contains anything which is irreducibly obscure and unintelligible and over which, consequently, it can have no dominion. But such lofty rationalism, grounded as it is in a mere illusion — the illusion that the complex is a mere appearance — such rationalism is of a very inferior type. Reason must acquire sufficient strength to retain its confidence in itself while at the same time being aware that things are complex and that their complexity is real.

For that there has to be a radical transformation in our educational system. It is only at the end of the eighteenth century that this need began to be felt. At this period a new era in our academic history began. It was the third and the last. Indeed, if we disregard the Carolingian era, which was a preparatory and preliminary period, the road we have travelled since the beginning of this expedition comprises two main stages. First there is the age of Scholasticism which runs from the twelfth to the fourteenth century, then the age of Humanism which runs from the sixteenth to the end of the eighteenth century. To the first period we owe the whole of our academic organisation: universities, faculties, colleges, degrees, examinations: all this derives from then. To the second period we owe that literary curriculum which until recent times has provided the basis for all our intellectual education. On the eve of the Revolution a third phase begins, in the course of which the attempt will be made to complement the study of literature with historical and scientific study. This phase, which began a century and a half ago is still with us. We have not yet emerged from it and it affects our very selves. It is upon the study of this phase that we are now about to embark.

chapter 23

The educational theory of the Realists

Its origins: Comenius, Roland and the Revolution

We are now on the brink of an entirely new phase — the final one — in the evolution of educational theory and, more generally, in the development of the peoples of Europe. From the very beginning of this book we have been consistently following a single intellectual path; we reached the climax in the last chapter with that improved and more rational brand of Humanism which found its most perfect expression in Cartesianism, in the philosophy of clear ideas, which has remained, and which in a new form ought to remain, as the basis of our national mentality. We are now going to tackle a contrary tendency. But precisely because the movement whose origins we are going to observe flows or seems to flow in a direction which is quite the opposite of the preceding one, it is important before going any further that we seek to gain a general perspective of it, in order to be able to demarcate properly the general pace of its progress. If we do this we shall be able to make up our minds whether these two currents really flow in opposite directions or whether, rather, they are not ultimately bound to meet again, to intermingle and to flow along one and the same path, however enlarged and transformed it may be.

I was arguing in the preceding chapter that the positive content of Humanist education consisted in getting the child to understand the most general aspects of the human heart and mind. This explains the ambiguous sense which was taken on and which, not without good reason, has been retained by the word 'humanities'. This is because the teaching of humanities constitutes an education in the study of man, since the environment in which the child is formed and developed consists exclusively of products of human thought. But the education of the previous era, that is to say of the Scholastic era, was not essentially different. The culture which reigned in the University at that period was not literary, it is true; it was exclusively logical. Now, what is the object of a training in logic, especially as this was conceived in those days, unless it is the study of man? It is not man as an integrated whole, such as he was envisaged by the Humanist, man in all the diverse ways in which he manifests himself through his moral activity as a creature of emotion and will as well as of thought; it is only man reduced to his logical side, that is to say pure intellect, to ratiocination; but it is still man and only man. If we go still further back beyond the Scholastic period to the Carolingian era, that is to say back to the age of grammar, it is still human thought which is being studied and taught beyond and beneath the material signs in which it expresses itself, beyond and beneath language. Moreover, we know that this period constituted only a preamble and a preparation for that which was to follow it immediately. Thus it was always man who was at the centre.

As for nature, it was always known indirectly as a result of the study of man. Things were not intrinsically interesting; they were not the object of a special study carried out for its own sake, but were only dealt with in connection with the human beliefs to which they had given rise. What people wanted to know about was not how the real world actually is but rather what human beings have said about it, that is, so to speak, from its human point of view.

Hence the primordial importance of the text, which is no less great under Scholasticism than it was in the Renaissance. This is because it was in the text that the thoughts and ideas of men were incarnated. Between the things of the world and the things of the mind falls the text, which acts as a partial veil between them. This power exerted by the text was so obsessive that the greatest minds, those who were most vividly aware of the real world as something vital, as something that would be of immense intellectual interest as a source of life if the mind could approach it more closely, even they did not manage to free themselves from the influence of the text: such was Rabelais. These people only lift this veil which conceals reality from them momentarily and immediately allow it to fall back into position. This mental attitude derives from such profound causes that we have been able to remark upon it from the outset. The oldest system of academic organisation which we know of is that which divides into two cycles all the branches of human knowledge, the trivium and the quadrivium. We have seen that in the archaic form this division and classification fulfil a function which is still relevant today. The trivium consisted in the teaching of those disciplines whose object is the various manifestations of human nature: grammar, dialectic and rhetoric. The quadrivium was the totality of the disciplines relating to things: that is to say, arithmetic, geometry, music, the science of sound and rhythm and astronomy. From this time onwards the distinction was thus made. We have seen that henceforth the quadrivium would occupy only a very limited place in education; it was the trivium which held the foreground, and it has never given up this position of predominance.

In this way we can explain a law to which I have frequently drawn attention and which, in fact, governs the whole of our academic evolution. This is the fact that from the eighth century onwards we have moved from one educational formalism to another educational formalism without ever managing to break the circle. In different periods this formalism has been successively based on grammar, on logic or dialectic, then on literature; but in different forms it has always been formalism which has triumphed. By this I mean that throughout this whole period the aim of education has always been not to give the child positive knowledge, the best available conception of the way specific things actually are, but to generate in him skills which are wholly formalistic, whether these consist in the art of debate or the art of self-expression.

The reason for this tendency, which is so pronounced, is that once the subject-matter of education had become man and man alone it was no longer able, as it were, to include knowledge in the strict sense. Because the study of nature was excluded from it, a whole source of positive knowledge — perhaps the most important one — was at a stroke banished. There remained only the study of man; and no doubt it is possible to conceive that man should form the subject-matter of a science in the strict sense. We know today that human nature is infinitely complex, that it has, buried within it, hidden depths whose existence ordinary people never suspect; we know that the way in which it presents itself to itself is deceptive, and that it offers those who study it a veritable harvest of positive knowledge. But this viewpoint is very new; it is a mere thirty or forty years old; at the very most it can be traced back to Auguste Comte.

For the Humanists nothing could be simpler than the passions which have motivated men since they first came into existence, or than the great truths which were regarded as fundamental, and consequently elementary, to all civilisation. From this it followed that what mattered in education was not the substance of these general features of the human spirit but rather the art of giving them expression, of translating the subtle distinctions between them into words. For the dialecticians of the Middle Ages man was something even simpler, since he was reduced to pure ratiocination, to a small number of very general concepts formed without content which could be readily applied to any and every species of subject-matter: the concept of substance and attribute, of essence and accident, of genus and property. As a consequence, what was difficult for them, what children were above all ignorant about, was less the nature of these general, formalistic concepts (about which there was not much to be said, since they were vacuous) than the art of making use of them in reasoning, and more particularly in debate.

Thus with us the cultivation of the intellect has been marked by an endemic formalism, because it has always concentrated more or less exclusively upon man. We must now enquire into why it has remained concentrated on this object exclusively, why for centuries education has so systematically turned its back upon the external world which is so close to us, which, whatever we do, plays such a great part in our life, and which, in the effect it has on our senses, constantly seems to be reminding us of its own palpable existence. Is it in the nature of all civilisations in their infancy to concentrate first of all on the study of man, and to neglect the study of the world? Classical civilisation developed in precisely the opposite direction. It was towards things first of all, towards the physical universe, that Hellenistic thought directed itself. All the great thinkers of Greece from Thales to the Sophists speculated exclusively about the physical universe; they were physicists. What they were striving to understand was the world; as for man, they seem to have felt no need whatsoever to understand him, and left him more or less systematically outside the scope of their speculation. It is not until Socrates, at a very late date, that the human mind becomes an object of reflection and consequently of education. Why then did Christian civilisation develop in the reverse direction? Why was it immediately attracted to man and to things human whereas, by contrast, it exhibited such great and sustained indifference towards the things of the external world? It is easy to see why the question is so interesting, even from the point of view of educational theory.

In the comparison with Greece we have taken the first steps on the road to a solution. If Greek thought was brought to bear first and in so exclusive a fashion upon the world, this is because at that time it was the world which was esteemed by public opinion to be supreme and sacred. The world, indeed, was considered as something divine or rather as the very realm in which divinities lived. The gods were not outside the world, they resided in things, and there was no thing in which they did not reside: *panta plērē theōn* — 'All things are full of gods'. In those days it was man, the human mind, which was regarded as something profane and of little value, Socrates himself reveals this, and he even invokes this profane character of the mind as the fundamental justification of the right to speculate with complete independence: here, he says, the thinker should enjoy complete freedom, for he runs no risk of trespassing upon the domain of the gods. For Christianity, by contrast, it is the mind, it is the consciousness of man, which is regarded as sacred and ineffable; for the soul, this principle of our inner life, is a direct emanation of the divine. As for the world, it is defined in terms of matter; and matter is something profane, vile, degrading, antagonistic to the spirit and the source of evil and sin. Between the mind and material things there is all the difference which separates the spiritual from the temporal. Thus God has disdainfully abandoned the world to the free endeavours of men, *tradidit mundum hominum disputationi.*

This remarkable contrast in the attitudes adopted by these two religions was in no wise fortuitous or accidental: rather it derived from a corresponding contrast in the principles which inspired them. The religions of antiquity were first and foremost systems of rites, the observance of which was essential in order to ensure the regular progress of the universe. In order that the seed should flower and produce an abundant harvest, in order that the river should flow, in order that the stars should complete their revolutions, the gods of the harvest, the gods of the rivers, the gods of the stars needed to be alive; and it was the rites which nourished their lives. Should these rites cease to be accomplished on the appointed days and in the prescribed manner, then the life of the whole universe would come to a halt. Thus we can see why the attention of the Greeks should be entirely directed towards the external world in which, as they saw it, the whole principle of existence was to be found.

By contrast, the Christian religion had its seat in man himself, in his very soul. It is essentially an Idealist religion: it is over the world of the mind and the spirit that its God seeks to acquire dominion, not over that of the body. To worship the gods of antiquity was to sustain their material life by means of offerings and sacrifices because on their life depends that of the world. As for the God of the Christians, he wants to be worshipped, as the formula has it, in spirit and in truth. For Him, to be is to be believed in, to be thought about and to be loved. Thus everything inclines the Christian to turn his thoughts inwards, since it is within himself that the source of life is to be found, that is, the source of true life, of the life which he regards as of supreme importance, spiritual life. Even the details of the practices of the cult compel him to concentrate upon himself in this way. The most common rite is prayer, and prayer consists in an internal meditation. For the Christian virtue and piety do not consist in material operations but rather in internal spiritual states; so he is driven to a perpetual watchfulness over his own being. Since he is under obligation to be examining his conscience constantly he must learn how to interrogate himself, to analyse himself, to scrutinise his motives; in a word, to reflect upon himself. Thus of the two possible poles of all thought — nature on the one hand, and man on the other — it was necessarily around the second that the thought of Christian societies would gravitate and so, consequently, would their educational system.

To sum up, with Christianity the world loses its confused primitive unity and becomes divided into two parts, two halves, to which very different values are ascribed: on the one hand, there is the world of thought, of consciousness, of morality, of religion; on the other, there is the world of mindless, amoral, non-religious matter. Now, religious, moral and intellectual activity constitute what is truly and essentially human. Since, by universal consent, the supreme goal of education is to develop in the child the seeds of humanity which he contains, it would never occur to anyone that nature and the natural sciences could be utilised to this end. They could only distract from it. Today it is this feeling which, whether in lucid or obscure form, is still decisive for those who continue to protest against all attempts aimed at increasing the part played in our educational system in the physical world and the sciences related to it. By explaining the universe to man (it is argued) we will not get him to understand that which it is of ultimate importance for him to grasp: his own nature. By teaching him the laws of physics or chemistry, we will not teach him how best to guide his thinking and to regulate his conduct. There even seems to be something contradictory and profane about thus seeking to educate conscious man in the school of nature and modelling the noblest part of reality upon the basest.

I shall not consider here whether this whole idea ought to be abandoned or whether, on the other hand, it is not to some extent justified and consequently contains something worth preserving; I postpone this problem for the time being because we shall encounter it again later. For the moment I am content to expound this conception as it confronts us in history, because it furnishes the answer to the historical question we have posed. We are asking ourselves what strange blindness could have afflicted man so that, even while being profoundly involved in his physical environment, he was able to attain to such a degree of detachment from it; how he could so divert his attention from the things which surrounded him, which pressed him on every side and upon which he so intimately depended. Well, the answer is that his attention was elsewhere; under the influence of prevailing ideas another object was absorbing him and obsessing him: this object was himself.

As a consequence of this exclusive preoccupation he interested himself in things only in as far as they were in some way relevant to the realm of the human. What he sought from them was not the things in themselves, it was rather his own self, that is to say the human events which occasioned these things, the ideas to which they gave rise, and the texts in which these ideas and these events were set down. Given these circumstances, we can not only explain the remarkably persistent indifference shown towards all knowledge relating to nature, but we can also easily foresee that it would only be possible to triumph over this indifference after encountering the most vigorous resistance. For to achieve this it was necessary to get man to see himself and things from a different point of view and, consequently, to modify the whole cast of his mind.

How was this transformation brought about?

In order that things might finally be able to capture people's attention, in order that the value of teaching children about them be finally recognised, public consciousness had to see in them a value which had for so long never been accorded to them. It is indubitable that the only social functions which things can directly further, since these constitute the object and the subject of their study, are those which, for convenience, we can designate by a phrase borrowed from Christian terminology, 'the temporal functions', those which are designed to sustain and develop the physical life of societies. If these functions which, in the view of Christian societies throughout the Middle Ages and the early days of the modern period, were regarded as being of an inferior order, finally came to conquer this disdain and to acquire greater dignity and importance, then both things and knowledge related to things (indispensable for the normal operation of these functions) could not fail to rise simultaneously in public estimation. It was indeed in this way that they finally became introduced into academic life.

A moment came, sooner here, later elsewhere, when moral and religious considerations were not the only ones which people took into account; when economic, administrative and political interests took on too much importance for it to be possible to go on treating them as insignificant matters which the schoolmaster need not bother himself about. There came a moment when what might be called the purely secular and amoral needs of society were felt too intensely for people not to realise the necessity of equipping children in advance with the means of satisfying them one day. Thus a new criterion became established in relation to which the educational value of different types of knowledge was henceforward measured. Henceforward they were judged not only against the yardstick of the highest moral goals which it is possible for men to pursue, but also in terms of the vital needs of society and the conditions which are essential for its effective functioning.

So a new perspective entered educational theory alongside the old one, although without excluding it. People were no longer exclusively concerned with producing good Christians — and I am using the phrase in its widest sense to include not only scrupulous practitioners but also people whose conscience and consciousness is thoroughly imbued with the great moral concepts which are fundamental to Christianity. People also wished to create good citizens who would be capable of usefully fulfilling the function which society would one day assign to them. Without preparing the child for any particular profession, people aimed to furnish him with knowledge which would be useful by enabling him to embark, under favourable circumstances, upon the profession which he would later select. It was felt necessary to supplement the purely spiritual training which he had hitherto been given, and to set beside it a temporal training which would the better prepare him for real life. To do this, it was necessary to force him out of this world of pure ideals in which he had been sustained until then and to place him in contact with reality and, in particular, with nature; and this was how the natural sciences acquired the educational interest which had so long been refused them. In expounding how this new form of teaching became part of academic life I am not claiming that this is the only means of justifying it; nor am I denying that this juxtaposition of two heterogeneous cultures has grave disadvantages. For the moment, I am simply describing; evaluation will come later.

It was in the Protestant societies, especially in Germany, that this new view of education first emerged; and, moreover, the German-speaking world remains the place where it finds most favour.

It is true to say that in its basic principles Lutheranism was fundamentally tepid towards Humanism. If Luther recommended the study of classical languages this was so that the preachers of the reformed religion should not appear inadequate to their task; it was so that during the century which witnessed the initial propagation of the taste for eloquence they should not give the impression of being backward barbarians. But, for his own part, Luther felt none of that enthusiasm for classical letters which was characteristic of Erasmus and the great Humanists of the Latin countries; and, with the exception of Melanchthon, all those around him felt the same. The fact is that Protestantism had a feeling for secular society and its temporal interests which Catholicism neither possessed nor could possess. If Luther demands schools it is, as he himself says, 'to sustain the external temporal order, *den weltlichen Stand*, so that men may govern the country well, and so that women can bring up their children well and run their households well'. He wants nothing to do with the old system: 'It is not my view that schools should be organised in the same way as those which have existed hitherto. We live in a different world and different things are required.' Moreover, he asks that young men be prepared for their future functions. Thus Humanism, in the Protestant countries of Germany, never exercised the same influence and the same authority as it did with us. From the end of the sixteenth century its influence and prestige were declining.

So the ground was prepared for the emergence of a new educational theory which, by contrast with Humanism, would seek in the world of things, in the world of reality, the tools of intellectual culture. From the beginning of the seventeenth century this educational theory was already in the process of becoming established. Ratke (who is better known under the name of Ratichius) was the first to protest against the place occupied by classical letters in education and against the years which children wasted in studying them. Of his successors the most illustrious was the great educational theorist of modern times, Amos Comensky, who was also better known in the Latinised form of his name, Comenius (1592–1670).

In the work of Comenius we find formulated in more explicit terms this same principle which I was expounding a moment ago and which is absolutely fundamental to the new educational theory; this is that, while it is of course important to educate people bearing in mind their spiritual life (the importance of which Comenius as a priest could not underestimate), one must also not lose sight of temporal and civil life. '*Scholae*,' he says, '*dum hominem formant, totaliter forment ut parem negotiis hujus vitae ipsique aeternitati aptum reddant*' (*Magna Didactica* 1657, XVIII II). 'When schools mould the man let them mould him in the totality of his being in such a way that he will have mastery over the functions which it will be incumbent upon him to perform in this life and that he will be ready for eternal life.' And elsewhere: '*Nihil tractetur nisi quod solidissimum habeat usum ad hanc et futuram vitam*' (ibid., 8). 'Let nothing be included unless it has genuine usefulness for this and the future life.' With respect to everything which is not concerned with religious and moral training it is considerations of immediate usefulness which should be paramount. *Nihil doceatur nisi ad usum praesentem* (ibid., XVII, 45). It is patently clear that the study of languages and literatures could in no way directly serve this practical end. What was important was to be familiar with things. One must completely overturn the methods which had hitherto been employed in the schools and which substituted texts for things. '*Non monstrarunt [scolae] res ipsas quomodo a se ipsis et in se ipsis sunt, sed quid de hoc et illo unus et alter et tertius et decimus quisque sentiat et scribat; ut maximae eruditionis habitum fuerit de multis discrepantes tenere sententias*' (XVIII, 23). '[The schools] have shown things not as they are by themselves or in themselves, but as this one or that one, or the third or the tenth person has felt and written on one topic or another, as if the highest learning had been to know the conflicting views of many.' Henceforth it was the opposite path that needed to be followed; books and texts should make for things and for reality in whose school the child should be placed directly: '*Summa huc redit: docendi sunt homines non a libris sapere, sed e coelo, terra, quercubus et fagis, id est nosse et scrutari res ipsas, non de rebus tantum alienas observationes et testimonia*' (XVIII, 28). 'In short: men should be taught not to know things from books, but from the sky, the land, the oaks and beech trees; that is, they should get to know and examine actual things, and not so much other people's observations amd evidence about things.'

Only the sciences can enable us to get to know the world. The sciences will thus come to play in schools the predominant role which has formerly been assigned to languages. The knowledge of languages will cease to be the ultimate goal of education; they will only be taught to the extent that they are useful either in practical or in scientific education. The national language and other modern languages will be taught in order to facilitate intercourse between people; classical languages will only be taught '*ob legendos libros sapienter scriptos*' (ibid., XXII, 1), in order to enable the child and later the man to make use of books written in these languages. Moreover, the part played by the sciences will become even more substantial because all of them are to be taught without exception. Scientific education will need to become encyclopaedic. Not, of course, that there could be any question of giving each child a thorough and exhaustive knowledge of all the sciences, nor even of only one or a few of them. But he had to have a schematic knowledge of each of them which covered at least those ideas most fundamental to them. For since he was destined to live in the world he could not afford to be ignorant of anything about the world, at least anything essential. It was impossible to know in advance what kind of things he would have to deal with; thus it was essential that none of them should catch him unprepared. 'Everyone,' says Comenius, 'who emerges from school and confronts the universe not as a simple spectator but as an actor (*quicumque in mundum, non solum ut spectatores, sed etiam ut actores futuri immittuntur*), must possess an awareness of all essential things as they are or as they are becoming (*omnium principalium quae sunt et fiunt fundamenta*)' (X, 1).

Here we have the idea of an encyclopaedic education which we have already found at each of the preceding stages of our journey, and which reappears on the very threshold of the new era upon which we are embarking. It is quite true, as I stated in one of the earliest lectures, that this idea has never disappeared from sight, and this persistence, this periodical returning, constitutes a remarkable phenomenon which it is essential to be aware of, and of which we shall certainly have to give an account. Already we can see that the further we advance the more this idea grows in strength and consistency. Vague, unstable, unformulated, in the cathedral schools where it finds expression only in the encyclopaedic character of the great academic manuals, it becomes even as early as the first universities a more self-conscious aspiration. Then, as we have seen, Rabelais and the great scholars of the Renaissance made it an object of glorious celebration but without experiencing, in their confused and tumultuous enthusiasm, the need to justify it with objective reasons. Now we have it presenting itself to us in the form of a systematic theory grounded in rational argument. Education should be encyclopaedic because it should prepare men for every possible kind of action.

Comenius even supplements this practical reason with another which is purely speculative. This is that knowledge in its entirety genuinely forms an encyclopaedia: it is a unity, it constitutes one and the self-same system, which, however ramified it may be, nevertheless grows in its entirety out of one and the same trunk: '*una encyclopedia in qua nihil sit non e communi radice ortum* (XVIII, 35)'. Science is a unity because the world is a unity. The logical relationships whereby things are united with one another are the nuts and bolts which hold together the different elements of the system and provide it with stability: '*Rationes sunt isti clavi, istae fibulae ... quae rem faciunt firmiter haerere*'. This time we are clearly in the presence of a great encyclopaedist philosopher; Comenius is a precursor of the great encyclopaedists of whom we shall shortly be talking.

These ideas of Comenius did not remain purely theoretical; they were the starting-point for a whole movement which very rapidly spread even beyond the borders of Germany. Everywhere in the Germanic societies the best minds felt the need to break away from the methods of the Renaissance, no less than with those of Scholasticism, and to educate children in the school of things. The great seventeenth-century German thinker, Leibniz, became the champion of this new conviction. He even goes as far as claiming that a taste for the real world is one of the distinctive features of German culture: 'I would willingly grant to the Italians and to the French, to Leo the tenth and to François the first, the honour of having reinstated the humanities (*restaurationem cultiorum litterarum*), provided that they in their turn recognise that the sciences dealing with reality (*die realsten Wissenschaften*) almost without exception originated in Germany.' Thus the movement came into being which culminated around the middle of the eighteenth century in the establishment of the first *Realschulen*, that is to say the first secondary schools in which the instruction given in matters concerning the real world, in things and the sciences which deal with these things, took the place of the purely literary instruction which had held pride of place until that time.

With us this movement — and it is important to realise this fact — began much later. France was from this point of view a century behind Germany.

It is true that Montaigne has sometimes been portrayed as the precursor of this new educational theory, whose origin would then need to be traced back to the sixteenth century. Up to a point he may appear to have anticipated the thinkers whom we have just been discussing. He too held bookish education in horror; he accorded no prestige to texts; he too demanded that children be placed directly in contact with things. But fundamentally this resemblance is more apparent than real. How indeed can we fail to be aware of the abyss which yawns between a sceptic such as Montaigne, for whom all science is an empty artifice, who has 'more swagger than strength and more foliage than fruit', and such thinkers as Comenius and Leibniz, who had such a lofty conception of scientific education. According to Comenius and Leibniz, if we must cast aside the texts in order to reach out directly to things this is because that is the only way of truly getting to know them, to know them in a scientific way. If Montaigne despises the written letter and traditional views it is not because he is filled with the scientific spirit nor because he has a taste for the experimental method: it is because of his scepticism; it is because he believes that there can be no true knowledge of things; all we have are sensations and impressions acquired by direct experience and only by direct experience. If then Montaigne stands out oddly amongst his contemporaries because of the practical cast of his mind (which derives perhaps from his Jewish origins), this is no reason for placing him in the same class as other thinkers who appeared a long time after the Baconian reformation and the ideas to which this reformation had given currency. Moreover, what is more characteristic about this educational theory is the social sense which is its driving force. It is concerned above all with equipping the child to fulfil his functions in society. Any such sentiment is entirely lacking in Montaigne's work.

It is only towards the middle of the eighteenth century that we French began to respond to this sentiment; and it becomes increasingly intense as the Revolution approaches. This was the moment when French society was becoming directly aware of itself, was learning to think about itself from outside the framework of all religious symbolism. It was coming to be held by individuals, in its own right and in its wholly secular form, in sufficient esteem for its needs and interests — even the purely temporal ones — to appear as pre-eminently respectable and sacred. Thus we see emerging and spreading with remarkable rapidity the new view of education which we have just been describing: all reflective persons at this period are unanimous in designating the essential object of education as being to ensure the effective functioning of society. 'Education,' says La Chalotais in his essay on national education, 'since its purpose is to prepare citizens for the state, must obviously be determined by the constitution and the laws of the state; education would be radically bad if it ran counter to the state.' As Prime Minister, Roland took up the phrase which constituted the title of La Chalotais' book and declared in 1783, in his 'Plan for Education' (page 8), that the moment had arrived 'for giving schools a form which would impress on public education the stamp, which was so valuable and which had been for too long neglected, of a national education.' 'Public instruction,' says Condorcet in his First Memorandum on the subject (*Works*, VII, page 169), 'is a duty of society, for it is the only way of putting everyone in their rightful place.' Talleyrand in a very fine passage from his report to the national assembly developed the same theme: 'One should,' he said, 'consider society as a vast studio. It is not enough that everyone should be at work in it, it is essential that everyone be in their rightful place; otherwise forces will work against one another instead of working in that harmony whereby they become multiplied .... The greatest of all economies, since it is an economy of people, consists therefore in placing them in their rightful situation; now it is beyond dispute that a good educational system is the first essential for achieving this (*Hippeau*, p. 41).' Everywhere, from Roland's premiership to the Convention, we find the same idea: namely, that the educational system and the organisation of social function should be closely linked. 'Let us imagine,' says a report presented to the Convention by the committee for public instruction, 'let us imagine the different professions and functions of society, those most necessary to our natural and political needs, organised into a general system according to the degree of intelligence and the nature and extent of education which they require. The art of education consists in providing a corresponding general system in which all of human knowledge is presented according to its nature and gradual development.'

In order to prepare children for their social functions, it is not enough to make them live in a world of pure ideals after the manner of the Humanists. They must be introduced to the things of the real world, for it is with the real world that they will have to deal. Hence the unanimous protestations against the education of the Humanists, which was accused, in Diderot's phrase, 'of having no goal other than the production of priests or monks, poets or orators (*Works*, VII, 431)', hence, as he puts it, 'the need for substituting for the study of words the study of things (ibid., 421).'

We have here the most characteristic feature of this educational theory. Because of the considerable place which it accords to the sciences, as we shall be seeing in the next lecture, one might be tempted to describe it as scientific by contrast with the literary educational theory of the Humanists. But this expression can give, and has given, rise to confusions. An educational theory imbued with the Cartesian spirit is also scientific. We have seen how different it was from the one that we are now studying; for the Cartesian educational theory, like the educational theory of the Humanists which sired it, confronts the child with pure abstractions, with entities which have been completely idealised. It is better to define the educational theory which was born with Comenius by using the word which served to designate the first schools in which it became institutionalised in Germany, and to call it Realist educational theory. This designation clearly marks the contrast which exists between it and that of the Humanists; they each gravitate towards quite different poles: one towards man in the abstract, the other towards the real world, towards things. In this way we can see the inspiration which was common to the educational theory of the whole eighteenth century, as well as what made it original. Even Rousseau's educational theory can be subsumed under this definition; for what is fundamental to Rousseau's doctrine is the idea that things, since they constitute an essential factor in our intellectual and moral life, should also be an essential factor in our education.

chapter 24

The Revolution

The Central Schools

We saw in the last chapter how the educational theory of the Revolution stood in marked contrast to what had gone before. From the beginning of our academic history, from the Carolingian period, education had had man as its exclusive subject-matter: sometimes considered solely in his capacity as a logical being; sometimes, with the establishment of the humanities, as an integrated whole; and it is this which accounts for the formalism from which educational thinking never managed to escape. Never, I believe, has human thought carried anthropocentricity so far. The educational thought of the Revolution turned in precisely the opposite direction; it was towards the external world, towards nature that it directed itself. It was the sciences which tended to provide the centre of gravity for education.

Up to that time children had been sustained in an environment inhabited by pure ideals, abstract entities; now the need was felt to educate them in the school of reality. The change was not simply a matter of degree or of dosage; it was not enough simply to be aware of the inadequacy of an education which was exclusively literary, and of the need to give some place to a different kind of training. What took place was a veritable right-about-turn; and what caused this was the importance which contemporary public opinion accorded to purely temporal functions which the Middle Ages and even the Renaissance had considered as being inferior in rank and dignity. The civil interests of society henceforth appear sufficiently respectable for education to concern itself with them. It was because Protestantism was already sensitive to the secular side of society that the Protestant countries provided the location in which this new educational theory originated. It was because eighteenth-century France acquired this sense that this same viewpoint emerged here at this time without, as far as one can tell, any direct borrowing or imitation having taken place, but simply because the same cause produced the same effect.

The nature of this kind of educational thinking which was to triumph with the Revolution shows clearly how one-sided and narrow is the way in which Taine had defined the revolutionary spirit. He saw in it only a form and, as it were, an extrapolation of the Cartesian spirit which, having been applied during the seventeenth century to the things of mathematics and physics, is supposed in the succeeding century to have expanded into the realm of politics and morals. And, of course, it cannot be doubted that the eighteenth century received Cartesianism as a legacy in just the same way as it has handed it down to us, and moreover it is a legacy which we must cultivate and not allow to decay. But the history of the development of educational thought shows us that, in addition to this inherited intellectual tendency, the eighteenth century also had another one which it developed for itself and which bears the stamp of the age. What is characteristic of it is the feeling for reality, the feeling for things, for the place which they occupy in our intellectual and moral life, for everything they are capable of teaching us. We have here a cast of mind which is quite opposite to that of the mathematician and the Cartesianism; if we leave this out of account, we can see only one aspect of the moral and political doctrines of the time, and consequently we are not in a position to understand them. We must not, however, lose sight of the fact that it is from Condorcet and the encyclopaedists that Saint-Simon, Comte and all the positive philosophy of the nineteenth century derived.

Between this orientation of the revolutionary spirit and the old spirit of the University there was a radical incompatibility. Never perhaps has there been such a striking discordance between the concerns of public opinion, its hopes and tendencies, and the state of education.

At this period, when illustrious men of learning were so numerous in all the different fields of natural science, when great discoveries were proliferating, when consequently the sciences inspired such great enthusiasm that people expected them to produce a complete regeneration of man and society, they had nevertheless managed to secure for themselves a place in the colleges only marginally more substantial than previously. Science teaching was entirely concentrated in the second year of philosophy. Here a little mathematics was taught, but not a word of natural history, not a mention of chemistry. As for physics, what was taught under this title was merely a form of abstract metaphysics. 'Almost everywhere,' says Diderot, 'in the name of physics people would wear themselves out in arguments about the ultimate elements of nature and the ultimate order of the universe.' Experimental physics finally infiltrated the classes only very sporadically. What was taught amounted to very little: a few ideas about movement and gravity, Mariotte's law, the equilibrium of liquids, and the weight of air. With the colleges so fundamentally out of tune with the public mind it was inevitable that they should appear with their antique organisation as simply so many obstacles to necessary progress; thus it was never even to occur to the men of the Revolution to preserve and use them for the new educational ends after which they were striving.

From the beginning they proclaimed the necessity of wiping the slate clean, of abolishing them completely, and starting out from basics to build an entirely new system which would accord with the needs of the time. It is not the case that this work of reconstruction was improvised. The question was posed as early as the constituent assembly and it subsequently remained permanently on the agenda. At each of the three great revolutionary assemblies plans for reorganisation were examined and debated, the reports were presented by persons of the greatest importance: by Talleyrand to the constituent assembly, by Condorcet to the legislative assembly, by Romme, Sieyes, Danou, Lakanal to the convention (*vide* Hippeau: *Public Instruction in France during the Revolution*). The works of the committee for public education, appointed by the Convention, were already on the point of publication and already covered many pages of quarto. However, it was only after the ninth Thermidor that this was brought to fruition. A law, dated year 3, which was modified a few months later after the third of 'Brumaire' in year 4, finally established the new institutionalisation of education, which had been so long expected, under the title of the 'Central Schools'.

Two different ideas dominate the entire academic achievement of the Revolution. First, there is the encyclopaedic viewpoint, which was held so dear by all the great thinkers of the period. Here we have a belief which we have already found expressed in Comenius, and which indeed is characteristic of the whole philosophical movement from Bacon and Hobbes to Saint-Simon and Auguste Comte: that science is a unity, that its different parts are interdependent and inseparable from one another, forming an organic whole, and that consequently education should be organised in such a way that it respects and even creates awareness of this unity. This accounts for the tendency to institute an academic system in which all the scientific disciplines would take their place according to a methodically organised plan. Talleyrand (who was not even an encyclopaedist) was already saying that 'education should be universal in its goals. The various branches of knowledge which it embraces may not be equally useful; but there is not one of them that cannot be genuinely useful, which cannot become more so and which ought, consequently, to be rejected or neglected. Rather there exists between them a timeless alliance, a mutual interdependence .... From this it results that, in a well organised society, although no one can succeed in knowing everything, it is nevertheless essential for everyone to have the opportunity of learning everything.'

Condorcet proceeds on the same basis at least with respect to those schools with which he intended to replace the colleges and which, under the new name 'Institutes', are the real prototypes of the Central Schools; which means that in his system they are the establishments where secondary education takes place. 'The third level of education,' he says (the Institutes were counted third because Condorcet wanted a hierarchy of two sorts of primary schools rather like upper and lower junior schools), 'deals with the elements of all the branches of human learning. Education ... is absolutely complete here .... Here will be taught not only what it is valuable to know as a man, as a citizen, in the interests of some profession to which one aspires; but also anything that might be of value regarding each of the major categories of profession.' All the sciences, all aspects of human study will have a place there.

However, it is clear even from this passage that practical and professional considerations were hovering over this whole organisation. The important thing was to equip the child to acquit himself usefully in the social function which it would one day fall to him to fulfil. Now, professional education is necessarily specialised. The knowledge demanded by one profession is useless to another. Polymathy becomes a futile burden, in as far as one is trying to get the pupil to cope with a restricted task. Two opposite tendencies were in conflict; yet the members of the Convention thought that it was possible to reconcile them. To do this they deliberately abandoned the system of classes as it had established itself in the colleges at the end of the fifteenth century, and they set about replacing it with an entirely new organisation. Each particular discipline provided the subject-matter for an autonomous course which was pursued year by year until it reached its natural end; it was run by one and the same teacher. There was thus a regular gradation from one year to the next within the same course; in other words, each course was divided into several sections corresponding to the number of years during which it would normally last. But the different sections of the course were entirely different from one another; they were not linked to one another as they are in our classes so that each pupil is obliged to progress at the same pace as his contemporaries in each of the subjects taught. In short, the former unity of the class became dissolved in a plurality of parallel courses. In this way the pupil who arrived at the Central School could either follow only one course, or several, or all of them (the time-tabling was supposed to allow for this simultaneity of study). He might belong in the first section for one branch of teaching and in a different section for another. Consequently it was easy for him, according to the preference of his family, either to have an integrated education or alternatively to select and combine the specialised courses which would be the most useful to him in his chosen career. It was he himself or his parents who determined his course of study.

Such a system goes so much against what we are used to that at first sight we are apt to be disconcerted; we will examine shortly what is to be thought about it. But at any rate, we must beware of thinking that the convention had recourse to it as a mere expedient, thought up at the eleventh hour and not adequately considered. The idea had been propounded for a long time and it was bolstered by the authority of the most influential men of the eighteenth century. Condorcet had already sponsored it in the legislative assembly. 'Education,' he says, 'will be divided into courses .... These will be so arranged that a pupil will be able to follow four courses simultaneously or else to follow only one. In the space of about five years, he will be able to embrace the totality of learning, if he has great ability; to limit himself simply to a part of it if he is blessed with a less fortunate make-up.' Before him, Talleyrand had foreseen the same arrangement and vigorously criticised the system of classes: 'One of the main changes in the organisation will consist in dividing into courses what used to be divided into classes; for the division into classes serves no function; it fragments teaching, and subjects the pupils each year, in dealing with the same subject-matter, to different methods; with the result that the minds of young people become confused. The division into courses is natural; it separates what ought to be separate; it delineates each separate part of the teaching process. It reinforces the attachment of the teacher to his pupil and establishes a kind of responsibility in the teacher which becomes a guarantee of his zeal.'

In 1782 President Roland, a moderate and thoughtful mind if ever there was one, was already expressing the same idea: 'The first difficulty,' he says, 'which occurs to me concerns the limitations and the uniformity of the plan which the University has expounded. In it I see all the young people embarking on the same career, following the same set of classes in the same number of years, and in a narrow space of time all striving towards the same kind and the same degree of knowledge; and yet amongst the young people assembled in the same college I see some whose circumstances are different and who should find different employment. The knowledge necessary for some may prove useless for others and differences of intellectual range, diversity of talent and taste, prevent all from progressing at the same pace and being attracted to the same studies.' He asks that 'each subject have its special teachers; each could even be taught in different courses in order to avoid confusion and working at cross purposes. That part of education which concerns morals would be common to all; only the curriculum would be different ...; it would offer the appropriate knowledge to the whole range of intellectual ability and temperament'. As a footnote, he tells us that this is not just his own idea; in particular he refers to a Discourse which was awarded a prize by the academy for floral games (literary competitions) and whose author was a college professor at Toulouse. Thus the idea had been in the air for a long time, and the diversity of the people who accepted and defended it makes it hard to believe that it was without any foundation. For the moment I merely note this; we shall return to the question shortly.

It is worth adding, moreover, that the principle of parallel courses which had been unreservedly written into the first promulgation of the organisational law (year 3) for the Central Schools, was somewhat attenuated and corrected after ten months' experience (the law of 'Brumaire' in year 4). The teaching carried out in these schools, which normally lasted for six years, was arranged into three cycles or sections which were superimposed upon one another. Pupils began in the first at twelve, in the second at fourteen, in the third and last at sixteen. The different subjects taught were shared out between three cycles so that no one could find themselves in two different cycles. Each cycle had its own set of subjects. Drawing was done in the first cycle and there was no question of its appearing in the subsequent ones; the physical sciences were reserved for the second and played no part in the two others (the result was that, since one cycle only lasted for two years, the teaching which took place in it, no matter what it was, could not last longer than that). But within each cycle the autonomy of each of the courses taught there remained intact. The pupil could, according to his pleasure, either follow all of them or follow only one. Consequently his was the final voice in determining his course of study. He had complete freedom to choose the subjects in which he wished to be instructed, except that his age determined the order in which he was to receive the instruction he had chosen.

Let us see now how the internal economy of this system worked.

It is characterised by the predominant place given to those disciplines which are concerned with things, with nature. In the first cycle two out of three courses were of this type: they were drawing and natural history. The second cycle was entirely devoted to mathematics and experimental physics and chemistry. Thus out of the six years which made up the complete course of studies there were four during which the attention of the pupils was almost exclusively directed towards the outside, towards the external world, towards the nature of things. It is indeed a complete reversal of the traditional system; and Fourcroy, in a report to the five hundred, could justly contrast the colleges of the old days in which 'one spent years regurgitating the elements of a dead language' with the new schools, of which there were then ninety, in which young people were encouraged to engage in 'more various and more attractive forms of study. Their active imagination, their insatiable curiosity is nourished by the spectacle of nature and its creations, of the mechanics of the world and the diversity of scientific phenomena. No longer will their intellectual faculties be restricted solely to the study of words and sentences; it is with facts, it is with things that we shall feed their minds.'

However, man was not obliterated in this new system in the same way that nature had been obliterated in all preceding systems. He constituted the object of study which filled the two final years of the courses, that is to say the third cycle. Thus it is only after having studied physical nature that the pupil embarked upon the study of human nature. Moreover, people strove to teach about man and matters human in the same spirit and using the same methods as with things material, that is to say scientifically; in other words the physical and natural sciences which predominated in the first cycles were succeeded by social and moral sciences which had just become established.

Two branches of learning were included. First there was general grammar. The study of general grammar was intended to replace the old formal logic taught in the philosophy classes of the colleges. Instead of describing the mechanism of thought in the abstract an attempt was made to study it and to cause it to be studied by means of the language in which, as it were, it had become crystallised. Thus in a new form, we have a restoration of the ancient conception of grammar which we encountered at the beginning of this history. It was grammar understood as an instrument for logical training.

In addition to man conceived of as pure understanding, the necessity was realised of getting the pupils to understand man as a social being; this was the prescribed goal of two other disciplines which combined to serve this same end: history and legislation. For the history in question was not supposed to consist merely in the teaching of a simple chronology of national events; it was a kind of universal history whose object was first and foremost to illuminate the way in which the great ideas which constitute the foundation of human civilisation became established. 'Above all,' writes the minister Quinette in year 7, 'it is crucial to get the pupils to observe the progress of the human mind at different times and in different places, the causes of its progress, of its aberrations and its temporary retrogressions in the sciences, in the arts, in social organisation, and also to get them to see the constant relationship which holds between human happiness and the number and truth of human ideas.' This historical education was supposed, as one man said who was in a position to observe the functioning of the Central Schools very closely, to furnish the teacher of law 'with the set of experiments which he needed to confirm or verify the general principles of the science' which he had to profess. Indeed law was taken to consist in a description and exposition of the general principles upon which contemporary law and morals were based. The best way of justifying such principles was to show the natural fruit which they had yielded in the course of their evolution in history.

But what of literature, which had only yesterday reigned supreme in education? It was not completely excluded from school but its role had nothing of the prominence which had previously been accorded to it. One course in Latin in the first cycle, one course in literature in the third, and that was all. The Latin course was designed not really to teach the language, which would have been impossible in such a short time, but primarily to supply an object of comparison so that people could better understand their national language. 'In order to learn what a language is,' says Lacroix, 'and in order to form a really clear idea of its forms, it is essential to compare its workings with that of another language.' Secondly, it was also hoped in this way to stimulate a taste for classical literature, which was 'the model for our own', although nobody on this account thought it possible to provide a knowledge of Latin which would enable people to dispense with translations. As for the course in literature, it was purely theoretical and concerned with literary aesthetics; it was restricted to instruction in 'the body of the rules established by the critics on the basis of a close examination of the production of genius'. It had absolutely nothing to do, as Lacroix puts it, 'with developing a talent for writing', which it was thought could only emerge after maturity. No exercises in composition were demanded, beyond the essays relating to the various courses. It is clear that with its scope reduced in this way the teaching of literature was little more than a remnant of its former self, sustained only by a final feeling of respect for an ancient tradition.

This then was the curriculum. We cannot fail to see how daring it was. Nowhere hitherto have we come across so radical a revolution. No doubt, with the Renaissance, we saw great and important innovations occurring, but they were still not on this scale. The Renaissance had preserved the colleges of the Middle Ages, their organisation, their system of classes, in the same form in which they had become established towards the end of the Scholastic period; in these colleges Latin was already taught, classical authors read and expounded; in short, it was enough to cram the work in logic into the two final years in order to make room for the poets, the orators and the historians. In the Central Schools, by contrast, everything was brand new: the academic groupings, the subject-matter taught, the methods used, the character of the teaching staff, all these were created out of nothing. For the first time an attempt was made to organise the intellectual and moral training of youth upon strictly scientific foundations. Not only was the attempt novel but it has never subsequently been embarked upon with such systematic rigour.

It is true that this boldness has been described as mere rashness and thoughtlessness. It has been said that if this educational system was so ephemeral — it only functioned for six years from year 4 to year 10 — this is because it was not constituted for survival, because it was based upon a viewpoint which was radically unsound. Certainly, as I believe and shall show, the external organisation of the schools, even if it did not make failure inevitable, nevertheless made success rather difficult. But I also believe that the curriculum contained some progressive ideas which are well worth recalling, and it is a matter for profound regret that they were nipped in the bud.

Intense criticism has been directed against the principle of substituting courses for classes. And no doubt the way in which this idea was interpreted justifies some serious objections. We cannot allow every family, according to its whim, to construct the course of studies for each child. A country, at least a country which has attained a certain degree of civilisation, cannot afford to forgo a certain shared culture which could never survive such extreme educational individualism. The institution of compulsory curricula which we saw produced for the first time in the mediaeval universities was a response to real needs which are still with us. A society in which education has become an important factor in social and moral life can no more abandon the educational system than it can the moral system itself to the absolutely arbitrary choice of individuals. If it is necessary that the curriculum take account of the needs of families it must, nevertheless, be first and foremost subordinated to more general and higher interests which, consequently, the families will not be fully competent to appreciate.

But if the absence of all rules has its dangers, regimentation which is too strictly uniform is fraught with disadvantages. The more we progress the more we feel that it is essential for our children not to be subject every one to the same intellectual discipline. The ever-increasing diversity of social functions, and the diversity of vocations and of aptitudes which results from this, demand a corresponding diversity in the educational system. It was this feeling which is still well-grounded that was expressed, albeit somewhat immoderately, not only in the academic system adopted by the Convention but also in the schemes put forward earlier by men such as Condorcet, Talleyrand and Roland. It is interesting to note that the need to diversify secondary education which has prompted our most recent academic reorganisation did not emerge yesterday. Its origins go back to the middle of the eighteenth century; and we shall have a chance of seeing that, ever since, this same idea has steadily gained in strength.

This is not all, for the reforms which the Convention was bold enough to institute need to be explained from another point of view as well. In order to deal as effectively as possible with the diversity of careers and skills, it might after all be enough to establish small teaching units within which the system of classes could be maintained with all its former rigour. But another factor intervened which changed the original nature of the class and so posed the problem which we are not perhaps ready to solve, but which will have to be tackled one day. Essentially the classroom with its indivisible unity presupposes a unity in the teaching. It is only completely justified when the teaching is concentrated on one subject-matter and one subject-matter alone, or on very closely connected subject-matters. Indeed a class is a group of children who are taught together. But the common nature of this instruction which they receive implies that they display a sufficient degree of intellectual homogeneity.

For them to be able to be taught at the same time and in the same way they must not be too far apart from one another intellectually. This homogeneity is easy to obtain when the teaching is restricted to a single discipline or to a few individual disciplines; for there is no difficulty in grouping children together who in this one unique respect have palpably progressed to the same point. This condition was satisfied in our former colleges. Only Latin was taught in them. Even when a little Greek and a little French were added the education did not, after all, demand a kind of aptitude other than the literary. This is no longer the case today when the most diverse and heterogeneous of disciplines are taught in our secondary schools; and already this heterogeneity was very considerable in the Central Schools of the Convention. From then onwards it was fallacious to suppose that the homogeneity necessary to one of these studies would necessarily be carried over to all the others. It is very common for the pupils who are most gifted in letters not to have the same aptitude for the sciences. So by what criteria are we to determine which class they should go into? The degree of their proficiency in letters? In that case they will lag miserably and futilely behind their fellows with respect to everything concerning the sciences. According to the extent of their scientific knowledge? In that case they will be wasting their time in literary exercises. The diversity of the subjects taught is thus difficult to reconcile with the rigidity of the system of classes. This is what the men of the Revolution were intensely aware of. And this same sentiment has been subsequently expressed by a number of good minds.

In 1868 Victor Duruy, while recognising that the idea might be difficult to put into practice, nevertheless commended it to the attention of Napoleon III. Ernest Bersot, a moderate thinker if ever there was one, also championed it. 'We would like,' he said, 'to get away from viewing the class as an indivisible unity comprising courses in letters, in history, in the sciences both mathematical and physical, a unity which forces the pupils to follow different courses for which they are not equally ready and which, when it is pitched at the right level for some, is too high or too low for others.' In the course of the investigation for the last inquiry into secondary education the same idea was expressed by several of the people who gave evidence and was categorically endorsed by the commission.

However, it was not completely triumphant. The problem seems, indeed, so complicated that any excessively radical solution must arouse legitimate doubts. The disadvantages of the class cannot be disputed. On the other hand, we must not lose sight of the fact that a group of children working together needs not only a certain degree of intellectual homogeneity; it also needs a certain degree of moral unity, a certain community of ideas and feelings, as it were a small collective mind; this would be impossible if the different groups lacked all fixity and stability, if from one hour to the next they broke up and formed themselves into different groups so that there were a thousand different ways in which they came together and separated. If the same pupils did not have sufficiently continuous contact with one another, if they did not take part in the same exercises, if they were not attached to the same men, subject to the same influences, if they did not live one and the same life, if they did not breathe one and the same moral atmosphere, the spirit of community would be missing. Everyone recognises how inadequate were the moral foundations of those old elementary mathematics classes, precisely because they lacked this unity, being composed of disparate pupils who came from every point in the academic spectrum, from the rhetoric form, from the introductory mathematics form, from the philosophy form, and from other forms.

The truth is that a class is not and should not be a crowd. We have here different requirements, which may even be in conflict, and both of which must be taken into account. At the moment, the only way that I can see of tackling the problem would be, instead of organising the different and unrelated studies in parallel series within the hierarchy of the classes, to group them according to their natural affinities so that each class was defined not by an ordinal numeral but by the nature of the studies which went on in it. This arrangement would be all the more natural because there exists a logical hierarchy amongst the different disciplines and education ought to respect it; moreover, the Convention was aware of this. At all events it is clear that the reforms which the Convention initiated were not the products of a kind of mindless day-dreaming. There existed then, and there still exists, an important problem which remains unresolved; the Convention must be given credit for having raised it even if the solution which was offered for it was not the kind which can be unconditionally accepted. It was by studying the educational theory of the revolutionaries that I became convinced that the system of classes constitutes a problem.

This does not constitute the limit of our indebtedness to it. Everyone recognises the great service which is performed by stressing the educational value of the physical and natural sciences and by according to them a place consistent with their importance. But what has been less remarked upon and what, nevertheless, deserved to be noted was the entirely novel way in which the Convention organised the teaching of the humanities. It was no longer literature which it employed for this purpose, it was again science; but it was science of a new kind. Whereas the natural sciences, although they had been long established, had waited for close on two centuries for the gates of the schools to open to them, the Revolution at a stroke introduced those sciences which had only just been born: the sciences of man and of society.

One might have said that these sciences were still in their infancy, and consequently not worthy of such an honour. And no doubt, given the rudimentary state in which we still find them, they were not up to coping with their task. But this was not a reason for excluding them. There was a case for seeking complementary

means of teaching children about things human without out-
lawing these sciences. Since these sciences suffice for adults,
why should they not have been valuable for children between sixteen and eighteen years old? In the state in which they were, they
were already full of fertile insights of the kind which would stimulate reflection in young minds and, consequently, they could
have been valuably used as educational instruments. In order to
grant to a discipline right of entry into school it is not necessary
for that discipline to have taken definitive shape — does this
moment ever arise anyway? It is enough that it should be capable
of profitably influencing young minds. I would add finally that
the place assigned to these sciences in the Central Schools was right
in accordance with their nature. It was fitting that they should
be taught after the natural sciences, since they were established
later. The ordering of the curriculum should reflect the order
in which the sciences being taught have developed historically.

Unfortunately, as I said at the beginning, all the fruitful ideas
which were contained in revolutionary educational theory were
tainted by the way in which they were put into practice, by grave
organisational flaws. The higher education which the Central
Schools gave children from the moment they entered presupposed
that they had already received a preliminary training of considerable breadth. Remember that they were not taught French; so the
assumption was that they had studied it somewhere else. Now,
below the Central Schools there were only the primary schools,
where what was taught was of an extremely modest nature. Between them and the Central Schools there was a gap which the
men of the period were very well aware of, although they did not
succeed in filling it. From another point of view we have already
pointed out how excessive was the lack of co-ordination between
the courses. This lack of co-ordination was intensified still further
by the complete absence of any internal direction; the schools did
not have a head. Even the aim of each course of study was only
very hazily established; to some extent each teacher tailored it to
suit himself. Add to that the difficulty of finding teachers for all
these new subjects. Remember that in the colleges of the *ancien
régime* neither natural science nor general grammar were taught.
Thus a staff had to be assembled impromptu which nothing had
prepared for this task. It was recruited from the most varied of
professions. Moreover, the choices were made by local panels,
which were not themselves always in possession of the necessary
competence.

All these defects, however serious they may be, would not
perhaps have sufficed to bring about the ruin of the Central
Schools (which seem, at least in certain areas, to have produced

satisfactory results), if they had not become the object of political passion. But the Central Schools were the work of the Convention; under the Consulate that alone was enough to discredit them. Moreover, they in no wise conformed to Bonaparte's educational views. Under pressure from him a law was passed on the eleventh of 'Floréal' in year 10 which abolished them, and which at the same time obliterated all the educational theory of the Revolution. The Central Schools were replaced by *lycées* and in addition small secondary schools which were a preparation for the *lycées* and which were called colleges. The organisation, the content and the methods of the teaching became once more what they had been under the *ancien régime*. The sciences only survived because of the military courses. Latin came to predominate once again. It was a return to the old system. Everything was to start again.

In sum, the achievement of the Revolution in the realm of education was more or less what it was in the social and political realms. Revolutionary effervescence was immensely productive of brand-new ideas; but the Revolution did not know how to create organs which could give these ideas life, institutions in which they could be embodied. It might have been because the revolutionary views were often excessive. It might have been because institutions cannot be improvised or plucked out of nothing, and (since those of the *ancien régime* had been demolished) the essential materials needed for reconstruction were lacking. It might have been for both reasons simultaneously that the Revolution proclaimed theoretical principles far more than it created realities. Even the attempts which it made to translate the theories into realities often redounded to their discredit; for since these enterprises generally ended in failure, the failures were taken as a condemnation of the ideas which had inspired them. These were, however, to survive the backlash which, albeit falteringly, occupied the greater part of the nineteenth century and which proved so difficult to resist and overcome. In this endeavour our finest intellectual forces were engaged throughout this period.

One might say in conclusion that about the only result of all this effort is to have brought us back to the point of departure, to have posed once more the educational problem — and I might add many others as well — in virtually the same terms in which it spontaneously arose at the beginning of the Revolution, except that we are able to take heed from the long experience at our disposal. The result is that the academic history of the nineteenth century was not very rich in innovations; it was a slow, gradual rediscovery of ideas which were already well known to the eighteenth century; consequently it need not detain us long.

chapter 25

Variations in the curriculum in the nineteenth century

Definition of secondary education

In the last chapter we reached the very threshold of the nineteenth century at the moment when the work of the Revolution, after a transitory existence for six years (year 4 to year 10), foundered on the rock of the Consular reaction. The Central Schools created by the Convention, whose perhaps premature originality we have witnessed, disappeared. The old academic organisation was reformed, using the partially new name of *lycées* and colleges. Lastly, Latin regained its old predominance. Apart from the fact that for sheerly practical reasons it was no longer possible to divest the sciences completely of the right of citizenship which they had won, the position reverted to what it had been fifteen years before, and everything had to be begun again.

This restoration came only a few years before a great event which dominates the whole academic history of the nineteenth century. I am referring to the merging of all the educational agencies in the country into a single organism, directly dependent upon the central power and exclusively responsible for education. It was by a decree of 7 March 1808 that the University of France was created. It was the corporative idea which the Revolution had sought to abolish in all its forms which was re-emerging; but in a more extensive form, transformed, adapted to the new circumstances of national life. The fragmented local corporations which had been the old provincial universities — corporations from which, moreover, primary teaching was excluded — were henceforth replaced by a single corporation which covered the whole country and embraced all aspects of academic life, all the schools and all the teachers of every type and of every level. It would certainly be interesting to explore what gave birth to this phenomenon, for it certainly did not emerge, fully-fledged, as the brain-child of Napoleon. It would be interesting to show just how it answered to needs which existed well before the Revolution and which had already found spokesmen in La Chalotais and Roland; just how, nevertheless, Napoleon sought to leave his own mark upon this new conception, by envisaging it as a vast lay congregation, a kind of civilian Society of Jesus whose general he would be; just how, through the force of circumstances, this newly conceived system was to elude what he hoped for from it and to form its own traditions and physiognomy and to acquire its own distinctive character in spite of the surveillance to which it was constantly subject. It would also be interesting to specify the causes which led to the suppresion of the state monopoly and to examine the consequences of this suppression. But however important these questions may be, they concern politics and the administration of schools rather than the history of teaching; they are not directly related to educational theories. So I shall leave them on one side and limit myself to tracing the way in which the content of the curriculum and the methods of teaching developed in the course of the nineteenth century.

What is immediately striking when one sets out to trace the history of the curriculum in the nineteenth century is its extraordinary instability. There were at least fifteen different sets of courses which followed one another. Gréard has resurrected all the promulgations, decrees and circulars which modified education to a greater or lesser extent; from 1802 to 1887 there were no less than seventy-five, of which seventy-four date from before 1870. The programmes are in a perpetual state of flux. One aspect of education, at least on the face of it, changes in the most capricious way: this is science education. Sometimes it expands so that it covers every level and is shared out more or less equally between the different classes; sometimes, by contrast, it is all concentrated into a single class, generally at the top; sometimes it is made to drop out of the compulsory curriculum and declines to the point of merely being an optional extra. Sometimes the sciences are combined with letters, sometimes they are kept apart from them. In short, their condition is one of perpetual nomadism.

This fact is significant and deserves to be borne in mind. People complain often enough today about the excessively frequent variations which have occurred in the curriculum over the past twenty years; and people even blame the current crisis in secondary education on these excessive fluctuations. It is clear that this lack of stability didn't come into being yesterday; it is not to be imputed to this or that personality or to this or that set of particular circumstances. Rather it constitutes an evil which has been chronic for the whole century and which is apparently the product of impersonal forces. Far from being the cause of the evil, it is its effect and its external measure. It does not create the evil; rather it reveals it. If so many diverse combinations have been tried out one after the other and if, from time to time, they have collapsed in ruin upon one another, this is because until very recently people refused to recognise the scope and the extent of the disease which they were seeking to remedy. People think that in order to get our secondary education re-established on solid foundations it would suffice to make certain felicitous changes of detail, to blend the disciplines taught into a better dosage, to increase the part played by letters or that played by the sciences, or alternatively to balance them sagely, when what is really needed is a change of intellectual orientation. Even if we had no other reasons for thinking this, these continual fluctuations would constitute our best evidence. Nothing is more futile than complaining immoderately about these incessant changes and recommending patience; one does not cure a fever victim by advising him to keep calm. But, as against this, it is time to put an end to these wanderings, to understand the education to which they lead, and to confront the problem with courage, in the form in which it arises and in its fullest extent. This is what we shall attempt to do in the pages which follow.

One factor in particular has contributed substantially to this extreme confusion: this has been the intervention of political concerns and prejudices in the formation of educational ideas. From the very beginning of this book we have seen that there was a kind of natural hostility between the spirit of classical antiquity and that of Christianity, and, throughout the whole period of history which we have traversed right up until the present, there has never been a moment, so to speak, when some learned Christian doctor has not appeared on the scene to point out the dangers with which faith was threatened by an exclusively literary culture, and especially by a culture which took all its materials from paganism. Now, by a strange twist of history, from the beginning of the nineteenth century, in the aftermath of the Revolution, a kind of bond of alliance was formed between Humanism and the Church. The champions of traditionalism, in religious as well as in social and political matters, rightly or wrongly saw in the old literary education the best support for what they regarded as sound doctrine, while, by contrast, for them scientific education was suspect. From that time onwards liberals of every persuasion and degree tended to espouse the contrary cause.

The result quite naturally was that, depending on which political party was in power, depending on whether it was by preference orientated towards the future or the past, education oscillated between these two opposing poles. The Consulate and later on the Empire had reserved for the sciences, and especially for the mathematical sciences, a place of some importance: arithmetic, geometry, algebra, trigonometry, surveying, some optics and astronomy were taught in the first *lycées*. The Restoration repressed all scientific education, first by restricting it to the upper forms of the second grade (rhetoric and philosophy), and finally and exclusively to the philosophy class alone. It survived only in the fourth and third grades in the form of lessons on natural history and, even then, the word 'lessons' was scarcely appropriate. For everything was reduced to treating twice a week of topics 'relative to the elements of the natural sciences'. However, in 1828 a more liberal minister, M. de Vatimesnil, took charge of the University; at once the sciences, which had been hitherto so compressed, expanded, came out into the open and found their way into all the classes. With the July monarchy they continued to make progress under the administration of Guizot, but with Villemain they began to lose ground, which, however, they regained with M. Salvandy. This toing and froing continued until quite recent times. In the aftermath of the war of 1870, Jules Simon, in a circular dated September 1872, delivered a harsh blow to the ancient methods of Humanism: Latin verse disappeared, written exercises and essays yielded some of their ground to expositions. Shortly afterwards a political reaction set in, with the result that there occurred a fresh educational reaction: once again the classical system was re-established more or less universally, until the country again switched political direction, around 1880.

In the face of facts as well established as these it is somewhat surprising to encounter an affirmation as categorical as the following: 'Classical studies have always had the honour to be suspect under despotisms .... There is a breath of democratic liberty which blows through classical studies and which is located nowhere in particular but is nevertheless everywhere and which remains in the soul as a latent force.' This utterance is to be attributed to M. Fouillée. Certainly I would not dream of claiming that cultivation of the humanities implies and necessarily imposes a particular political attitude. But still the association of the Humanist spirit with the spirit of traditionalism does indeed seem to be incontestible.

The reason for this curious alliance is not difficult to grasp. No doubt there is justice in the view that, since the achievement of the Revolution was precisely that it instituted a system of education whose foundations were exclusively scientific, science remained, as it were, tainted in the eyes of certain people. However, this alienation derives from causes which are more profound and more respectable.

According to Laprade the opponents of Latin culture could only be 'imperialists, atheists, revolutionaries, socialists'. According to Archbishop Kopp, 'every retreat from classical culture has the effect of shaking the foundations of Christianity'. The reason was in fact, as we have seen, that between literature, in which is expressed the noblest forms of activity of the human mind, and the sciences, which determine and record the laws of the physical universe (since by the sciences we ordinarily understand only the natural sciences), there stretches all that great distance which separates mind from matter, the sacred from the profane. The consequence is that not only for any Christian but also for anyone who has the feeling for what is genuinely and specifically human about man (for what characterises him and gives him his own unique physiognomy amongst other creatures) to rear a child exclusively in the school of the sciences is to depersonalise him, to profane him, to prevent him from developing his true nature. Consequently, once the educational problem consisted essentially in opting between literature and the sciences, it was natural that, on this account, literature, despite the anxiety which it had once inspired, benefited from the repulsion inspired by the sciences and came to be considered as offering the only education which was capable of sustaining a truly human state of mind. By contrast, for anyone who has a vivid feeling for the material necessities of life, for the importance that must be attached to them, for the need not to leave men empty-handed confronting the world of things, any education which is not primarily scientific will inevitably appear inadequate for its purpose.

As long as this antinomy is not resolved, as long as people fail to understand that there are not two orders of values which are at once opposed but mutually incomparable, and between which it is, consequently, necessary decisively to choose, it is inevitable that people's minds, according to their temperament, will incline in their entirety in one direction or the other. Hence this perpetual pendulum effect which we can observe throughout the educational history of the nineteenth century, and which depends upon the individual men who are in charge of events. The only way of putting a stop to this is to find a way of causing these two kinds of education, which up till now have seemed to be facing in opposite directions, to become reconciled to one another or to strive together to one and the same goal.

From among all these tendencies which have followed one another in such chaotic and contradictory fashion, there stand out by their very persistence a few key ideas which only underwent temporary eclipse that they might reappear immediately afterwards and establish themselves afresh with increased vigour, thus testifying to the urgent and constant nature of the needs to which they were responding. This is most notably the case with the idea that, in order to match up to the diversity of careers and vocations, education itself should renounce its ancient unity and become diversified. We observed the birth of this idea in the second half of the eighteenth century; it has never subsequently dropped out of view.

'The unity of French society,' Saint-Marc Girardin was writing in 1847, 'is the fundamental cause of the University. The University should be one, because society is one ... and it ought to be diverse in its education because modern society is essentially diverse in its labours.' As early as the period of the Consulate, people had been forced to concern themselves with organising a special education for candidates for the military life; in this from a certain age science courses took the place of courses in humanities. But this system was tried in only one establishment, the *Prytanée français*, which had been established in the buildings of the Louis-le-Grand college. The system was not made general. However, under the July monarchy, in his 'Memoir on secondary instruction in the kingdom of Prussia', Cousin takes up the idea again. According to the plan which he expounded in his work, grammar schooling would bifurcate into two separate halves. In one, classical culture would continue to be developed along traditional lines; in the other scientific education would predominate over literary education although it would not exclude it. It is true that when he became minister, Cousin did not dare to put this plan into action in its entirety; but from the fourth grade onwards he organised a whole system of courses which allowed the pupils who so wished to leave purely literary classes and to devote themselves primarily to the sciences.

The system later established by the Minister, Fourtoul, on 10 April 1852 is still known as the 'bifurcation system', but it was in no wise an improvisation; rather it was the culmination of a whole progressive series of developments. By this system, which lasted until the ministry of Duruy, pupils divided into two categories from the fourth grade onwards, some studying Latin and Greek, others Latin and sciences. We have here the prototype of our Latin and sciences curriculum whose origins reach back across the systems of Fourtoul and Cousin, and so go right back to the *Prytanée français*, at the beginning of the century. The system of bifurcation left in the minds of the people who administered or experienced it such bad memories that this precedent is scarcely designed to inspire confidence in the future of our present attempt, but it is unjustifiable to draw conclusions from the results of this first experiment regarding the one which we are currently engaged in. We must, in fact, distinguish the principle which may be sound from the way in which it was given application.

1852 saw the very beginning of the Second Empire, that is to say that it was a time of real intellectual depression. In order to prevent the re-emergence of liberal ideas the government handed out education with an anxious and mistrustful niggardliness. An attempt was made to cut out from teaching anything which might be of educational value and provide intellectual fortification; briefly, they sought to sterilise teaching. It was not only bifurcation, but also all the educational methods of the time which left these memories of extreme gloominess. However, it was the system of bifurcation which suffered as a result. Add to this the fact that children were forced to make their choice much too early (in the fourth grade), and that the children in each of the two groups received part of their literary education in common even though such a study could not be the same for both groups, and we have more than enough to explain why the idea of bifurcation was for so long discounted, inspiring such hostile prejudice, we shall also be able to prevent ourselves from giving in to this prejudice too easily and from confusing the principle with its practical application at a particular time.

Besides, this course of study, which borrows its subject-matter half from classical literature and half from the sciences, was only an attenuated form of Humanism. The need to establish a curriculum which owed nothing to classical literature, was, as we have seen, a need that emerged in the eighteenth century, deriving from causes too fundamental to prevent its being vividly felt again in the nineteenth century. One could not fail to realise that there were social functions whose importance was incontestable and for which this very special kind of training seemed to be completely useless. In 1821 the regulation allowed third-grade pupils who did not intend to enter the faculty grades to move after the third grade to study courses in the sciences and in philosophy, where they received special lessons on modern history. This was the starting-point for a new type of curriculum, for a curriculum without Greek and Latin, to give it a provisional negative definition. These special courses were developed in 1828 by M. de Vatimesnil, elaborated by Guizot, who, at the very least, devised a plan for creating a curriculum 'appropriate to professions and social situations which are not necessarily linked with scholarly studies but which are important by virtue of their number, their vigour and their influence for the strength and security of the state'. This was what was then called the intermediary curriculum, the theory of which Saint Marc-Girardin set out in his book on *Intermediary Instruction and its Relation with Secondary Instruction* (1847). This intermediary curriculum Victor Duruy made a reality in 1865 under the title Special Secondary Education. The very use of the expression 'intermediary' or the somewhat self-contradictory juxtaposition of the two adjectives 'secondary' and 'special' to characterise the new curriculum bears witness to the fact that it was somewhat vaguely conceived of.

In fact two different objectives were simultaneously assigned to it, which were difficult to reconcile with one another. On the one hand, people wanted it to be a substitute for certain children for the old classical education, that is why they wanted it in varying degrees to fulfil the same function of providing a general cultivation of the mind. But at the same time it was intended as a preparation for particular careers and professions and consequently, to some extent, had a special character. This ambiguity was certainly more than somewhat damaging to its success. And yet, for a very long time this curriculum oscillated uncertainly between these two objectives, whose incompatibility we shall see more clearly presently, until in 1890 a new regulation finally settled the question at a stroke by deciding that henceforth it would cease to be special and technical and would become classical. This is how the modern curriculum was born which the programme of studies of 1901 definitively integrated into the complex system of classical education which is simultaneously a multiplicity and a unity.

We have now reached the most recent stage of academic organisation. We can see how, at least in its general principles, it is linked to forms of organisation which preceded it, how it emerged from them in a kind of regular evolutionary pattern. It remains for us now to discover what kind of spirit shall inform it. Here we are going to emerge from the past and enter the future. For this spirit does not yet exist; to us will fall the task of creating it.

If we wish to proceed methodically, we shall only be able to anticipate this future by making use of the lessons which emerged from the past, which we have just been studying. It is thus a propitious moment to recall them. We have observed a series of historical phenomena; let us see what ideas they may justify us in forming about what secondary education is, and about what it should become in the future.

First of all, what are its objectives and limitations?

The preliminary and purely negative observation (whose importance, however, we shall soon see) is that secondary education has never had an essentially vocational goal. Neither in the age of Scholasticism, nor under the Humanist regime did the teacher in the arts faculty seek to turn his pupils into members of a particular profession. In the eighteenth century, it is true, statesmen and educational theorists felt the need of creating greater harmony between the nature of education and the exigencies of real life; they concerned themselves with giving pupils access to an education which was more closely related to certain professions, from which classical culture could only deflect men's minds. But despite the practical concern which predominated, perhaps excessively, in the organisation of the Central Schools, these never became technical schools preparing pupils to embark upon the same particular job. The pupil who had taken courses in drawing or in physics or experimental chemistry was, of course, in a better position subsequently to follow such and such a profession than if he had received a purely literary education: but he did not learn this profession at the Central School.

Education should nevertheless so shape the mind that it is capable of benefiting from this kind of training later on. If it does not prepare the mind of the pupils for a particular profession, it facilitates their readiness for such a preparation. If this were not the case, if there were no continuity between secondary education and professional training, the former would constitute a kind of parasitic organisation which was without any social reality; for man is socially useful only when he plays his part in the work of the community, that is to say when he exercises a profession whatever it might be. The college of the *ancien régime* did not, of course, turn out doctors, priests, statesmen, judges, advocates or teachers; but in order to become a teacher, an advocate, a judge and so on it was considered essential to have been through the college. From another point of view, one can see from these very examples that if college allows access indirectly to certain professions, it does not do so for all of them indiscriminately. If then we know which were those professions for which secondary education constituted the preliminary initiation and what were their distinctive features, it will be very easy for us to establish the object of this education.

There is a whole group of these professions with which we are well familiar and which, quite certainly, constitute the principal, if not the unique objective of secondary education. For with university, specialisation begins; it moulds people with particular functions in mind: doctors, teachers, scholars, advocates, administrators. In addition to this, we know what are the links which unite secondary education with higher education, links which are so close that these two kinds of education have for centuries remained inseparable from one another. The first is and has always been the natural and necessary mode of entry into the second. What is characteristic of the function for which university prepares people is that these functions cannot be learned by mere mechanical training; rather they require theoretical training, which is indeed the very thing which is essential to them. In order to prepare young people for them one does not start by teaching them certain movements; rather they are taught ideas. Of course every profession is concerned with action and with practice. But in these professions theory is necessary for practice; it is an essential element; sometimes (as with the scientific professions) it constitutes virtually the whole of them. In order to be able to fulfil these functions it is not enough to possess technical skill, one must in addition know how to think, to judge and to reason. A certain degree of development of the reflective faculties, the speculative faculties, is quite indispensable. The reason is that in all these fields practice is too complex and depends on too many factors, too many variable circumstances, for it ever to be able to become something mechanical and instinctive. It must be guided by the light of reflection with every step it takes.

The development of the power of reflection is presupposed by higher education but is not generated by it. Here we find the specific and indispensable object of secondary education: it consists essentially in arousing the speculative faculties, in exercising them, in strengthening them in a general way, without however committing them to any vocational tasks. The college does not teach a trade, it develops aptitude in judgment, in reasoning, in reflection, which is especially necessary in certain trades. It is in precisely this that its function has always resided. Depending on which kind of reflectiveness seemed the most important — for there are several quite different kinds — the procedures followed have varied; but the goal has remained the same. When the art of judging and of reasoning was assimilated to the art of debating, dialectic constituted the unique subject-matter of secondary education; but this was because it was considered to be the only way of training the mind in a general way. Next it was an understanding of literary matters which was by preference cultivated, that was regarded as embodying the supreme form of intelligence. The specialised nature of this training should not cause us to lose sight of its general character. Indeed this character has never been so pronounced. For since in literature human life in its entirety and, indirectly, nature itself find expression, a literary education gives people an understanding of everything. Was this not the distinctive feature of cultivated gentlemen of the seventeenth century?

Perhaps by linking secondary education so closely with the professions we have been speaking of, we are running the risk of cutting it off completely from careers in industry and commerce? Not at all. For our thesis to entail such an exclusion we would have to agree that these professions require no speculative and theoretical training. Now, if one thing is certain, it is that they are becoming increasingly aware of a need for such training. At least, the managerial functions in industry and commerce can less and less afford to ignore it. No doubt there was once a time in these professions when technique was learned exclusively by practice, by habituation, by application; but nowadays this technique seeks to imbue itself with the theories of science at the same time as science itself is increasingly tending spontaneously to renew all the techniques which for so long were grounded in tradition, unreflectingly accepted. Even now the schools in which future industrialists and future businessmen are moulded are indistinguishable from the schools of higher education in the strict sense; and perhaps the day will come when they take their place in the regular ranks of the University with all the other special schools which the Revolution created and which tradition has sustained. Let us not then be impeded by differences in labelling. Manifestly reflectiveness is penetrating more and more into this sphere of human activity as into so many others; it follows that the young people who aspire to these professions must also themselves be taught to reflect: they need to go to college no less than the future judge. At least, the only differences between them in this respect can be differences of degree.

If from this point of view a secondary education can be valuable at least to some future professionals in economic life, yet it should not and it cannot, without losing its identity, be organised with these professions specifically in mind. To avoid betraying its own nature it must not take as its aim the preparation of people for a life in industry or commerce, any more than one in the law or the army, since its essential characteristic is that it does not initiate people directly into any particular profession. This does not mean that I am disputing the value of the industrial or commercial schools in which future practitioners in industry and commerce are moulded directly on leaving primary school. On the contrary I believe that within these careers there are certain functions which need not theory, not highly-developed speculative faculties, but practical qualities; and there are grounds for arousing and exercising these qualities without delay in children who have a greater aptitude for them than they have for reflection. It is only that, although these schools follow directly after primary schools as do our colleges and *lycées*, we must beware of confusing them with secondary schools as we have just defined them. For each kind of school is orientated in a quite different direction; they must employ quite different methods and draw inspiration from a quite different spirit. Each constitutes a category of educational establishment which it is of the utmost importance to distinguish.

If, failing to recognise these differences, we lump them together under the same headings, we run the risk of talking about both of them at once and consequently of no longer knowing what we are talking about. It is this confusion which has resulted in the fact that people have often confused two very different questions: First, how should we organise an education especially designed for commerce and industry? Second, is it possible to develop a genuinely secondary education which would nurture the reflective faculties in a general way, but which does not include Greek or Latin? And people have thought that having solved the first question the second was also solved by the same token, or *vice versa*.

By secondary education we mean exclusively that education which prepares people for the University and which is specifically defined by the absence of any immediate vocational concern. The features of this education in the whole gallery of our academic system are thus sharply defined. How it is to be distinguished from technical education and from schools concerned with practical application, we have just explained. Like higher education it is directed towards the reflective faculties, but it develops them in a general way whereas higher education makes use of them in a specific form, and in this way we can distinguish the former from the latter. The line of demarcation with primary education is perhaps more vague. Primary education does not prepare people for vocations; it too, at least today, aims to arouse reflection to the extent that in these times no one can be without it. Thus when people think that classical languages are not necessary to secondary education, it is difficult to say where one of these kinds of education ends and the other begins. There are only differences of degree, which are virtually imperceptible at the frontiers. There is nothing less justifiable than the barriers which currently separate these two kinds of school; they are barriers constructed exclusively out of illegitimate prejudices and we must hope that they will be broken down.

In that case, are we not reverting to a formalist educational theory after we have condemned it? The general aptitude for reflection, judgment or reasoning, is, so it would seem, an aggregate of entirely formal habits which are independent of any specific subject-matter. Up till now we haven't even claimed that the secondary school should teach this rather than that, these pieces of positive knowledge rather than others. Must it not be the case that we regard the nature of these pieces of knowledge and their importance as secondary matter, and that our educational ideal is going to turn out to bear a strange resemblance to that which was pursued in the schools of Scholasticism or the colleges of the Humanists? Is it not going to consist in fashioning the mind in a general kind of way, rather than in furnishing and nourishing it?

By no means; for it is impossible to teach a mind how to reflect if there is no specific object for that reflection to fix itself upon. The reflection does not take place in a void. The mind is not an empty vessel which can be directly moulded in the same way as one moulds a glass, which one subsequently fills up. The mind is made for thinking about things, and it is by making it think about things that one fashions it. Right thinking is a matter of thinking aright about things. It is by confronting the intellect with the reality which it should reflect that one can teach the mind how to tackle it in such a way as to form correct views about it. The object of thought is thus an essential factor in the education of the intellect; it is impossible to cultivate the mind by purely formal exercises. The role of the objects, of the subject-matter of teaching, is consequently even greater in importance because the right way of reflecting upon things varies according to the nature of those things. One does not reflect upon things mathematical in the same way as one does about things in the physical universe; and again the way reflection operates upon these things is different from the way it operates upon things in the world of biology, and so on. In short, there are diverse forms of reflectiveness which are a function of the objects to which it is applied. There are different techniques to be mastered which the mind cannot grasp except by making contact with the different kinds of reality with which it is confronted, and in accordance with which it must fashion itself. So necessary is this that in truth there has never actually existed a formalist educational system in the strict sense of the term. Always it has proved necessary to make the child reflect about something, in one case about the abstract forms of pure understanding, in another about matters literary, about the general aspirations of the human mind and heart.

In these cases the subject-matter to which reflectiveness was applied was infinitely tenuous and transparent in texture; the knowledge which it comprised constituted a very small body of information; it was even, in a sense, composed of abstractions, of intellectual concepts, rather than objectively given realities existing outside the mind. It is in this sense that one can describe this kind of education as 'formalist'. But let us apply thought to solid, consistent and resilient objects, to objects from which we have much to learn, and which the mind is forced to reckon with, according to which it must fashion itself; and we can maintain the essential principle that secondary education ought first and foremost to train the mind, without thereby making ourselves liable to the serious charge of formalism.

There are two and only two categories of object to which it is possible for thought to be applied. They are persons on the one hand, and nature on the other; the world of consciousness and the physical world. That these two kinds of object should have a place in education follows demonstrably from everything which we have said hitherto. But there remain two great questions. First, there is no problem about how to set about getting men to reflect about nature. It is by getting them to study the natural sciences. But to what disciplines should we have recourse in order to give people a knowledge of people? Secondly, what relations exist between these two kinds of education? Are they entirely foreign to one another? Do they have different aims? Is an understanding of the world of persons directed towards moral ends, while the natural sciences are geared to temporal and material ends? Or perhaps they are rather preconditions of each other and the physical sciences are necessary for an understanding of persons? This is what we shall examine in the following chapters by way of conclusion to our entire exposition.

chapter 26

Conclusion (I)

Education and the world of persons

In the preceding chapters we have established the following propositions. First of all, that the object of all secondary education is to arouse and develop a capacity for thinking without trying to tie it down to any one particular vocation; it follows therefore that the whole concept of a secondary education system designed to give only a specialised training for particular jobs, say in commerce or industry, is radically incoherent. Having made this conceptual point, we at once added that it is impossible to exercise a capacity for thinking in the void: it has to be directed towards particular objects of thought. The only way of developing the capacity for thought is to present the mind with particular things to think about, to teach it how to come to understand them, to approach them from the direction in which they may most easily be grasped, to demonstrate to it how best it can tackle them in order to arrive at clear and distinct conclusions. Thus when I say that we must cultivate the capacity for thought, I certainly don't mean that we have to submit the mind to some vacuous, because purely formal, culture; what we need is to discover those elements of reality upon which the mind ought to be exercised, for it is these elements of reality which must determine its development. The object of cultivating the mind can only consist in the acquisition of a certain number of intellectual habits and attitudes, which enable the mind to form adequate conceptions of the most important kinds of things. The habits are necessarily a function of the kinds of thing with which the mind is dealing, and they differ when different kinds of thing are involved. Thus the supreme problem in educational theory is that of knowing towards what kinds of thing the public thinking should be directed. And this, of course, is to ask a question very far removed from the formalism which has dominated and continues to dominate secondary education.

There are two and only two main types of thing which are possi ble objects of thought: human phenomena and natural phenomena, the world of the mind and the world of physical things. The first question, then, which we have to ask is also the most important: how in schools are we to teach those things which have to do with man, the 'humanities' strictly defined.

This education concerned with the study of man does not have to be created *ex nihilo*. It has existed in our schools for centuries, and there was even a very long period when it was the only kind of education given in them. We have already seen that the great service rendered to education by the Humanists, not to mention the Scholastics, was precisely to make pupils think reflectively about matters human, seen from a particular point of view. The time has now come for us to evaluate this education which still has not been replaced, to ask why it no longer answers to the legitimate needs of the modern world and how, consequently, it needs to be changed.

It was based on two fundamental principles.

The first asserts that human nature is universally and eternally the same: in its essence it does not vary from one age to another, from one environment to another. It was regarded as self-evident that to the questions of how to think about the world and how to behave in it there is a single right answer which holds true for the whole of the human race. In other words, humanity is not the product of history, not something which acquired its present form only very gradually, after a long process of evolution, and which will be required to continue adapting and re-adapting itself indefinitely. Rather was its form determined once and for all at the outset, and it will be encountered in exactly the same form wherever men shall live. As for the diversity amongst men with which history confronts us, this was said to result exclusively from the fact that this fundamental human nature had never been able to establish itself in its most pure form; everywhere it is overlaid by the parasitic vegetation of diverse prejudice and superstitions which falsify and corrupt it, and which consequently conceal it from the observer who sees only the surface variations, not the true inimitable fundamentals. The most barbaric peoples are those whose humanity has been most completely buried beneath this layer of alien alluvial deposit. The most noble societies are those in which man has been most successful in setting free and making manifest his essential nature as it truly is. It was this hidden but unchanging essential human nature that the eighteenth-century *philosophes* were seeking to uncover beneath all the deceits and artificialities of different civilisations; for this was the unshakeable rock upon which alone they could construct their political and moral systems. Anything else struck them as being like shifting sands on which nothing solid could be built. Moreover, this idea was far from being the invention of the eighteenth century: if one really wished to research into its origins one would have to go back to those makers of Roman law who had already developed the notion of a legal system which would be equally valid for the whole of humanity. In any case, the idea is fundamental to Christianity, since the doctrine of original sin implies that human nature has become corrupt as the result of a particular contingent event, so that it might recover its pure form through the benefit of the Redemption. But whatever the history of this idea may be, it is certain that it was universally believed from the time of the Renaissance onwards; that while the humanists utilised and relied upon it, they did not invent it.

Granted this principle, there was and could only be one kind of education with respect to the world of persons. This consisted in confronting the child with the inimitable unity which is human nature and making him sensible of what it is like. But where can we find it, how can we get hold of it? For a Christian, Christianity alone possesses an adequate conception of what man is; hence it follows with faultless logic that Christian doctrine alone should be used in educating children about human nature, and no other body of doctrine should be allowed to supplement it. However, we have already seen that Christianity, whatever else it may have had, never enjoyed a situation in which it was sufficient unto itself. In order to produce minds receptive to Christian ideas, these minds had to be cultivated, in other words they had to be initiated into a civilisation which had already been established. The only civilisations which were even possible candidates for this role were classical civilisations, especially the Latin; for it was in the Roman Empire that Christianity had developed, Latin was the language of the Church, and there were undeniable affinities between Latin thought and Christian thought.

It was wholly natural, therefore, that people came to see Rome as a society created by Providence, in which for the first time man had succeeded in achieving self-awareness, a knowledge of his true nature, and consequently of the principle on which true morality and true religion are grounded. 'Providence,' says Rollin, 'after having demonstrated in Nebuchadnezzar, in Cyrus, in Alexander, how easily she can overthrow the mightiest of empires, has been pleased to establish one and one only quite different in kind from all others ... whose power was the fruit of all the greatest human virtues, and which on these grounds deserved to become the model for all other governments.' Not, of course, that Latin civilisation had succeeded in completely purging itself of those errors which would only be finally dissipated in the light shed by

Christianity; but it was enough to leave these in the shadows and to fill out the gaps which they created by means of the teachings of the Church. It remained no less true that in Rome essential human nature had expressed itself in its most near-perfect form. Here we have the second postulate of Humanism: that the excellence of the classical writers, but especially of the Latin writers, constitutes the best possible academy in which to study the world of human nature.

So important is this postulate that it is still the major argument invoked by present-day defenders of this system of education. People still claim that the eternal verities found their most definitive expression in Rome. 'In morals,' says Bréal, 'there are some truths which have not needed to be stated twice; centuries ago they found definitive expression such that there is no question of reviewing them: they are taken for granted by all reflective people .... All the commonplaces of classical wisdom about the sanctity of duty, contempt for goods acquired by mere luck, the whole background of ethics, of social conscience and the idea of honour, do not appear in the works of modern writers precisely because they are all in the writings of the classics and they are rightly regarded as needing no reiteration.'

These then are the two postulates of Humanism. Whereas it was natural that they should appear as self-evident truths to the seventeenth and eighteenth centuries, today they can no longer be reconciled with the findings of research in history and the social sciences. This is why, whatever services this education in the humanities may have rendered in the past (and that such services were rendered is beyond dispute), and however great was the advance constituted by confronting the mind with man, not merely reduced to the logical part of himself but with man as a complete and integrated whole, we nevertheless today need a different conception of man, and a different approach to the study of him. But the concept and the approach do not have to be created from scratch. They are gradually and spontaneously emerging from the advance of ideas, and all we have to do is become more keenly conscious of them.

First of all, it is clear that the kind of supremacy accorded to Rome is totally lacking in historical foundations. Latin civilisation is in no way entitled to a position of pre-eminence. Was not the Greek civilisation infinitely richer? In Rome creative originality is really only to be found in the realms of law and political organisation, whereas the fecundity of the Greek genius appears in an immense diversity of forms: in art, in poetry, in history, in philosophy, in science. How impoverished, cold and arid does Roman religion appear when compared with that magnificent proliferation of myths which we owe to the Greeks. Such comparisons could be multiplied. If there ever has been a society where human beings succeeded in realising to the full their essential nature, it is far more plausible to locate that society in Athens rather than in Rome. This is why at the beginning of the nineteenth century certain German humanists like Herder and Wilhelm von Humboldt took the view that, in order to remain true to the very principles of Humanism, it was necessary to overthrow Latin civilisation and replace it with Greek. In this attempt they failed, and Greek civilisation has always remained in the background of human culture. Moreover we are nowadays familiar with other great civilisations which are well worthy to be compared with those of classical antiquity. Can we really believe, for example, that to study the marvellous complexity of Indian civilisation would be of less educational value than studying that of Rome, that the humanity which it enshrines is somehow of an inferior quality? As history and archaeology extend the scope of their discoveries, we come to see more and more clearly the narrowness of wishing to mould man exclusively or almost exclusively on the model of that atypical and limited civilisation which belonged to the people of Rome. Nor was this exclusiveness any more than marginally limited by the few borrowings from Greece usually to be found in the Humanist educational system.

Whatever may be the case concerning this particular issue, let us return now to the fundamental idea on which the whole system was based. Something called 'human nature', unique and immutable, is assumed to exist. Man has had this particular nature ever since he came into being, and it is only his lack of self-awareness which has prevented his true nature from expressing itself freely. This assumption constitutes the most flagrant contradiction of everything we know from the study of history. Far from being immutable, humanity is in fact involved in an interminable process of evolution, disintegration and reconstruction; far from being a unity, it is in fact infinite in its variety, with regard to both time and place. Nor do I mean simply that external forms of life vary, that men do not everywhere speak the same language, wear the same clothes, or observe the same rituals. Rather I mean that the fundamental substance of their way of conceiving the world and conducting themselves in it is in a constant state of flux, which itself varies from place to place. The view that there is one single moral system valid for all men at all times is no longer tenable. History teaches us that there are as many different moral systems as there are types of society; and this diversity is not the product of some mysterious blindness which has prevented men from seeing the true needs of their nature. It is, rather, simply an expression of the great diversity in the circumstances under which collective living takes place. As a result those sentiments which we would dearly like to believe are the most deeply rooted in man's congenital make-up have been wholly unknown to a host of societies. This happened not merely as a consequence of some kind of aberration, but rather because the conditions necessary for the genesis and development of these sentiments simply did not obtain.

Our whole present-day moral system is dominated by the cult of the individual person. To the Greeks and the Romans this was quite unknown; this sentiment did not take root in the soil of the city-states because it ran violently counter to the whole institution which characterised these societies. In other words, it could not have germinated in these societies without introducing a principle which would have led to their destruction and eventual death. If there is one thing that seems to us to be an essential and eternal part of human nature it is mutual affection between parents and children; and yet there are societies in which this bond is so weak that the legal structure of family life bears no trace of it, quite simply because other social groupings have taken the place of the family as we understand it. There are other societies in which the bond holds between the child and his father rather than his mother, and still others of which the reverse is true. It all depends on whether the need of the social organism to survive leads the family grouping to centre around the father or around the mother and her relatives.

Thus nothing could be further from historical truth than the assertion that the cardinal truths of our ethical system found definitive expression in what was said by the sages of classical times. Of course if we detach the maxims which we find in the works of classical writers from the social context in which and for which they were written, if we eradicate from them the stamp of time which they so patently bear, we shall be able to contrive artificially a few commonplaces which can be applied to modern society. But we shall only be able to transform them in this way by destroying their true character, by emptying them of their original content and spirit, in such a way as to leave only the outward form. Ideas such as those of the fatherland, patriotism, honour, humanity, work or courage mean something quite different to us from what they meant to the ancients. Compare even those moral concepts which seem most closely related: how great is the distance which separates them. How vastly different are the eudaemonic ideal of Stoic ataraxia and the Christian ideal of self-denial and holiness.

What I say of the ethical domain is no less true of the cognitive.

If there is one principle which to us appears essential to all forms of thought, it is the principle of non-contradiction. If a judgment is self-contradictory we regard it as being a denial of itself and consequently worthless. Now, there are in existence symbolic systems which in the course of history have played a role as great as, if not greater than, that of science but in which this principle is violated at every turn: I refer to the symbolic systems of religion. Myths constantly treat of beings which at the same moment are both themselves and not themselves, which are at once single and double, spiritual and material. The notion of a single substance capable of infinite division while yet neither diminishing nor ceasing to be the same unified whole in each of its parts; this notion, although it violates the principle of the conservation of matter and energy, is at the root of a wide variety of beliefs and practices which even today can be found amongst a large number of different peoples. There are even different systems of logic which have followed one another or co-existed but which were by no means arbitrary, being all of them equally grounded in the nature of reality, that is in the nature of different societies. For, in proportion as different societies needed to give expression to their consciousness of themselves and the world in religious and mythical forms, in proportion as some religious system was indispensable to their survival, there emerged a parallel need to operate a system of logic which necessarily could not be that which informs scientific thought.

If this is the case then it is easy to see that Humanism was totally misguided in its attempt to teach children about human nature in general, for there is simply no such thing. Human nature is not a specific reality which one finds more in evidence here rather than there, in this literature or that civilisation, and which consequently has a tangibility of its own. It is rather a construct of the human mind and an arbitrary construct at that; for we have absolutely no means of saying what it consists of, how it is constituted, or where it begins and ends. We have just seen in fact that feelings which we regard as the most supremely natural, and ideas which we would be inclined to regard as indispensable to the normal functioning of any kind of thought, have, as a matter of quite normal course, been completely absent amongst whole peoples.

In fact 'man', as Humanist teachers portrayed and continue to portray him, was no more than the product of a synthesis between Christian, Roman and Greek ideals; and it was these three ideals which were used to mould him, because it was these three ideals which had moulded the consciousness of those who expounded him. This explains why there is something abstract and relatively

universal about him, for he is the product of a kind of spontaneous generalisation. Yet for all its generality, this ideal is still
idiosyncratic and transitory, expressing the very special circumstances in which European civilisation developed, and especially
that of our own people. There is consequently no justification
whatsoever for presenting it as the only ideal conception of man,
the only one which expresses the true nature of man; it stands, on
the contrary, in very definite causal relationship to a particular
time and a particular place. If then we wish to give our pupils
some genuinely objective notion of what man is really like, and
not merely a portrait of how he was ideally conceived at some particular moment of history, we shall have to set about it quite
differently. We shall have to find some means of making him
aware not only of what is constant in human nature but also of
that element in it which is irreducibly diverse.

But, it will be objected, if we make the diversity of human
nature the basic subject-matter of education, if we choose this as
the focus on which to direct our pupils' attention, we shall be
bringing into the foreground all those aspects of the development
of the human race which are the most idiosyncratic, accidental,
contingent and ephemeral. What intellectual merit can there be
in that? What value is there in knowing that at some place or
other, among some people or other, some peculiarity has been
noticed in their moral or religious life; and that this peculiarity
was implicit in the transitory condition of the local social situation
at the time? Indubitably if we restrict ourselves entirely to acquainting our children with some more or less titillating curiosity,
some more or less surprising relationship between phenomena,
we shall ourselves be forced to conclude that this method of teaching people about man can only become more scientific at the cost
of being completely stripped of any educational value. My answer
to this is that from a study of the infinite variety of human nature
— and this need not even necessarily be exhaustive — there are
lessons to be learned which are of immense educational value. For
the result of such a study is to give us a picture of man quite
different from that which the Humanists presented us, and one
can scarcely deny that this would constitute a supremely important achievement.

If human nature is so diverse, if it is liable to variations and
transformations the possible multiplicity of which cannot be
determined *a priori*, then unquestionably we can no longer continue to conceive of it as a single reality specifiable in clear-cut
categories, capable of being formulated once and for all time. The
reason this view of the matter is so attractive to us is the tendency,
very deep-rooted within us, to think that the only true form of

humanity, genuinely worthy of the name, is that which emerges in those civilisations which we have got into the habit of investing with the significance of a private cult. But the truth is that if, in our attempt to form a picture of man as he really is, we concentrate solely on one particular and allegedly superior people, our view of man becomes severely narrow and distorted. Of course, there is a sense in which we can describe this form of humanity as superior to that of less advanced peoples, but this does not make these latter any less human. All the feelings, all the states of mind which find expression even in inferior cultures, are nevertheless still essentially human, deriving from human nature, and manifesting certain aspects of it: they show us what it is capable of becoming and creating under specific circumstances. In the myths, legends and skills of even the most primitive peoples there are involved highly complex mental processes, which sometimes shed more light on the mechanisms of the human mind than the more self-conscious intellectual operations on which the positive sciences are based.

As soon as we have fully grasped the infinite variety of the systems of thought which man has thus developed from the raw material of basic human nature, we realise that it is impossible to say, at any particular point in history: here is manifested the essence of human nature; here we can see how it is constituted. For the immense wealth of what has been produced in the past is precisely what makes it illegitimate for us to assign a limit in advance to what man is capable of producing in the future; or to assume that a time will come when, man's capacity for creative innovation being exhausted, he will be doomed merely to repeat himself throughout all eternity. Thus we come to conceive of man not as an agglomeration of finite specifiable elements, but rather as an infinitely flexible, protean force, capable of appearing in innumerable guises, according to the perennially changing demands of his circumstances. Far from its being the case that humanity in its entirety achieves full fruition at some one particular moment of history, there is in each of us a multitude of unrealised potentialities, seeds which may be dormant in the ground for ever, but which may also blossom into life if called upon by the force of circumstance. The *personae* which humanity currently adopts may once again be submerged; new ones may be born and old ones, fallen into desuetude, may be reborn in new forms adapted to the new conditions of life. This is the picture of man which history paints for us; and it differs dramatically from that implied in and propagated by the traditional Humanist education.

But the value of seeing man this way is not of a purely theoretical kind; for, as we should expect, our conception of man is also capable of affecting our conduct.

One reason why we often shy away from relatively novel social enterprises, even when we are more or less lucidly aware that they are essential (and this incidentally is why even the most acute minds are inclined to be neophobic), is that we conceive of human nature as something which is narrowly and rigidly circumscribed; and consequently it appears to us to be essentially hostile to any innovation of real significance. The limits within which it is capable of change seem to us to be extremely narrow. We believe, for example, that the conception of human desire on which we base our present-day system of ethics describes essential and immutable features of human nature; and consequently any reform which depends on a relatively radical modification of human desires most easily strikes us as a dangerous and impracticable utopianism. While it is obvious that human nature cannot become just anything at all, it is equally certain that the limits to what it can become are set very much farther back than is suggested by the crude examination on which popular opinion is based. It is only because we have got so used to it that the moral order under which we live appears to us to be the only one possible; history demonstrates that it is essentially transitory in character. For by showing that this moral order came into being at a particular time under particular circumstances, history justifies us in believing that the day may eventually come when it will give way to a different moral order based on different ethical principles. Amongst all the advances accomplished in the past, there is scarcely one to which this *ne plus ultra* argument has not been raised in opposition; and yet historically evolution has always played havoc with the restrictions which men have sought to impose on it. When we reflect on these past experiences, we ought to become very suspicious of claims to be able to restrict the possible scope of evolution in the future.

To sum up, human nature as it manifests itself in history is above all something which we can and should credit with amazing flexibility and fecundity. We need not fear that this conviction will cause men's minds to swing abruptly from neophobia, which is one kind of evil, to what is a different but no lesser evil, namely revolutionary excess. What history teaches us is that man does not change arbitrarily; he does not transform himself at will on hearing the voices of inspired prophets. The reason is that all change, in colliding with the inherited institutions of the past, is inevitably hard and laborious; consequently it only takes place in response to the demands of necessity. For change to be brought about it is not enough that it should be seen as desirable; it must be the product of changes within the whole network of diverse causal relationships which determine the situation of man.

Another practical consequence of this view consists in impressing upon us the fact (which follows from the previous point) of how little we know ourselves. When we contemplate the history of the modes of human behaviour, thought and feeling, all of which are so different from one another and from those to which we are accustomed, and yet which are characteristically human, rooted in human nature and expressive of it, how can we fail to realise that we contain within us hidden depths where unknown powers slumber but which from time to time may be aroused according to the demands of circumstances? This extended and expanded view of humanity makes us realise more clearly how impoverished, flimsy and deceptive is the one yielded by direct observation of ourselves; for we must candidly admit that there exists in us something of all these styles of humanity which have historically succeeded one another, even if we are not currently sensible of the fact. These men of former ages were men like ourselves, and it is consequently impossible that their nature should be completely foreign to us. Similarly, there live in us, as it were, other men than those with whom we are familiar. This proposition is confirmed by the findings of modern psychology, which reveal the existence of an unconscious psychic life beyond that of consciousness: a life which science alone is gradually managing to uncover, thanks to its special methods of investigation.

But the important thing to see is how much more convincing is the historical evidence for this proposition. For history exposes us to a large part of all these unknown riches which we bear with us. It enables us to become concretely aware of them. We will act quite differently depending on whether we believe that we can attain complete self-knowledge by a simple act of self-examination, or whether we realise, rather, that our most apparent characteristics are also the most superficial. For in the latter case we are less liable to yield to motives, ideas and feelings which brush against our consciousness as if they were the whole of ourselves, whereas we know that we are in fact made up of much else besides, which we do not directly perceive but which it is nonetheless important to take into account. We become aware that to achieve real self-knowledge, and in consequence to act knowing what we are about, we must approach the matter in a quite different way: we must treat ourselves as an unknown quantity, whose nature and character we must seek to grasp by examining (as is the case with external things) the objective phenomena which express it, and not by giving heed to those so transitory and unreliable impressions of inner feelings. This could be proved by taking the example of a choice of vocation, which is often made at random though it ought to be guided by objective considerations based on observation.

It is plain that this method of teaching about the world of persons is a far cry from merely collecting curiosa. From it a new conception of human nature emerges; and this conception is not just an abstract idea designed to enrich the corpus of the speculative sciences, but a whole new cast of mind with which we need to impregnate the intellect and thereby the will. I said at the beginning of this work that what our education suffers from most is the fact that the teacher can see no clearly defined goal towards which to strive. Here we have a first goal which deserves to be methodically and systematically sought after. It contains everything which is necessary to attract someone engaged in an activity which he would like to regard as useful.

But how are we to attain this goal? This education in the world of persons, via what disciplines and with what methods is it most suitably carried out?

I reply that first of all the principal condition — certainly necessary and to some extent sufficient — for carrying out such an education, is to realise the need for it. Anyone who is determined to teach about these things will easily find a suitable means for doing so. For despite official curricula, every subject-matter can be used to this end. Nevertheless some subjects are more easily adapted for this purpose than are others. What are they?

If the psychological and social sciences were more advanced, they would be the most obvious candidates for this role. To them would fall the task of enabling us to understand human nature, just as it is the goal of the physical and biological sciences to enable us to understand the nature of material objects. However, given the rudimentary state in which they are at present they are in no position to serve our purposes. An idea of the kind we have been discussing cannot be implanted in people's minds, so that it points them in a specific direction, by means of the few abstract, fragmentary and disputable propositions which the cultural sciences have succeeded in setting forth. Since it is the spectacle of human diversity, as it manifests itself in history, which is to evoke this conception, it is to history that we must have recourse. Historical and social studies are close relatives and they are destined eventually to merge with one another.

By history we must understand not the history of all the peoples of the world (such rapid surveys make no profound intellectual impression), but at least the history of several peoples, selected with discrimination from amongst those which differ from the ones with which we are directly acquainted. For, I repeat, it is essential to take the pupil out of his own country, to acquaint him with men other than those to whose ways he is accustomed. Two kinds of people in particular seem to suit this role ideally: those of Greece and those of Italy. They are at once very different from ourselves and at the same time they are of special interest to us on account of the special ties which unite us with them. This history would benefit from being illuminated by that of other societies, even those which are considerably less advanced. For these lower forms of humanity survive into Greek and Roman civilisation; both Rome and the Greek city-state have roots which penetrate deep into the world of the barbarians and even beyond, with the result that they contain numerous ideas and customs which can only be understood by setting them beside those which we find in full flower amongst much less advanced peoples. How many instructive parallels could thus be made along the way, which would at least give the pupil a glimpse of types of humanity over and above those which he was studying directly. But of course we must be on our guard against presenting to him all these practices and beliefs as things bizarre which are the product of human aberration: rather we must give him a feeling for their rationale, make him aware that they are natural, and elicited by a certain disposition in the order of things.

I include in this historical education the teaching of the relevant literatures, which seems to me an inseparable part of it. For it is in the literatures that the moving principle of the civilisation becomes definitively articulated, at least as long as science has not become an essential feature of the general culture. It is not enough for the teacher to talk in a general way about the manners, the ideas and the institutions of a people: the pupil must touch them with his own hands, must see them alive in the surviving documents; or, at least, in those where those ideas and practices are depicted most vividly. This is what ought to be the main object of the study of literatures. When they are only used to mould taste, one may well ask if the time taken is worth the benefit which results. At bottom they have always been used for something else: namely, to arouse and exercise this feeling for things human, which the Humanists to their lasting credit were always supremely concerned to cultivate. And indeed there is no other way in which this sense of the human can be acquired.

Let us then continue the work of the Humanists, but transforming and revitalising it with new ideas. Let us use the classical literatures not to familiarise the child with this abstract and generalised ideal of man, which was cherished in the seventeenth century, but to show man as he is, with his almost limitless capacity for change, in the extreme complexity of his nature which is capable of manifesting itself in an immense diversity of forms. Just as the literatures will be studied in a different frame of mind, they will be able to be studied by different methods. For if a literature is to be used as a means of getting to know a civilisation, a knowledge of the language in which that literature is written may still be useful, but it is no longer essential. A knowledge of the language is valuable as a means of getting closer to the ideas one is striving to grasp; but as soon as the essential thing ceases to be an appreciation of the aesthetic values, a translation can to a large extent — and especially at the level of the first initiation in the secondary school — take the place of the text. Thus we can see how secondary education might achieve one of the main aims which it has always pursued without making compulsory a study of the two classical languages. Thus understood, a study of the civilisations and literatures of antiquity will have approximately the same effects as if the Latin and Greek languages were taught.

If it is necessary for us to have an idea of the diversity of the human types which have succeeded one another in the course of history, which indeed still coexist today (for they exist wholly or partially even in our very midst), it is clear that there is one type of humanity which it is of crucial importance that we understand, namely our own: the one towards which we tend to aspire, the one which we as Frenchmen and, more generally, as members of civilised society in the twentieth century take as our model. This is the aim which an education in our own history and literature ought to serve. This too should be used above all as a means of initiating us into a particular civilisation: our own. It should steep us in an understanding of the elements out of which it is constituted; and, because our own history and literature are closely bound up with those of the peoples to whom we are closely linked, foreign literature and history should serve to mitigate the over-narrow exclusiveness which would otherwise be endemic in the teaching. But however great the value of this education based on modern studies, it will still be to some extent distorted if it does not take its rightful place in the educational scheme, if it has not been prepared for by other studies. We cannot understand present-day humanity except in relation to that which has preceded it. This is why an education in the world of persons which was restricted exclusively to a study of the history and literature of modern peoples, would completely fail in its task.

chapter 27

Conclusion (II)

Education and the world of nature: the sciences
The development of logic by means of languages

The problem of secondary education, as we habitually pose it, consists almost entirely in the institution of more or less methodical enquiries into the relative educational merits of the arts and sciences. Thus formulated, there can be little hope of an objective solution, for it is far too vulnerable to personal preferences. Everyone inclines towards the dictates of his own temperament. This is why these debates most frequently degenerate into conflicting pleas for and against, depending on whether the protagonist's own intellectual bent is more towards aesthetic subtlety rather than scientific precision, whether he is more interested in artistic emotions than in positive knowledge, or *vice versa*. As you have seen, we have been concerned to pose the question in quite different terms. We have not been enquiring whether we should educate through the medium of the literary disciplines rather than through that of scientific disciplines, but rather what aspects of reality it is most appropriate to teach. The fact is that forming the mind, which is the ultimate aim of secondary education, is not a matter of training it in the void by means of formal gymnastics. It consists in getting it to acquire the essential habits and attitudes, so that it can fruitfully confront those different aspects of reality with which it is ultimately destined to deal, and so that it can make sound judgments about them. These attitudes can be acquired by the mind only when it is made to face things directly, as they are and as they operate. It is by practising doing this that the mind will acquire the structures it needs. This is why the crucial question is to find out what objects it is appropriate for the intellect to tackle. There are two major categories of things which it is essential for man to understand: the first is man himself, the second is nature. Hence the two great fields of study: on the one hand, the humanities, human minds, the manifestations of consciousness; on the other, the physical universe.

That man needs to understand man, it is superfluous to demonstrate. This need has been seen so clearly that, until very recent times, response to it has been excessive: at the end of the eighteenth century, secondary education still consisted entirely in the study of humanities. In this area, therefore, we only need to continue a tradition which has long been consecrated by custom; but we must continue it by transforming it, in such a way as to harmonise it with the progress of our knowledge and the needs of the present day. The teachers of humanities in the Jesuit colleges and in those of the University only gave to their pupils a simplified picture of man, truncated and reduced to a few very general states of consciousness and a few simple, universal ideas. But the truth about human nature is that it is highly complex, and it is this complexity which we need to teach. Not that it is either possible or desirable to deal with all the elements involved, whose number is infinite; such a task, which is in any case unrealisable, goes beyond the bounds of secondary education. What we have to do is to imbue the child with a feeling for this complexity. We have seen how it is only by setting a study of the history of ancient peoples beside that of our own, of ancient literatures beside modern ones, that we can succeed in evoking this feeling – without its being necessary, for all that, to make children learn the languages in which these literary monuments were written. It is by learning to understand ideas, customs, political constitutions, forms of domestic organisation, ethical and logical systems other than the ones he is used to that the child will become aware of the vital richness of human nature. Thus it is only from the historical perspective that we can appreciate the infinite variety of the potentialities of human nature. It is for this reason that it has seemed to us desirable to extend our historical study of the secondary school as far back as possible. I even went so far as to express the wish that a teacher might be familiar with peoples other than those of Greece and Rome, so that he might be able to give his pupils at least some awareness that beyond this particular manifestation of the human spirit, there are others, which are again different, commonly regarded as being 'less advanced', but which nevertheless are worthy of investigation because they too constitute manifestations of the human spirit. He will have a ready opportunity for doing this, since the societies of the classical world had roots in these allegedly inferior cultures and still bear the marks of these origins. How lamentable it is, therefore, that in two out of four of the branches of our present-day (1902) classical education, history and literature play virtually no part! The study of mediaeval and modern history and of the corresponding literatures cannot possibly provide a substitute. It is a grave mistake to think that in order to understand man it is sufficient to study him in his most modern and developed forms. We can only understand him by analysing him; and we can only analyse him through the medium of history. There is, therefore, a serious gap in the curriculum we actually operate at present, and we must be aware of this gap in order to find ways of bridging it.

We come now to the second main branch of learning which we have distinguished: the study of nature.

We have seen how it came to acquire the rights of citizenship in our academic system: it was for reasons of a utilitarian kind relating to specific professional requirements. It was the increasing importance in economic life, around the middle of the eighteenth century, of industry-centred professions which created awareness of the need for a kind of education for young people, to prepare them better for these professions, from which, it was felt, Humanism could only put them off. This is the reason why, historically, this branch of learning was introduced into our schools; but does it follow that this is the only reason we can offer for continuing with it?

If there were indeed no other reason, we should have to make it the exclusive province of aspirant engineers, industrialists and business men. Now, no one would deny today that some scientific education is essential for those who are going to be magistrates, lawyers, historians, men of letters, or statesmen; in a word, without such education, a man is inevitably regarded as being intellectually incomplete. This is the first reason for suspecting that a scientific education must have some other *raison d'être*. Moreover, if the teaching of science cannot be justified in any other way, we shall have to resign ourselves to the fact that it is an inferior kind of teaching, virtually lacking in any educational value at all. No one seriously doubts that teaching is educational only in as far as, by its very nature, it has the capacity of exerting a moral influence on the way we are and the way we think; in other words, in as far as it effects a transformation in our ideas, our beliefs and our feelings.

A subject-matter which limits itself to providing us with knowledge which will give us a greater control over the world of things may well by of use in enabling us to increase our material prosperity; but it can in no way affect our interior life. The Christian concept of education is far from being without justification: if the symbolic language in which it has enveloped itself is no longer acceptable as scientific truth, underlying these symbols there is nevertheless a profound truth we ought not to abandon. If the human mind, freed from dogma, cannot concede that there exists in us a supernatural guiding principle which is an emanation from the divine, it remains true – and empirically true at that – that human consciousness is still for us the single most important fact about the world, that which gives it incomparable value, and to which, consequently, everything should ultimately be related. Moreover, it remains true that the function of education is first and foremost to educate the human being, to develop the seeds of humanity which we carry within us. But an education whose sole aim is to increase our mastery of the physical universe is bound to fail in this central task. This explains why science teaching still has such low status, and is regarded as of only secondary importance in our educational system. It is seen merely as an optional extra. Cold, languishing and lifeless, it is dragged or rather towed along behind the study of the arts; and hardly anyone sees any inherent link between these two types of discipline. As long as science is conceived of in this way, as directed exclusively towards the external world and to things which have nothing to do with us, it is impossible that the subject will be humanised and revitalised.

But this dichotomy is a false one, which depends on nothing to do with reality but solely on the way in which we conceive it. It is a hang-over from the past. Far from its being the case that between the disciplines which deal with the world of persons and those which deal with the world of things there is a great gulf fixed, the fact is that they mutually imply one another and converge on the same end. It is because people fail to recognise this underlying unity that they can plausibly deny the educational and indeed the moral value of a scientific education.

In the first place, since man is a part of the universe, one cannot abstract him from it without denaturing him and without truncating him. He is not a self-sufficient entity, but a part of the whole in which he fulfils his special function. He can consequently understand himself only if he has some understanding of nature and the relationship in which he stands to it, since it is his environment and he is dependent on it. This is why even the most idealist religions, even those which make thought and the life of the mind supreme, even those which value it inestimably, still have some sort of cosmology. They do not restrict themselves to teaching man about the diverse elements within himself, they also inculcate in him a certain way of conceiving of the universe so that he may be able to take his place in it. Our secondary school curriculum, just like our primary school curriculum, is secular nowadays; but if it is to take the place of the religiously orientated curriculum, which it has a rightful claim to replace, then it must still be able to provide the same services. It too will consequently have to concern itself with teaching man about nature, in order that man may understand the part he himself has to play within the natural order.

It is far from being the case that the science teacher should, in the manner of someone telling the rosary, restrict himself to a recitation of geometrical theorems, physical laws or chemical formulae. What is far more important is that he should instil in the minds of his pupils a number of general concepts wich will enable them to construct a picture – which will vary with respect to the degree of its vagueness and incompleteness, depending upon the child's age and the progress of scientific knowledge at the time – of the nature of that external reality to which the child is related in so many different sorts of way. Seen in this light, science teaching takes on a wholly new significance, since it becomes naturally and necessarily the complement of studies in the humanities.

For example, there is a belief which, depending on whether or not we hold it, whether or not we are deeply and powerfully convinced of it or whether our conviction is only superficial, completely alters the way we conduct ourselves and the way we think we ought to conduct ourselves: this is the belief that the universe is determined. Depending on how we envisage the world, we develop quite different conceptions of the part we have to play in it, and consequently of what we ourselves truly are. The world will appear radically different depending on whether it is conceived of as being governed by the arbitrary whim of fate (as in ancient times), or by a benevolent personal Providence, or at the other extreme by laws of necessity which we can do nothing to alter. On the other hand, it is not enough, if we are to deal adequately with the concepts of necessity and determinism, that they be expounded haphazardly in lessons whose subject-matter and treatment are primarily abstract and philosophical. The pupils must have come to ascertain the truth about natural necessity, not in a general but in a particular sort of way, just as humanity itself gradually came to understand it in the course of its history, by observing the clustering of phenomena according to necessary connections deriving from the nature of things. This understanding must have come slowly and progressively, intermingled with all the other threads of our thoughts so that it is everywhere present. It will not do then if it is taught late in the day by the philosophy teacher; it is the business of science teaching itself to ensure that it gradually comes into focus and impregnates the mind by slow and continuous influence.

Not only is nature the immediate theatre of activity as far as man is concerned: he is himself inseparable from it because it is in nature that he has all his roots. The human race is only one amongst the animal species; and it is impossible to understand anything about the former if one isolates it from the whole process of evolution. However one resolves the problems which are posed in this sphere, whether one accepts the transformist solution or its alternative, it is impossible to form any concept of human nature whether true or false unless one takes into account its relationship with the rest of the animal kingdom. Moreover, if consciousness is our most distinguishing feature, it can exist only with an organic substratum upon which it is dependent; and it is essential for pupils to be able to understand this dependency. It is essential then for them to understand this organism with which the moral life is so thoroughly intermingled. But consciousness is related not only to the domain of the organism: it is also linked, no doubt less directly but still very closely, to the whole of its cosmic environment. In particular, the way in which human beings group themselves on the surface of the earth, the configurations that are created by these groupings, or to be more precise the form and structure of human societies, their density, their extent, the commercial activity which takes place between them and consequently the level of their civilisation: all these depend on the nature and disposition of the land. Here we have precisely the essential subject-matter of geography, especially of what is known as human geography, that is the study of these relationships of dependence. There is nothing which science can teach us about the way we ought to conceive of the total habitat of humanity, the Earth, which does not affect the conception that we have of ourselves. As Auguste Comte quite rightly pointed out, the old anthropocentric conception of man was finished once the law of universal gravitation had been discovered and we knew that the Earth, far from being the centre of everything, is but a minute fragment of a universe which is infinitely greater and which is itself lost in a multitude of similar universes.

This is not all: there is another point of view from which the sciences are necessarily involved even more directly in any genuinely human education. As I have said, the educational value of the study of literature resides not solely in the aesthetic merits of the works. If this were the case the domination of our own academic system which has for so long been exercised by Latin would be inexplicable. The value of these works is that they show man in all his aspects and consequently reveal his nature. But the sciences are also human achievements; they too are a product of the mind, and consequently manifest its nature. Science is human reasoning in action. Once we have empirical science, literature can no longer constitute the exclusive subject-matter of even a purely human education, for there is a whole area of humanity which is being excluded. If it is essential for us to know the extreme diversity of feelings which have stirred the human heart, that we should have lived them through thought, as well as the great moral religious and aesthetic beliefs which men have held, it is no less important that we should be initiated into the advances and procedures whereby human reason has progressively taken control of the world.

This initiation is not of purely theoretical and speculative interest; these processes of scientific thought must be known not simply for the satisfaction which knowing them provides, but in order that we can assimilate them ourselves. Science contains ways of thinking and reasoning which we cannot learn in any other school and of which we should know nothing if science did not exist. It is a mistake to think that all the logical faculties, all the intellectual operations which science uses, exist in us ready-made; and that it is consequently only a question of becoming aware of them, of exercising them, and of applying them, as the Scholastics thought. If this were the case, would logic have undergone all the successive variations which it has seen in the past? Did man have any idea of what the inductive method was, or experimental reasoning, before the experimental sciences became established? Even in the seventeenth century a man like Bacon only had a very vague and vacillating notion of induction. Similarly it was only when the mathematical sciences had reached a certain degree of development that the nature of deductive reasoning was fully understood. Indeed there is no science whose principal advances have not consisted in the fortifying, refining and perfecting of the logic of its own procedures. There is a whole area of logic which is by no means the least complex nor the least important, and whose discovery was the result of science and certainly did not precede it. Consequently it is only by living the scientific life that we can acquire an understanding of this logic. This is because science is not the work of isolated individuals; it is the product of co-operative enterprise in which scientists of all kinds and of all places come together. Thus it represents, at each moment of its history, a kind of résumé of human experience as this has been concentrated and accumulated year after year, from generation to generation. Its intellectual worth is consequently and quite naturally infinitely greater than that of individual minds operating on their own and without recourse to anything other than themselves. This explains why it is from science that we have everything to learn; in science we find a kind of exemplary rationality which is the ideal model upon which our individual rationalities should seek to model themselves. Philosophers have often speculated that, beyond the bounds of human understanding, there is a kind of universal and impersonal understanding in which individual minds seek to participate by mystical means; well, this kind of understanding exists, and it exists not in any transcendent world but in this world itself.

It exists in the world of science; or at least that is where it progressively realises itself; and it constitutes the ultimate source of logical vitality to which individual human rationality can attain.

Teaching of the sciences serves not only to render the world familiar and, consequently, to perfect our understanding of man; it is an additionally invaluable tool in the development of logical thinking. And here we have the means of filling the serious gap – which we have had occasion to note – in our secondary education. In fact, we have seen how the training in logic which had been instituted by the Scholastics was swept away by the Humanist revolution without anything being put in its place. Now, it is difficult to regard as being entirely normal an educational system which interests itself so little in the development of those faculties which make for logical thought. Of course, there is no question of going back upon our unequivocally expressed condemnation of Scholastic formalism. Scholasticism was a response to an age in which the experimental method was unknown, and in which thought could only make contact with external reality via the medium of those opinions which men formed concerning it, by confronting these opinions with one another by means of argument. Today, thanks to the experimental method, we can reason about things directly and without any intermediary; new forms of argument have been born, a new kind of training in logic has become possible, that training which is generated by scientific life itself. In order for this kind of training to become organised and as fertile as can be expected it is, in addition, necessary that the teacher feels the necessity of it. He must, that is, realise that his job is not confined to expounding the particular results of the science for which he is responsible; he must also and above all explain the methods, the mental operations, the logical mechanisms of which these results are the product. The methodology of the sciences, which today is touched upon in the philosophy class alone, should not be divorced from the teaching of the particular sciences. On the one hand, only he who has practised the sciences is equipped with the necessary competence to render its methods intelligible. On the other, this method can only be really understood by the pupils if they see it in action, if they have it explained to them at the same time as it is being applied, if they are trained to practise and apply it themselves. It will thus be up to the teacher of the sciences to teach the methods which he uses, the reasoning underlying them, and the principles upon which they are grounded. Unfortunately, we know only too well that in this sphere everything remains to be done.

Training in this kind of reasoning is all the more valuable because it can be put to work not only in the study of material things but in the study of man himself. The idea, indeed, is becoming increasingly well established that man is not a world within a world, that he is not separated by a void from the rest of the universe. Increasingly the tendency is to see the human domain as simply the natural domain which, of course, has its special features just as the biological domain has its special features by comparison with the domains of physics and chemistry, but which is subject to the same essential laws as the other realms of nature. If that is the case there can exist no special privileged procedures for understanding it, no mysterious avenues which allow us to dispense with the tortuous and toilsome roads which physicists, chemists and biologists are forced to follow in their investigations. If human reality is a reality like any other, then in order to discover its laws it will not be enough to turn oneself inwards, to meditate internally and to make deductions. Rather must one observe it in the same way as we observe things in the external world, that is to say from the outside; we must experiment and make use of deduction or, if experimentation in the strict sense is in practice impossible, we must find a way of setting up objective comparisons which can fulfil the same logical functions.

These new methods and the key ideas from which they derive: where can they be learned except at the school of the sciences, which have already advanced them to such a high degree of perfection? Everything points to the fact that the great gulf which still separates the study of physical nature and the study of human nature is now nothing but a relict which is destined to disappear. The day will soon come, and we must seek to hasten it, when the idea of trying to educate an historian or a linguist without first of all initiating him into the discipline of the natural sciences will appear to be a veritable aberration. It is obvious that, to the same extent that we think it necessary to adopt the same attitude in regard to ourselves as the scientist adopts in regard to things, we must train our children in the *lycées* to take up this essential attitude towards the world of persons. A sound scientific education seems to be an indispensable condition of all truly human education.

Thus the study of the sciences, far from constituting a kind of intrusive and alien element in our educational system, far from being an outsider to it and a threat to its economy, is in reality a valuable auxiliary, and an essential element in the older humanistic education which for so long was completely predominant. Although it is orientated towards the outside it leads us away from ourselves only to bring us back to ourselves; but it brings us back armed with, and enriched by, precious insights which cast new light upon our own nature. Between these two kinds of discipline there exists close solidarity. This solidarity is even more absolute than might appear from what has already been said, for it is reciprocal. Not only is it the case, as we have just seen, that natural science helps us to understand mankind better; but the study of things human, in addition to being intrinsically indispensable, is also a necessary preparation for the study of the world.

Indeed, the logical training which emerges from the practice of the positive sciences is not enough on its own; it presupposes something else which is more elementary and which must be sought at a different source. In order to derive value from an initiation into the natural sciences one must already posses a certain mastery over one's own thinking; one must have already acquired a certain aptitude for clear, distinct and coherent thought. This requires a whole education which must begin before scientific education, and which must be pursued for many years in parallel with it.

Naturally, thought presents itself to the mind in a global and confused form. It is not an organised series of clear ideas, not a chain in which the rings are firmly linked to one another; rather it is that the diverse representations which we experience simultaneously are lost amongst one another so that we cannot say where one begins and the other finishes. They are so intimately interpenetrated that they exchange their identities. The affective state in which we find ourselves at any given moment adds its own colouring to the ideas with which our consciousness is filled at the time, so that everything seems sad or gay to us depending on whether we ourselves are feeling sad or gay. Impressions vary completely, depending on those which have gone immediately before: this is known as the law of contrasts. In this way the images which an object may have left in our memory come to mingle with the sensation which we are presently experiencing so that together they form a confused whole in which it is impossible to distinguish what derives from the past and what is due to immediate experience.

This vagueness reaches maximum intensity in the child, who cannot distinguish sensations from one another, who cannot even locate them at specific points in space. Because this confusion is fundamental it permanently inheres in the natural movement of thought. When we reflect on a subject or a question, what we notice first of all are vast blocks of vague ideas, of representations which are synthetic and consequently confused. Logical thought, by contrast, is made up of specific conceptions capable of being formulated by definitions which map the boundaries separating them from related but different conceptions, and which, by means of such a limitation, avoid the mix-ups, the interpenetrations, all the symptoms of contamination by illogicality whose consequence is confusion. Between the point of departure and the point of arrival, between spontaneous thought in the state of nature and logical thought which is reflective, self-disciplined and self-conscious, there is thus a great gulf fixed. How has man been able to bridge it?

Principally by means of language. It is words that introduce distinctions into the thread of our thinking. For the word is a discrete entity; it has a definite individuality and sharply-defined limits. In order to express our ideas by means of words we must separate them out; we must shatter the natural nebulousness of our thought and resolve it into its elements. In a sense, language does violence to thought; it denatures it and mutilates it since it expresses in discontinuous terms what is essentially continuous. This is why it is true to say that we never succeed in fully expressing our thought; it's because the contents of consciousness cannot be translated by language except approximately, just as the continuity of geometrical sizes can only be approximately expressed through the series of numerals. Of course, it would be quite erroneous to say that language must do everything, that it is the sole agent of distinctiveness and clarity. Nothing can absolve consciousness from the task of grasping a confused collection of thoughts, of isolating it, of concentrating upon it all the light which it can command, and of illuminating it in such a way as to make plain the unperceived elements of which it is composed. It is this tentativeness and concentration which are the active tools of all intellectual analysis. However, the results of this analysis would remain remarkably precarious, they would very soon evaporate, and thought would return to its original state of confusion, if they were not cemented by words; for words give them a consistent and individual existence which enables them to survive. From another point of view, in order to think clearly and distinctively it is not enough to analyse our ideas. We must additionally bring back together the different elements which we have dissected in order to reconstruct the natural whole to which they belong. This reconstruction does not consist in assembling things mechanically from the outside; for these fragments of thoughts are parts of a living whole. They vibrate in unison with one another, they call out to one another, they are mutually sympathetic and converge upon one another; between them there exists all kinds of relationships, relationships which may run parallel, be those of dependency, be oblique or otherwise. But how could we represent to ourselves with anything approaching clarity these niceties (which are so complex and so fleeting) if we had not had at our disposal the

artifice of language, of verbal flexions, of grammatical agree-
ments, of rules of construction, and even special terms to express
certain of these relations (notably prepositions and conjunctions)?

If we owe to language the introduction into our mind of distinctness and logical organisation, the study of languages is obviously the best way of accustoming the child to distinguish and to
organise his ideas logically. It is by making him reflect on words,
meanings and grammatical forms that we can best train him to
think lucidly, that is to say to grasp the elements and relationships
of thought. It is this which constitutes the great service rendered
by the linguistic exercises which still play such a large part in our
classes. There is no question but that, from this point of view, the
classical languages offer special advantages. Precisely because the
classical peoples are far removed from ourselves in time, their
manner of analysing their thought was very different from our
own; and it is this very difference which renders Latin and Greek
an exceptionally effective stimulant for this special kind of
reflection. A French word, an English word and even, most commonly, a German word overlap exactly, at least in the generality
of cases, and this overlapping is bound to be constantly increasing. The result is that transposing a term in one language into the
other can be done easily and almost unconsciously. The case is
quite different with Latin and Greek. Here the pupil is forced to
make a quite special effort in order to become aware of the
thought expressed by the words he is translating from French into
Latin or *vice versa*. This fact alone trains him in the making of distinctions and the habit of clarity. Similarly and for the same
reason the practice of translating Greek and Latin from and into
French, because their grammar is so very different from our own,
forces the child to be constantly engaged in logical analysis; he
must be perpetually aware of relationships which exist between
ideas as these are expressed through grammatical forms.

But it is not the case that Latin and Greek are irreplaceable. It is
possible to find valuable substitutes for these classical exercises.
Whatever may have been said about it, I do not believe that we
should place too much confidence in living languages; first of all,
there is the reason I have just indicated, namely the ancestry which
these languages have in common with our own. And then there is
the reason that the use of direct methods demotes translation and
prose composition to secondary roles and, by definition, virtually
excludes all exercises in transposition. But what would be possible
would be deliberately to institute methodical and repeated
exercises in vocabulary. Why not train the child to a perpetual
awareness of the meaning of the words he is using? It would be
necessary somehow to get him at each age to define the terms in

his vocabulary, to stimulate him incessantly and by every means available to make himself conscious of his ideas. Moreover, these exercises would be more beneficial for not being undertaken haphazardly; the words to which his attention would be directed could be grouped rationally according to their etymological relationships or according to the relationships of their meaning, depending on the particular case: all the possible combinations must be used. A whole discipline, of which I can do no more than sketch the principle, is waiting to be instituted with this goal in mind. It could prove most fruitful if it were applied systematically and methodically.

Similarly, instead of the automatic logical analysis which is required by classical prose translations, we could have recourse to repeated exercises in logical analysis in the strict sense, provided this did not consist in something that was merely arid, blind and mechanical. There is nothing more instructive than getting children to understand how a proposition or a sentence is made up, how the elements which comprise it tie in with one another, how certain of them gravitate in the orbit of the others, how some of them command while others are commanded. We should inculcate this understanding in them by way of repeated exercises in which, however, repetition does not render the exercise of intelligence otiose. In short, grammatical culture, rightly understood, ought to regain something of the place which it used to occupy in our schools, and which it has long since lost.

These initial exercises constitute only a first stage which we must get beyond as quickly as possible. From the sentence and the proposition we must move on to paragraphs. We must confront the child with a piece of developed writing and incite him to resolve it in its elements. The lessons which he is given in history or other subjects should be conducted with the same end in view. They should be constructed in such a way that he can clearly see the composition. In the first place, we would begin by showing it to him, not by means of summaries which are compacted and hence indigestible, but by means of plans which would show clearly how the thought was linked together; in other cases we would encourage the pupil to discover this for himself. In a word, we must take as our overriding concern during the early years the constant multiplication of opportunities for letting the child dissect and reconstruct his own thinking. In this way we shall arrive progressively but without haste at stylistic practice proper. For stylistic training should be understood, first and foremost, not as a means of teaching children to write elegantly and eloquently, but as a more complex exercise in analysis and logical synthesis. If we need to get him to deliver narratives in his own language, it is not only so that he may know how to express himself gracefully; it is above all because there is no better way of teaching him to speak lucidly, and this is a consequence of the special role which language plays in intellectual life. And as the habit of lucid thought is a prerequisite for the study of the sciences it is clear that a training in style is no less essential for scientific education than for so-called 'literary' education. This is why the study of style — that is to say of grammar and of language — constitutes the common basis of all education.

When I began this work, my principal object was to pose the problem of secondary education as a unity. We are today in a position to see what is the source of this unity; it is man. All education is necessarily anthropocentric, which is something the Humanists understood full well. However, man is only a part of the universe and he cannot be detached from it. From this it follows that an education in things human presupposes an education in the things of nature. Since the relationship between nature and man is not solely one of neighbourliness but rather of close kinship, since man exists in nature and emerges from it, not only do these two kinds of education complement one another, they also interpenetrate one another, they act and react upon one another. They exchange good offices with one another so that the study of nature finds in the study of language — which is something supremely human — an essential preparation; and the study of man discovers in the study of nature some key conceptions and the methods with which it ought to be informed. Thus if these two kinds of discipline can be unequally developed; if it is possible in particular cases to lay emphasis now on the one, now on the other; if, in this regard, there is a case for introducing a certain amount of diversity into the academic system, there can still be no education which is capable of omitting either the one or the other.

In this way we can see the sense in which education ought to be encyclopaedic. The idea of encyclopaedic culture we have seen surviving and developing with such persistence from the earliest origins of our academic evolution that it is impossible that it should be a mere fantasy. It constitutes a response to that very profound insight that the part cannot be understood without some conception of the whole from which it emerges. However, the only form of encyclopaedic knowledge which is both desirable and practicable is not that about which Rabelais, for example, used to dream; nothing is more a waste of time than the attempt to cram the entire subject-matter of human knowledge into the brains of young people. But what is possible is to acquaint their minds with all the diverse intellectual attitudes with which they will need to be equipped when one day they come to confront the different categories of things. Under these conditions an encyclopaedic education would not need to be either over-ambitious or overloaded.

Thus we come quite naturally to the word, to the formula, which sums up this educational ideal and which will constitute our conclusion. Our goal must be not to turn each one of our pupils into a perfect polymath but to render, in each one of them, the faculty of reason comprehensive. Humanism, in its most elevated form, in its Cartesian form with Port-Royal, the Oratory and their imitators, set itself the task of moulding the reason; but it was the reason of mathematicians who could only see things in simplified and idealised form, who reduced man to clear thinking and the world to its geometrical forms. Still today, we must remain Cartesians in the sense that we must fashion rationalists, that is to say men who are concerned with clarity of thought; but they must be rationalists of a new kind who know that things, whether human or physical, are irreducibly complex and who are yet able to look unfalteringly into the face of this complexity. Our children must continue to be trained to think lucidly, for this is the essential attribute of our race; it is our national quality, and the qualities of our language and our style are only a result of it. But we must give up mistaking simple conceptual combinations for reality as a whole; we must feel more vividly the infinite richness of reality, we must understand that we can only succeed in thinking about it slowly, progressively and always imperfectly. This should be the goal of the triadic culture which is implied by an education concerned with the development of the whole man through the most effective methods: linguistic culture, scientific culture, and historical culture, such as we have defined them.

Index